VIRGIL THOMSON

VIRGIL
THOMSON
BY
Virgil Thomson

A DA CAPO PAPERBACK

Library of Congress Cataloging in Publication Data

Thomson, Virgil, 1896-
    Virgil Thomson.

    (A Da Capo paperback)
    Reprint of the 1966 ed. published by A. A. Knopf,
New York.
    Includes index.
    1. Thomson, Virgil, 1896-   2. Composers—United
States—Biography. I. Title.
    [ML410.T452A3 1977]   780'.92'4 [B]   77-23407
    ISBN 0-306-80081-0

ISBN: 0-306-80081-0

First Paperback Edition

This Da Capo Press paperback edition of *Virgil Thomson*
is an unabridged republication, with a few minor
corrections by the author, of the first edition
published in New York in 1967. It is reprinted
by arrangement with Alfred A. Knopf.

Published by Da Capo Press, Inc.
A Subsidiary of Plenum Publishing Corporation
227 West 17th Street
New York, New York 10011

Acknowledgments

FOR PERMISSION TO QUOTE from letters, poems, and articles, I wish to thank the following: Mrs. Böske Antheil for a letter written me by George Antheil in 1925; Mrs. A. Everett Austin, Jr., for letters written me in 1933 by A. Everett Austin, Jr.; Mrs. Alfred H. Barr, Jr., for letters that she wrote me in 1932 and 1939; Mrs. William Aspenwall Bradley for a letter written me by William Aspenwall Bradley in 1933; Mrs. Bagg and Angus Davidson, administrators, for two poems by Mary Butts (*Pagany,* I:2 [1930]; II:3); Mrs. Theodore Chanler for a letter to Kathleen Hoover written by Theodore Chanler in 1948; Aaron Copland for letters written me in 1931, 1932, 1939, 1943, and 1954; Marian Morehouse (Mrs. Cummings) for a postcard written me by e. e. cummings in 1940; Edwin Denby for letters written me in 1929 and '30; C. Dewitt Eldridge for a letter written to his family in 1938; Roy Harris for a letter written me in 1930; Lou Harrison for a letter written me about 1964; John Houseman for a letter written me in 1939; Georges Hugnet for letters written me in 1930 and '33, for an article entitled "Virgil Thomson" (*Pagany,* I:1 [1930]) as translated by me into English, and for his poem "Enfances" (*Pagany,* II:1); Minna Lederman (Mrs. Mel Daniel) for a letter written me in 1938; Pare Lorentz for a telegram sent me in 1937; Henri Sauguet for a review published in *L'Europe nouvelle,* 1931, and for his musical portrait of me; Mrs. Gertrud Schoenberg for a letter written me in 1944 by Arnold Schoenberg; Daniel C. Joseph, administrator, and Donald Gallup, literary executor, of the Gertrude Stein Estate, for letters written to me and to Georges Hugnet by Gertrude Stein and for her "Poem Pritten on Pfances of Georges Hugnet"; Mrs. J. Sibley Watson for a letter written me in 1930; Yale University Press, New Haven, Connecticut, for a stanza from Gertrude Stein's *Stanzas in Meditation*.

For the loan of pictures used herein as illustrations, I wish to thank Mrs. Böske Antheil, R. Kirk Askew, Jr., Mrs. Ross Lee Finney, Mrs. Roy Thomas Gleason, Johana (Mrs. Roy) Harris, the Harvard University Records Office, Philip Johnson, King's Chapel (Boston), Lincoln Kirstein, Suzanne Peignot (Madame Lauboeuf), the Estate of George Platt Lynes, the New York *Herald Tribune,* Lee Miller (Lady Penrose), Miss Dorothy St. Clair, Henri Sauguet, James Soby, the Yale University Library, John Cage, Annette Dieudonné, and Nicolas Nabokov.

For assistance in preparing the manuscript of this book for publication I owe untold gratitude to Briggs W. Buchanan, Professor Richard Burgi, Jason Epstein, Maurice Grosser, Robert Offergeld, Herbert Weinstock, and Gavin Young, all of whom have read it with sharp eyes for both taste and clarity.

New York, 1966   VIRGIL THOMSON

A Note on the Illustrations

PHOTOGRAPHS of René Crevel, Janet Flanner, James Joyce, and Pierre de Massot by Berenice Abbott; photograph of George Antheil by Bain News Service; group photograph of Virgil Thomson, Walter Piston, Herbert Elwell, and Aaron Copland by Thérèse Bonney, also the photograph of Virgil Thomson with Gertrude Stein; of John Cage by Bob Cato; of Kristians Tonny's monoprint portrait of Virgil Thomson by P. Delbo; of Dr. Frederick M. Smith by Straus-Peyton; of Virgil Thomson (frontispiece) by William Gale Gedney; of King's Chapel, Boston, and its graveyard by Haskell; of Virgil Thomson by the *Herald Tribune;* of Geoffrey Parsons by New York *Herald Tribune*-Fein; of Florine Stettheimer's model theater and of Marcel Duchamp's portrait of her by Peter A. Juley & Son; of Frederick Ashton by Ker-Seymer, London; of Pare Lorentz by Dorothea Lange; of Constance Askew, Alfred Barr, and Alexander Calder, also the group photograph of John Houseman, Pavel Tchelitcheff, Aline McMahon, and Orson Welles, by George Platt Lynes; of Maurice Grosser and of John Houseman by Lee Miller; of the quai Voltaire by André Ostier; of Mary Butts, Pablo Picasso, Mary Reynolds, and Virgil Thomson (following page 54) by Man Ray, of Lincoln Kirstein by Leonie Sterner; of Bernard Faÿ and Philip Johnson by Carl Van Vechten; of *Four*

Saints in Three Acts by White Studio; cartoon by Henri Charles Strauss from *Saturday Review;* "Peanuts" comic strip, United Feature Syndicate. The author wishes to thank all those who granted permission for the use of these materials.

The photographs are to be found after pages 54, 150, 278, 406.

Contents

VIRGIL THOMSON

Missouri Landscape
with Figures

To anyone brought up there, as I was, "Kansas City" always meant the Missouri one. When you needed to speak of the other you used its full title, Kansas-City-Kansas; and you did not speak of it often, either, or go there unless you had business. Such business was likely to be involved with stockyards or the packing houses, which lay beyond the Kansas line in bottom land. The Union Depot, hotel life, banking, theaters, shopping—all the urbanities —were in Missouri.

So was open vice. One block on State Line Avenue showed on our side nothing but saloons. And just as Memphis and St. Louis had their Blues, we had our *Twelfth Street Rag* proclaiming joyous low life. Indeed, as recently as the 1920s H. L. Mencken boasted for us that within the half mile around Twelfth and Main there were two thousand second-story hotels. We were no less proud of these than of our grand houses, stone churches, and slums, our expensive street railways and parks, and a political machine whose corruption was for nearly half a century an example to the nation.

Kansas, the whole state, was dry. And moralistic about everything. There was even an anticigarette law. Nearly till World War II, one bought "coffin nails" under the counter and paid five cents more per pack than in Missouri. Though Kansas had always been a Free State and supported right in Kansas-City-Kansas a Negro college, most of our colored brethren preferred Missouri, where life was more fun. The truth is that Kansas was Yankee territory, windy and dry, with blue laws on its books; and the women from there wore unbecoming clothes and funny hats.

As for the food, a touring musician described a hotel steak with "I drew my knife across it, and it squeaked." As late as 1948, motoring west with the painter Maurice Grosser, I caused him to drive in one day from Slater, in Saline County, Missouri, to Colorado Springs, 714 miles, by insisting one must not eat or sleep in Kansas. He had yielded, he thought, to mere Missouri prejudice. But when we stopped once for coffee and a hamburger (safe enough), and noticing under a fly screen some darkish meringue-topped pies I asked the waitress what kind they were, she replied, "Peanut butter," he says I turned and simply said, "You see?"

I learned in my grown-up years how beautiful Kansas can be in the middle and west, an ocean of mud in winter and of wheat in summer, with a rolling ground swell underneath and a turbulent sky above, against which every still unbroken windmill turns like a beacon. I came also in those later years to respect her university at Lawrence, especially for music, and to read her free-speaking editors, William Allen White of Emporia, Ed Howe of Atchison. I have wished merely to point out here, in telling what life was like on the Missouri side, that any Southern child from there inevitably grew up making fun of Kansas.

Such fun, of course, was chiefly made in private. Publicly our city was for tolerance. As a multiple railway terminus, it offered welcome equally to old Confederates, to business families from Ohio and New England, to German farmers, brewers from Bavaria, cattlemen from Colorado and the West, to miners, drummers, and all railroaders, to Irish hod carriers, Jewish jewelers, New York investors, and Louisiana lumberjacks, to school teachers, music teachers, horse showers, horse doctors, to every species of doctor and clergyman and to many a young male or female fresh off the farm. In such a cosmopolis mutual acceptance was inevitable. So also was a certain exclusiveness, based on contrasts in manners, morals, and religion.

In my family's case, these conditionings were home-based in "Little Dixie," a central Missouri farming region bounded north, northwest, and northeast by the Missouri River and centered commercially round Boonville, Marshall, and in early days the river town Miami. This district had been settled in the 1820s and '30s by planters from the eastern counties of Virginia and further populated after the Civil War from northern Kentucky. My Virginia great-grandfather Reuben Ellis McDaniel had brought with him in '41 from Caroline County a household of thirteen whites and sixty Negroes. In Missouri he grew hemp and tobacco, traded in staples for his neighbors, raised a family of twelve, took part in the founding of colleges and Baptist churches, sent his sons by river boat to Georgetown College in Kentucky. My Thomson great-grandfather, also a Virginia Baptist, had preceded him by two decades. My mother's people, settled in Kentucky since the 1790s, did not come till nearly 1880.

Farmers my people were, all of them, with an occasional offshoot into law, divinity, or medicine, rarely into storekeeping, never into banking. Baptists they were too, and staunch ones. I do not know when it got started in Virginia, this business of their being always Baptists, though family records show persecutions for it in the eighteenth century. And certainly there had long been Baptists in Wales, where many came from. It may be that the Welsh ones (and my mother's people seem virtually all to have borne Welsh names) were Baptist when they landed, a Captain John Graves in 1607, a Gaines shortly after. But the Scottish Thomsons (arriving a century later) and the Scotch-Irish McDaniels may well have been converted in the colonies. In any case, all were Baptists, every forebear of mine known to me, and after the Civil War Southern Baptists.

The third historical fact dominating my childhood—after three centuries of mid-Southern slave-based agriculture and of belief in salvation by faith plus total immersion—was the Civil War. I never heard it called in those days anything *but* the Civil War, either—except for short simply "the war." And I was brought up on it. My grandmother Thomson was a Confederate war widow; all her brothers had fought on that side too, one being killed. My great-uncle Giles McDaniel had at nineteen escaped from the Federal prison in St. Louis, where my grandfather lay dying, returned to his family, made his way from Missouri to Canada and thence to Virginia, where he joined Lee. The Thomson great-uncles, as well, all had war histories. And since Grandma, who was a quietly wonderful storyteller, regularly spent the winter with us in Kansas City, it can be imagined in what detail the war was reviewed as lived through on a Missouri farm by a widow with three small children.

Grandma Thomson, born Flora Elizabeth McDaniel in 1830, was already seventy in my earliest memories of her. These picture her short and slender as to frame, dressed in blacks, grays, or lavender, carrying outdoors or to church a reticule (small handbag with a reticulated metal top that opened like a row of x's), and wearing a bonnet (crescent-shaped small hat, covered with flowers or jet, which sat on her parted hair just forward of the bun and was held there by ribbons tied beneath the chin). To others she appeared as a gentlewoman not hesitant of speaking up to anyone, black or white, afraid, indeed, of nothing at all save God's anger and of crossing city streets.

Quincy Adams Thomson, born in 1827, must have owed his pre-names to the presidential incumbent, since he had no family connection to Massachusetts. Like Flora McDaniel he was one of twelve children, and when they were married in 1856 he was twenty-nine. At this point he acquired land from his father and built a house.

Not long afterward, Flora developed an eye condition that required her, for a specialist's care, to travel to Palmyra, near Hannibal. Arrived, she wrote her husband of her pregnancy by saying that on the boat she "would have enjoyed [his] society so much, and besides I had something to tell you about which I will only say it gave me pleasure and leave you to guess."

A month later she is "trying to be patient" till they can be "reunited . . . at no very distant date." Then the next day,

> I received your letter this morning saying you had already started for Kentucky. It was probably better for you to go than Asa [one of his brothers], but if I had been at home I do not know that I would have consented to the arrangement. After all, I should perhaps be thankful you are going to Kentucky instead of Kansas, for though I could never blame you for responding to a call of duty from your parents or country, it would be hard to give you up even for a time.

She adds in postscript, "I wish you had written more about the Kansas excitement. I hear but little said about it here and have no idea what they are doing in Saline [County] and feel anxious to know."

This is all one reads right then, in her letters or his, about the coming troubles; but in October 1857 one of her brothers writes him from College Hill (Columbia, Missouri):

What has become of Kansas? I can learn nothing from the newspapers. Sometimes I see a piece saying something about it, and very likely before I put the same paper down I see it contradicted. Can learn nothing for certain. Wish you would let me know when the election is to come off, or if it is over, what was the result of it: I do hope that the Missourians are not so foolish as to let it be taken from them (though I do really think they deserve it). Is Gov. Walker for or against the south?

By the end of 1861 the war was on. And Quincy Adams Thomson, wiry and passionate, looks in photograph like a hothead. A letter of September 3, 1861, written to his brother Asa, who was by that time with the Confederate troops, recounts the state of the war at home and of the absent brother's farm.

Your horses look very well considering the work they have done. I broke your highlander mare, as you desired, and let a man in Col. Price's regiment by the name of Granville Botts have her, as you ordered, and I have no doubt but you have seen her before this time. . . . I do not intend to let any more of your horses go, because you have not any more than you need for your farm. . . .

There has been much excitement here since you left. I have been from my business a great deal. We are still very fearful that the Federals will over run this County before you all can get here. May the Lord forbid it, though we don't deserve to be treated so well. Our trust is in God for the success of our cause, which is the cause of religious and political Liberty. Two of my brothers have been spared to get home from the scene of conflict and death safely, and I pray God that my other Brother may not only be thus highly blessed, but that he may come home to tell us that he has become the soldier of the true and living God.

This last refers, I presume, to Asa's unconverted state.

Eventually eleven of Quincy's brothers and brothers-in-law served the Confederacy. At this time my grandfather himself was thirty-four and twice a parent. One year later, when he left for the war, his wife was carrying her third child. Four months later still, he was dead. A group of some six hundred Confederate volunteers, mostly from Saline County and in large part friends, relatives, and neighbors, mounted on their own horses and in many cases accompanied by their Negro servants, had organized themselves into a regiment, elected one of their number temporary colonel, named others as officers and noncoms, and set out southwest to join General Sterling Price. Within a few days the regiment was surprised by Federal cavalry, captured, and shipped in open boxcars to a prison in St. Louis, arriving there on Christmas Day. Epidemic diseases broke out. Giles McDaniel escaped by blackening himself with a burnt cork. Most remained, awaiting transfer to the Confederate side in exchange for Federal prisoners. In January my grandfather died, probably of typhoid; and his body, shipped to his wife in Saline County, was buried in the graveyard of their country church. My father, born on January 12, was lifted up for one long look at his male parent. Later, from being so vividly told and re-told the event, he almost remembered it. He was a redhead named Quincy Alfred, and he came to look very much like his father.

Flora Thomson had been expected to join her father for the duration. But on that point she was firm. She stayed on her farm, ran it with her own Negroes, not all of them available after Emancipation, and brought up her babies. If marauding troops came by, Blacklegs or Scalawags, she offered them food, which they would have taken anyway, and beddings-down in the hay barn. She never locked her door, esteeming such precaution distrustful of God and futile against armies.

By the mid-1870s she was moving her family winters to Liberty, Missouri, some twenty-five miles north of Kansas City, seat of a Baptist preparatory school and college named William Jewell, of which Reuben McDaniel had been a founder. Here my father studied Latin, English literature, and natural philosophy (as physics was called then); his brother Reuben read law; and his sister Leona (or "Lonie") was got ready for Stephens College, a Baptist female seminary at Columbia. But in those postwar times, with ex-soldiers going all wild and with several of her brothers drinking far more than any gentleman or farmer should, Flora Thomson had added to her canons of Southern Baptist upbringing a clause about total abstinence. No liquor crossed her threshold, nor was it served in her children's houses. I have seen my Aunt Lonie's husband hide blackberry brandy in the carriage house and swallow aromatics after taking it rather than face her on the question.

My father, the youngest, was the first to marry. My mother was eighteen, he twenty-one. His passion was romantic and intense, remained so till his death at eighty-one. Though he had a redhead's temper, I never heard him raise his voice to her. To be her husband was for him as proud a privilege as to be a Baptist or a farmer. For he loved farming too, loved land, loved growing things, loved ingenuities done by hands with wood and stone, loved everything about life in the country from Monday's sunrise to Sunday's dinner with guests brought home from church. His mother, respecting his needs, divided her land, gave him his share. Young Quincy thereupon built a frame cottage and moved into it with his bride.

My mother, though born on a farm in Kentucky (in 1865) and removed to Missouri at fourteen to live on another, had never known a farm life's loneliness. Her father, Benjamin Watts Gaines, born in 1832, had lived in a wide Boone County house full of children and visitors. The Civil War, less passionately viewed, I gather, in northern Kentucky than in central Missouri, had passed him by. Along with his brothers, he had offered himself to the Confederate troops; but he was refused for lacking two fingers. He does not seem to have insisted on showing them how remarkable a shot he was with the other three. Nor did he let the Federals draft him. He simply passed up the war, stayed home, and built a family. After bearing him seven children, his wife Mary Ely Graves died of a "galloping consumption"; and it was chiefly the sadness of her loss that caused his removal to Missouri in 1879. Here he again married a Kentucky woman, Elizabeth Hall, who gave him three more children. When he was not much over fifty, he sold his farm and built a house in nearby Slater. He never did a stroke of work again except for gardening. He lived to be a hundred.

As with so many Kentuckians, life at his house was a never-ending party. My mother, Clara May, from growing up in such a house and visiting in others like it, had been all her life a hostess or a guest. Young Quincy from across the road, with his strict devotion to a widowed mother, his relentless theological integrities, and his intensely romantic feelings about everything (indeed, I suspect there were in him, and in his father, possibilities of wildness), was polarized by the complementary characteristics of a young woman who, though she possessed many graces and all the household arts, knew only one rigor, that of speaking always with tact.

They were married in the fall of '83; and their first child, Ruby Richerson, came two years later. All that summer of '85, with my father constantly out of the house on farm work, Mother had been much alone for the first time in her life. At twenty, pregnant and terrified, she acquired an ineradicable distaste for the country. What tactful softening up of my father's hard passion for the soil went on in the next few years one can only guess. But he did decide eventually on selling the farm. And so they moved to a tiny village called Nelson, where with his newly realized capital he set up a hardware store and tin shop.

The tin shop used his skills in tinkering, repairing, roofing, stove-piping, and the like. Making houses come to life was as good as tilling the ground. But he had no instinct for trade, no skill in collecting monies owed him. And so in about six years he had nothing left. It was probably the depression of 1893, as much as his own inexperience, that brought to an end his adventure in storekeeping. But he never mentioned the famous Panic to me, may not even have been aware of its relation to him; I learned of its existence years later from a history book. But by 1894, and no question about it, he had to move.

The move he made was that of many another farm boy in trouble; he took his family to the city and looked for work. The city was Kansas City (Missouri, of course), and the work he found was as a conductor on the cable cars. For over a year he shared houses on Brooklyn Avenue near 24th Street with my Aunt Lula, Mother's sister, and his boyhood friend, my Uncle Charlie Garnett. Then he took a flat of his own at Tenth and Virginia, where on November 25, 1896, his last child was born, a son named Virgil Garnett.

Thirty-five years old, with a wife and two children in his charge and with no money at all save a modest wage, he did not look, to prosperous Saline County, exactly successful. I do not think, however, that my father had ever had much respect for success or any undue aspiration toward it. His mother had prayed for him to hear the "call" and become a preacher. He himself had early become resigned to not hearing it. Always a worker for the Kingdom and early a deacon, he aspired to little earthly reward beyond being a son, husband, and father. Also, if possible, a householder, since life in rented premises (especially in a flat, where there was not even a flowerbed to dig in) seemed to him no proper way. But to buy or build a house he needed credit, and for credit he needed a steady job. The cable cars offered no such security, since their franchise even then was running out. So he took civil service examinations and was appointed to the post office. With a job involving tenure, he could borrow money. His sister Leona was married to a man of substance who had already bought from my grandmother her remaining property, replaced her pre-Civil War small farmhouse with a larger structure, and offered a perpetual home in it to both his wife's mother and his own. He now lent my father, against mortgage, $3,000 for building a house. Thereupon a small lot was purchased on Wabash Avenue, at 2613, and a two-story frame house raised, my father being his own architect and contractor.

From here we moved some ten years later to a slightly larger house in the same block. Surrounding both were yards good for growing flowers and fruit trees and every vegetable. My father arranged his post office working hours so to have daily a half day for gardening. He either rose at five and gardened till noon or went to work at five and gardened all afternoon. He "improved the place" also, building a stone cellar, putting in a furnace, wiring for electricity, painting, paper hanging, roofing, shingling, There was nothing about a house and yard he could not do with joy.

Mother was happy, too, because she could have company. Grandma Thomson came for a long stay every winter, arriving with sacks of chestnuts from my Uncle Will Field's trees and with a telescope valise full of quilt pieces. My cousin Lela Garnett, who would also spend winters with us, brought a piano into the house and gave me lessons on it. It was Lela who taught me, at five, to play from notes. Before that I had only improvised, with flat hands and the full arm, always with the pedal down and always loud, bathing in musical sound at its most intense, naming my creations after "The Chicago Fire" and similar events.

Mother's half sister, Beulah Gaines, would come too, a pretty girl who laughed and danced. She could play anything at sight, delighted the other grown-up young that way, who loved to stand round her at the piano and sing songs. There were sometimes whole house parties of girl cousins and their chums. Where they all slept I do not know, certainly in one another's beds, possibly some on the floor. Cooking went on too, lots of it, and for weeks at a time dressmaking, for Mother could make anything out of cloth, even to tailoring a coat. And there was china painting. From fifteen my sister Ruby had had lessons in that and in water color. From eighteen she received pupils in both and executed orders, firing her china in a gas kiln that stood in the basement. She filled the house with artifacts, earned her own money, and when the Garnett piano went away bought one for me to play and practice on.

A first cousin of my mother's, an amateur violinist, would sometimes play all evening with Lela accompanying; and I remember rolling on the floor in ecstasy at hearing for the first time in real string sound the repeated high F's of the *Cavalleria Rusticana* Intermezzo. By the time I was ten I was playing waltzes and two-steps and schottisches for my sister's friends to dance to. I had learned also by that age to dance the grownups' dances and to play their card games.

Card games and dancing had been brought into our house by my mother's half brother, Cecil, who had come, just out of Slater High School, to work in Kansas City and to live with us. Handsome, full of jollities and jokes and card tricks, playing the banjo, knowing songs and darn-fool ditties, sophisticated about girls and adored by them, he filled the house with a young man's ease and laughter. And not long after Cecil came, his high school chum also arrived from Slater. Being at work, they paid for their board; and every night's dinner now was a company dinner, with steak or chops, hot breads, three vegetables, and dessert. Afterwards the boys got exercise by playing catch or wrestling. In winter there was sometimes reading aloud; the year round, almost always singing.

It was after the boys began to live with us that the larger house was bought. Sometimes their number grew to three or four.

Eventually the group withered away, with Cecil going to work in California. Then after my sister's marriage in 1913, she and her husband took two of the upstairs rooms, furnished them with their own things, and lived there for ten years. So that still there was dinner every night and lots of company. My father had for joy his house and garden; my sister had her artisan's life and no house-keeping; I had my music lessons and piano; my mother her Ken-tucky-style hospitality, so skillfully contrived that she was almost never seen at work and so prettily administered that life seemed to be, as she had always thought it should be, one long party.

Nobody remembers being a baby, but I remember being a child of two or three and growing from there to school age. Against the backdrop of my father's small but comely house and on a stage peopled by characters of all ages, I took my place quite early as a child performer. I was precocious, good-looking, and bright. My parents loved me for all these things and for being their man-child. My sister, eleven years older, looked on me almost as her own. My relations were pleased at my being able to read and sing songs and remember things. So with all this admiration around (and being, in spite of the praise, not wholly spoiled), I early seized the center of the stage and until six held it successfully.

Beyond our residential neighborhood there were forays into the great world of downtown, of department stores with their smells of dress goods and with their stools that one could whirl around on. I was taken every October to the Carnival parade and carried home by my father sound asleep. But the greatest adventure was going to the depot to meet somebody, usually my grandmother. For this we traveled either on a cable car that went over a cliff and down a steep incline or on an electric one that went through that same cliff in a black tunnel. At the depot itself there were men with megaphones singing lists of railroad lines and towns and numbered tracks. As for the trains, their engines looked so power-ful, in motion or at rest, that I did not dare go near them with-out holding tightly to my father's hand. Even thus, my fear was awful. There was no identity at all between these monstrous ma-chines and their toy images that I cuddled every night in bed.

My mother's sister Aunt Lillie Post could play, with all their pearly runs intact, variations on "Old Black Joe" and "Listen to the

Mocking Bird." She did not consent to do this very often, being out of practice; but when she did, she evoked a nostalgia that I could know to have some connection with the prewar South. It was all very polished, poetic, and deeply sad. But saddest of all was a song my mother sometimes sang as prepayment for taking a nap. It was "Darling Nelly Grey," and I could never listen to the end without tears in my throat. All other music, though a joy, was merely sound. But these souvenirs of an earlier Kentucky, rendered by women who remembered, no doubt, its Arcadian landscapes, their father as a young man, and their mother early dead, had over me a power so intense that, as with my terror of the engines at the depot, I could almost not bear for it either to go on or to stop.

When I was only two, which I do not remember, and again when I was five, which I do, my father took me to Saline County for showing me off. I stayed at my Aunt Lonie Field's farm, with peafowls on the lawn, visited in Slater my Grandpa Gaines and Grandma Betty, spent nights in other houses, got chummy with a cousin of my own age, Bessie Field, attended my Grandma Thomson's seventy-first-birthday dinner, came home a traveled one.

Since my father's parents had both been born into families of twelve, my father possessed at this time more than fifty first cousins. My mother's extant aunts and uncles and cousin connections would have seemed almost as numerous had not most of them lived in Kentucky, whence they came to visit us less frequently. In my own right I had eight aunts and uncles plus five more by marriage. From my first cousins and the children of my parents' cousins to my grandparents, with their own large numbers of brothers and sisters, my childhood was surrounded by a company that included persons of virtually every age and disposition. It is not to be wondered at that having long appeared successfully before such a vast and varied public, I arrived at my school years self-confident, cocky, and brash.

Some of this expansiveness may have come from living close to Kansas. My cousins from Little Dixie, I must say, had none of it. In any case, in September of 1902, when still five (I would not be six till Thanksgiving), without the prelude of kindergarten or the benefit of any parental presence (my cousin Lela Garnett went along to enroll me), I entered first grade at the Irving School, on Prospect Avenue at Twenty-fourth Street, wholly unafraid and ready for anything.

2

A Kansas City Childhood

ON MY SECOND DAY AT SCHOOL I got into a fight. That was a surprise to me, and so was the outcome. Physical brawling had not been part of our family life; nor had my father ever shown me, even in play, the stances of pugilism. Neither had I been taught to fear aggression. It simply had not occurred to me ever that I might be attacked, still less that I might be led on (for this may well have been what happened) to attack another boy. In any case, I did find myself, just off schoolyard limits, engaged in fisticuffs. I also found myself losing the match. Then somebody separated us. Neither bore any marks. But my surprise was definitive.

It was definitive because it made clear to me, not yet six, that I was going to have to find other ways toward gaining respect than the head-on physical encounter. A boy named Maurice Baldwin, just as bright as I and just as small, early chose the athletic way. He could always out-wrestle or out-box a boy of his size and out-pitch at baseball many a taller one. But he spent all his out-of-school time keeping up that muscular command. My own choice was simply not to compete. This choice kept me mostly out of fights and always free from broken bones. It also left me time for music and reading. And if it often brought me the taunt of "sissy," it caused me to grow strong in other ways of defense and attack, psychological ways, and in the development of independence.

Nor did it make me an outcast from friendships. My closest associate from nine to thirteen, a half-Canadian boy named Percy Taylor, had attached himself to me in the fourth grade. He was a strong boy and thoroughly adventurous, but formal sports were closed to him because of defective eyesight. The overcompensation of lenses, on the other hand, had made him a facile reader. So together we shared boys' books, historical tales, Dickens, dime novels, fairy tale collections, Webster's Unabridged, and the encyclopedias—all the common reading matter of children except popular science, which interested neither of us. We skated together (in Missouri, that was mostly on rollers), captured moths and butterflies, went fishing (which I found slimy and slow), and took enormous walks.

With Percy's older brother and some more boys we played cave man, raided back porches, stole useless objects at the dime store, and slept in a tent. As we approached pubescence, we pooled our information and shared experiments. Then, after manhood had come firmly to us all, we separated as casually as travelers off a train. No sentiment had been involved; no attachments remained —only a crystal residue, indissoluble in memory's private stream, of the fabulous boyhood years from nine to twelve.

These years had taken place in the first decade of this century, when there were as yet no movies, radio, or television. Our mass-produced entertainment consisted wholly of books and of the Sunday comics. We lived in a middle-class neighborhood in a middle-sized Middle Western city, our whole existence as permeated by rural residues as our residential blocks were checkered with vacant lots; and every car line ended in the country. Downtown there were theaters and big stores and, we had heard, whorehouses. We were proud of all these; they made us feel citified. But in our neighborhoods we lived a small-town life centered on school and church, with lots of play and reading life thrown in. And neither the play life nor the reading, though no doubt watched over, was officiously guided. We thought we were making up our own amusements; and for the most part we probably were, though our games, of course, like all children's games, followed a seasonal calendar as unalterable as the equinoxes.

Our clothing too followed folkways of our time and place, our middle-of-the-world social class. Till the age of twelve we wore knickerbockers, ribbed cotton stockings (black), soft-collar shirts, ties, and coats, in winter always high shoes laced up by means of both eyelets and hooks. On Sundays the collar was stiff and collar-buttoned, the suit of dark blue serge. And since every Sunday suit, unless outgrown, came to be worn for "every day," we were likely to be in blue a good deal of the time. In cold weather we wore overcoats, sweaters being thought a bit roughneck except for athletes; and one winter large fur gauntlets were the fashion. In spring we wore dark blue skullcaps known as "dinks," the tougher types affecting tan felt hats with brim pinned up on one side by a brooch, in Teddy Roosevelt's "rough rider" style.

Since none of us had much spending money, we would walk three miles of a Saturday to the public library, pooling our carfare nickels for chocolate bars or potato chips. We changed our books, robbed the dime store, ate something sweet or salt, and as often as not walked home again. In the summertime we went on country walks or watched professional baseball through knotholes in a high board fence, though for myself I cared as little for spectator sports as for being a competitor. Those boys whose families permitted, and who could scrape up twenty-five cents plus carfare, would go to a Saturday matinée at the Gillis, a melodrama theater playing *Chinatown Charley, No Mother to Guide Her,* and similar classics. Then the following Saturday, in the loft of somebody's carriage house, that same play would be produced in brief, from memory, at ten pins for a place on a plank or one cent for a box seat, literally a wooden box.

Stories of violence and sudden death came later to be exploited by newspapers, during the approach to World War I, as a way of getting people worked up against the Germans. But well through 1910 and beyond, the cowboy world of song and story was still alive; and in the gambling joints of Cripple Creek and Leadville, only a night away by train, gun play was far from extinct. Real violence was easily available to young men who felt the need of it. And country boys, from the age of ten, all carried shotguns for banging away at rabbits and for immobilizing a rattlesnake or skunk. Youth's taste for violence in literature was not starved either; it was merely catered to less massively than now. And my childhood years in Missouri, for all their seeming peacefulness, were contemporaneous both with the Wild West's own Indian summer and with the final flourishing of Victorian blood-and-thunder on the stage.

I was six when I first went to the theater; my sister took me. The play, *Miss Petticoats,* was about a young woman whose father so nicknamed her because her dead mother had called her in French something that sounded like that. I could not follow very well the events of the spectacle; but I loved everything else about it—the dressy clothes, the make-up, the lights and painted scenery, the impersonating of character and simulations of feeling. That night, before going to bed, I put on the show. After that, my sister took me to matinees when she could, though never often enough for me. From the time I first entered a theater—and for all the masses of well-dressed people, the strangeness of the lobby, the chandeliers, the gold, the curtain, the seats that flopped down and up—I never felt anything but completely at home in any theater, backstage or out front.

My own appearances on stage were chiefly musical, playing the piano in student recitals or executing a duet with Helen Walley, the girl next door, at a Grand Army veterans' society to which her grandfather belonged. Once I appeared as William Tell in a scene from Schiller's play, and with an unloaded crossbow shot the apple clean off Ted Sherwood's head. I was not, however, a prodigy performer, merely a willing one.

Actually I had had no lessons in elocution and very poor ones in music. After my cousin Lela Garnett got married, my sister exchanged with certain music teachers china painting for my piano lessons. The first of these was a well-born but ignorant woman who firmly corrected my tendency to play by ear rather than from notes, without giving me any sound training at all in either solfeggio or note playing. The other was a young man whose brother was an actor and who was himself an opera fan. He got me to reading the stories of the operas, put me through the piano score of *Faust,* and taught me to execute quite stylishly, I thought, Leschetizky's arrangement for left hand alone of the Sextet from *Lucia di Lammermoor.* With him I also stumbled my way through bits of Liszt. And diving into any opera score with a splash, I swam with equal delight in the limpidities of *Fra Diavolo* and bathed in the turgid stream of *Parsifal.* I had already played in duet form the chief Italian overtures; and I had begun to frequent summer band concerts for hearing (scored in brass) the great operatic set-pieces and for being ravished on weekly Wagner nights by the most luscious harmonic experience that exists.

By the time I was eleven I had a gluttonous musical appetite and what I took to be vast experience. Actually I had not yet heard a symphony orchestra or a string quartet or an opera, though my acquaintance with opera music, through piano scores and band arrangements, included much of that time's current repertory. And I could play, well or badly, not only Paderewski's Minuet and the pieces by Cécile Chaminade that all students learned, but also some easy Liszt and Mendelssohn and a page or two out of Chopin, as well as a chunky choice of popular songs and lots of ragtime.

These last had come into my repertory through my sister's friends. Whenever they rolled up the rugs, I was requisitioned. It was hard, at nine and ten, to keep a steady beat; but I learned to do it. And because I did it I was allowed to be with the grown-up young. Life among the mating set seemed more romantic to me than the parties that included other ages, for it made me feel almost grown-up. With them, if only for one hour, I could leave off being a brat.

All this time there went on my mother's life of constant cooking and dressmaking and having company, Ruby's life of painting china and firing it in the gas kiln and having pupils, my father's self-contained and happy continuity of working in the garden and of making household additions and of never being absent from church. My school, my piano practice, my play and reading life kept me more occupied than most children. But I also went to church; I had to be ill to get round my father's rule about that. And since I was never ill (rarely missed school a day a year), I went regularly to Sunday school at half-past nine and stayed on for church. In my adolescent years I came to enjoy two of my Sunday school teachers, women only just enough older, say ten years, to make them a civilizing influence. Also, in my adolescent years I played the organ in other churches than Baptist ones and got paid for it. Professional status was at all times a joy, as was indeed, for the most part, church music itself. But I never at any time took to religion. In the Baptist view I am not even a Christian, having never experienced conversion or undergone baptism. I have never felt inferior to the believers, or superior; I simply am not one. Churches are not my home. In the choir room or in the organ loft I earn my fee. But I cannot be a customer; this was always so, is still so. It has nothing to do with the fact that a major part of my music has been either composed for liturgical use or inspired by hymnody.

The loyalties formed in my preadolescent years lie elsewhere than to Bible reading and preachers. They are to music, companionship, and hospitality. The hospitality stems from central Missouri, which was my father's home, and from northern Kentucky, my mother's. Also from a legendary Virginia, as known through my grandmother and her brothers. From this classical mid-South, seemingly so gentle, come my arrogance and my unhesitating disobedience.

Naturally, in a place as Yankee-versus-Rebel conscious as Kansas City, I kept mostly to myself what nostalgias I may have felt for a way of life I had not known anyway and which certainly had never existed in quite the way that anybody still living remembered it. There was nothing left to defend that had not already been defended with lives, and nothing to give up that had not long since been taken away. But slave-owners anywhere, I think, do have, like their slaves, a "tragic sense of life," a fullness in courage and compassion that has made of so many Southerners good soldiers and good judges. Myself, I owe to my Civil War forebears at least my rebelliousness.

However, at twelve I was more bumptious than rebellious. And I had become, moreover, successful at being a schoolboy. My father, as reward for a report card of all A's, though I do not recall it as unique, bought for me a ticket to hear Paderewski's piano recital, my first big-time music event. I went alone, remembered everything, literally every note, including the false ones. And when I was graduated from the Irving School in June of 1909, he gave me his own gold pocket watch.

That same summer there opened near by the first film house to serve our neighborhood. The price was five cents; the show, which repeated itself all evening, an hour long. The program, changed nightly, consisted of an "illustrated song," sung to piano accompaniment and colored slides, and two short films—a drama and a comedy. I must have gone every night. One evening just before opening time, someone came to the house asking if I would substitute for the regular pianist. I went; I played; I earned a dollar, my first receipt from any professional action.

Since the pianist in those days never knew ahead of time what the films were to be, he had to fumble his way through the first show while watching the screen. After that he could with luck hit certain passages on the nose. For comedies one played animated popular music, not disdaining a topical reference such as "I Love My Wife but O, You Kid!" For the dramas one used slower stuff. Being unskilled in improvisation, I simply played pieces I knew while a trap drummer underlined the rhythm and added "effects" such as cowbells, horses' hooves, bass drum thuds, and cymbal crashes. His flyswatter, always at hand in summer, could be useful too for light drum taps. It was soon to become, in fact, under the name of "brush," standard drummers' equipment. My first performance as a film accompanist could not have been brilliant. But I did substitute a few more times that month; and once, appearing in answer to a want ad, I was allowed by a none-too-confident manager to play through an evening at a tent show.

And then, as if these grandeurs were not enough, my Uncle Will Field took me to New York. It had always been his habit in August, when the crops were in, to go somewhere. This year my aunt was not feeling well; and my cousin Bess, inveterately train-sick, hated travel. Determined on getting away from his farm all the same, he telegraphed to invite my company, got it with alacrity. That night I took the Chicago and Alton "Hummer" at six, which picked him up in Slater at nine; and at eight in the morning, having slept in a sleeper and eaten cake there, I was in Chicago.

Since my uncle did not like staying long anywhere, for two weeks we kept on the move. We took a white steamer to Petoskey, Michigan, stopping for a swim at the beach hotel where he had spent his honeymoon, went on to Mackinac Island at the head of the lake and from there through two more lakes to Buffalo, where we drove in a carriage past lovely Victorian houses and admired Niagara Falls. Next we took a train to Albany, where we visited the capitol and its million-dollar staircase of white granite. Then, progressing majestically by day boat down the Hudson, we arrived in New York to stay at a hotel in Times Square.

For a youngster who read regularly *The Green Book* and other theater magazines, this locale was heaven, as all those ladies waiting in lobbies, so beautifully dressed and made up, I knew to be angels, though I did not think them pure. I must have seen lots of New York in three days; but what I remember most clearly is Times Square—its theaters (all closed), its restaurants (very expensive), its hotel lobbies, gloriously lighted and beflowered. The Claridge, the Knickerbocker, the Astor were dazzling to see. We stayed at the less glorious but stylish-enough Cadillac, on the Seventh Avenue corner of Forty-third Street. The electric signs, more elaborately narrative than today's, were a show in themselves. There were well-dressed spenders, too, and lots of carriages, even motor cars. I had never had so intensely the feel of being at the center of something.

Traveling by ship to Norfolk, Virginia, I entertained a salon full of admirers by playing and singing, was rewarded with a plate of fruit by a Negro in white jacket. I also got my first taste of sea-sickness.

In Norfolk, the Negro market women in bright bandannas selling highly colored fruits were almost too picturesque to be true. So were the damp ancient churches and colonial graveyards. At Richmond's Jefferson Hotel trout swam in open channels. At Gordonsville bandannaed Negro mammies brought to the train the hugest platters I had ever seen, piled high with fried chicken and with Jeff Davis pie (a confection of sugar and cream and egg yolks), both to be eaten in the hand. At Charlottesville we called on a distant cousin and drove to Monticello. Then we went home, stopping only in St. Louis to change trains. Uncle Will got off at Slater. I arrived in Kansas City just in time for the first day of high school, still only twelve years old, still small for my age, and still in short trousers.

3

A Musician's Adolescence

THAT FALL THREE DECISIVE THINGS HAPPENED: I acquired a musical mentor; I appeared in print as an author; and I fell in love. The object of my love, with black hair and brown eyes, had been something of a trophy in third grade. There had even been written proof, "Dear Virgil, I love you. I cannot live without you." (It was always the girls, never the boys, who wrote.) But after she had moved away at the end of one school year, no tie remained except for a memory of dark beauty and red hair ribbons.

Then five years later, in high school classes and on the Brooklyn Avenue streetcar, which we both took every morning, the bright sight of her as a young woman of perhaps thirteen (hair ribbons outgrown) made me suddenly to know the bond intact. But who was bound to whom was not the same; this time it was I who could not "live without." She showed no signs of sharing my disturbance, strictly preserved a neutral friendly way. Essays at dates were brushed off too, with tact. I could not by any means provoke an empathy. So my passion fed in secret and on what I took for suffering, nourished itself that way for three long years, till I had turned fifteen, after which time it gave place to youth's euphoria. And soon our geographic separation was to leave only, as before, an image of dark beauty, set permanently this time as my natural magnet.

My debut as an author was no less unhappy. The assignment had been to write a story. And though by this time I had read surely some several hundred works of fiction, I found myself quite sterile for creating one. And so I kidnapped. I copied no lines, but I did retell a tale I had read in a magazine. It was a good tale (a comedy-of-errors type), and I must have told it not badly. Well enough that my English teacher proposed submitting it to the school paper. I could not say no; I did not say no. It was offered with my consent; it was accepted; it was published. And then catastrophe fell. Within the week I was denounced by a fellow student. The facts were undeniable; I did not deny them; and an editors' apology was printed the following month.

No student, no teacher, ever mentioned the incident to me. But in my sophomore year I was not elected to a club. At the end of my fourth year I decided to stay on for another, and that year I did join a society. I also attended an advanced course in composition that I had petitioned into existence. It turned out to be (they were popular then) a course in short-story writing; and a piece I wrote for it was again published in *The Central Luminary,* this time without apology, though the tale itself was plainly, to me, modeled on *Trilby.*

The truth is, and I learned it from these experiences, that I have no gift for imaginative writing. I can describe things and persons, narrate facts. But I do not assemble my pictures and my people into situations where they take on memorability, which is what storytellers do. Nor can I make a language change its sound or words their meaning, which is the faculty of poets. Language, to me, is merely for telling the truth about something; and it was during my high school years that I learned to use it that way.

The teacher most responsible for this training was an old maid cheerful and small with a face like a bulldog. For Miss Ellen Fox grammar was a way of life, and so was promulgating teetotalism after the precepts of Frances Willard. She was a New Englander but not a dour one, a lover of laughter whose own laugh was like a bark. And I never saw her show weakness. One day when from some fault of weather there were no streetcars, she merely got up earlier and walked the five miles to school.

She would mark themes in the left-hand margin with proof-reader's signs such as *p, d, gr, tr, lc, Cap,* and the like. But the writer had to unmask for himself just where within that line the error lay. And not till every fault had been removed would she accept a piece of writing as work done. No credit was given for unusual excellence, no stigma attached to mediocrity. You did your work or you didn't; when you had done it you got an *A*. At the end of term, if you had done three-fourths, you got a *B;* for one-half, a *C;* one-fourth, a *D;* less than that, an *E* for failure. Her standards of usage were those of any reputable publishing house, her authorities Webster's dictionary and Crabb's *English Syno-nymes.*

Many found her unreasonably severe. But there is no other way than the hard way (meaning the complete way) to acquire a mastery, as I was already learning from my music teachers; and I am grateful to Ellen Fox for making me prove to myself that it is always possible, if you work at it, to make both sense and grammar. I am inclined, indeed, to credit whatever precedence the sciences have achieved in today's schools over the humanities to the fact that the sciences are still viewed as disciplines, whereas teaching in the artistic branches does tend, I fear, to encourage doodling.

Going back to my freshman status, with its burdens of unrequited love and literary delinquency, scarcely more promising was my first appearance as an actor. This took place in Sheridan's *The Rivals,* in which William Powell, three years my senior, played the male lead, I the drunken butler. Powell's gifts were already commanding—a fine bass voice, clear speech, some grace of move-ment, and above all, presence. I had no such on-stageness, and I was not especially unhappy to find that out. Actually, though I made then no resolve on the matter, I have never since essayed impersonation.

The preceding summer had brought me an encounter that opened the way to eventual decision regarding music as my voca-tion. This had happened even before my baptism by films and before my grand and glamorous trip to the East. At one of the nightly band concerts in Electric Park I had been spoken to by a musician whom I knew by sight as the tenor soloist from Calvary Baptist Church, where my father was a deacon. With Robert Leigh Murray, a well-washed roly-poly man in his middle thirties, our conversation was all of music. There began at that moment, indeed, a dialogue that was to go on almost without interruption for ten years. This started by his asking my musical accomplishments; and when he learned how superficial they were and how poor was my instruction (for he knew, or knew of, the silly opera buff who had been teaching me), he said right off, as if taking me over, that if I wanted to be a pianist I must have proper lessons.

I do not know how often I saw Mr. Murray that summer, but by fall he was established in my parents' confidence, and in mine, as the mentor of my musical progress. He saw to it that I did have proper lessons and eventually that I earned money to pay for them. He also taught me to play his accompaniments and paid me at commercial rates for doing so. For the next six years we rehearsed at least two evenings a week; and I accompanied always his banquet dates and out-of-town recitals, sometimes playing alone a Beethoven sonata or group of pieces by Schubert, MacDowell, Debussy.

My first proper lessons were from Moses Boguslawski, a pianist of Lisztian brilliance. They ceased when my father could no longer afford them. The next summer, paying for them myself, I went to a friend of Mr. Murray's, Gustav Schoettle, a cultivated Rhineland German, who threw in harmony gratis. The next summer I went to Rudolf King, a Leschetizky pupil, who put me through some tough technical studies and got me to playing solos in public. My heaviest practice took place during the summer. In the winter I went to school, worked for Mr. Murray, played occasionally in public, practiced without guidance.

I also had, at thirteen, organ lessons from Clarence Sears, of Grace Episcopal Church. My original interest in the organ had been monetary, to earn during the summer five dollars a Sunday substituting at Calvary Baptist for Mrs. Jennie Schultz. But the architectural splendors of Grace Church (now the Cathedral of Grace and Holy Trinity) were attractive to an adolescent; and Mr. Sears, to provide experience of the Anglican liturgy, had proposed that I assist him at Sunday services. To this arrangement my father, not willing to see me escape from Baptist influence, had consented only on condition that I attend Sunday school at Calvary beforehand. And Clarence Sears made it worthwhile by giving me more to do than just turn pages. As soon as I had learned my first solo, something by Sir John Stainer with an easy pedal cadenza, Sears, at the end of a Sunday morning service, the exited choir having sung its offstage "Amen," slid off the bench, saying, "Play your piece." I did, and that made me an organist. I continued for about a year to assist him at the instrument and later, when my voice had changed, sang with the choir. He was an excellent teacher and straightforward in his ways, ever treating me as an adult and a colleague. My lessons went on till I left for war in 1917 and for a time in 1919 after my return. But after the first years I no longer helped at services; I was having church jobs of my own.

I think I was fourteen when the awareness of vocation came to me. I do not remember how the subject arose; but somehow, in conversation with my mother, father, and sister—a discussion of my studies and my future—I found myself declaring that there was no use their thinking I was not to be a musician, that I was one already, that music was my life and always would be.

Now the family had never been in the least discouraging about music. I imagine that even then their chief aim was to find out my intuitions of destiny. Well, they found out; and so did I. The vehemence of my statement so surprised me, indeed, that before there was time for any reply I burst out crying and fled upstairs. From that day my musical vocation was never questioned. My father, in fact, though music did not speak to him (he was virtually tone-deaf), seemed ever afterward to accept it for me as related to the ministerial call that his mother had hoped would summon him but that somehow had passed him by.

Five days a week I went to the Central High School at Eleventh and Locust Streets, a turreted red sandstone building from the 1880s just on the edge of the business district. It was hardly a step from the big stores and the theaters; and since classes were over before two, it was easy to linger downtown for looking in shop windows, for reading at the public library, for attending a concert or matinee.

From 1909 to 1917 I saw all the shows. No, not quite all, because burlesque was not my passion, nor vaudeville. But I went to all the full-length plays and musicals, the operas, the concerts, and the ballets. At the Auditorium, seat of our resident stock company, and at Convention Hall, where mammoth attractions played, I could get in by selling candy or by ushering. At weekday matinees elsewhere I paid twenty-five cents for a gallery seat, saving this up out of my weekly lunch-and-carfare allowance of $1.25. For concerts (minimum a dollar) I was dependent on Mr. Murray, who sometimes had free seats in connection with his work as a piano-store executive and who would often take me with him to an evening performance. For several years he also took me to Chicago at the Christmas vacation, where we would stay at a hotel and go to the opera every night, afternoons to the art museum, to recitals, and to plays. He profited as a singer from these excursions and took satisfaction from their benefit to me, for he had assumed the guidance of my musical development, being rewarded only by affection and by my delight in his adult companionship.

It was on the first of these trips that I acquired an admiration for Mary Garden's artistic powers that to this day has not relaxed. Melba and McCormack had voices more classically beautiful; Minnie Maddern Fiske and Sir Johnston Forbes-Robertson could act better to speech. But only Garden (working with certain conductors and fellow singers) has ever in my lifetime produced so homogeneous a blend of words and music. That kind of group workmanship has disappeared from the lyric stage; and French opera, the repertory in which it shows to best advantage, has in consequence lost much of its appeal. As Garden herself said to me in Paris on the verge of World War II, "Opera as you and I knew it is dead."

Opera was anything but dead, however, in my 1914 understanding of it; and it was for wrestling with its most impressive embodiment, the Wagnerian, that I essayed getting a grip on it by means of Wagner's own intellectual instruments. Some of the urgency, of course, with which I began that fall to read German philosophy was due to the war itself. For the next three years, till our country had finally opted for a side, the war put us all under such persistent propaganda pressures that in self-defense one had to try (hopefully) to find out for oneself who these military Germans were. That they were the countrymen of Bach and Beethoven was in their favor. That their present-day music was losing world leadership, forcing them to accept condominium with Russia and France, I strongly suspected. And I was sure that between Beethoven's death in 1827 and that of Brahms in 1897 some radical (and possibly fatal) transformation had taken place in German music that one could hopefully come to understand through following its polemics. My eighteenth birthday, in November, would find me immersed in these. But already, during the summer of 1914, the time had begun for me when thinking about music and reading about it were to be no less an urgency than making it.

This intellectualization of my music life was further aided by my next piano teacher, a woman of somewhat higher cultural attainments than her predecessors. The others, however consecrated, had been just musicians. E. Geneve Lichtenwalter had graduate degrees (an M.A. at least) and read non-fiction books. She also composed, and the texts she chose for her vocal works bore literary distinction.

To pay for my weekly lessons, which cost $2.50, I had taken a $25-a-month job as page at the public library; and it was there that I came upon the absorbing narrative that is Richard Wagner's *My Life*. Although Miss Lichtenwalter, to whom I showed my discovery, knew it for not exactly the whole truth about this amazing genius, she merely remarked, "You must also read his enemy Nietzsche." So I went to the philosophy stacks, found the complete works there in English, began at the beginning. From *The Birth of Tragedy* (a hymn to Richard Wagner) to *Thus Spake Zarathustra* and *Ecce Homo* (self-praise in dithyrambs) by way of all those middle works in which he debunks his former hero, I read, in the order of their composition, the whole set. It took me a year.

Meanwhile I was capturing lions. There was Mrs. Hannah Cuthbertson, my sister's painting teacher, a handsome woman of fifty whose toleration of me initiated a still unended series of friendships with painters that was later to furnish the ambience and norm of my Paris life. There was James Gable, too, an impoverished Englishman and friend of "Cuffbutton" (as eventually I was allowed to call Mrs. Cuthbertson), a generalized man of letters, Eton and Oxford trained but without original talent, who had known as a young man everybody artistic and literary in London or Paris, including Wilde and Douglas and all the painters, and who had been everywhere, read everything. With thus as part of my circle a painter and a writer, in Mr. Murray a vocalist of distinction, and in Geneve Lichtenwalter a pianist-pedagogue of the highest aims, I began to use the hospitable habits of my family for getting all these into conversation. In high school days I had been host to the brighter young at Sunday suppers, and Mother had always encouraged my inviting for dinner anyone I wished. Now I mixed the ages more, hoping, I think, to create and to sustain a symposium of the arts.

In 1915 our local board of education opened a junior college in the newly vacated premises of old Central High School. So I resigned from the library and became a freshman, still living at home, of course. In college, since I found banal the clubs that others organized, I designed my own, got myself elected president, ran it my way. I also started a college magazine and very largely wrote that. It was Midwest-oriented, after the Chicago poets I admired, Masters and Sandburg and Lindsay, but also explosive and polemical, like my other admirations, Shaw and Mencken. I am not impressed today by its college-boy brilliance, but I remember much sport being had at its making.

More significant, or so they seem now, are two less clearly motivated matters. One is the slow progress over the next two years, on the part of myself and of my country, toward getting into the European war. The other is a friendship with a Mormon girl.

Alice Smith, great-granddaughter of the Prophet Joseph Smith, was a fellow student. Her father, Dr. Frederick Smith, president of the Reorganized Church of Jesus Christ of Latter Day Saints, in Independence, Missouri, was a man of learning, also a religious executive both physically and intellectually powerful. His spiritual powers, though sufficient for a modern churchman, rarely went the length of prophecy, albeit on one occasion, when opposed by a majority of his bishops, he did, after prayer, order their retirement with the phrase, "This is the voice of inspiration." As such, his solution was accepted; and as such the gesture served him that first time, in later life perhaps a few times more. He was no habitual prophet anyhow. He was an administrator, a sociologist, and a student in psychology of Morton Prince and G. Stanley Hall. Alice's mother was a gracious lady with tact and wit, inveterately not very well and inveterately my protector.

Not that I needed much protection. Alice, monumentally proportioned and as a consequence lacking a little the experience of boys, was finding out, as I was, that unless one is destined to mate early, intellectual friendships are perfectly possible. She was pretty enough too, indeed not unlike those massive creatures that for a time after World War I Pablo Picasso drew and painted. Having always been a big girl, she was not imprisoned by her flesh; she moved with grace. As for the mind, it was quick like her mother's, tireless like that of her father. For me she was a mirror, also a pupil, someone to educate and to protect a little against being blighted by a virtually indigestible religious inheritance. In any case, we took each other on in good faith, read books together, reviewed each other's manuscripts, made jokes, cooked a little; and I manipulated the Doctor by direct attacks tempered with good manners into relaxing the Mormon conventions about female subservience that were still being held up to his two daughters, out of reaction no doubt to the fact that there was no question of their being applicable to his wife.

Alice wrote in later years a memoir of these times in which she described my criticism of her writing as being "sometimes a little harsh and . . . always delivered with a combination of omniscience and patronage that was hard to take." Also that "he wasn't at all reticent about the fact that he expected to be a great man someday."

At the beginning of World War I, in 1914, Americans had tended in the main, I think, to favor neutrality; few west of the Atlantic seaboard wanted the violence to spread. On the contrary, they wanted it stopped, and not by more violence, but by negotiation. Besides, our fellow citizens of Germanic roots were not, in their instinctive sympathies, anti-German. By 1915, however, "pro-German" had begun to be a dirty word; and by 1916 "neutral" meant pro-Ally. From then on, and with that year's mutinies in Europe put down, our progress toward participation was unstoppable. I am not making any political point in this review of history, merely reciting it as a background against which my own actions took place.

These came to be moved, as I went on growing up, by a desire to get into the fighting. All those millions being killed, the sinkings at sea, the filth and vermin of trench life, the pictures of bayonetted guts and burst Belgian babies, everything about it made it seem, to a boy just going twenty, a lovely war. You wanted to be a part of what so many were experiencing, to try yourself out, prove your endurance. You certainly did not want the war to end without your having been through something. You wanted it to go on till you could get there.

At what moment the civilian officers' training camps were opened,

I am not sure; I think in the fall of '16. There was one at Plattsburg, New York, I know, and another at Fort Leavenworth, Kansas. I applied for admission to the latter and was refused. Toward January of 1917, American participation being by then a matter of short delay, I enlisted in a National Guard regiment. There were two of these in the neighborhood, an infantry one in Kansas City and a mounted artillery outfit in nearby Independence. I chose artillery on account of the horses; one could drill with them evenings, go riding Saturdays. I liked being around horses, or thought I did; and joining the Guard made me part of the war. Shortly afterwards, from March 17, when the President and Congress made their declaration, I knew that I should be inducted eventually, along with my regiment, into federal service. So I put my mind back on studies and prepared to pass a pleasant waiting time.

As soon as the college term was over I went with a high school comrade, Ross Rainsburg, to Ann Arbor, Michigan, where he was a student, being also employed nights at a film theater. Once there, I enrolled for courses in gas engines and math and took a job at Ross's movie house. Here I shared with an instructor from the university's Music School both a grand piano and a pipe organ. For comedies we played the usual ragtime and topical songs; for drama we alternated in classical repertory or improvised. Sometimes we improvised together. Neither of us made any use of the cue sheets that were beginning to be furnished with long films.

I also made an attempt to get myself sent overseas with the Ambulance Corps, which turned me down in Allentown, Pennsylvania, on a mistaken diagnosis of flat feet. This enterprise had involved getting myself discharged telegraphically from the Missouri Guard regiment on grounds of having left the state. I also, being that far east, took a trip to New York, where I almost enlisted in the Navy. I was quite ready to take the oath and would have done so had not three sailors at the Brooklyn Navy Yard pleaded with me. I had gone there to be interviewed by the Chief Bandmaster. When the sailors in his office asked my purpose, I replied I had been sent from a recruiting stand on Broadway, where I had seen a poster about bandmaster training. At this, they stared at one another till one said, "He looks a nice kid. Shall we tell him the truth?"

The truth turned out to be, according to them, that there was no assurance at all of a school assignment, that once signed up, I might be shunted off to ship work or to an office, that if I wanted musical advancement I should stay civilian, and that if I wanted real war I should keep out of the Navy. I still rather wanted that course in band conducting, but the sailors' frankness had shocked me back to my original line of quick overseas involvement. So I decided not to wait for the Chief Bandmaster, thanked the boys in white uniform, took my subway to Manhattan and my train west. In early August, back in Kansas City, I met another high school friend, George Phillips, a premedic student. So together we joined the Medical Detachment of my original artillery regiment, now federalized and soon to be heading for camp.

My proto-military maneuvers, going on for a year, had all been known to my family. And the family offered no encouragement, raised no objections. Before my second and final enlistment I had gone to the post office to ask my father's consent. He did not refuse it, simply brought me up to date. "I have been planning to offer you the other house," he said, "if you will sell it. With the money from that you could go away to college." I answered that though going away to college had formerly been what I wanted most of anything, just now I was asking permission to join the army. His reply to that was that on any decision so important to myself he would neither urge me nor stand in my way.

I was to know later that he approved. How could he not? His own father, after all, had been a soldier and so had every other male of his father's generation, as well as of all those earlier ones in earlier wars. Being in a war whenever there was one seemed to him a natural thing. It seemed so to me too. Only in my case, and perhaps it had been that way in other generations, my yearning toward novel experience was a major motive. Neither then nor later did I have much interest in whether any country involved in the war, including my own, was right or wrong. War, I already knew, could not be reasonably viewed as an extension of ethics. After eighteen volumes of Nietzsche and ten of *The Golden Bough* I could only think of it as myth-in-action; and acting out myths was a mystery that I had as much right as any other man to get involved in.

4

My World War I

FOR THE NEXT SIXTEEN MONTHS I lived in uniform. Also in several states—Oklahoma, Texas, New York, Louisiana. But for the immediate next six weeks I lived at home. My regiment, renamed 129th Field Artillery, was not ready for being sent overseas, or even to camp, being short by federal standards in men, officers, and equipment. While waiting for the last to be supplied by Washington and a camp prepared, we stayed in Kansas City, built up the personnel. For the time being, though we all had uniforms, there was no drilling.

Convention Hall had been requisitioned as headquarters, and some of the boys from out of town were bunked there. We took our meals at a restaurant, paid in chits, kept office hours. The Medical Detachment of the 129th—consisting of three officers, called Surgeons, and some fifteen enlisted men, two of whom were graduate pharmacists—received the sick from eight to five (chiefly venereal cases) and vaccinated everybody. George Phillips, whose family had moved to Lee's Summit, a farming suburb, came to stay with my family during the waiting period. We were thus together all the time, remained so later at camp, and never at any moment lacked for things to talk about. At this time, however, we used to like of an evening to wind our woolen puttees very smooth, put on our broad campaign hats at the level, and go adventuring among the downtown young women who had sugar daddies.

Camp Doniphan, near Fort Sill, Oklahoma, to which we were removed about October, was a desert paradise of sun and dust, high winds, and hard ground. So hard was the ground that for setting up the square tents in which, by eights, we were to pass the winter each peg had to be driven into a hole dug out with a pickax and for thirty minutes softened up with water. Also, it was cold that winter, fifteen and twenty below for weeks on end. Even the bread froze, had to be cut with a meat saw. And the dust storms, which penetrated everything—your clothes, your shoes, your gloves, your fur-lined goggles—blew just as hard in cold months as in others.

Fair weather, however, could be beautiful, with the dust that hung high in air creating displays at sunset such as I had not seen before, nor have I since. And the Wichita Mountains to our north, a glory of barren shapes at any time, served on calm afternoons as objective for horseback rides. Our objective almost any evening was the village of Lawton, twenty miles away, a prairie tank-town that we went to simply to be going somewhere, standing in line an hour for a poor meal or a soda, two hours for a good hot bath. The jitneys that took us there were buggy-topped high-riding Fords, which would set a straight course across the billowing land, just as if it were open sea, and which in high winds could easily capsize.

During that fall and winter our division was beaten into right military shape. But no assignment came for overseas. It seemed that all the forces except for a few regulars and Marines, sent as tokens, were having to wait it out in camp till ships and tanks and guns and shells were ready for a great joint moving. Indeed, the American Expeditionary Force that at the end of 1918 turned a stalemated trench war into victory was nowhere seen in Europe before late spring, more than a year after war's declaration. While we waited, draftees were sent in for enlarging our numbers, and some unsatisfactory officers were replaced. One of our most effective officers was Captain Harry Truman of Company D, whom I never met, though I knew well his First Lieutenant George Arrowsmith, a sometime beau of my sister's, who later, as dentist, moved with the President to Washington. Meanwhile bright fall had turned into cold winter and that into spring before at last, in June, the outfit sailed.

But long before that, I had left, having got myself transferred to aviation. There must have been, among the swelling troops, a shortage of flyers, for my application, made at the end of November, when I came of age, was processed so rapidly that within the fortnight I was ordered to Kansas City for tests and an interview. This last was brief; and at its end I was accepted charmingly (yes, that is the word) by an examining officer who asked me just one question—about the compression-and-expansion cycle of a gas-engine cylinder—then, when I seemed to hesitate, gave me the answer. By mid-January I was in Pilots' Ground School at the University of Texas.

I had outsmarted myself by leaving the regiment, which saw England and France that summer and by fall was fighting in the Argonne. On the other hand, I had got what I wanted just then, activity. Though for the next eleven months I was never to be in danger and rarely in discomfort, I was not ever again to be bored by the war, because my abilities were being used; and my life was in consequence brimful of novel experience, of adventure. I never became fully a pilot, however, because before that could have occurred the war department found that it had a glut of pilots and did some foot dragging. Anyhow, though wings were highly esteemed, I knew now that I wanted, more than I wanted to fly, to be doing something interesting all the time. And that is what started happening the day I became a cadet.

My two-month stay in Austin, Texas, began cold, with frozen rain on all the trees and all those hilly streets, and ended eight weeks later with spring full-blown. During that time there had been no dullness and no leisure. I wrote to Alice Smith March 21:

> We have worked here harder and steadier than I have ever done in my life, I think. From 5:30 in the morning till 10 o'clock at night we drill and study. The drill is our salvation; if it weren't for the two or three hours a day we spend at that we would go mad. The rest of the time we take rapid-fire lecture notes. At night we learn the day's notes in order to make room in our minds for the next day's. . . . The work is entirely a matter of hearing everything and remembering it all. . . . Everybody passes a quiz in every subject every week

or else busts back a week. More than one bust and a man leaves the school.

It was at just this time that the Army discovered its excess of pilots. Francis Poindexter, an athletic top sergeant from my Kansas City regiment, had in preceding me to Austin by two weeks gone straight from there to flying school. My class, just that much too late finishing, was sent to a cadets' concentration camp in Dallas. After a month there of all-day drill and rifle practice, I was a fair shot at clay pigeons, but thoroughly restless. So were the others, all the several thousands of us lodged in frame barracks at the fairgrounds.

At this point a choice was offered. We could either wait for assignment to a flying school or go immediately, if our academic record was good, to Columbia University. There we would learn radio telephony, a new method supposedly better than Morse code for controlling artillery fire from the air (the chief use for aviators in World War I). We would not be trained as pilots till after the three-month course; but the chance of an early overseas assignment was at least as good as that of the still untrained ones, maybe better. Naturally I applied, and so did many others. Out of them all, about thirty were selected, mostly men with credits in engineering; and within a day or two we were off to New York.

Here began a third military phase. My time with a regiment of the line had been tolerable for its physical activities, also as a schooling in democracy. The ground school, designed for an elite, had been no less than absorbing by the completeness with which it occupied both mind and body. New York was to offer delights wholly independent of the military experience but come by, in large part, through being a soldier.

Learning the theory of the vacuum tube and the wiring complexities of a "wireless" telephone was no less rigorous under the instruction of Columbia's professorate (including, as I remember, the famous immigrant inventor Pupin) than the engine and airplane work done earlier at Austin. But by this time I was used to stuffing the mind and could do it fast. I could even take time out to teach equations to a buddy. And all the time New York was lying round us, like heaven in our infancy, and awaiting us on week ends.

We were lodged in a semicircular gymnasium behind the library and fed in a cafeteria just above that. We swam in a pool that underlay our sleeping quarters, drilled in the athletic field. An hour and a quarter were allowed for the evening meal before we were due at 7:15 to study under guard in the philosophy library. And since the regular nourishment (something put out by a lunch-counter chain) was the most offensive I had yet encountered, with my buddy of the time, Leland Poole, I used to frequent as often as funds allowed a nearby rotisserie, La Parisienne, where in the window chickens turned on spits.

New York, unlike the other cities I had been to, was in love with the armed forces. And by the spring of 1918 (which I witnessed twice that year, having just come from Texas) New York was organized for showing them a good time. There were dozens of free canteens, dance halls, hostess houses, libraries, reading and writing rooms, bureaus for picking up theater tickets, church par-ties for meeting girls, and dinner invitations. And the women one met this way—music students, art students, grand ladies, chic debs, working girls—were having the same fun we were. I formed at this time a permanent connection with two households that seemed to have adopted both Leland and me, old New York families that lived in four-story houses, had servants, and dressed for dinner.

I furthermore had friends from Kansas City. Cuffbutton was living with her lawyer son in Elizabeth, New Jersey; and the literate world-traveler James Gable, in warrant officer's uniform, was editing a Navy magazine at Cape May. Also, two girls of my own age, one of whom I had known since second grade, were studying piano with famous teachers and living almost next door, on Claremont Avenue. Through these young artists I came to know others, both young ones and older ones, and to experience from the inside New York's music life. This was no different in kind from Kansas City's, any more than the families I came to know were very different from my own in social attitudes. It was merely that New York seemed to offer, in every domain of excellence, more and better. One did not have to fight one's way to quality. Big Time there—musical, social, intellectual—flourished and passed for natural; beauty and distinction were not alien ideals, but a way of life.

On May 21 I wrote to Alice Smith:

I have been here a month now and will remain two more, receive a commission as Squadron Radio Officer (probably a 2nd Lt.), fly 5 weeks at Fort Sill, and go across. I am very glad I chose this course, as the fellows I graduated from the ground school with may not be sent over for two years. . . .

Alice, you would love New York in wartime. . . . Saturday was the Red Cross parade. It took from 1:30 till twenty minutes of eight for it to pass; and of course Fifth Avenue was beflagged as only Fifth Avenue can be when it wants to turn itself out. There were nurses and nurses and nurses and ambulance units and boy scouts and home guards and women knitting and more nurses and such a lot of bands. There were bands playing "Onward Christian Soldiers" and bands playing "They Go Wild, Simply Wild over Me," and bugle bands, and a French band that limped and wore blue spiral leggings. . . .

Two months later, also to Alice, I summed up the New York adventure as "a grand lark." In addition,

my ability to do a couple of parlor tricks on the piano . . . got me places I should most likely never have seen in civilian clothes. . . . I saw a little of the homes of the idle poor and visited in those of the busy rich . . . withal learned many things. As Mr. Gable said when I went to see him in Philadelphia, "One always feels very sophisticated after a sojourn in New York, doesn't one?"

Fort Sill, my next place of residence, had since my earlier stay there lost Camp Doniphan and acquired a flying field. It had also acquired the comforts of a well-run war. It had not lost, however, its outrageous climate. For December's ten below we had now, believe it or not, 120 in the shade without any shade. We got up at half-past four, did desultory flying till half-past one (my pilot's book shows very few hours), ate, spent the afternoon lying on our bunks and cussing, toward sundown bathed and dressed and walked out, usually to the hospitable chintzy bungalow of the American Library Association, where we had tea or supper. After a while we were commissioned and sent away—though not, as promised, to Europe, merely to Louisiana, for playing in the air with wireless telephones.

In this soft aqueous jungle where giant mosquitoes that could bite through any blanket flew in V-shaped squadron formation, our own flying was minimal, mechanics' ranks being decimated by an influenza called in flying circles "hispano-sneeza." We met the Southern girls at dancing parties and were taken by them in motorboats up bayous, where sunset's ever-changing afterglow would last for hours on the waveless waters. We also played bridge at the Officers' Club. And talked about the flying we were not doing.

In less than a month I caught the current flu, which went less hard with us in the South than with those in the North. I wrote Alice that I found being ill

disgusting . . . well, not entirely, after all, because it got me out of some disagreeable work and gave me a week's mild adventure in the hospital, where I was starved and sweated and purged and rubbed and examined and bathed by a nurse. . . . One day, when I tried to walk, I fainted. That too was interesting, because I had never fainted before.

I returned to barracks ten pounds lighter, all of which I got back by eating a pound of chocolates a day for ten days and not moving from the bridge table. At the end of that time, along with twenty others of my radio-telephony class, I was ordered overseas, with home leave on the way.

Geneve Lichtenwalter gave me a party; Mr. Murray had me photographed in uniform; and I went to church on Sunday with my father. The next seven weeks, spent in New York, were pure play, accompanied, the last five of them, by the frustration of having quite literally missed the boat. I say literally because I had been assigned to a ship, had acquired all the proper equipment (including trench boots from Abercrombie and Fitch and a camel's-hair sleeping bag), and said good-by. Then came the two Armistice Days, the false-news one on November 9, the real one two days later. The false one had been fun, the celebration of it spontaneous. The real one was strictly for civilians. All such were justly joyous at the ending of an awful thing. But for many among the sailors and the military who might have felt romantic, like myself, about adventure, or who were certainly, many many of them, happier to be away from home than back there, or who were not at all eager to leave off being paid—for all sorts of us the riot was a little sad. We had not planned our war that way, but wanted it to go on till we ourselves cried, "Hold, enough!"

And now it had become, through its sudden ending, a dead story. Phillips wrote from France that the boys who had for a year cried, "When are we going over?" were now whining, "When do we go home?" As for myself, in less than five weeks, which is good speed, I had resigned my commission, received my discharge, and gone back to my father's roof.

Here I took up my past and reflected my future. I returned to organ lessons and to the piano. Since the church where I had played just before the war did not choose to give back my job, I got me another. And mid-January, at the second term, I again took up classes at the junior college. Back at my own matters I felt older, more grown-up. I was also thinking hard about getting away, going East again or maybe to Europe for studies.

I had not always of late years been sure whether music should, or properly could, be used as a breadwinner. Perhaps some other form of writing might be my destiny. But with my return to music itself, to piano and organ and choir conducting, I knew where my joy was and would always be—in the sound of music and in making it sound my way. All the same, I was twenty-two and must be getting about the rest of my education. It was already late, but not too late. With money I could manage everything.

Just on the chance, I wrote my uncle for a loan, was refused. It was my friendship with the Smiths that resolved the matter. The good Doctor, a professional himself, knew well my problem; but it was his wife who thought up the solution.

This was to be, simply enough, a loan from the Mormon Church. There was a fund in the church's budget for training teachers. Young Mormons borrowing money from this could either pay it back or teach it out. I protested that I had no intention of teaching in a church college. Mrs. Smith laughed and said she could not imagine me there. Alice urged too; she must have. In any case, Dr. Smith proposed the matter, though not as the "voice of inspiration"; and since the Prophet's mantle still lay over him, no effective objection could be raised. Later, when it seemed I was not likely to repay the $2,000 I had used in my first year at Harvard, Dr. Smith was reproached. As a matter of fact, this debt was one of several matters on which he found himself so strongly attacked by his bishops that he needed inspiration, and got it, to remove them from office.

It was nearly twenty years before I cleared up that debt, and then reluctantly. At the time I had no plan for paying it; all that concerned me was getting East. And Mrs. Smith had said, "I'll make it come out right."

Two other events from that spring remain vivid, my trying out of a drug and my grandmother's death.

The drug had been given me by Dr. Smith. Passing the previous winter, for his wife's health, in the Southwest, he had made inquiries about a hallucinogenic cactus known as peyote. As a student of man's higher powers, notably those of second sight and prophecy, he had read about this plant in Havelock Ellis. In New Mexico he had observed it among the Indians, who eat the dried bud with religious intent, certain Catholic ones taking a tea of it for Communion. He had also tried it out himself at the ceremonies and had experienced its characteristic excitation to feats of endurance and to colored visions. He had informed himself further that the essential drug of it was "neither injurious nor habit-forming." He had described his experience to me and, when I asked if I might try it too, gave me five bumpy little buttons, less than an inch across and hard as wood, saying, "I suggest you take these at night. Just chew them up and go to bed."

I did exactly that, though the taste was so horrid, especially where tough crumbs stuck in my teeth, that eventually I vomited. This clearing of the stomach relieved the nausea without interfering with the drug. The effects, full visions each as complete in color and texture as a stage set, began slowly to appear before my closed or open eyes, then came more rapidly till two hours later they were flashing at least twice every second, with no delay involved in their complete perception. Each one, moreover, had a meaning, could have been published with a title; and their assembled symbolisms or subjects, though not always sequentially related, constituted a view of life not only picturesque and vast, but just as clearly all mine and all true.

I had gone to my room for taking the peyote about eight o'clock, and its full effects were in operation by ten. These continued without letup till around eight the next morning, when I dressed and went about my errands with no fatigue. The last four hours had been a grand prophetic view, always in color, of what my life and future were to be. I saw this in pictures, all symbolic, all quite clear as to meaning, and all arranged in chronological order by decades, even sometimes by exact years of my age.

Though this experience had been in every way splendid, I did not try to reproduce it till somewhat later. I described it to Dr. Smith, of course, an itemized report having been his price. It remained the price when next year I shared the drug and its adventures with Harvard friends. In the next three years I spent a peyote night perhaps ten times. And all were surprising, all visually sumptuous. But in none did the heavens so definitely open as they had done for me that first time, alone in my room.

It was in that same room that my mother woke me one morning with the news of death. My grandmother Flora Thomson, spending the winter with us as usual, had several months earlier taken to her bed. Since there was nothing observably the matter with her, nothing but everything, and since she was in her eighty-ninth year, it seemed clear that she was not to be on earth much longer. She had little to leave behind, having long ago distributed her land and little by little, in the years she had been a widow, spent most of the little money she had had. All the same, she wished to leave a legacy, however small, to me. I was her only male grandchild, and I had been a soldier like her husband. So she sent for her nephew Lex McDaniel, who was a lawyer, changed her will, and bequeathed me one hundred dollars.

Shortly afterward she ceased to be aware. Her speech, however, kept following familiar patterns. She would pray aloud: "Forgive us our sins and come to see us soon." When she died asleep, late in March, we took her to Saline County for burial beside her Confederate soldier, waiting since 1862 in the graveyard of their country church, called Rehoboth. On the morning of the funeral there arrived by train, for paying her last call on "Miss Flora," a Negro woman of near Miss Flora's age who had in early years belonged to her. This visit was the last to be received by a woman who for the last half of her nearly ninety years had herself been ever a visitor. Indeed, as departing guests are wont to do, she had just made, leaving my father's house, a gift to his youngest child. And it was with that in cash of my own, against some private need, that I left home that August for the promised land of Cambridge, Massachusetts.

5

Harvard,
Jumping-Off Place
for Europe

HARVARD HAD BEEN CHOSEN for my especial needs, which were three—good keyboard lessons, available in Boston; training in harmony, counterpoint, and composition, said to be excellent at this university; and full access to its arts and letters. My ultimate aim at this time was to become an organist and choirdirector in some well-paying city church and from there to pursue a composer's career.

In Cambridge, on the first day I took a room; on the second I acquired a piano and a piano teacher. The room was in a college-owned house, kept by a Mrs. Brown, at 12 Oxford Street; the piano was a medium-sized grand, bought on time; the teacher was Heinrich Gebhard. I inquired about organ teachers too, but found the best ones all vacationing. And since I still had lots of time to spare (four hours a day at the piano being quite enough), I engaged a teacher for French conversation and in a coaching school brushed up on Cicero, in this way getting ready both to pass the French reading-test and to satisfy a Latin requirement. Of an evening I covered the Boston suburbs and shore drives in the sidecar of a summer school student also residing at Mrs. Brown's. And on

Labor Day week end I visited wartime New York friends at Sullivan, Maine, in their immense "cottage" overlooking from on high Frenchman's Bay and the island of Mount Desert.

After term began, time stopped; and for the next two years it had no flow. I did my studies, sang in the glee club and in the daily choir (being more often than not engaged on Sundays elsewhere as organist). For exercise, unless the Charles was frozen, I mostly rowed, sometimes on a lightweight crew, more usually in a single shell. I attended plays in Boston occasionally, always the symphony concerts and the many recitals of ancient and modern music offered free to Harvard students at Paine Hall. As often as I could I went to New York, where I still had wartime friends who lived in style and where, invited out, one dressed for dinner. This costume change, along with a tail coat for singing in the glee club, had been acquired from a Beacon Street tailor for the exact amount of my grandmother's legacy.

The director of the chapel choir and of the glee club was Dr. Archibald T. Davison, known as "Doc," thirty-four, smallish, sandy-haired, and balding. A Scottish disciplinarian of relentless mission, he had already transformed the college glee club from an adjunct of the Mandolin Club into a virtuoso choral society; and he was proceeding in the next few years, through the Graduate School of Education, to transform throughout America music instruction in the schools. It was during my time that he first offered his course (with singing laboratory) in the History of Choral Music. Some years later he was to found today's main model among courses for laymen, known nationally as "Harvard's Music I." A man of great personal reserve (he lived with a widowed mother and did not marry till she died), he had few close friends, just a hand-picked student or two. All the same, he was companionable, much loved, and with younger people quite gregarious. For three years I was his aide and substitute at the Appleton Chapel organ, in conducting the chapel choir and glee club, and for teaching his courses. I was the first, in fact, of a long series of musicians to be marked indelibly by him; and I remained for two decades quite possibly the finest choral conductor of them all.

My faculty advisor was the composer Edward Burlingame Hill, for whose Modern French Music I had signed up in my first term. The next year I assisted him in that course, also in the general

History of Music, later in a History of Russian Music. Orchestration I learned only from him. Aloof but not unfriendly, tall, fifty, athletic, well-to-do, and French-trained, he was a Bostonian's ideal of the gentleman-artist. But there were also in him a straightforwardness of statement not unlike my father's and a thoroughness of knowledge certainly related to that of his own father, a chemistry professor and the son of a Harvard president. My friendship with Mr. Hill and with his family long outlasted my attachment to Doc Davison. We wrote each other letters, paid visits, talked of music and musicians forever, until his death, in fact, in 1960.

It was during those first two years that I came to know S. Foster Damon, slender, pale poet with a blond mustache, at that time instructing in English A while preparing privately, since Harvard would have none of it, the book that was to open up the language of William Blake. Foster was a composer as well as a poet and a scholar—also a close associate of Amy Lowell, whose biographer he became in the 1930s. I do not remember how I first knew him; but I do remember long walks and talks; and I remember his bringing me music and books that he thought I ought to know. Some of these, such as the critical writings of T. S. Eliot and the Irish tales of James Stephens, I found merely informative or charming. Others changed my life. Among these last were the piano works of Erik Satie, a pile of them four inches high, and a thin small volume called *Tender Buttons,* by Gertrude Stein. I returned these favors by introducing him to peyote, which we would take together, sometimes with another poet and English A instructor, Robert Hillyer. Foster has often re-appeared in my life and almost always with gifts in hand, the most remarkable of these being a facsimile collection, with Damon's notes, issued in 1937 at Brown University, of one hundred American popular songs from before the Civil War, a source that has helped me ever since to evoke early times in composing for films and dramatic spectacles. After his wife had lost her mind and the neighborhood urchins of Providence would come to jeer, he built a playroom in his basement, invited them in. For Foster Damon was inveterately an opener of doors.

Among my Harvard musical contemporaries the closest in musical understanding was the organist Melville Smith, brainy and birdlike, a chirruping and twittering companion who could also peck. Melville had a relentless hatred of the bogus and a nose for quality. It was he who in Paris discovered Nadia Boulanger as a teacher ideal for both our needs and led me to her. There was also my almost-homonym Randall Thompson, like myself an acquirer of the choral-writing techniques. And there was Leopold Mannes, who with Leopold Godowski, both of them sons of famous musicians, both of them amateur photographers too, took out in their college days a patent on color photography that led them later to the Eastman laboratories and to perfecting a type of film now known as Kodachrome. A slightly older student from the suburbs, Walter Piston (born Pistone), was by gift the best musician of us all. He had a good mind, too, and firm opinions. But, as for so many of Italian background, both life and art were grim, without free play.

It was the epoch for ankle-length coonskin overcoats, if you could afford one, and for soft brown hats crushed shapeless. Under these we wore for most occasions gray herringbone, its cut the timeless Ivy League three-piece, for formal informality the period's golf togs, which were plus-fours, plaid stockings, and brogues. From late November to March we flapped around a snow-clogged universe in unbuckled galoshes. For Symphony Hall we took a rattling articulated prepayment streetcar known to college boys as "parlor-bedroom-and-bath"; for downtown errands, then as now, the subway. Since Cambridge was a gastronomic desert, on Saturday nights we mostly went to Boston—to the Athens (Greek), to Jake Wirth's (German) to Durgin-Park (steaks), to Hung Far Low (in Chinatown), and to the Boston Oyster House. Speakeasies having not yet appeared, Harvard at the turn of the twenties was almost as dry in practice as in principle. One easy binge was Hostetter's Stomach Bitters. Less effective were the meads and hydromels I brewed with the aid of my massive British landlady from recipes found in a seventeenth-century cookbook, *The Closet of Sir Kenelm Digby, Kt. Opened*. More successfully achieved after the same book's formulas were perfumes for pipe tobacco compounded of ambergris and aromatic herbs.

For all the cultural advantages of Boston, plus its lovely sky line made soft and feathery by chimney pots and its sometimes tolerable food, I never really felt at home there or quite at ease. New

York, a boastful city, let one swell up. But in Boston, even still, no one expands; the inhabitants seem rather to aim at compressing one another. From my arrival there, I had felt that over all New England, save Maine perhaps, there hung a crowd of enemies to man, of circumvolant Calvinistic warlocks no part of my theology. And I grew to understand the need for placating these every century or so with human flesh and blood. In seventeenth-century Salem those killed off were kin and neighbors; during the Civil War, slaveowners resisting reform; right then, though I did not know it, there was coming a need again (first felt in Boston, where in 1919 the police force went on strike) to stop something in its tracks (this time, revolution) through the sacrifice of two Italian immigrants. The sky, so blue on coldest days, the bright white snow, the grass, the lakes, the sea—nature in general seemed not the enemy, though rarely did it bless. But in the wary eyes of everyone and in the necks that never turned around, one could feel the fear that makes them all take exercise, put money by, study forever, and worship ancestors. For me the exercise and study were just fine, though economy as such I scarcely thought a virtue. As for ancestors, I had plenty myself; and I learned early to keep silence on that subject in the drawing rooms, since referring to anything that might have happened before 1620 was almost as if one had blasphemed.

Boston's own silence treatment administered against blasphemy I witnessed at an Appleton Chapel Sunday service. Just at the end of the sermon a young Hindu in blue serge stood suddenly on the first step of the chancel. Rapidly, quietly, distinctly, he said he was Jesus Christ and that he had chosen wisely, he hoped, this place and time for announcing his return, adding that since his identity might be doubted, he would show us in his hands the scars of nails, and in his feet. So far, no one had moved. But as he bent down to untie his shoe, Doc Davison from the organ pealed forth a hymn, which the choir and congregation rose to sing. At the same time the young man was led backstage and from there by outside path to the front steps, whence a professor from the medical school whisked him off in a car. Benediction pronounced, those present exchanged good mornings over the postlude and went off to Sunday dinner. Though for thirty seconds we had been held breathless, neither on this occasion nor afterward did I ever hear this Second Coming mentioned.

Before the end of my first year I had found a quite good organ job at a family-endowed church in a family-owned town south of Boston—North Easton, Massachusetts, seat originally of a shovel factory, now of seven handsome estates all belonging to people named Ames, descendants of the early shovel-maker. There I enjoyed a fair organ, a fair choir, and a fair salary, also a two-month summer vacation. I would go there by train on Saturdays, rehearse, sleep, play one service, eat, come back. On the train I marked papers or did my philosophy reading, finding rail noises good for concentration, just as many of the less music-minded were finding it a help, when studying, to put on radio headphones. I kept this job till I went to France in 1921, and I never got bored with it or quarreled with my minister. In that academic year, my second, I had earned my keep and not done anything unpleasant either, for besides my church job, which paid, I think, $800, I had an assistantship in the music department worth $500, as well as scholarship money.

The summer of 1920 began with the Chapel choir at Commencement exercises singing Josquin des Prés from the top of Sanders Theater to the Belgian war hero Cardinal Mercier. I had stayed on in Cambridge during July, reading and riding, spent August on Frenchman's Bay with my New York friends. I wrote music too, my first inditings, chiefly songs and choral pieces, one of the latter to see print two decades later. In September I went on a wild-goose chase to Missouri. President Lowell had passed me for a Rhodes scholarship at Oxford (though heaven knows why I wanted it); and so had Frank Aydelotte, then a professor at M.I.T. and chairman of the American Committee. When those in charge of the Missouri selection asked for an interview in St. Louis, I decided to risk the fare. It was the president of our state university who received me; and like my examining officer for aviation school he asked one question, "Where are the Virgin Islands?" (just acquired by the United States and in the news). When I replied, "I've no idea," he thanked me and rose, later selecting someone from his own university.

Going on to Kansas City, I found George Phillips, six months back from France, the first of my own contemporaries describable as belonging to a "lost" generation. Not that there was anything personally lost about him. It is simply that Phillips, destined by choice for medicine, had been twice interrupted in his studies, once for a year and a half on the Mexican border as a militiaman, while the regular army invaded Mexico, and later by two years in the Field Artillery. Four years, or nearly, taken out of his medical schooling had lost him for the profession, just as a similar time-out in France had removed many a soldier from the trade in which he would from eighteen to twenty-two have been passing his apprenticeship.

This state of their being lost to a chosen profession is what Gertrude Stein's *hôtelier* Monsieur Pernollet had meant when he said of the returned French soldiers, "*Ils sont tous une génération perdue.*" And that is what Miss Stein told me she had meant when she later applied this remark to American war veterans. As quoted by Ernest Hemingway, who was not at all lost to newspaper reporting, since he had gone right back to it, the term was supposed to mean, I think, that something in the war experience had rendered many permanently rootless. This idea, although obviously true, is nevertheless somebody's mistranslation, for had the Bellay hotel-keeper meant that, he would have said, "*une génération* de *perdus.*"

But George Phillips was really lost to medicine; and though he became a successful journalist, he never got to use, save as an amateur, his instinct for diagnosis by compassion. I have no reason to suppose that he regretted. I merely use his case for pointing out how an observation mainly sociological got turned into a literary slogan.

I have said that for two years time stopped, as indeed it often does in the years just after twenty. Following the showy end of adolescence (for it is easy to cut a figure at nineteen), there are likely to be some vague years spent just working, before one re-appears in the world at twenty-six? My own time underground, unless we count war years, was short of average. I had been late going in, prompt coming out—although for three years after I was twenty-five, so displaced had been youth's order of events, I made no break with my immediate past.

That past can be identified with my plan for being professionally an organist, my future with abandoning in 1925 all intercourse with the instrument. The growing distaste for any such career was to begin in Paris, where I turned twenty-five in 1921. The replacement of a mainly liturgical view of music, begun in Kansas City at Grace Church, by a more secular view, French-oriented—though this too had its roots way back, in my early contacts through Geneve Lichtenwalter with the piano music of Debussy and Ravel and through Mr. Murray with the opera repertory of Mary Garden —had taken place chiefly in Cambridge. Partly through Davison, himself French-trained, but even more through the views and musical ways of E. B. Hill, which were French to the core, I came in my Harvard years to identify with France virtually all of music's recent glorious past, most of its acceptable present, and a large part of its future.

It was consequently no sudden or disconnected event, as going off to Oxford would have been, for me to move to France in 1921. On the contrary, it appeared to me as natural, though it happened through no planning on my part. It had already been decided in the spring that the glee club would take a trip abroad that summer. It also happened that two traveling fellowships named after music's founder at Harvard, John Knowles Paine, had lately become available. Melville Smith was already using one in Paris. The other I could have if I promised to return after one year and finish my degree. Giving traveling fellowships to undergraduates was not customary; but my good friend Hill was chairman that year, and Davison was warmly disposed. Had the regular chairman, Walter Spalding, not been absent on sabbatical, the vote might not have gone through, since he and I had never quite got on, I disdaining somewhat his courses, he correcting me without cease for my uppishness. But he *was* away, and I *was* appointed, and I *did* stay abroad the next year.

It was in anticipation of this absence that my father and mother came to visit me in Cambridge. That was in late spring, and the weather was fine. Mother enjoyed the rhododendrons in the Yard, my father the feastings on fresh lobster. He was also courtly to a Southern lady, the mother of Oliver Payne, my glee club roommate, who gave parties for them and took them places. One evening, on a ship of the Outside Line, we passed at sunset through Cape Cod Canal and slept aboard. In New York I showed them off to both my bohemian and my stylish friends; nothing went wrong. Nor were they displeased, either, with their first trip East. They went home by way of Kentucky, soon after I had sailed, having shipped ahead my books and music.

6

The First Time
I Saw Paris

W E HAD BEEN DETAINED in Le Havre all day on ceremonies and garden parties, so that after an evening train ride through the Frenchest countryside there is, it was going on eleven when at the Gare Saint-Lazare we climbed into horse-drawn buses, especially mobilized, and set out for the rue de Vaugirard. But dark comes late the twenty-first of June; and Paris lamps, some arc-light and some gas, mixed with the dying daylight to produce a luminosity half white, half green. And as from my perch in the upstairs front seat there rolled by like painted scenery the Madeleine, Concorde, Chamber of Deputies, I recognized their every detail. This well-known species of illusion I had experienced exactly once before, on first entering in Kansas City, at the age of ten, the Willis Wood Theatre. It does not happen many times to anyone; but when it does, it stamps upon a color-photographic image the memory of something personally possessed.

The adventures of that two-week stay in Paris—lunching with Maréchal Foch, a tea with Joffre, elegant parties at private establishments and a shocking push at the presidential palace, a masked ball at the Opéra, ballets by Milhaud and Cocteau and all six of Les Six at the Théâtre des Champs-Elysées, singing three packed-house concerts in the Salle Gaveau and conducting at High Mass in Saint-Eustache—all these were to characterize the trip. And after two months of similar occasions in eastern France, Alsace, the

Rhineland (still occupied by American troops), Venice, and the Italian east coast (where in Pesaro I conducted a whole concert), I felt very European and almost ready for settling down (with cane and spats) to a Paris winter.

Actually, when the tour disbanded in Geneva, I stayed on in Switzerland for a fortnight and then spent four delicious weeks in England, two of them at Oxford. There in High Street digs right next to Magdalen I wrote some articles promised to *The Boston Transcript* and with an American girl, unoccupied just then by absent Oxford, viewed all the other colleges and gardens. She also taught me to punt. There too I bought a British bicycle with hand brakes and set off alone, shipping my trunk to Southampton, where, after ten days of sight-seeing cathedrals and landscapes, I took ship for France.

Once more it came over me, though not as a recognition, that sense of owning completely the thing seen, when in a bright September morn at five, having left my bike and luggage at the port, I climbed the cobbled streets of Saint-Malo. I was climbing toward French breakfast with a view. And as I climbed, stepping around tiny women in black beating small laden asses with large sticks and exorting them with cries, I found myself, though just from England, saying, "Thank God to be back where they speak my language." In later years I used to say that I lived in Paris because it reminded me of Kansas City. And Paris can present to anyone, of course, since it contains all possible elements, an image of his origins. In my case, I now learned, not only was Paris to be my new home town, but all France, so little did I feel alien there, was to be like another Missouri—a cosmopolitan crossroads, frank and friendly and actually not far from the same geographic size.

Thus meditating, I progressed possessively through my new-found land (and because of Henry Adams, by way of Mont-Saint-Michel) to Paris, where, although it was to be my home, I still had no house. And this I started looking for while waiting for my lessons to begin. I knew they were to be with Nadia Boulanger, since Melville Smith, who had discovered her that spring, had convinced me she was just right for a Harvard American. But as she would not be in town before October, there was a month during which I could look around. Temporarily staying with a French family, I walked the whole of Paris that lovely fall, pricing rooms and practicing my French, till I finally settled down at 20 rue de

Berne in a *maison meublée* chiefly inhabited, like all that street, by daughters of joy.

Nadia's mother, Madame Ernest Boulanger (Princess Mychetsky), delighted in my compromising address. I valued its freedom to make music at night, when my neighbors were out, dining late or dancing, love-time for kept girls being afternoon. And there was a hideous, kindly chambermaid, who washed my socks and all day long on varicosed legs climbed the five flights of circular stairs, bringing me hot water at any time, a tray if I were ill. I was in walking distance both of Boulanger and of a Swedish church where I could practice the organ. My fifth-floor room (with *cabinet de toilette*) contained, in addition to bed, mirrored wardrobe, and two chairs, a grand piano mounted on blocks and fitted with organ pedals. This I had procured on hire; and at this I worked out fugues by Bach, perfected later in practice at the church. Here too, since the leg-supporting blocks that gave room for the pedal keyboard also raised the height, I used to compose or write counterpoint standing up, using for desk the piano's level top.

Nadia Boulanger, then thirty-four, taught harmony at the Conservatoire, organ-playing and counterpoint at the Ecole Normale de Musique. A tall, soft-haired brunette still luscious to the eye, she had already resigned womanly fulfillment and vowed her life to the memory of her sister (a gifted composer early dead), to the care of her long-widowed mother (who had married her elderly voice teacher at eighteen), and to musically bringing up the young. A certain maternal warmth was part of her charm for all young men; but what endeared her most to Americans was her conviction that American music was about to "take off," just as Russian music had done eighty years before. Here she differed with the other French musicians, who, though friendly enough toward Americans (we were popular then), lacked faith in us as artists. I joined her organ class of three, to which Melville had procured me a scholarship from the Ecole Normale, and also took private lessons in strict counterpoint, showing her, as well, my pieces, which were beginning to pour out. The other organist beside Smith and myself was a gaunt Norwegian lad named Hessenberg. A third American, studying privately, was Aaron Copland, who had discovered her for himself the preceding summer at the just-opened Conservatoire Américain in Fontainebleau.

Above: My Virginia great-grandfather, Reuben Ellis McDaniel, born in 1799, brought his family and slaves to Missouri in '43.

Above left: Giles McDaniel, Reuben's son, at eighteen, in Confederate army uniform.

Below: Flora Elizabeth Thomson, his daughter (1830–1919), my grandmother as I knew her.

Below left: Quincy Adams Thomson (1827–1862), my father's father.

Below: Flora Thomson and her children —Reuben Yancy, Leona Townsend, Quincy Alfred.

Above: Quincy Alfred Thomson (1862–1943), my father, at about the time he moved to Kansas City.

Below left: Clara May Gaines Thomson (1865–1957), my mother, as a young married woman.

Below: Wedding photo, 1883. May is eighteen, Quincy twenty-one.

My cousin Lela Garnett in 1902. She gave me my first piano lessons. I called her Cuz.

Ruby, my sister, who was eleven years older than I and a china painter. She bought me a piano and paid for my early lessons.

Beulah Gaines, my mother's half sister, who gave piano lessons. She lived in Slater but came to see us often.

Cecil Gaines, who came to live with us at seventeen, was a lady-killer, knew card tricks, and played the harmonica.

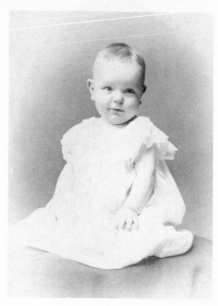

Mother, sixty-two, with Benjamin Watts Gaines, her father, ninety-five. She lived to be ninety-two, he one hundred, both in command of their faculties to the end.

The author of this memoir at eleven months.

V.T. at twelve, in 1909. V.T. at seventeen.

Left: Mrs. Hannah W. Cuthbertson, my sister's art teacher, who later designed Chinese rugs in China. *Above:* Alice Smith, monumental Mormon comrade. *Below left:* My piano teacher, Geneve Lichtenwalter. *Below:* Dr. Frederick Madison Smith, psychologist and religious executive, grandson of the Mormon prophet Joseph Smith.

Right: As an aviation officer cadet, I studied wireless telephony at Columbia University and weekends went out in society.

Below right: In Claremont Avenue, where I knew girl piano students from Kansas City.

Below: After August 1918 I was a shavetail in the Military Aviation.

Left: Dr. Archibald T. ("Doc") Davison, professor of music at Harvard, conductor of the glee club, organist and choirmaster of the chapel, a trainer of choruses and choral directors, my mentor for three years.

Below left: The composer Edward Burlingame Hill, from whom I learned music's history by helping him (for pay) to give his courses. He also taught me to orchestrate in the French manner. We corresponded till his death in 1960.

Below: The Harvard Glee Club at Milan cathedral, 1921; V.T. in front row holding hat.

King's Chapel, Boston, and its graveyard.

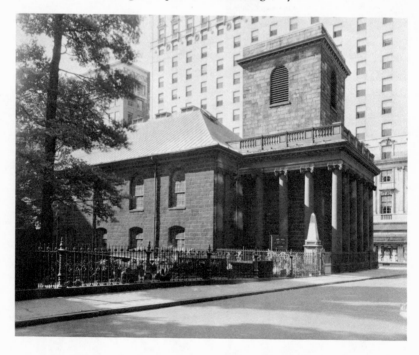

It was through Bernard Faÿ, a young history professor who had studied at Harvard and who had instigated the glee club's invitation to France, that I made acquaintance with France's newest wave in music and letters. At his family's wide, low-ceilinged flat in the rue Saint-Florentin I met at tea Darius Milhaud, Francis Poulenc, Georges Auric, and Arthur Honegger, all near my age and all well disposed to accept me as a colleague. There came there also my revered Erik Satie, and Marcelle Meyer, pianist, married to the actor Pierre Bertin. And there were musical evenings at the Bertin flat, boulevard du Montparnasse, where Marcelle, athletic like the women on the banknotes, and Poulenc, holding his elbows in and his wrists up like a dancing pig on a postcard, played music by Satie and by Satie's young friends. At the Faÿs' there would be sometimes the poet Jean Cocteau, also Bernard's young painter brother Emmanuel, the very young actor Marcel Herrand, and the very very young novelist Raymond Radiguet, then eighteen (to die at twenty). With Radiguet a certain ease of intercourse developed, with Emmanuel (also just two years ahead of death) exchange of confidence almost without reserve.

In late December, when the public frequentations of Cocteau moved to a bar in the rue Boissy d'Anglas named after a ballet score by Milhaud, *Le Bœuf sur le toit,* a young American painter from Missouri, Eugene McCown, whom I had introduced into the Faÿ circle, was engaged to play jazz on the piano. There was very little jazz in Paris then. The establishment housed two rows of tables, perhaps ten in all, with a piano and a bar at the far end. One drank there champagne for luxury, whiskey for style, or the white wines of Alsace, home base of the host Moyses; but one did not dine there (not yet), although after a theater or concert one could have thin sandwiches or thick *fois gras en croûte.*

Against pale tan cloth side walls hung two large pictures by Francis Picabia, both painted on the finest linen canvas and both of them examples of Dada art. One contained, below its larger-lettered title *L'Œil cacodylate,* the brushed-in signatures of a half-hundred friends. The other bore glued-on incrustations—in an upper corner a Swedish match box (empty) joined by a meandering twine cord to, in a lower corner, a printed invitation (no longer valid) to a party at the house of the once-beauteous opera singer Marthe Chenal. It also bore this legend exactly: *M. . . . pour*

Erik Satie
(*Drawing by Picasso*)

Erik SATIE peint par
lui-même, avec une pensée:
« Je suis venu au monde très
jeune dans un temps très vieux. »

celui qui le regarde. Against the pale and very French decor, and to McCown's unquestionably American dance music, Cocteau received on almost any evening. The world that he received was chiefly French, since the English did not discover Le Bœuf till Easter, since the international vice crowd was in Berlin, and since

Raymond Radiguet, 1903–1923
(*Drawing by Picasso*)

the artistic and literary Americans were crowding the cafés of Montparnasse. Cocteau's group, well-to-do and upper-class, represented a conversation about the arts among people well-off enough to be making them or rich enough to buy—neither of which, in the still stringent postwar times, could the impoverished very much do.

A Dada tone was then the stylish tone for advanced artists and for the art-minded. Even the well-established Pablo Picasso, whom I first encountered at this time, had adopted Dada's debunking attitudes. As explained to me by Emmanuel Faÿ, the Dada principles were simply that all is convention, that all conventions have equal value (or none), and that an artist is therefore free to work in (or invent, if he can) any convention whatsoever that may please him. And Tristan Tzara, the Dada spokesman, had defined all art a "private bell for inexplicable needs."

Such a declaration of independence from commerce, the academies, and all other entangling alliances was congenial to my natural rebelliousness. I loved the climate of it, its high, thin, antiestablishment air. And though Dada, as a movement, had already been declared dead by its founders (how could so pure an attitude survive?), for me it offered an ethical ideal, as well as an expression of my inmost temper: so relentlessly (in the eyes of many) frivolous, at the same time so resistant to being governed. I think all Americans are a little Dada-minded. What else is our freewheeling humor, our nonsense, our pop art? And how else can one explain the deep excitement created, well before Dada, by the painting of Marcel Duchamp and the poetry of Gertrude Stein?

If Dada, an aristocratic frame of mind, was a shade right-bankish in its allegiance, music too was a matter of neighborhoods. The ninth and seventeenth *arrondissements*, overflowing to the eighteenth and the eighth, housed virtually all the musical residents. (They still do.) For this reason Montparnasse, though full of convivial Americans, friendly painters, and wild poets, was not my hangout. I knew its cafés and many of their pew-holders; but it was all too much like Greenwich Village to offer me much novel education. So I stuck to my slopes-of-Montmartre music errands and to visiting in friendly houses further west, to operas and concerts for enlightenment, to bicycling in the Bois for exercise. And often, for dining well at almost no cost, I would join up with my own quieter bohemians at the Rendezvous des Mariniers, a tiny bistro on the Ile Saint-Louis.

Before I came abroad, H. T. Parker, reviewer of plays and music for *The Boston Transcript,* had given me a "To Whom It May Concern" letter stating that I was his paper's correspondent. Through entrusting this to Bernard Faÿ, who had connections at the Foreign Office, and through his passing it to Paul Morand, an undersecretary, I early received entry privileges to all spectacles and musical occasions. I had already sent off from Oxford some pieces about the spring season, especially the Ballets Suédois, where I had seen *Les Mariées de la Tour Eiffel,* by Cocteau and Les Six, and Milhaud's *L'Homme et son désir*. I reviewed that fall the Opéra's revival of

Berlioz's *Les Troyens*. In the spring I was to cover that of Debussy's *Le Martyre de Saint Sebastien,* with Ida Rubinstein as mime; and

Les Six by Jean Cocteau (center); clockwise from lower left: Germaine Taillefer, Louis Durey, Georges Auric, Francis Poulenc, Darius Milhaud, Arthur Honegger.

I wrote about Schoenberg's *Pierrot Lunaire,* sung by Marya Freund, led by Milhaud; Schubert was on the program, the first music performed in German since 1914. But my piece that changed history was the one about a series of orchestral concerts conducted at the Opéra by Serge Koussevitzky, since this article set in motion a train of events that ended in his appointment as musical director of the Boston Symphony Orchestra.

The train of events was simply this. My article, appearing early in 1922, stimulated interest among the trustees, already considering the replacement of Pierre Monteux, serving since 1919, who, though thoroughly successful in Boston, did not draw full houses in postwar New York, always Germanic and now again turned anti-French. The following season, therefore, they sent their observers to Paris for the Koussevitzky series and, finding his concerts every bit as impressive as I had told, engaged him for the fall of 1924. In July of 1923 H. T. Parker had written, "I owe to you the only available pictures of Koussevitzky, . . . and the trustees of the Boston Orchestra have meditated on your article about him." That Koussevitzky credited me with influence in his appointment was clear from the bosom-pal, run-of-the-house friendship he bestowed upon me in Boston the following year.

In the spring of 1922 I was told again that there was to be no retaining my fellowship, though Doc Davison did send me, from a fund that he administered, more money ($350, I think); and he also caused me to be engaged for the following season as organist at King's Chapel, Boston.

I repaid him by securing, through the enterprise of a choral society president (who mobilized as sponsor Davison's organ teacher, Charles-Marie Widor) a minor decoration, Officer of Public Instruction. (I still have the letters of the lady who managed this. We had tried for the Legion of Honor; but the time for giving him that, when he was appearing with his glee club, had gone by.) For my support next year, in addition to the job at King's Chapel, I was to have the Naumburg Fellowship and my usual assistantship. Meanwhile, planning to stay on well into the summer and to get work done in some healthful countryside, I went off, come June, for a month in Austria.

Austria at that time was not easy to get into; how to do that was taught me by Slater Brown, e. e. cummings's buddy of *The Enormous Room*. You went to Zurich first, where you went to the American Consul, who sent you to the Austrian Consul, who gave you a visa. Then you took a train to Buchs, the frontier, where you could buy an Austrian railway ticket for almost nothing; and you were in Austria. At Brown's suggestion I settled for the Vor-Arlberg village of Imst, where there was a fine view, also a mountain to climb and a hotel providing room and board for fifty cents a day. I went alone, was later joined by Eugene McCown and a vastly companionable fiction writer, John Mosher. Already at the hotel were Matthew Josephson, slender serious American poet, and his ever-laughing wife, chestnut-haired Hannah. Still later, after I left, came Tzara, Jean Arp, Max Ernst—the Dada general staff. Eugene and I wore, for kicks, Tyrolese costume, the kicks taking place in a shelter hut near the top of our mountain, the Müttekopf, where in leather shorts and to the music of zithers we danced the native *Schuhplatteln*.

I did some work too, orchestrating in sketch Schumann's Symphonic Variations. I had to do these all over again in Cambridge, since Mr. Hill did not find them satisfactory. I think myself that they were not, and I know now that orchestration was the branch in which Nadia Boulanger's teaching was less than perfect. Back in Paris, I stayed till mid-August, working at the organ, writing music, and buying books. One was *Ulysses,* by James Joyce, just off the press at Shakespeare and Company. Others were eighteenth-century technic-treatises suggested by Boulanger—de Nardis, for instance, and a two-volume in-folio Choron. Then there were French books, recommended by Emmanuel Faÿ and Radiguet. I still own among these *Le Bon Apôtre* by Philippe Soupault, Cocteau's *Le Potomak,* Gide's *Les Caves du Vatican.* I had read the Proust volumes (there were then only two); and long ago, even before arrival, I had resigned from Anatole France. I had not yet begun on the French classics, nor had I set foot in the Louvre; but I felt at home with France, its music, its food, its people, its reading and writing. And when in late August of 1922 I embarked at last for New York on a ten-day French Line ship in company with two sad returning exiles, Cuthbert Wright, a writing friend, and Helen Winner, estranged wife of another, I knew I should be back.

7

An End to Education

ACTUALLY THREE YEARS WERE PASSED before I returned to Paris—the first of these in Cambridge, the second in New York, then another in Cambridge, where from 12 Oxford Street I also carried on my Boston life. Besides my organ lessons with Wallace Goodrich, this took place chiefly at King's Chapel. In that granite Greek temple, pre-Revolutionary, seated in its still older graveyard on Tremont facing Beacon Street, I enjoyed a modern four-manual organ and a paid chorus of twenty-four male voices trained to *a cappella* singing. My predecessor, Dr. Richard Cabot—a medical man, a philosophy professor, and a musical amateur devoted to Davison—had induced the congregation to accept Appleton Chapel repertory; and I extended freedom further by teaching my choir to sing plain chant (in Latin) and the Holy Thursday Improperia, or Reproaches of Christ to His Church (which are partly in Greek). And at the organ, still bearing its crown and miter, I played the full organ reportory, from Frescobaldi by way of Pachelbel to Roger-Ducasse and Vierne.

I held three choir rehearsals a week, one of them just before the Sunday service; and I played a short noon service every day, as well as an organ recital on Saturdays. At the noon services, frequented chiefly by lunch-hour strays, I tried out the more recondite pieces and sometimes improvised, using the most advanced discord techniques I knew. Regularly there were weddings and funerals, remunerative and no trouble. That is to say, funerals were no trouble because they could not be planned very far ahead and because they lasted only twenty minutes. Since the congregation there tends to be fairly old, I did not have many weddings; but there were regularly four funerals a month, except in November and April, the pneumonia months, when there were nine each.

For both weddings and funerals I found it convenient to play Bach, avoiding thus both sobs and sentiment, the entrance and exit pieces that I used most often being the Canzona in D and the Prelude and Fugue known as "Judgment Day." In that cultured set-up no one ever asked for Mendelssohn or *Lohengrin*. About the only observance imposed at all, beyond the eschewing of styles folksy or "common," was avoiding verbal reference to the Trinity. The Virgin Birth, Vicarious Atonement, Adoration of the Holy Sacrament, all of theology's most protested points might be the subject of motet or chant, provided one avoided the mystery of Three in One. There was method, however, behind this liturgical eccentricity.

The land beneath and around King's Chapel had been granted in the 1680s "by K. William and Q. Mary" to be used in perpetuity for services of the Church of England. Nevertheless, at the time of the Revolution, when other Church of England parishes merely broke with the Bishop of London, King's Chapel, the first Episcopal church in New England, became the first Unitarian. But in order to prevent plate and property from being inherited by Trinity parish, it was necessary to keep to Church of England services, or something like them. So the rector of the time slightly rewrote the Prayer Book; and the clergy kept right on wearing its same black gowns with starched lawn collar-tabs. And in that hand-carved white Corinthian interior, blazing with daylight from high windows and cozy with box pews cushioned in rose damask, there still takes place a routine indistinguishable from that of many an English church, save that the Trinity is just not mentioned and that the choice of anthem texts and of their musical setting is so permissive, so culture-conscious, and so catholic that the service, though by its origins Low and Broad, seems to yearn toward sumptuosities virtually Roman. Only a few years ago, on the 275th anniversary of the Church's founding, at a concert given there of music by its former organists, the examples chosen from my work were a Latin Mass (complete with Nicene Creed) and a *Stabat Mater* for soprano solo and string quartet, composed to a text by Max Jacob in French.

For presenting in public my new Paris allegiances, sometime toward spring I gave a concert in Paine Hall at which I offered, out of friendship for my teacher, a choral work by her sister Lili Boulanger, *Pour les funerailles d'un soldat*. Also (and this was the real purpose of the concert, a public program of the Harvard Musical Club) a complete performance, the first in America, of Erik Satie's *Socrate*. This work, still rarely performed, consists of three dialogues out of Plato (cut for length, of course) in the French version of Victor Cousin, set to music for one or more solo voices with orchestral or pianoforte accompaniment. I have subsequently given *Socrate* in other ways; but on this occasion I used a tenor soloist, Joseph Lautner, and played the piano part myself. We prepared the piece for months and gave, I think, a lovely reading. In any case, we liked it; and so did H. T. Parker, who reviewed it. I must say that I have over a forty-year period changed that reading very little, though I have given the work many times—in New York, Paris, and Los Angeles.

Initiated by Foster Damon to the delights of Satie, in Paris I had found him stimulating Milhaud, Poulenc, Auric, Cocteau, Picasso. And I knew his music as the test, almost, of any composer's really inside twentieth centuryness. I did not know yet, though I suspected, that built into it is an attitude of reserve which by avoiding all success-rhetoric has permitted the creation of a musical reality as real as an apple or a child. I did know that its way of speaking, as if nobody were there, was the kind of communication that I liked. I had not in Paris sought companionship with Satie, wishing to get inside his music first, then make my homage later through performance. That way we might find something real to talk about, and a conversation so begun might extend to my own work. Since Satie died before I returned to France, I cannot know what friendship with him might have brought. I only know that during an acquaintance with it of more than forty years his music has never ceased to be rewarding. People take to Satie or they don't, as to Gertrude Stein. And if I have long been associated publicly with the work of both, that is because I was so involved with it in private that the rest was merely announcing my engagement. And if I did not make many converts ever, I at least exposed lots of people to contagion.

The rest of my work that year was academic. With Hill, in solo seminar, I orchestrated piano works by Schumann, Fauré, Debussy, and myself. I also helped him give a brand-new course in Russian music. I gave all Hill's courses, in fact, when he was ill for a month. For the glee club I arranged a mixed-voice work by Lili Boulanger, *Vieille Prière Bouddhique.* I assisted Davison in his Choral Music course, also substituting for him many times at morning chapel. I always sang in chapel weekdays, because that took only a quarter of an hour and because the musical experience was so lovely. While Doc's mother was dying I gave from his notes the choral music course; and after she died I took the glee club on its spring tour, since he did not feel at that moment like conducting publicly or traveling in company.

That year I joined a club. I had earlier been asked to a fraternity but declined. I had never aspired to join the richer groups; but this was my kind of club, a fair eating place (something anyone needed in Cambridge) frequented by a mixed set, artistic and scholarly. Shortly after the war a leftist group had got together under the name of Harvard Liberal Club and leased a house, their *raison d'être* being the discussion of current events. I had not bothered to participate, though asked, because current events, as such, were not my interest. I had found out in high school anyway that liberalism was not liberal, but a doctrinaire position just left of center. (Maurice Grosser put it that "all liberals had had unhappy childhoods.") Many must have shared my lack of interest, since the club remained small and, in spite of aspirations to a world-wide view, parochial. Then suddenly, during my year abroad, it had expanded into a culture group. Two of my Harvard Glee Club buddies, politically conservative types themselves, had made over the membership for diversity of interest. Joining up for eating, I plunged into a world cosmopolitan, cultured, in every way congenial.

Above the main floor of the house, where lay only kitchens and the dining room, there were a sizable parlor and two floors of bedrooms. These last came to be occupied by a group of older members—graduate students and younger instructors—known as "the house party." And this nucleus plus certain associates who, though not residing on the premises, had the run of the upstairs, welded themselves together intellectually and built themselves into one another's lives in a way that years, careers, and matrimony have not undone. This conversation among the arts and sciences became decentralized when the house-and-tutorial system was adopted at Harvard, its chief remaining members becoming Tutors and House Masters. Its recentralization came still later in the Society of Fellows, where the talk is today, I think, the finest anywhere. In 1922, and for the five years following, such talk was available in Cambridge every afternoon at the Liberal Club house party, upstairs over bridge and tea at all the seasons, on long walks up the Charles in spring and fall.

Its leaders were the historians Garrett Mattingly, Allen Evans, and John Coddington; an English major, John Knedler (now Dean of the College at New York University); the physicist (crystalographer) Alan Holden; the painter (naturalistic) Maurice Grosser; the art historian (Sumerian seals) Briggs Buchanan; the historian of achitecture Henry-Russell Hitchcock; and the maker of documentary films Henwar Rodakiewicz. Closely associated were Alexander Mackay-Smith, now a Virginia horse breeder; Oliver Cope, a Boston doctor; Henry Francis, curator of painting in Cleveland; Carleton Sprague Smith, music librarian, and Lincoln Kirstein, editor and poet (later ballet organizer), who was soon to paint the dining room with all-over murals representing steam pipes budding into flowers. Charles Poletti, subsequently lieutenant-governor of New York, used to wait table.

Late in the spring of 1923, Bernard Faÿ came back to Cambridge for lecturing and for launching his first book about Franco-American history, bringing with him his brother Emmanuel, suffering from unrequited love and fed up with France. The Faÿs were a tribe of bankers and solicitors, ultra-bourgeois by financial position and ultra-Catholic through their mother (née Rivière), one of whose brothers was an archbishop (at Aix-en-Provence) and the other (later bishop of Monaco) then pastor of the stylish Saint-Thomas-d'Aquin. Emmanuel was thin-skinned and slender with a nose so high and a head so narrow that he seemed to be all profile. He was strong in mind, weak in body, intense from withheld emotion, in manners sweetly reserved, as if smiling over pain. He loathed the Catholicism of his family.

I showed him Boston and New York. He was alone in New York when I went West. In October he died. Bernard had gone back to France. Though in New York myself, I had neglected him that week; and so had others. It was cold weather. And a lady of means who had commissioned him to paint a room had changed her mind when she learned that paint and canvas alone (the best was all he had thought to use) would cost more than she cared to spend. So one evening in his Stuyvestant Place lodging he took sleeping pills and lay down by an open window. Found unconscious in the morning, he was removed to a public hospital, where, still unconscious, he died of pneumonia. And in the short time between his being carried away and the sealing of his room, his pictures disappeared. Avery Claflin, his brother's closest friend, and Roy Larson, then a young newspaper man, instigated a police inquiry and carried out on their own some questionings in the house. Not a scrap of actionable information, or of painting either, ever turned up. A small sheaf of drawings is all that remains today from this gifted artist and ever-so-touching young man. Shipped back to France against his written wish, he was given Catholic burial from the Eglise de la Madeleine.

While the same year's spring had been coming to an end, I myself was deep in unrequited love, with all love's classic symptoms of distraction. My passion, like all my intensely conceived ones, came to nothing. The only need for mentioning it here comes from its influence on my academic behavior. When it came to the three-day examinations known as "generals," which one had to pass with distinction in order to be graduated A.B. *magna cum laude,* or even *cum,* I took them casually, did both well and badly, wrote the best exam in orchestration ever seen, according to Hill, and the worst, said Clifford Heilman, in fugue. What proved to Walter Spalding that I should have taken his course in Appreciation was my referring, wrongly of course, to an Introduction in Beethoven's Fifth Symphony. Spalding did not like my counterpoint either, though I was expert at both the Bach kind and the strict kind. He had never quite approved of my having learned the latter at all, especially from a woman. I do not suppose that my exams were better than reported, for certainly both Hill and Davison would have protested any unfairness toward me. But in Spalding's letter informing me of his regret that the department could not recommend me for distinction, I did sense a grain of triumph at the results of my having almost never followed his advice. And no mention was made of the fact, learned by me only later, that a college record containing no mark lower than a B would have entitled me to *cum laude* anyway. My only disappointment, really, was that I was not to have for the following year my $1,400 traveling fellowship. So I left for home without waiting for commencement, receiving my diploma there by mail.

Walter Spalding, evidently regretful of my plight, wrote offering a $1,500 fellowship which had become available through the Juilliard Trust. I could do anything I wished with the money; naturally I would go straight to Paris. But on my passage through New York in late September for a routine interview on the matter, my third-class passage on the *Paris* already engaged, I fell into a tempting opportunity. Chalmers Clifton, pupil and bosom friend of E. B. Hill and a comradely chap (who had been gracious to me in Paris and praised my pieces), had one year earlier accepted to direct the American Orchestral Association, a training orchestra for young players. For the season of 1923/24 he was adding a conductors' class; I could join it if I wished. I did wish and I did join. It was the errands involved .with that, in fact, with cancelling my berth and getting settled, that caused me to neglect Emmanuel Faÿ during the mid-October days before his death.

In Clifton's conducting class I learned how to digest an orchestral score; and I conducted several—a Beethoven and a Mozart symphony, I think, a Weber overture, and some French works. And I learned, for participation purposes, to play most of the percussion instruments. Rehearsals took place at the red brick Liederkranz Hall on Fifty-eighth Street. Impatient sometimes with just sitting there, I occupied myself by writing exercises. For I was taking lessons again, this time from an Austrian-trained Italian, Rosario Scalero, who, having no faith in French music-teaching, was putting me through strict counterpoint again. Indeed, so skillful had I become at all the contrapuntal species that I could compose invertible eight-part choruses in one key while the orchestra rehearsed Beethoven in another.

I was not the best conductor in the class, though I had a natural beat. That beat, in fact, schooled to the finical finger-work of choral directing, resisted taking on the looser patterns required for coordinating instruments of differing speech-lag, such as oboe and tuba, kettle drum and flute. It was not till in the 1930s, conducting in an opera house, that I began to be able to relax before an orchestra; and in order to do so I had had to erase the choral beat from my reflexes. I know now that the great orchestral leaders, though they all give choral works, can rarely be trusted to train a choir; and just as certainly, great choral conductors like A. T. Davison or Robert Shaw have seemed never to be quite at ease with instruments.

Since Rosario Scalero disapproved my Harvard-and-Paris approach to composition, I never showed him any of my pieces. I was writing a good deal of music, all the same, including a sizable *a cappella* Mass. And I profited eventually from Scalero's insistence on the "normal" harmonization of a chorale, though I resisted it at the time, Paris having taught me that no such harmonization exists save in the German academic mind. I realize now how right Scalero was whenever I test today's composing students in the colleges. Their counterpoint is fair; they can sometimes orchestrate; but their skill in thoroughbass is virtually nil.

In private Luigi Silva, also studying with Scalero at the Mannes School, would back me up, though not before the Germanized Italian. The cello was Luigi's instrument, and he was already a virtuoso. He gave me cello lessons when I would practice. I liked the ear training of a nonkeyboard instrument, but my hands were too small to be stretched effectively. I gave up in the second position. I did acquire in Silva a string-playing mentor, however, the first of several. Two others came into my life that winter, Lillian Fuchs, the viola player, and her violinist brother Joseph. For anything I needed to know about the viola or the violin they were available. They still help me in private with string writing, play me in public.

I began in the spring of 1924 to write about music in magazines. It was H. L. Mencken who got me started. Feeling a little bit the urge to write (and to be paid for it), I had gone to see him and asked for advice, suggestions. "Write me an article," he said, "answering the question, 'What is jazz?' Everybody talks about it; nobody defines it." So I did just that; and he published it in *The American Mercury,* the first attempt, I believe, to describe jazz in technical terms. Primed by two young friends who worked for the Condé Nast publications, I also wrote a piece for *Vanity Fair.*

It was quite the thing to write for *Vanity Fair*. Frank Crownin-shield, its editor, by publishing photographs of modern art and literary texts by Erik Satie, Jean Cocteau, Gertrude Stein, Colette, and e. e. cummings, had proved that an organ for advertising luxury products is a good place to show far-out culture. He liked my writing and found my up-to-date musical information exactly what his readers needed. For the next year I wrote him a piece about music every month, and only twice was I rapped on the knuckles.

Once was about a title I had proposed, a joke on the magazine's fashion column "What the Well-Dressed Man Will Wear." When I called a piece about the coming season's novelties "What the Well-Dressed Mind Will Hear," it was printed under another title. The second occasion was an article making fun of orchestral conductors. Mr. Crowninshield, in declining to publish it, wrote that the subject was pretty recondite for his magazine, ending his letter, "You must remember that nine tenths of our readers live outside of New York, many of them in the state of Kansas."

I had called orchestral conducting, after *The Seven Lively Arts* by Gilbert Seldes, an "eighth lively art" and remarked that Leopold Stokowski, "panting in a frock coat over the love music from *Tristan* was giving his own show, just as if the director of the Louvre were to exhibit himself, posed and breathing through his nostrils, before a Rubens Venus." When the piece, which I later sold to *The New Republic,* appeared there as "The New Musical Mountebankery," B. H. Haggin wrote in, denouncing me for hav-ing turned criticism into "a ninth nonsense art."

The Juilliard Fellowship had lasted one season, that of 1923/24. I had no more money, and I had not returned to France. I was offered at that time by Hill my former assistantship, and by Davi-son the organ at the Harvard Theological School, a post that carried salary and lodging. Before I arrived in Cambridge, however, Doc had given the post to someone else. He had figured rightly that I was not to be around for long and that he might as well make some other protégé his heir apparent. Wallace Woodworth was the new one, and he stuck. But the director of the Theological School, considering that I had been treated less than fairly, gave me a free room anyway.

I still had my *Vanity Fair* pieces for income, and I went on working for Davison as well as Hill. The job of arranging mixed-

voice choral repertory for men only, a chore formerly done by Doc
himself, was beginning to be farmed out, often to me. In addition,
a Boston music publisher was getting ready to issue these arrangements under the Harvard Glee Club's name. In the course of
checking the musical text of a Palestrina motet, "Adoramus Te,"
I found no printing of it earlier than 1836. When I informed Doc
of this and asked him where he had got it in the first place, he
admitted that he had taken it from the 1836 volume, showing me
at the same time a later book in which it was ascribed to "a contemporary of Palestrina." "But the cadences we sing," I said, "are
not the same as those in either book." "I have restored them," he
replied, "to what Palestrina must have written." When I suggested
that it might be embarrassing to publish the piece as Palestrina's
work on no more authority than either of us had been able to
find, he pointed out that it would be equally embarrassing to
change the attribution. So I said no more. Though in many editions
it is still "by Palestrina," musicological studies have now ascribed
it, I think, to Agnielli.

Neither did I protest when an arrangement I had made of the
Fête polonaise out of Chabrier's operetta *Le Roi malgré lui* was
published without my being asked, paid, or named. I do not know
what other male-voice arrangements by other helpers may be
grouped in the same edition under Doc's editorship, but I was
amused when he told me some years later, and in all innocence,
that he was receiving quite large royalties from the Glee Club
collection.

Nadia Boulanger came to America that year for giving organ
recitals and some lectures. In New York and in Boston she played
the solo organ part in Aaron Copland's First Symphony, a work
composed especially for her. When she asked me how I liked it,
I replied that I had wept. "But the important thing," she said,
"is why you wept." "Because I had not written it myself," I answered. And I meant that. The piece was exactly the Boulanger
piece and exactly the American piece that several of us would
have given anything to write and that I was overjoyed someone
had written. For joy also had been there in my tears.

At the beginning of Koussevitzky's tenure in Boston he had
been happy to see me and declared friendship. When I wrote in
The Boston Transcript an analysis of Prokofiev's *Scythian Suite,*
which he was introducing that season, that the work's dazzling

final pages were possibly more successful than its earlier movements, he took umbrage. His wife Natalie stopped speaking to me
for six weeks, and he himself kept a wooden face during that time.
Then he relaxed; he could not hold a grudge. But she never smiled
at me again. He got angry at me later many times, usually for my
having written something about him that he did not like; but
we always made up. Once I got mad at him for trying to tell
me how not to write a piece. I even, on account of his discourage-
ment, held back performance of the piece. Then twelve years later
it started being played. That was my Symphony on a Hymn Tune.

By late winter of 1925 I had another church job, again in a
family-owned factory town, Whitinsville, near Worcester. The chief
estates there were all owned, like the factory that made cotton mill
machinery, by families named Whitin or Lasell. Two members I
found I knew already, the son of one Lasell family, Philip, and
the daughter of another, Hildegarde Watson. Hildegarde and her
husband, J. Sibley Watson, were close to e. e. cummings; and
Watson was a backer of *The Dial*. Hildegarde's mother, Mrs.
Chester Whitin Lasell, was two years later to become my patron.
That spring I made weekly trips to Whitinsville, lunching usually
with the Lasells after the service. The atmosphere was wholly unlike that of the Ameses' town, which had been ever quiet, smiling,
Arcadian. Here one felt hysterias and tensions. At the frame
residence-hotel where unmarried workers lived, South Europeans
mostly, there were flamboyant waitresses with dyed red hair. And
they too were grim; nobody laughed. At the houses on the hill,
where my protectors lived, there were good wines, pictures, books,
every charm and cultural convenience; but there too nobody
laughed. After a long and weary spring I quarreled with my minister, got myself fired, went off to Paris via Kansas City.

In Missouri I wrote music; played the organ at Alice Smith's
marriage to a Mormon religious executive, an Englishman; gave
orchestration lessons to a Negro composer (teacher at a college on
the Kansas side), holding these on the front porch warm mornings, just to show off my race relations. For my future life in
Europe I had a ticket, a little money, and a request from *Vanity
Fair* for articles. This time I sailed with Sherry Mangan, a comrade
from the Liberal Club—poet, classical scholar, and Irishman of the
world who was also by way of becoming a gargantuan gourmet.

8

Antheil, Joyce, and Pound

IN 1921, EUROPE ITSELF had been my objective. That was where
the good teachers lived and all the best composers—Stravinsky,
Ravel, Schoenberg, Strauss, Satie, and masses of ingenious other
ones, especially among the French, from the aged Fauré, Saint-
Saëns, and d'Indy through the middle-aged Florent Schmitt and
Paul Dukas down to Darius Milhaud, not thirty, and Francis
Poulenc, just eighteen. Already twenty-four myself, I had then
been needing to finish learning before I could get on with music
writing. In 1925, four years later, only the musical pouring out
was urgent; everything else I did got in its way. Organ playing,
teaching, and conducting I had practiced successfully; but I did
not want to go on doing any of them. They filled up my waking
mind with others' music. When I remarked this to E. B. Hill,
he declined to press me, like my father on the subject of going
to war, pointing out that if I cared about such things I could
easily have a professor's career at Harvard, with no doubt a composing and performing life as well, but that if I needed just then
to compose only, I had every right to follow my impulse. It had
never been my habit to relinquish a thing while learning to do it,
but rather to give up only that which I had proved I could do.
(A mastered branch could be picked up again.) In quitting at
that time teaching and performance, I set for all time my precedent,

incorrigibly to be followed in later life, of walking out on success every time it occurred.

My return to Europe in 1925 was therefore both a coming to and a going from. I was coming to the place where music bloomed. I was leaving a career that was beginning to enclose me. I was leaving also an America that was beginning to enclose us all, at least those among us who needed to ripen unpushed. America was impatient with us, trying always to take us in hand and make us a success, or else squeezing us dry for exhibiting in an institution. America loved art but suspected distinction, stripped it off you every day for your own good. In Paris even the police were kind to artists. As Gertrude Stein was to observe, "It was not so much what France gave you as what she did not take away."

But even Eden charges room and board. And in resigning from self-support off two byproducts of my musical education, I had kept a third as ace in hole, that of writing about music. This, I made believe to friends and family, was the least demanding of all and the most remunerative, would therefore be the least inhibiting. I believed this myself for a while; but when I got to France I never wrote again for *Vanity Fair* or for *The New Republic* or for Mencken's *American Mercury,* though all wrote me they awaited pieces, as did also *The Dial* by way of its new editor, Marianne Moore.

The money I had come abroad with in September, exactly $500, was gone by April; but I did not tell my family that, because I did not wish to worry them or put my father to undue sacrifice. Actually, after a bad time in the fall of '26, I did ask him for $100, which he sent without question. That winter and spring I had also small gifts from friends and eventually a commission. In the summer of '27, again destitute, I saved the life of Jessie Lasell, Hildegarde Watson's mother. Out of gratitude she sent me $125 a month for about three years. There were briefer patrons, too, and an occasional fee for performing my music. All in all, I lived for eight years "without turning an honest penny," as I put it. Or a dishonest one, for that matter. For whenever I borrowed money I paid it back. You have to do that when you are poor, to keep your credit.

Living again in the rue de Berne, so far my Paris base, little by little I established outposts across the Seine. The first of these was at 12 rue de l'Odéon, where I already knew Sylvia Beach and was a frequenter of her hospitable bookstore, Shakespeare and Company. And it was there that I made friends with the composer George Antheil, truculent, small boy-genius from Trenton, New Jersey, and the very personal protectorate of Sylvia, James Joyce, and Ezra Pound.

I envied George his freedom from academic involvements, the bravado of his music and its brutal charm. He envied me my elaborate education, encouraged me to sit out patiently the sterile time it seemed to have brought. In a *pneumatique* of November 12, he wrote, "Let me say what I said last night, that I believe in you more than I believe in certainly any other American, and perhaps even a lot more of other nationalities." Antheil's warmth and admiration cheered me through that worried fall, until by January I was deep in a three-movement piece.

George was composing that winter a *Jazz Symphony* for some twenty-two instruments. His *Ballet mécanique* was finished, awaiting its premiere till the piano manufacturer who had had the rolls cut should be able to solve the problem of synchronizing sixteen pianolas, the number George had set his heart on for producing a loudness matching that of the large percussion group. The work eventually achieved public performance but without mechanical synchrony or quite sixteen pianos. Meanwhile he would play the rolls on one piano, pumping hard to keep up enough wind pressure for sounding all the notes at maximum; and in his low-ceilinged one-room flat he managed to make quite a racket.

For composing in tranquillity he had hired a room around the corner and put in it an upright piano not mechanical. Here he composed daytimes, going home for lunch and dinner with his tiny Hungarian wife, Böske, in their room above Sylvia Beach's bookstore. I used to spend the night sometimes in the narrow hotel room, just opposite the barracks of the Garde Républicaine, and be wakened by the sounds of horses' hooves as the troop pranced through the gates to exercise. I slept there because by Christmas I had moved to Saint-Cloud, where Theodore Chanler had lent me an apartment.

Teddy, then eighteen, represented an experiment in upper-class male education, since he had opted, just out of school, for becoming a composer without taking time out for college, but wholly through studying with Nadia Boulanger and living in Europe. From Christmas till April that year he would be visiting his mother in Rome. The two-room flat in Saint-Cloud that he had invited me to occupy was at 66 avenue de Versailles, on the top floor of the topmost house of the topmost hill; and its view was panoramic. This included the distant Sacré-Cœur and the nearer Eiffel Tower, on which at night there was played out in lights, putting Times Square to shame, a repeated drama of being struck by zigzag yellow lightning, then consumed by red flames, after which white stars and comets appeared and finally the name of the sponsor, Citroën.

A friend from the Liberal Club, Maurice Grosser, in France on a Harvard fellowship and practicing to be a painter, came there to stay with me and share expenses. These were minimal, since the wife of the landlord, himself a retired butcher and devoted vegetable gardener, would send up lunch at cost. Then after a morning's work and a tasty meal, we would walk, breathing damp fresh air, in the Saint-Cloud forest on leaf mold and under trees all green moss on their northern sides, full at their tops of gray, ball-shaped mistletoe. Or we would walk along the Seine and round the Longchamp race track in the Bois de Boulogne, sometimes to Paris itself, or to Versailles for cakes and tea, and then walk back.

Sometimes still other friends came out for lunch, the writers Janet Flanner, Sherry Mangan, Victor Seroff (then practicing to be a pianist and living just below at Boulogne-sur-Seine). Every week I went to town by train to show Nadia Boulanger my progress on a piece called Sonata da Chiesa. I also made sketches for my Symphony on a Hymn Tune; but these I did not show her, knowing that once the Church Sonata was finished my time of lesson taking would be over. I also went to Paris at other times for seeing people, going places, doing things; and it was when I loitered too late to catch the last train back from Saint-Lazare that I would spend the night in Antheil's room at the Hotel de Tournon.

I often loafed at Sylvia Beach's shop, where I had the privilege of borrowing books free. And I went to parties at her flat, also in the rue de l'Odéon, shared with Adrienne Monnier. If angular Sylvia, in her boxlike suits, was Alice in Wonderland at forty, pink and white, buxom Adrienne in gray-blue uniform, bodiced, with peplum and a long full skirt, was a French milkmaid from the eighteenth century. At her bookstore opposite Sylvia's, La Société des Amis des Livres, she published a magazine, *Le Navire d'argent;* and under the same imprint a French translation of James Joyce's *Ulysses,* by Valéry Larbaud, was about to be issued. When the book was ready, Adrienne invited Picasso to illustrate it. He demurred, probably out of friendship for Gertrude Stein; but he did consent to read it, a thing he rarely did for any book. After he had returned the manuscript, he comforted Miss Stein, "Yes, now I see what Joyce is, an 'obscure' that all the world will understand" (*"un obscur que tout le monde pourra comprendre"*).

Joyce and Stein, I must explain, were rivals in the sense that, viewed near by, they appeared as planets of equal magnitude. Indeed the very presence of them both, orbiting and surrounded by satellites, gave to Paris in the 1920s and '30s its position of world-center for the writing of English poetry and prose. Hemingway, Fitzgerald, and Ford Madox Ford; Mary Butts, Djuna Barnes, and Kay Boyle; Ezra Pound, e. e. cummings, and Hart Crane worked out of Paris and depended on it for judgment, as often as not for publication too. And all were connected in some way to Stein or Joyce, sometimes to both.

The stars themselves came together just once—briefly and both consenting. That was at the house of the sculptor Jo Davidson. And since Joyce was by that time almost blind, Miss Stein went into another room to meet him, rather than that he should be led to her. But when they had approached, exchanged greetings and good-will phrases, they had nothing to say to each other, nothing at all.

It was through Sylvia Beach that I first met Joyce (at her flat, I think). But it was more in company with Antheil that I used to see him. When during the spring of 1926 Antheil's music and mine began to appear together on programs, Joyce always came to hear us and never failed to tell me that he liked my work. That the compliment was sincere I had no reason to doubt; that it was pleasing to me, coming from so grand a source, no one need doubt. Nevertheless when in the mid-1930s, after my opera *Four Saints in Three Acts,* for which Gertrude Stein had written the libretto, had received some recognition, Joyce offered me his own collaboration, I demurred, as Picasso had done, and for the same reasons.

I did not feel like wounding Gertrude Stein, or choose to ride on both ends of a seesaw.

What Joyce proposed was a ballet, to be based on the children's games chapter of *Finnegans Wake*. He gave me a hand-printed edition of that chapter, with an initial designed by his daughter Lucia; and he offered me, for the final spectacle, production at the Paris Opéra with choreography by Leonide Massine. I did not doubt that a ballet could be derived from the subject. My reply, however, after reading the chapter, was that though anyone could put children's games on a stage, only with his text would such a presentation have "Joyce quality." I did not add that in place of the pure dance-spectacle proposed, one could imagine a choreographed cantata using Joyce's words.

It was from a literary source that I had first heard of Antheil, an article in *La Revue de Paris*. And the writer of that had quoted from another work of letters, Ezra Pound's book *Antheil and the Treatise on Harmony*. Antheil was being launched, in fact, by Pound, past master at launching careers (though before this, only for poets). Joyce, Monnier, Beach, the world of Shakespeare and Company, all were fascinated by Antheil's cheerful lack of modesty. He was in fact the literary mind's idea of a musical genius—bold, bumptious, and self-confident; he was also diverting. The resistance to Antheil came from music circles. In spite of the rue de l'Odéon publicity and in spite of a gift for blowing his own horn, George had not broken into the concert programs, even the modernistic ones. His chief glory came from the still unperformed *Ballet mécanique*, composed originally to accompany a film of that name designed by the painter Fernand Léger but early detached from it. Besides this music and an unfinished *Jazz Symphony*, his repertory consisted of a half-dozen songs, a youthful piano piece entitled *Airplane Sonata*, a Symphony for Five Instruments, and a String Quartet. For Ezra Pound's violinist friend Olga Rudge he had written also a Sonata for Violin and Piano, percussive throughout and with bass drum laid on at the end. And he was composing that spring and summer of 1926 a Symphony in F, to be played the next season in a concert organized by himself. I rather think, however, that his first Paris concert performances came through me.

The Société Musicale Independente, founded in 1909 by Gabriel Fauré, was still active, with Ravel, Koechlin, Casella, Falla, Stravinsky, Schoenberg, and Bartók on its board. Boulanger, a member of the program committee (and with Walter Damrosch, her colleague at Fontainebleau, available for bringing in Americans to subsidize it), had conceived the idea of a special concert, outside the regular subscription, devoted to young American composers. On the program were to be my Sonata da Chiesa, for five instruments, piano pieces by Herbert Elwell, a song with flute and clarinet and two pieces for violin and piano by Aaron Copland, a piano sonata by Walter Piston, and a violin-piano sonata by Theodore Chanler. All the works except one of Copland's violin pieces were receiving their first performance anywhere; all were to be played by first-class artists; and all were the work of Boulanger's pupils. Adding the Antheil String Quartet was my idea; and that too was to be a first public performance.

All these pieces were characteristic of the newest in American talent, as well as of postwar Parisian ways, which is to say that they applied old-master layouts to contemporary melodic inspirations and harmonic concepts. My way of doing this, also Antheil's, was derived from the latest works of Igor Stravinsky; the others had theirs more from Boulanger, who was both an organist conditioned to Bach and a pupil of Gabriel Fauré. A certain unity of musical method, nevertheless, underlay personal variations and gave to the concert a recognizable impact, just as fine executions gave it brilliance. There were lots of people present, lots of laudatory reviews later, along with some shocked ones, the latter mostly with regard to my Church Sonata, which consisted of a chorale, tango, and fugue and made funny noises.

My report on the concert to Briggs Buchanan, my chief confidant, itemizes:

1. The audience was distinguished,
French music represented by Boulanger, Florent Schmitt, Louis Aubert, Albert Roussel, Inghelbrecht, others.
Society as mentioned in the program [a long list of patrons and patronesses].
French criticism by Paul Le Flem, Boris de Schloezer, André Coeuroy, Raymond Petit.
American music (though their works were not played) by George Foote, Walter Damrosch, Edmund Pendleton, Roger Sessions, Blair Fairchild.

American critical intelligentsia by Pierre Loving, Gilbert Seldes, Manuel Komroff, Ludwig Lewisohn.

American diplomacy by the military attaché (in dress uniform), tone-deaf but serious in the performance of his assignment.

James Joyce also appeared. He never goes out.

2. The performances were uniformly excellent.

3. The program was impressive, though long and tiresome. (Six first auditions are too much.)

The most impressive work (by number of players engaged, novelty of form, and strangeness of noises produced) was the *Sonate d'Eglise* by V. Thomson. Second in importance on the program (though, in my opinion, not inferior in quality, probably even superior) was the String Quartet of George Antheil. The other works, more modest in pretension, less well realized in style, but all genuinely musical in conception and not bad to listen to, were distinguished by the second movement of Chanler's Violin Sonata, which is a real piece."

And of my own piece:

In general one may say that leaving out about two ill-advised experiments, the instrumentation is unquestionably a knockout. The chorale has a genuinely new idea. The other movements decently satisfactory. The faults are a dangerous rigidity of rhythmic texture in the chorale, an excessively contrapuntal style in the fugue, and an immature comprehension of the profundities of classical form. The work manifests, however, a mind of great strength and originality. The public awaits (or ought to) with eagerness Mr. Thomson's next work, a symphony in the form of variations on an American hymn tune.

Hardly any time after this concert, I was taken to a chubby and personable young woman who was in the mood to entertain artistically. Alice Woodfin, a musician herself but also a frequenter of society, was the go-between. Mrs. Christian Gross, sugar millionairess and wife of the First Secretary of the American Embassy, had a palatial flat on the Champ-de-Mars at 1 avenue Charles-Floquet—also so much income and so little technique for spending it that when buying Catherine the Great's emerald necklace at Cartier's she had modestly asked if it would be all right to pay at the end of the month. She thought it would be lovely to have concerts of my music at her house; and when I suggested sharing these with Antheil to make the repertory larger (also, his name was better known than mine), she was overjoyed. Four weekly concerts were therefore announced (with tea before and champagne after), Antheil's strong-arm squad, commanded by Ezra Pound, taking care of the guest list and handling finances.

The programs, elegantly performed, contained my Sonata da Chiesa, conducted by Vladimir Golschmann, and Five Phrases from the Song of Solomon, accompanied by percussion and sung by Alice Mock. Antheil's chamber works were also exposed; and a final gala at the Théâtre des Champs-Elysées presented for the first time publicly his *Ballet mécanique,* played with lots of percussion including two airplane propellers, but only one mechanical piano. I did not attend this concert, since no work of mine was on the program and since I was a little disturbed by George's and Ezra's secrecy with regard to material benefits. Ezra did say to me, on a bench in the Luxembourg Gardens: "If you stick around with me, you'll be famous." But in view of how domineering he was, I was not very interested in being made famous by him, nor in sticking too close; and he must have felt this. In any case, our brief association soon ended. A decade later Ford Madox Ford recounted that at one of Mrs. Gross's musicales Ezra had pointed me out: "You see that little man there? That's the enemy."

That fall an orchestral concert was held in the Salle Gaveau at which Antheil's Symphony in F had its *première.* Golschmann conducted; and everybody was well paid, including, I believe, the press. As for me, I had received from Mrs. Gross at the end of our series a check for $500, this to be considered as commissioning a work. I wrote the work but was never able to deliver it, because by fall she had left her fine flat, her husband, and her children and eloped with a Mexican. As innocent at musical patronage as at social climbing, she did not again, to my knowledge, essay either; rumor had it she remained content with love.

Sometime that spring I had written to Briggs Buchanan regarding the winter just past that Antheil had been its "chief event."

For the first time in history another musician liked my music ... said hello. Somebody recognized what I was all about. Or recognized that I was about something worth looking at. Imagine my gratitude. More particularly since this support and admiration came from the first composer of our generation (of this there isn't any doubt) and was supported by deeds. I must admit that the encouragement has been mutual, that the contact has bucked up George just as much as me, perhaps more. The point remains, Antheil is the chief event of my winter. He has admired me, he has quarreled with me about theories, he has criticized my pieces, he has consulted me about his, he has defended me to my enemies, to his enemies, to my friends, to his friends. . . . He has talked, walked, and drunk me by the hour. He has lodged me and fed me and given me money. At this very instant he is trying to persuade a rich lady to give me money instead of to him, although he is perfectly poor himself.

For this effort I had only Antheil's word, for the name of the lady not even that. It is true that he had once given me, at his wife Böske's suggestion, when I was destitute, 500 francs ($20). It is also true that we were companions and believed in each other. My estimate of him as "the first composer of our generation" might have been justified had it not turned out eventually that for all his facility and ambition there was in him no power of growth. The "bad boy of music," as he was later to entitle his autobiography, merely grew up to be a good boy. And the *Ballet mécanique,* written before he was twenty-five, remains his most original piece.

New York heard this work on April 10, 1927, along with the Jazz Symphony, at a Carnegie Hall concert vastly publicized and vastly disastrous to Antheil's career. In despair he acquired lung spots; in a long Tunis vacation he cured them. A few years later, after a not wholly successful essay at German-language opera (entitled *Transatlantic* and produced in Frankfurt), he returned to America, where for the rest of his life he earned his living, took care of his health. The living was made not only by writing music, which he did for Hollywood films with some distinction, but also by writing for newspapers on subjects unrelated to music. He conducted a syndicated column of advice to the lovelorn, basing his answers on the probable influence of certain endocrine glands (thymus, thyroid, pituitary, adrenal) over the questioner's destiny. And during World War II he wrote astonishingly accurate military prophecy for a newspaper editor, Manchester Boddy, of the *Los Angeles Daily News.* He also composed one striking ballet (on a Spanish subject out of Hemingway), several English-language operas, and six symphonies.

Earlier that season, in late June of 1926, Ezra Pound's opera had been performed in a stylish execution before a stylish intellectual public at the Salle Pleyel in the rue Rochechouart, where Chopin and Liszt had played. The text was François Villon's *Testament;* and the orchestra contained a *corne,* or animal's horn, five feet long, that could blow two notes only, a bass and the fifth above it, but with a raucous majesty evocative of faraway times. The vocal line, minimally accompanied, was a prosodization of Old French, which Ezra was said to know well. The music was not quite a musician's music, though it may well be the finest poet's music since Thomas Campion. For one deeply involved with getting words inside music, as I was, it bore family resemblances unmistakable to the *Socrate* of Satie; and its sound has remained in my memory.

I had been heart-warmed through a cold and dismal autumn, that year of my return, by the affection of a poet, Sherry Mangan, and sustained in my musical hopes by the faith of a composing contemporary, George Antheil. My music's steady flow had finally begun on the heights of Saint-Cloud through the generosity of the younger composer Theodore Chanler and the companionship of the painter Maurice Grosser. Toward the end of spring, back in Paris, I had experienced for a short time complete poverty. After that had come performances of my work, and these had led to money enough for getting through the summer. With my patron's gift of $500 I went off at the end of July to Thonon-les-Bains, near Évian, where I wrote music and rowed on Lake Geneva. I also met there a Frenchwoman forty years older who became my close companion for thirteen years (not mistress, not pseudomother, but true woman friend ever jealous and ever rewarding) till her death at eighty-three on the eve of World War II.

Langlois, Butts, and Stein

LOUISE LANGLOIS (NÉE PHILIBERT) was slender, wore her gray hair short, and smoked constantly. Born in Besançon (Place de la Préfecture), she practiced the historic courage of the Franche-Comté along with the indefatigable letter writing of the French educated classes. Her father, born around 1800, had brought up nine children and at eighty got another on the chambermaid. Louise, the youngest legitimate one, was the darling of her next older brother, a naval officer, later admiral. All their grown lives they wrote each other every day. She married late, he never. Her husband, Dr. Jean-Paul Langlois, had been a professor of physiology. Her friends were chiefly men of learning and general staff officers, powerful people, busy people, all running something. Her closest man friend outside the medical and military clans had been Lucien Herr, librarian and later director of the Ecole Normale, Alsatian exile from 1871, long-time chief of the Socialist party, guide and counselor to Jaurès and Léon Blum. Herr's widow once lent me for a month their farm-house retreat near Montfort-l'Amaury, where I learned from the abundance of Beethoven and of books about Beethoven in his private library the meaning of this composer as a freedom prophet for socialists of the Second International. Madame Langlois's constant traveling companion summers was a woman physician, Russian by birth, who addressed her both ironically and affectionately as *"Princesse."*

Surrounded from childhood by persons of power and brains, she had early become adept, as an academician said of her lately, at attaching to herself men of quality. (*"Elle a toujours eu le don de s'attacher des hommes de valeur."*) She must have suspected me one of those, because after a brief exchange of courtesies between us in a hotel hallway, she set herself out to become my friend; and within three days I was taking regularly my after-lunch coffee with her and her companion. We also took sight-seeing trips together, swapped books, played bridge. By the time we had got back to Paris we were as chummy as a child and its grandmother. Christian Bérard, who came from that kind of people himself, asked in astonishment, after one encounter, "How ever did you *meet* a Frenchwoman of that class?"

Actually that class, the upper-bracket professionals, is the one with which I have always got on best. Even in France, with its secretive family life, I had been received without abrasions in exactly such a clan, the Faÿs, almost as a member of it. There, in an atmosphere at once of friendship and formality, being asked to dinner when there were no other guests and only everyday foods or to tea when we sat down to it in the dining room, twelve strong around a special cake, I had recognized my Missouri grandparents and my Kentucky great-aunts, with their taffeta shirtwaists and diamond earrings, their involvements with religion and church, their sumptuous cooking.

With Madame Langlois (and I never called her anything but that) there was no misunderstanding about important matters. We viewed art, families, friendships, ethics, learning, politics, and patriotism with a closer consanguinity than might have been thought possible, given the distance that lay between us in age, geography, reading, upbringing, and language. Watching her behavior was always a lesson. At her husband's graveside she had refused to shake hands with Alexandre Millerand, President of the Republic, because he had failed to support her husband's research program. The manservant in her boulevard Saint-Germain apartment had shown devotion during her husband's last illness; and on account of her gratitude for this she could not fire him, thought he was stealing both money and furniture. So she gave up her apartment, pensioned him off, and went to live for the rest of her life, ten years, in a hotel. Again, crossing the Place Denfert-Rochereau alone on February 7, 1934, when masses of students, fascists, paid hoodlums, and police were involved in a far from spontaneous repeat of the previous day's Place de la Concorde "massacres," she said to the cop who had warned her she must not venture beyond the sidewalk, "I walk where I choose." And she crossed without harm, on her way to play bridge with Mary Reynolds, Marcel Duchamp, and one of her lovely old generals, Filloneau. Just as Roman Catholicism was her faith and France her country, moral elegance and personal bravery were her habit, affection and friendship her daily rite and virtually sole occupation.

Philip Lasell had come from America that fall and taken a room next to mine in the house at 20 rue de Berne. Gifted for many things but working at none, Hildegarde Watson's cousin was a playboy of wondrous charm. For him I served as guide to the intellectual life, though he also used in this way Jean Cocteau, Mary Butts, and the young French novelist René Crevel. In December, leaving for the South, he dramatized his departure with what I described to Buchanan as

> a sort of ethereal Proustian quarrel (a marvelous quarrel conducted with the greatest dignity and the nearest to an open display of affection that we have ever allowed ourselves, a sort of tearful but indignant graduating exercise, Philip doing his best to be hard toward the institution he was so fond of, and the best he could achieve being to offer me his ten Picasso's from which he has never been separated more than three days since he bought them in 1923).

The quarrel being no more than a gesture of temporary farewell, the gift was refused, though the framed gouache prints (five of musicians and five of card players) remained on my mantel for some months. Much later, leaving for America, he offered them again; and this time I accepted a gift but chose, since I could have whichever I preferred, a painted sculpture by Arp made out of wood. René Crevel got the Picassos, which I was happy to abandon. Having lived with them, I knew they were not my magic. The Arp is still with me and gives happiness. The quarrel was so void of significance that I joined Philip in April in the South, and it was through him that I came to know Mary Butts.

Mary was an Englishwoman of gentle birth, a roisterer, and a writer of intensely personal fiction. She was also quite handsome, with her white skin and carrot-gold hair. Her favorite dress was sweater and skirt (the British national costume); and she was fond of wearing, under a tipped-up man's felt hat, a single white jade earring, dollar-size. Like all the well brought up English, she got up in the morning. (Young Americans like to stay up late and sleep till noon.) Every day, too, she wrote with pen in large notebooks. She kept herself and her house very clean and roistered only when the day was done. Then she would have tea, toddle out to a café, meet friends, go on from there. The toddling was due to a knee that if not carefully handled would slip out of joint. It did not interfere with dancing in the walk-around fashion of the time or with a reasonable amount of country walking. What Mary liked most, however, come six of an evening, was a long pub crawl—going with loved ones from bar to bar, dining somewhere, then going on, tumbling in and out of taxis, fanning youth into a flame. Come midnight she would as leave go home and write.

I used to call her "the storm goddess," because she was at her best surrounded by cataclysm. She could stir up others with drink and drugs and magic incantations, and then when the cyclone was at its most intense, sit down at calm center and glow. All her stories are of moments when the persons observed are caught up by something, inner or outer, so irresistible that their highest powers and all their lowest conditionings are exposed. The resulting action therefore is definitive, an ultimate clarification arrived at through ecstasy. This kind of experience, of course, is the very nut and kernel of classic tragedy; and Mary liked using it for leading people on till they shot the works. There was no evil in her; her magic was all tied up to religion and great poetry. But she was strong medicine, calling herself in joke my "unrest cure." And she was sovereign against my juvenile reserves, my middle-class hypochondrias, my *"pessimisme américain,"* as Kristians Tonny was to call it. (She used to say that a European young man, waking up in the morning, opens the window, breathes deeply, feels wonderful, while his contemporary from America will close the window, then rush to a mirror and look for signs of decay.)

Accustomed as I had been from my earliest times to strong home remedies, and knowing well the advantages of ecstasy, I still did not like having my emotions manipulated; my resistance to the machinery of Southern Baptist conversion had not made me an easy mark. Nor could Mary's history of men quite recommend her. Marriage to a poet (John Rodker), a daughter by that marriage, escape from it to the continent with a tall Scot who practiced black magic and took drugs, the ensuing death of the Scot, an unforgiving mother, a demanding literary gift quick to bud but slow to ripen—all this had made her a strong woman, as her natural warmth had made her a good one, her classical education and high breeding (granddaughter of William Blake's friend and patron Captain Butts) a sweet and lively one. But none of it had trained her for mating with a musician. Nor could I at thirty take on for long a greedy and determined *femme de lettres* some seven years older. The mental powers were too imposing, the ways inflexible. We had lovely times together, warmths, clarities, and laughter. Then bickering began; and though our separation was not casual, by the time the year was out we were not meeting. That was in 1927. When she died in 1937 I felt almost like a widower.

In one poem Mary had declared her theme:

> From ritual to romance
> Two mediocrities:
> That is to say, without the high-strung moment
> Which in the transition, the passage,
> Undoubtedly occurs.

In another her nostalgia:

> O Lord, call off the curse on great names,
> On the "tall, tight boys,"
> Write off their debt,
> The sea-paced, wave curled,
> Achilles' set.

And back in her own south country, she had pronounced her prayer for abundance:

> Curl horns;
> Straighten trees;
> Multiply lobsters;
> Assemble bees.

It was through Mary that I knew the opium world, at least that part of it which comprised our friends. If I had encountered the drug at twenty I should certainly have tried it. At thirty I was afraid. But I respected its users and did not show disapproval. For the next five years I shared many a pipe vicariously. Once I held a friend's hand through withdrawal. I still enjoy the sweetish smell of the smoke, not unlike that of maple syrup cooking.

My friendship with Gertrude Stein dates from the winter of 1925 and '26. Though addicted from Harvard days to *Tender Buttons* and to *Geography and Plays* (almost no other of her books was yet in print), I still had made no effort toward the writer. I wanted an acquaintance to come about informally, and I was sure it would if I only waited. It did. Having heard in literary circles that George Antheil was that year's genius, she thought she really ought to look him over. So through Sylvia Beach she asked that he come to call. George, always game but wary, took the liberty, since he had been sent for, of bringing me along for intellectual protection, writing to me in Saint-Cloud a *pneumatique* that said, lest I hesitate, "we" had been asked for that evening. Naturally I went. Alice Toklas did not on first view care for me, and neither of the ladies found reason for seeing George again. But Gertrude and I got on like Harvard men. As we left, she said to him only good-by, but to me, "We'll be seeing each other." And still I made no move till late the next summer, when I sent her a postcard from Savoy, to which she replied.

I was thirty that year; and there had been dinner at Josiah Lasell's flat in the Palais Royal. At Christmas, according to my accounting of it to Buchanan, I attended

> two family dinners, great rowdy affairs with punch and champagne and children and movies . . . of Charlie Chaplin and turkeys from Lyon as big as sheep and plum puddings from London and mince pies from a swell Negro restaurant. And an eggnog party in the afternoon. A Xmas Eve tea with Bernard [Faÿ] and Sherwood Anderson. A Xmas Eve party at Gertrude Stein's with carols and a tree and a great Xmas cake with ribbon and candles on it. A dance Xmas night at Nancy Cunard's with Eugene [McCown] and the hard-drinking artist set.

On New Year's Day I took Miss Stein a musical manuscript, the setting for voice and piano of her *Susie Asado*. Reply was instant:

> . . . I like its looks immensely and want to frame it and Miss Toklas who knows more than looks says the things in it please her a lot and when can I know a little other than its looks but I am completely satisfied with its looks, the sad part was that we were at home but we were denying ourselves to everyone having been xhausted by the week's activities [actually that was the day she cut off her hair] but you would have been the xception you and the Susie, you or the Susie, do come in soon we will certainly be in Thursday afternoon any other time it is luck but may luck always be with you and a happy New Year to you always
>
> Gertrude Stein.

My hope in putting Gertrude Stein to music had been to break, crack open, and solve for all time anything still waiting to be solved, which was almost everything, about English musical declamation. My theory was that if a text is set correctly for the sound of it, the meaning will take care of itself. And the Stein texts, for prosodizing in this way, were manna. With meanings already abstracted, or absent, or so multiplied that choice among them was impossible, there was no temptation toward tonal illustration, say, of birdie babbling by the brook or heavy heavy hangs my heart. You could make a setting for sound and syntax only, then add, if needed, an accompaniment equally functional. I had no sooner put to music after this recipe one short Stein text than I knew I had opened a door. I had never had any doubts about Stein's poetry; from then on I had none about my ability to handle it in music. In the next few months I made several Stein settings, the last being a text of some length entitled *Capital Capitals,* composed for four male voices and piano. This is an evocation of Provence—its landscape, weather, and people—imagined as a conversation among its four capital cities, Aix, Arles, Avignon, and Les Baux; and it takes upwards of twenty minutes to perform. But long before that was composed, I had asked Miss Stein to write me an opera libretto, and we had sat together for picking out a subject.

The theme we chose was of my suggesting; it was the working artist's working life, which is to say, the life we both were living.

It was also my idea that good things come in pairs. In letters, for instance, there were Joyce and Stein, in painting Picasso and Braque, in religion Protestants and Catholics, or Christians and Jews, in colleges Harvard and Yale, and so on to the bargain basements of Gimbel's and Macy's. This dualistic view made it possible, without going in for sex unduly, to have both male and female leads with second leads and choruses surrounding them, for all the world like Joyce and Stein themselves holding court in the rue de l'Odéon and the rue de Fleurus. I thought we should follow overtly, however, the format of classical Italian opera, which carries on the commerce of the play in dry recitative, extending the emotional moments into arias and set-pieces. And since the eighteenth-century *opera seria,* or basic Italian opera, required a serious mythological subject with a tragic ending, we agreed to follow that convention also, but to consider mythology as including not just Greek or Scandinavian legends, of which there were already a great many in operatic repertory, but also political history and the lives of the saints. Gertrude liked American history, but every theme we tried out seemed to have something wrong with it. So that after I had vetoed George Washington because of eighteenth-century costumes (in which everybody looks alike), we gave up history and chose saints, sharing a certain reserve toward medieval ones and Italian ones on the grounds that both had been overdone in the last century. Eventually our saints turned out to be Baroque and Spanish, a solution that delighted Gertrude, for she loved Spain, and that was far from displeasing me, since, as I pointed out, mass-market Catholic art, the basic living art of Christianity, was still Baroque. And Maurice Grosser was later to remind us that musical instruments of the violin family still present themselves as functional Baroque forms.

Our conversations about writing an opera must have taken place in January or February of 1927, for by March 26 Miss Stein had "begun Beginning of Studies for an opera to be sung." "I think," her note went on, "it should be late eighteenth-century or early nineteenth-century saints. Four saints in three acts. And others. Make it pastoral. In hills and gardens. All four and then additions. We must invent them. But next time you come I will show you a little bit and we will talk some scenes over."

The same day, "The saints are still enjoying themselves." Four days later they had gone firmly Spanish. "I think I have got St. Thérèse onto the stage, it has been an awful struggle and I think I can keep her on and gradually by the second act get St. Ignatius on and then they will be both on together but not at once in the third act. I want you to read it as far as it has gone before you go...."

Going refers to my departure for the South, where a little bit with Philip Lasell but mostly with Mary Butts I stayed till May, wrote *Capital Capitals,* also some organ variations on Sunday school hymns. Alice Toklas must have decided by this time not to dislike me, because Gertrude's letters contain warm messages from her (referred to now as Alice) and constant declarations of Alice's admiration for my music. I had in fact become a member of the household and had begun introducing into it my close associates.

I began with three poets—the Frenchman Georges Hugnet, the Belgian Eric de Haulleville, and the American Sherry Mangan, plus the French prose writer Pierre de Massot, who wrote very beautifully but very little. My painter comrades at this time were Christian Bérard, Leonid Berman, Eugene Berman, and Kristians Tonny. I knew also Pavel Tchelitcheff, but so did Gertrude. Leonid she never took up with. Tchelitcheff, Bérard, and Eugene Berman (or "Pavlik," "Bébé," and "Genia") were in full reaction against cubism and striving steadfastly to express, as Picasso had loved to do two decades earlier, tenderness, mystery, and compassion. Pavlik and Bébé painted only people; Genia preferred deserted architecture. Leonid's subject even then was ships, the sea, and fishermen. Tonny, much younger, was a virtuoso draftsman of Flemish fantasy.

All these young painters, along with the poets, came later to be termed neo-Romantics; and their movement had influence not only among the twenty-to-thirty-year-olds but also among the older artists. Picasso himself, about 1930, essayed to take over the mystery, humanity, and ink blots of Bérard; but he could never quite get back for use again the compassion he had felt when young and poor. So he turned to the harsher and more calculated spontaneities of surrealism. Gertrude Stein, affected by us all, began at this time a series of landscape books that initiated the slow return to emotional content and naturalistic speech that were to give such impressive results at the end of her life. In mid-April of '27, still writing on *Four Saints,* she had sent word that "the opera has given me lots of ideas for a novel I want to write one." And in July, with the opera barely finished, she wrote of "progressing with my novel," *Lucy Church Amiably.*

The movement's literary mentor was Max Jacob—poet, painter, satirical storyteller, Picasso's friend from early youth, a Jew from Brittany, a penitent, a Catholic, and something of a saint. Max who had seen Jesus twice—in 1909 on his own Montmartre wall, at Montparnasse in a cinema five years later—was mean and generous, envious and kind, malicious and great-hearted. Most important of all, he could speak straightforwardly, whether ridiculing bourgeois ways or recounting religious experience. Gertrude, who had known him in prewar days, had long since ceased to receive him, on account of his uncleanly person and bohemian ways, which at that time had included sniffing ether. After his martyrdom at German hands in 1944, she spoke of his work with respect and admiration.

The group had no mentor for painting, could have none, because the only artist its members admired wholeheartedly was Picasso; and he was not available to the young. On the contrary—dyspeptic, worried, watchful—he led his life in terror of them, his all-seeing eye and whiplash wit alert to every prey. When Gertrude hung a neo-Romantic landscape by Francis Rose, he asked the painter's name and then the figure. To her reply that she had paid 300 francs ($10) he muttered, half-smiling, "For that price one can get something quite good."

The painters of our group, no father to guide them, developed unsteadily. As draftsmen, all were strong; in painting it is doubtful whether any ever grew to be a master. Three of them, however—Bérard, Tchelitcheff, and Eugene Berman—became world-figures in stage design; and Tonny has decorated many a wall. Leonid Berman alone, remaining strictly an easel-painter, continued to view his seas and their folk, his complex interpenetrations (under a quivering sky) of land and water, with the directness of his early vision.

The poets led less glorious careers. Sherry Mangan was a man of parts, a classical scholar, a lover of women, fine food, and drink. Yet for all his indomitable persistence, he became, as poet, a sterile virtuoso (which can happen with the Irish). So he turned to sex, marriage, book design, journalism, and revolution (as a Trotskyist), in all these domains cutting quite a figure. But in spite of his mastery of the literary forms, he was a failure in them all. He met death in Rome at sixty with an expression of surprise on his handsome face, though he had written me within the week, "There is so little time." Eric de Haulleville died earlier, around forty. He had written well, received awards. The poet in my Paris grouping who failed least toward his art, the one with whom I was most closely associated at this time and who was also most elaborately bound to Gertrude Stein, was Georges Hugnet.

Hugnet was small, truculent, and sentimental, a type at once tough and tender, of which I have known several among the French. (The conductor Roger Désormière was like that; so is today the composer Pierre Boulez.) Self-indulgent early about food and drink, by sixty Hugnet suggested a miniature Hemingway. At all ages his conversation has been outrageous and, if you like outrage, hilarious. Rarely have I heard matched the guttersnipe wit with which he can lay out an enemy. His poetry is liltingly lyrical, pleasingly farfetched as to image, and sweet on the tongue. His most striking contributions to letters, all the same, have been histories of the Dada and surrealist movements and a still unfinished memoir of Paris intellectual life under the German occupation.

I knew Georges in 1926, took him to Gertrude early in '27. He was beginning then, since no one else was doing it, to publish his own poetry and that of his friends, his father (a furniture manufacturer with taste in letters) staking him to the costs. The books came out in limited editions with illustrations by distinguished modern artists. Sold by subscription, they paid their way on condition that nobody receive royalties and the publisher take no salary. Under the imprint Editions de la Montagne, Hugnet brought out that year books by himself, Théophile Briant, and Eric de Haulleville. Others followed by Tristan Tzara, Pierre de Massot, and Gertrude Stein. This last was a collection of ten word-portraits accompanied by drawn likenesses of the subjects, the texts appearing in both English and French, the translations produced by Hugnet and myself. The subjects were:

	drawn by
IF I TOLD HIM: A COMPLETED PORTRAIT OF PICASSO	*himself*
GUILLAUME APOLLINAIRE	*Picasso*
ERIK SATIE	*Picasso*
PAVLIK TCHELITCHEFF OR ADRIAN ARTHUR	*himself*
VIRGIL THOMSON	*Bérard*
CHRISTIAN BERARD	*himself*
BERNARD FAY	*Tonny*
KRISTIANS TONNY	*himself*
GEORGES HUGNET	*E. Berman*
MORE GRAMMAR GENIA BERMAN	*himself*

Translating Gertrude Stein had been Madame Langlois's idea, and she had worked out with my aid a piece called *Water Pipe* (*Conduite d'Eau*). The original of this had been printed in the first number, dated February 1927, of *larus the celestial visitor,* Sherry Mangan's magazine, of which, according to the masthead, I was "editor in France." And the translation had been read aloud before a literary gathering at the house of Miss Natalie Barney, salonnière from Ohio, Remy de Gourmont's "*amazone.*" This was at an after-tea program devoted to Miss Stein, where I also sang my settings of *Susie Asado* and *Preciosilla.* Madame Langlois attended as well to honor the poet, encountering there an old friend, the historian Seignobos, who was so dumbfounded at meeting her in a salon several ways far-out that he blurted, "What are you doing *here?*" right in front of the hostess-amazon.

Another acquaintance of Miss Barney and of Gertrude Stein, the Duchesse de Clermont-Tonnerre (a member of Miss Barney's feminist literary group that called itself l'Académie des Femmes, also a writer of memoirs under her maiden name, Elisabeth de Gramont), paid honor to us by having performed at her house in the rue Raynouard, during a *Grande Semaine* costume party, our cantata *Capital Capitals.* Getting ready for this occasion, I had holed up in a hotel on the rue Jacob (my definitive move to the left bank), where I made ink copies for the four men to sing from and where I rehearsed them letter-perfect for the event. In the last days my bass took sick; and since replacement was not feasible, I ended by singing his solos from the piano. The party was very handsome, with the garden paths outlined in blue cup-candles and behind bushes a quartet of hunting horns. But the residence, an eighteenth-century gatehouse, was not large; and when the billionaire great beauty Ganna Walska arrived in a *robe de style* six feet wide and surely ten from toe to train, the duchesse, meeting her at the door, exclaimed, "But you know the size of my rooms. Go right out to the garden." And there all evening, in bright white satin, bare-breasted and bejeweled, she paraded like a petulant peacock. The Misses Stein and Toklas also came, having delayed their summer exodus by over a month.

All that winter and spring, while I was serving Gertrude Stein as translator, impresario, music setter, and literary agent, she was working for me too, trying to find money for me to live on while our opera got composed. She had done her best with Miss Etta and Dr. Claribel Cone, art collectors from Baltimore; and I had played music for them to no great cash result. Nor had her efforts with a rich friend from Chicago, Mrs. Emily Chadbourne Crane, yet turned to money. She had consulted the sculptor Jo Davidson about other prospects; and he had called up right away Miss Elsa Maxwell, whose life work was showing people how to spend money. Miss Maxwell immediately invited me to lunch at the Ritz, where at a table of twelve I sat between her (Oh, yes, at her right) and a Roman principessa and where, between cocktails and bridge, she outlined for me in detail a custom-made career, which she herself was to take in hand right off.

The first item of this was to be a commission from the Princesse Edmond de Polignac for a work to be performed the next season at one of this lady's regular musical receptions. The last item was to be a production of my opera at Monte Carlo in the spring of 1929, two years thence. And we were both to lunch with the princesse the next Saturday. The Monte Carlo deal appeared to me more credible than the other, because Miss Maxwell was employed at that time by the principality of Monaco as a promoter of its gambling casino, hotels, and beach. It was due to her work and presence, indeed, that the Côte d'Azur, formerly just a wintering place, was beginning its fabulous life as a summer resort. There she might indeed have been able to throw weight, perhaps even to give orders. But the princesse (née Winnaretta Singer) was not only socially stable; she was quite accustomed to making up her own mind and was herself a musician.

I do not know whether Miss Maxwell's plans encountered resistance, or whether she had been bluffing all the time. I do remember that the lunch in the avenue Henri Martin never came off and that within a week after the one at the Ritz, Miss Maxwell made six engagements with me in three days and failed to appear at any of them, leaving word the last time that she had quit Paris. Jean Cocteau, to whom I told the story, offered to write the princesse himself explaining that I was not to be judged from my acquaintances in café society. But I discouraged this, doubting she had ever heard of me.

Cocteau, who had known me since 1921 but who had just lately decided to become acquainted also with my music, now came, at the invitation of Mary Butts, to my narrow room in the Hôtel Jacob, where, accompanying myself at the piano, I sang him *Capital Capitals,* all four voices. The work pleased him, he said, by its solidity, "like a table that stands on its legs, a door one can open and close."

As I reread letters written at that time, I am struck by the intensity with which Miss Stein and I took each other up. From the fall of 1926, in fact, till her death in July of 1946 we were forever loving being together, whether talking and walking, writing to each other, or at work. Once for a four-year period we did not speak, having quarreled for reasons we both knew to be foolish; but for the last two years of even that time we wrote constantly, our pretext being business. I translated into French with Madame Langlois *Water Pipe* and *A Saint in Seven,* with Georges Hugnet *Ten Portraits* and excerpts from *The Making of Americans.* I also produced from among my friends a publisher, Sherry Mangan, who printed her work extensively, or caused it to be printed, including the parallel versions of Hugnet's *Enfances* and her English paraphrase of it, which later appeared as *Before the Flowers of Friendship Faded Friendship Faded.* I set to music *Susie Asado, Preciosilla, Portrait of F. B., Capital Capitals,* and a film scenario written by her in French and entitled, not quite grammatically, *Deux Soeurs qui sont pas soeurs*. Also two operas, both of which

First page of *Film: Deux Soeurs qui sont pas soeurs* by Gertrude Stein, music and ms. by V.T., the instrumental part being a portrait of Basket I, the poodle whose acquisition provided the story.

she wrote for me on themes thought up by me. The eventual performance and musical publication of these works was, moreover, brought about by me in every case, though at all times she did her best to further both our interests. She even offered the services of Picasso as stage designer for *Four Saints,* a collaboration which I declined, preferring to remain, except for her, within my age group. I did, in fact, right then beseech Bérard to consider designing an eventual production, though at that time he had not touched the theater; and he said yes with joy, began instantly giving off ideas.

All these maneuvers, I remind myself, had to do with a work not yet in existence, for the opera's libretto, begun in March, was not completed till mid-June; and at that date there was still not any music. There could not have been; I had not seen the text. I was given this almost complete at the end of June, but I did not receive the whole libretto till a month later. When she sent it from the country, I was still at the Hôtel Jacob et d'Angleterre without a penny. By the time it reached me I had embarked on an expedition that was to keep me from composing for several months.

This began as a motor trip through Brittany and Normandy with Hildegarde Watson's mother, Mrs. Chester Whitin Lasell, and a teen-age grandchild, Nancy Clare Verdi. It turned into a two-months' caring-for-the-sick when Mrs. Lasell came down in Rouen with an ear infection. By good luck, and through my friendship with Madame Langlois, I was able to command, in August, out-of-town and out-of-season visits from a first-class otolaryngologist. When eventually the mastoiditis had been cleared up without surgery, Mrs. Lasell was grateful, became for several years my patron. In late September she returned to Whitinsville. In October I ordered clothes and looked for a flat. By November I had taken a studio on the quai Voltaire and begun composing *Four Saints in Three Acts.*

I 7 *quai Voltaire*

THE QUAI VOLTAIRE is a row of eighteenth-century houses standing between the rue des Saints-Pères and the rue du Bac and
looking across the Seine to the Louvre. Just above it sits the seventeenth-century Institut de France, arms open like a miniature Saint
Peter's for receiving daily its college of lay cardinals, the forty
"immortals" of l'Académie Française. A farther short walk up-
stream brings the medieval world—the Conciergerie, Sainte-
Chapelle, and Notre-Dame. Downstream one passes the 1900 Gare
d'Orsay and the eighteenth-century Hôtel de Salm (Palais de la
Légion d'Honneur) and looks across to the Tuileries Gardens before arriving at the Chamber of Deputies and Place de la Concorde,
both dominating from on high excellent swimming-baths that sit
in the Seine without using its water. The situation could not be
more central or more historical.

Number 17, where I went to live in 1927 (permanently, as it
has now turned out), consists of two houses, each with its courtyard and concierge, plus a three-story pavilion known as *l'atelier
d'Ingres,* where the grandmother of our concierge's husband was
said to have posed for *La Source.* In the second of the larger houses,
dating from 1791 and built over the ruins of the fifteenth-century
Abbaye des Théatins, I occupied, five stories up, a furnished studio
complete with bath and with a view that included Louvre, Opéra,

and Sacré-Cœur. The concierge of the first house, Madame Jeanne, took care of it. She took care of me too, washing my woolens, receiving my messages, ordering anthracite coal for my *salamandre,* and in general looking to my comfort. Her sister, Madame Elise, concierge of the second house, came later to cook for me (and first class she was); but at this time I had no kitchen, only an alcohol stove for making coffee or tea.

The first house was L-shaped; and my landlord, Dr. Ovize, though not its owner, lived there with his wife on the top floor behind a twelve-foot-wide terrace dominating three fourths of the city. The second house, where I lived, was also L-shaped; and, completed by the Ingres studio, it enclosed three sides of a generous courtyard, turning the back of its principal wing to the Hôtel du Quai Voltaire, at number 19. Madame Elise, my concierge, only slept in this house; she spent her days helping out Madame Jeanne and preparing sumptuous meals for Madame Jeanne's husband, a bonded messenger for the Bank of France. And as if to bind further the two houses, their cousin Berthe (as a live-in servant she could not be called Madame) was maid to my next-door neighbor, the poet Lucie Delarue-Mardrus; and Madame Mardrus herself, ex-wife of an Arabic scholar, Dr. Jesus-Christ Mardrus, was the close friend of Madame Ovize. As a further connection, she shared literary and feministic consanguinities with my friends Miss Natalie Barney and Elisabeth de Gramont, Duchesse de Clermont-Tonnerre.

Berthe, costumed in black, was a schooled servant who addressed one in the third person. When I knocked on her kitchen door one day to ask how to make a mayonnaise, she began, "Monsieur will take a bowl and an egg. Monsieur will break his egg and put into his bowl the yellow only." Though forty or more, she was not afraid of stairs, always running down to find Madame Mardrus a taxi, then climbing back by the steep circular service stairs. Dark men from the Auvergne carried fifty-pound sacks of coal up that stairway too.

Madame Elise was tall, heavy, and beautiful, with blue eyes and white hair. She smiled constantly, unless cooking. Then she would hover, fluttering like a hen and barely breathing, as out of her left hand she would take with three fingers of her right a pinch of something and throw it in, then wait still breathless, as if listening, till she divined the gesture a success. When I began to cook she told me many secret things; and occasionally I taught her an American dish. This she would never put into repertory until her brother-in-law had pronounced it good. And she did not think it right not to eat soup. Thus I discovered that no dinner was too much work if I allowed her to make soup also—which she did well, cooking it always very slowly, while she mended, tending her sister's lodge.

The studio was octagonal and twenty feet tall, with high windows on the north and northeast facets, which were covered at night by rose-colored floor-length curtains, padded to keep the cold out. The walls and carpet were a golden tan; chairs, table, and dish-cabinet, all from Louis-Philippe times, were of mahogany. A velvet-covered plain couch was my bed. At the top of some long stairs were a balcony and a very large bath-dressing room. This had two windows (one with my finest view), its own heat (gas), and its mechanism (also gas) for heating water, plus a clothes-closet. I had brought with me some Chinese water colors and a Persian chess table (gifts of Mary Butts) and the abstract sculpture by Arp (gift of Philip Lasell). Almost immediately too there was a large Bérard, a man's portrait much larger than life painted in almost-black blues over candlewax modeling (a gift from Bérard out of his first one-man show). There was Chinese tea from Boston (via Mrs. Lasell). I acquired a rented piano from Pleyel. And I had new clothes, the first in several years, for with the first gift of money from Mrs. Lasell, before she put me on allowance, I had ordered at Lanvin three suits, an overcoat, and six poplin shirts with matching underdrawers. I paid for these in cash, made friends, forever after having credit there.

I said one day to Gertrude, "We are poor as anything and feeling quite bohemian, and yet we all wear suits and ties and hats. What did Picasso and Max Jacob wear when they were young?" But she did not remember, and so she asked Picasso. "Caps," he replied, "and sweaters, except for Max, who was a dude," then remembering further, "but we bought our sweaters at Williams's [British sport shop]."

Madame Jeanne, my caretaker, had black hair and flashing eyes; and though less monumental than her sister, was more striking. I have seen her image on the portal of an eleven-century church (Saint-Lô), along with those of Anatole France and of an ever remembered old French taxi driver. She was in fact as basically French as anyone I ever knew; she *was* France. She could barely read; she believed America to have been discovered by Lafayette; and the store called Old England she would write phonetically in French as Olden Gland. All the same, reciting the injustices of Madame Ovize toward her sister, she was Sarah Bernhardt, Réjane, Marie Bell. She was also Corneille and Racine, for what is the language of these at its most lapidary but the basic French of kings and concierges? *"J'admire ton courage et je plains ta jeunesse,"* says the monarch to the hero of *Le Cid* ("I admire your bravery and pity your youth"). And the young Oreste in *Andromaque* confesses, *"Mon innocence enfin commence à me peser"* ("My innocence begins to be a weight").

Of my sculpture by Arp Madame Jeanne had asked, reasonably enough, what it represented. And when I answered that I had no clue, she settled the matter with, *"C'est une idée d'artiste."* And when to her inquiry about a crystal that looked like pink flowers, I answered that such forms, found in the Sahara, were known as *"roses du désert,"* she observed philosophically, putting it back on the shelf, *"C'est intéressant tout de même la nature."* For humane understanding she was Madame Langlois's equal; and in her mastery of the tactful remark she could match my mother.

In my first week some composer had been playing me his newest piece, a long, loud, and highly discordant work. The next morning a letter came from my poet-neighbor Lucie Delarue-Mardrus that was a cry of pain. I answered with an invitation to tea, and she accepted. Tall and dark-haired, with soft brown eyes, she was a Norman from Honfleur, poet, painter, even something of a musician. It was around her music making that we made our pact. She liked to practice the violin from twelve to one; and I agreed not to mind music at that hour, since I would surely be shaving, bathing, and dressing to go out. During the earlier morning, when I might be using the piano, she agreed to do her writing in a room from which she could not hear my music. Early afternoons we both were out. Late afternoons she would tolerate whatever she might hear, since she now knew that what came through my walls would always be some dialect of music. I proposed not playing evenings after ten, but she said that music could not be heard from where she slept. So we became friends and began to visit, sometimes at her flat when all six of her tall dark sisters would arrive from Honfleur, sometimes at mine when there were literary people, still oftener at Dr. Ovize's, where there would be lunches lasting for hours, with music afterwards. Here I would play and sing my own, or I would play two-piano Mozart with Madame, a chihuahua-size Jewess from Algiers with deep shadows under green eyes and a mop of bright red hair teased into a headlight.

On November first I had taken possession; on November second I began Act One. Very shortly after, I composed my first song in French, a setting of four poems by Georges Hugnet that were not related to one another save by their lilting metrics. Henri Sauguet gave it the title of *La Valse grégorienne,* on account of its chant-like intonings and archaic harmony. The French found in it no prosodic fault, insisted I sing it for them all the time. It was so successful, in fact, that I went no farther just then with setting French. I had my *Four Saints* to be getting on with.

In the early Boulanger days I had trained myself to write music without instrumental aid, had come indeed to prefer working that way. For the opera I found myself working differently. With the text on my piano's music rack, I would sing and play, improvising melody to fit the words and harmony for underpinning them with shape. I did this every day, wrote down nothing. When the first act would improvise itself every day in the same way, I knew it was set. That took all of November. Then I wrote it out from memory, which took ten days. By mid-December I had a score consisting of the vocal lines and a figured bass, a score from which I could perform.

On Christmas night I performed Act One for close friends only. The party that went along with this performance grew out of a Christmas box sent at the request of Mrs. Lasell by Rosa Lewis, King Edward VII's former cook, owner of the Cavendish Hotel, clubhouse for London's millionaire bohemia. It contained three massive objects—a *fois gras en croûte,* a Stilton cheese, and a plum pudding. By having sent in to go along with these a salad of apples and peeled walnuts, an aspic of chicken, and some champagne, I managed to offer a lap supper to twelve people. What effect my music made I was not sure. Gertrude Stein was pleased, of course, and Alice too. Everybody, in fact, seemed buoyed up by the opera's vivacity. Tristan Tzara told Hugnet he had been deeply impressed by a music at once so "physical" and so gay. I had wondered whether a piece so drenched in Anglican chant (running from Gilbert and Sullivan to Morning Prayer and back) could rise and sail. But no one else seemed bothered by its origins. On the contrary, they had all undergone a musical and poetic experience so unfamiliar that only their faith in me (for they were chosen friends) had allowed them to be carried along, which indeed they had been, as on a magic carpet.

What gave this work so special a vitality? The origin of that lay in its words, of course, the music having been created in their image. Music, however, contains an energy long since lost to language, an excitement created by the contest of two rhythmic patterns, one of lengths and one of stresses. A pattern made up of lengths alone is static, and the stuttering of mere stresses is hypnotic. But together, and contrasted, they create tension and release; and this is the energy that makes music sail, take flight, get off the ground. By applying it to the text of Gertrude Stein, I had produced a pacing that is implied in that text, if you wish, but that could never be produced without measured extensions. Speech alone lacks music's forward thrust.

The theme of *Four Saints* is the religious life—peace between the sexes, community of faith, the production of miracles—its locale being the Spain Gertrude remembered from having traveled there. The music evokes Christian liturgy. Its local references, however, are not to Spain, which I had never seen, but rather to my Southern Baptist upbringing in Missouri. It does not do, this music, or attempt to do, any of the things already done by the words. It merely explodes these into singing and gives them shape. Poetry alone is always a bit amorphous; and poetry as spontaneously structured as Gertrude Stein's had long seemed to me to need musical reinforcement. I do not mean that her writing *lacks* music; I mean that it *likes* music. Much of it, in fact, lies closer to musical timings than to speech timings. The rigamarole ending of *Capital Capitals,* for instance, I have always felt to have small relation to Spenser, Shakespeare, Milton, or Keats; but I do recognize in its peroration-by-repetition the insistences of a Beethoven finale.

If it is the relation of music to words that makes opera in two senses moving, it is the relation of instrumental accompaniment to vocal line that makes an opera resemble its epoch. The singing line from Monteverdi to Alban Berg shows surprisingly little change, because with conscientious composers the words-and-music factor, even through language differences, is a constant. You have only to think of Purcell's *Dido and Aeneas,* Mozart's *Don Giovanni,* Wagner's *Tristan und Isolde,* Bizet's *Carmen,* and Stravinsky's *The Rake's Progress* to realize that the history of the lyric stage is largely the history of its changing instrumental accompaniment.

Now the *Four Saints* accompaniment is as odd as its text, so odd, indeed, that it has sometimes been taken for childish. In fact, many persons not closely involved with either poetry or music but mildly attached to all contemporary artwork by the conviction that it is thrifty to be stylish have for more than thirty years now been worried by my use of what seems to them a backward-looking music idiom in connection with a forward-looking literary one. That worry can only be argued against by denying the assumption that discord is advanced and harmoniousness old-fashioned. Not even the contrary is true, though the production of complete discord through musical sounds (the only kind of discord that is not just noise) has been practiced since before World War I. The truth is that only artists greedy for quick fame choose musical materials for their modishness. In setting Stein texts to music I had in mind the acoustical support of a trajectory, of a verbal volubility that would brook no braking. My skill was to be employed not for protecting such composers as had invested in the dissonant manner but for avoiding all those interval frictions and contrapuntal viscosities which are built into the dissonant style and which if indulged unduly might trip up my verbal speeds. Not to have skirted standard modernism would have been to fall into a booby trap. On the contrary, I built up my accompaniments by selecting chords for their tensile strength and by employing in a vast majority of cases only those melodic elements from the liturgical vernacular of Christendom, both Catholic and Protestant, that had for centuries borne the weight of long prayers and praises and of that even longer fastidiously fine-printed and foot-noted contract that we called the Creed.

I set all of Stein's text to music, every word of it, including the stage directions, which were so clearly a part of the poetic continuity that I did not think it proper to excise them. And for distributing all these parts among the singers I assumed a double chorus of participating saints and two Saint Teresas (not alter egos, just identical twins); and I added as nonsaintly commentators, or "end men," a *compère* and a *commère*. Though I had Gertrude's permission to repeat things if I wished, I no more took this freedom than I did that of cutting. She was a specialist of repetition; why should I compete? I simply set everything, exactly in the order of its writing down, from beginning to end.

Act Two was composed and written out by the end of February; and Acts Three and Four (for *Four Saints in Three Acts* is merely a title; actually there are thirty or more saints and four acts) were finished by summer and written out in July. Generally I worked mornings, sometimes also in the late afternoon. Always I went out for lunch and usually for dinner, unless I had a guest or two, in which case I had *cordon bleu* food sent in from the Hôtel de l'Université. This was a good quarter of a mile from door to door; but a dainty waitress would trip it twice, bearing her platter up five flights with soup and roast, a second time with dessert. When I had grippe a nearer restaurant would send a waiter up four times a day, twice to take the order and twice to deliver it. Otherwise, once out of the house and down my stairs, I usually stayed out till five or so on errands or walks.

Lunch was likely to be at a bistro on the rue Jacob called La Quatrième République, its title an irony left over from immediate postwar idealism. There one encountered almost always the singer Victor Prahl, usually Janet Flanner and her novelist companion Solita Solano, sometimes the reporter Vincent Sheean. The food, excellent and very cheap, was served downstairs by a portly *patron,* upstairs by a domineering waitress who had no fatigue in her as she ran up the circular staircase, or patience in her busy life for Americans who dallied over menus. "*Yvonne la terrible,*" Janet would call her. When one young man, mixing his salad, put in a whole teaspoonful of mustard, she teased him harshly, "You must be in love."

My walks that winter were chiefly with Russell Hitchcock, who had come to live near by in the rue de Lille and who was writing his first works on architectural history. Just as earlier and later I walked with Maurice Grosser in the woods outside of Paris from the forests of Rambouillet and Saint-Cloud clean round to the Bois de Vincennes, I walked the city itself, every quarter of it, with Hitchcock. I had done this by myself years earlier, looking for a lodging, but now I saw it from another view, for he could read it like a history book. This is not easy, since French house design has changed little since the seventeenth century. But ornament has changed with almost every decade; and a particular treatment of stone—smooth, rusticated, or vermiculated, with or without indentations—has marked the larger epochs of style. Involved at this time with Romantic architecture, Russell would love to point out, in contrast to the airy neoclassical design under Louis XVI of the customs barriers at the Porte de la Chapelle, the willful heaviness in the same epoch of Saint-Philippe-du-Roule, almost as massively weighted for romantic expressivity as the Napoleonic Place du Caire, with its trophylike sphinx façade, and the Chapelle Expiatoire, pious Restoration memorial to the executed monarch Louis XVI and his Queen Marie-Antoinette.

Red-bearded and not slender, speaking loudly because he was himself a little deaf, and always dressed with flamboyance, Russell attracted considerable attention; but he pleased the French by his knowledge of their country, by his elegant manners, which were formal without being lugubrious, and by his air, at once *bon enfant* and *gros jouisseur,* of having a wonderful time. He interested very little Gertrude Stein, more Georges Hugnet, who translated his early brochures for publication, a great deal Madame Langlois, who could spot a proper scholar when she saw one. It was through Russell that I first knew the academician Louis Gillet and his wife, who, having young ones themselves, liked other young ones to be about and who had as country house (except Sundays, three to five, when it was on show) the Château de Challis, near Ermenonville, which belonged to the Académie Française and of which Monsieur Gillet was curator. It was there, in fact, that Louise Gillet was married in the medieval chapel to music of mine. The residence itself had been a moated castle till its eighteenth-century owner, romantically attached to contemplating the Gothic but less so to living in it, had it transformed by dynamite into a ruin and then built himself a modern (Louis XV) house, from which his guests could view in comfort the ivy-clad reminder of times past.

With Henri Sauguet I also walked, but more for poking around slums than for mastering history. We showed each other our music, shared adventures and addresses, bound ourselves together by an unspoken credo (based on Satie) that forbade us to be bogus either in our music or in our lives. In the spring of 1927, coming from Villefranche with Lasell and Mary Butts, I had joined Sauguet at Monte Carlo, where Diaghilev was putting on *La Chatte,* his first ballet. Georges Hugnet too I saw constantly—also Henri Cliquet-Pleyel and his wife Marthe-Marthine. Cliquet was hollow-cheeked and looked Hispanic, save for the large, soft eyes, which could be only French. His wife was plumpish, blond, the classical soubrette, alert and sex-minded, also a singer of remarkable musicianship. With Hugnet and Kristians Tonny—blond, muscular, and Dutch, with the sea at the back of his eyes—we constituted a *petite famille* for dinners and laughter. Cliquet was a pianist of unusual facility, a sight reader of renown, and a composer of willful banality. His music was a tender parody, his life a slavery to potboiling jobs. Marthe too was not ever to be prosperous; she had thrown away her singing career for marriage in Rumania, and she could not fight her way back. She and Cliquet, though attached relentlessly, did each other no good. He would go into tantrums in which he burned his manuscripts or destroyed pictures with razors (*"colères de faiblesse,"* Madame Langlois called them); and she would take to red wine, quarts of it a day. Yet they remained for me gentle companions and colleagues of impeccable solidarity. Around 1928, Hugnet wrote a long poem about the Emperor Commodus, which Cliquet made into a cantata. Cliquet also composed an operetta with book and lyrics by Max Jacob, *Les Impôts.* This was a parody of every operetta in the world, and both verses and music were exquisite. When Cliquet died at seventy, in 1963, he had just completed a work called (actually) *Concerto posthume.* The earlier large works such as *Commode* and *Les Impôts,* not yet found, may have been destroyed by him in some frenzied fury.

Hugnet that winter went on publishing, usually poetry books. Tonny continued to draw and to experiment with paint. The three of us together made a gift for Gertrude which was a set of poems by Georges put to music by me and bound up in a cover that Tonny had drawn on silver paper by stylus pressure only. The full title of the offering was *Le Berceau de Gertrude Stein, ou le mystère de la rue de Fleurus, huit poèmes de Georges Hugnet mis en musique par Virgil Thomson sous le titre de Lady Godiva's*

Waltzes. Godiva was Gertrude's private name for her Ford, of which the cough and tripping rhythms dominate the piece. Marthe-Marthine first sang it publicly at a concert of my works in May of '28. Georges also made a film that spring in collaboration with a Belgian nobleman, the Comte d'Ursel. It was called *La Perle* and is a Dadalike fantasy that prefigured the surrealist films of Luis Buñuel. For its appearance at the cinema Aux Ursulines I arranged my *Valse grégorienne,* to please d'Ursel, for the five-piece orchestra that accompanied the show.

Lots of people came in and out of my flat that first year, and sometimes there were large parties. For one of these Bernard Faÿ invited a galaxy of literary stars and aged princesses. At another, Scott Fitzgerald stood up on my anthracite-burning *salamandre* with such shaky balance that both he and the stove just missed decline and fall. The novelists Marcel Jouhandeau and André Gide used to appear. Also León Kochnitzky, poet and professional traveler. Not Antheil, who was in America. Nor Ernest Hemingway, whom I never asked. He was part of a Montparnasse hard-liquor set which, though thoroughly fascinated by itself, was less interesting to people not also drinking hard liquor. Robert McAlmon I did find interesting; I also esteemed him as a writer; but just like Hart Crane, who was around for a while and whom I also admired, he was too busy drinking and getting over it to make dates with. Both were better when casually encountered. Mary Reynolds, the queen of American Montparnasse, came often, also Olga Dahlgren, a Philadelphian abroad, and my own painters, of course—Kristians Tonny, Bérard, and Leonid and Eugene Berman. Also a Swiss writer unbelievably impoverished, not always clean, not always sober, his mind ingenious, his talk both learned and funny—Charles-Albert Cingria, who lived in an unheated garret room with a fifteenth-century spinet, a bicycle, and five hundred books and who wrote in the most beautiful French prose small brochures about large historical questions, such as the rights of rhythm in Gregorian chant.

So what with parties and people, with new clothes and stable measurements (for I patronized a Russian gymnast who could keep me at 135 pounds), and with the opera advancing by leaps, time stopped once more. Nothing seemed to be going on, because everything was going right. In April Mrs. Lasell appeared, wholly recovered from her mastoiditis, returning with her brother and sister-in-law from an African trip. She was pleased with my flat and with my general industriousness, as well she might have been. Never before had I worked so fast or so well as I was doing in this comfortable place and with enough money to live more easily than before (just a little more easily, but that made the difference). Anyone could see that I was in phase, that my guardian angel was on the job, and that 17 quai Voltaire was not only the "strange packet ship" that Lucie Mardrus called it; it was for me in every way a magic locale. I did not tell Jessie Lasell that Gertrude's Chicago millionairess Mrs. Emily Chadbourne Crane had at Gertrude's extreme insistence also become temporarily my patron. But that was in part why I was doing so nicely—so nicely indeed that I thought it about time I gave a concert of my works. And I proposed this to Mrs. Lasell; it would cost $500. She thought the idea sound, gave me the money, went home happy. I had also promised to visit her in America at Christmas.

Europe after 1925

IT IS EASY TO KNOW that the 1920s were different from the 1930s. What is not so clear in America is that the first decade of the twenty-year World War armistice also had two parts. At the beginning of 1926 I was writing from Paris to Briggs Buchanan, my constant correspondent from college times, that "jazz (highbrow or lowbrow) is a dead art already." I was wrong, of course, since in the 1930s the swing beat was to develop, in the '40s bebop, and in the '50s the "progressive" or "cool" manner, for something happens to jazz in every decade. I was right, all the same, in judging that its basic forms and procedures were not to evolve any further; and they have not done so.

The early twenties, which brought jazz to maturity and to world-wide fame, had also brought fresh subjects into fiction. They gave us, for instance, *Main Street;* the luxury-loving, liquorous world of Scott Fitzgerald; and the chief theme of Ernest Hemingway's high period, which was an American soldier's wartime behavior as reviewed in the peacetime ambience of an Anglo-American bar in Montparnasse (Le Select). The American writers in general, I think, at home or abroad, tended to continue throughout the twenties (and some well into the thirties) their picturing of a world that did not change. For them the early twenties had to go on because they were not finished with writing about them.

And journalists kept licking their chops over the "jazz age" long after the Charleston had become a standard feature of American life. This dance coming up in 1925 was quite without relation to the real "jazz age," which since 1912 had practiced a slow, almost motionless dancing in close position. On the contrary, the Charleston's alert tempo and Caribbean beat (of ⅜ – ⅝) led not to petting in public but to the jitterbugging that was to mark the late 1930s, even to disengaged elegance, as in the Lambeth Walk.

For Europeans, the early 1920s offered nothing to cling to. In 1925, when our blockade of central Europe ended (a withholding of food from regions threatened by revolution), the fabulous financial inflation of Germany and the equally fabulous sex-inflation of Berlin began their decline. Ernst Křenek's opera *Jonny spielt auf,* a backward look at Germany's own "jazz age," was finished in 1926. And by that time Alban Berg's *Wozzeck,* forward looking in its compassionate social content, had already been performed (in December of '25). It was at the mid-twenties, or just before, that Arnold Schoenberg codified his way of writing music into the twelve-tone-row technique, also a forward-looking operation, since it encouraged the world-wide composing of nontonal music, offering a rule of thumb virtually foolproof to facilitate a previously recondite practice. This music was to take its place from that time on as part of the new romanticism and eventually, after World War II, to encircle the globe.

In France a new thing had appeared in painting when Bérard, Tchelitcheff, Kristians Tonny, and Leonid Berman, exhibiting as a group in 1926, drew attention by omitting from their work allegiance to cubism. In the same year Jean Arp, at the Galerie Surréaliste, showed nonfigurative sculptures involving curvaceous forms, distinctly a novelty in the abstract discipline. The year 1925, the year of Erik Satie's death, was also the year in which his young protégé Henri Sauguet, in a remarkably engaging short operetta called *Le Plumet du Colonel,* dared the use both of curvilinear melody and of harmony unrelated to Stravinsky's practices, as well as the straightforward expression of sentiment (without irony). That was the year too in which a Paris World's Fair devoted to Les Arts Décoratifs proved how "modern" (and "modern" meant looking back to cubism) the design of textiles, glass, furniture, wrought iron, and the like could be, leaving the painters on whose work these applications were based in the embarrassing position of seeing their dearest innovations, because of their success in industry, rendered useless henceforth for easel-painting. James Joyce, like the American fiction writers who surrounded him (and like the American poet T. S. Eliot, already captured by the admiration of tied-to-the-past young critic-poets), had opted for a career to be built on his own past. His *Work in Progress* (to be entitled *Finnegans Wake*), appearing in *transition* from 1927, was clearly, as to both method and theme, an extension of *Ulysses*. Neither from Eliot, struggling to survive in London's waste land on what Sherry Mangan was to call "the lotuses of prose style and Anglican theology," nor from the great Joyce himself, now nearly blind, would one know that the epoch had changed.

But it had. From here on out, the tone, whether violent or suave, was to be romantic. In July 1927 I wrote Buchanan:

> As I began to observe a little while ago, a new generation exists. Cocteau says it became possible about the middle of January [almost the date when Stein and I had formed our opera project]. No one knows why, but it suddenly did. Mary [Butts] says, "The good chaps are beginning to get together again." Anyway, six or a dozen people have suddenly begun to function. Poor Antheil (I am sorry) is not among them.

By the same month's end in 1928 my opera was finished; and Sauguet's ballet *La Chatte,* a wholly neo-Romantic work, had been successful in the Diaghilev repertory for over a year. Also I had given a concert of my works, the first one-man show to be offered by anyone, I think, of what I firmly believed, as did Sauguet and the other members of our neo-Romantic group, to be the newest music that there was.

This concert took place in the refurbished Salle d'Orgue of the Old Conservatory, the Napoleonic one near the Folies-Bergère, its organ of that period having recently been made usable. I had chosen this hall for its novelty value (people like going to an unfamiliar place) and also for the possibility of showing off my previously unheard Variations and Fugues on Sunday School Hymns. Actually almost none of the music on my program had been performed publicly except the Sonata da Chiesa, given two years earlier, though Five Phrases from the Song of Solomon, for soprano and percussion, had been heard privately at Mrs. Gross's musicales and *Capital Capitals,* for four men's voices with piano, had been offered just a year before at the Duchesse de Clermont-Tonnerre's costume ball. The Song of Solomon had been given in New York that spring at the first of the new Copland-Sessions concerts, and *Capital Capitals* was to be heard next year in the same series. Absolute novelties included a group of concert-songs in French—*La Valse grégorienne* and *Le Berceau de Gertrude Stein,* both to poetry by Georges Hugnet, and three poems by the late Duchesse de Rohan, a naïve writer often unconsciously comical whom certain French compared to the naïve painter, Henri (le Douanier) Rousseau.

The French songs had been substituted for a group with texts by Gertrude Stein because my soprano, Alice Mock, though she had sung the Song of Solomon earlier and welcomed an occasion to be heard in it publicly, refused to be associated with the Stein texts. So, rather than let a participating artist censor my program, I engaged another singer. Unable, however, to find an English-speaking one of Miss Mock's quality, I coached Marthe-Marthine phonetically through the Song of Solomon, which finally came off quite well. I did not think it wise, all the same, to expose her to the comedy risks of pronouncing Stein with a foreign accent. So I did for Marthe what I had declined to do for Mock, gave her a batch of songs to sing in French.

Actually my verbally animated French songs were better suited to Marthe's soubrette appearance and rhythmic exactitudes than they would have been to the statuesque beauty and mellifluous vocalism of Miss Mock. André Fleury (now organist of Saint-Germain-des-Prés) played the Sunday school variations; and Roger Désormière conducted the Church Sonata. The *Capitals* were sung by English-speaking males, accompanied by Edmund Pendleton. All the performances were perfect (though the French did not much care for Marthe-Marthine's blonde staginess), and the audience was intellectually select. Cocteau, Marcel Jouhandeau, and Cingria gave literary tone; Roy Harris, Boulanger, and Jennie Tourel the musical. There were painters too (I remember Pierre Roy), the rector of the University, Charlety (mobilized by Madame Langlois), and all sorts of up-to-date young. At the end of the evening Sauguet and Bérard made scandal by quarreling on the sidewalk, not about my music but about Bébé's going off with friends to smoke opium, an indulgence Sauguet could not tolerate. Gertrude Stein was there, of course; but Joyce did not come, since Gertrude was on the program, he not. The press was divided between those who found in my work "exquisite sonorities" as well as "a strong religious feeling boldly expressed" and those who heard in it only "a maximum of cacophony" and judged my whole effort as "no doubt sterile, certainly exaggerated." Gaston Hamelin, one of the players in my Sonata da Chiesa, had taken a fancy two years earlier to the piece and wanted very much to put it on in Boston, where he played first clarinet in the Symphony. Learning that I planned an American trip for the next season, he made a firm engagement to produce the work at a concert of the Boston Flute Players' Club, if I would be there to rehearse it and conduct.

For all the seeming effectiveness of this one-man concert, including a lively press, its afterglow in music circles was not warm. And I could not blame so definite a reserve on Marthe-Marthine's lack of a Franco-funereal singing style. Any in-the-know public could have shrugged that off. It was me they were not taking on. Nobody said so in my presence; but I could feel it, smell it, know it for true that my music, my career, my position in the whole time-and-place setup was something the French power group did not choose to handle. I was not being suppressed, not for the present; that effort was to be made four years later. But certainly I was not being adopted. Nor were any of the power-circle benefits—such as a commission from the Princesse de Polignac or from Serge de Diaghilev—to be coming my way. I was clearly not grist either for the French immortality-mill or for international snob-bohemia.

I am sure that the treatment I began to receive at this time from the talent scouts of both machines, a treatment courteous but reserved, was from their point of view wise and in the long run for me beneficial. It kept me an American composer and removed temptation toward trying to be anything else. A French composer I could never be anyhow; I had always known that. It was all right to be a foreigner working in France, but not a pseudo-Gallic clinger-on. I had not gone to France to save French music, but merely to improve my own. And come to think of it, as I did a great deal in the ensuing weeks during a long grippe-cold (probably acquired for that purpose), I considered the creation of an American music by myself and certain contemporaries to be a far worthier aspiration than any effort to construct a wing, a portico, even a single brick that might be fitted on to Europe's historic edifice.

The matter of living abroad was discussed a good deal in those days, and every so often some New York journalist would throw at you the Latin term expatriate. Other parts of America did not seem to care much where you lived, but Easterners could be jealous of Europe. As Russell Hitchcock put it, none were so upset by our spending all twelve months there as those who went abroad each year for six. It was assumed, moreover, that unless one was in Europe for study or business, one was there for the fleshpots only. Actually, save perhaps in Berlin, those were no more lively there than here. And Paris is not a hard-drinking town, never was. In fact it was the generally hygienic Paris routine—to bed by midnight and up by eight, love-making chiefly in the afternoon, with two tasty meals a day, some calisthenics, lots of walking, a little wine, no hard liquor and no telephone—that was my life. And I flourished on it, did lots of work, free from New York's pressure to conform.

Paris can admire you and let you alone. New York withholds its admiration till assured that you are modeling yourself on central Europe. This is still true; a French musical influence is by definition heretical and only that made in Germany (or to its east) esteemed worthy. As H. L. Mencken put it, "There are two kinds of music, German music and bad music." Right there was my reason for living in France. I believed then, and still do, that German music, after being blessed above all others and having led the world for two hundred years, had failed to keep contact with our century, that it had long since become self-centered, self-regarding, and self-indulgent. If American music was about to take off, as I also believed, any allegiance to contemporary Germany would have to be carried as dead weight. It was not that value had been stripped from the classic masters, but rather that the live tradition in Germany was no longer authoritative, even about performing those masters. And as for German composition at its most advanced—as in the work of the Austrians Schoenberg, Berg, and Webern—this seemed to me to combine the progressive and the retrogressive in a most uncomfortable proportion. The serial technique offered a strict counterpoint valuable for channeling a too-facile flow; but it also assumed as normal the textures of nondifferentiated counterpoint—a position of retreat from the highly differentiated part-writing of Stravinsky and Debussy, not to mention that of the classical symphonic masters, Mozart and Beethoven and Schubert. For modern harmony the Germans seemed to me tone-deaf, and as for rhythm, children. I did not know just when and how the great tradition had got lost; and the Germans themselves, in spite of Hitler's final stamping it out, have not admitted to this day its disappearance. But I knew the state of music in central Europe for decadent, and I was not having any truck with it.

As an American I had to keep contact with Europe. The new music growing up in my country was being pushed by German-trained musicians and German-culture patronage groups into paths I thought quite wrong for it. By keeping away from these Germanic pressures (and Paris was the only major center where one could do that) I could perhaps through my own music remind my country that it was not obliged to serve another country's power setup.

For the German-Austrian musical complex was still, in spite of a World War lost, in possession of such a structure. The music publishers of Leipzig, Berlin, Mainz, Augsburg, and Vienna were still rich in copyrights and in classical editions. They worked, moreover, in the German way, which is by cartel agreements—price-fixing, dumping, and pressures on the performing agencies. The latter were numerous and powerful, symphony orchestras and opera houses chiefly; and though these enjoyed some autonomy through their sources of subsidy—which were the central government, the separate states, and the cities—they were designed nevertheless for the encouragement of German musicians, for the protection of German publications, and eventually for the world-wide distribution of both. This situation, like the musicopedagogical machinery that had taught us all, had grown up after the nineteenth century had discovered what a gold mine in every sense were the classical masters. And the whole organization of it was central Europe's immortality machine. It was a conservative machine, its main merchandise Beethoven. Later composers like Brahms and Richard Strauss were tails to that kite. And Schoenberg the modernist, though a technical innovator, had kept his expressive content as close as possible to such standard Germanic models as the dreamy waltz, the counterpointed chorale, and the introverted moods of a *Liederabend*.

The French power setup was less massive, less imposing, less intolerant. Its immortality machine was not built for music anyway. France's culture market was for literature, art, and luxury products. And though her music publishers owned sound theatrical properties by Gounod, Bizet, and Massenet, their symphonic and recital repertories, running from Berlioz through Saint-Saëns, Fauré, and Franck to Debussy and Ravel, contained few best sellers; nor were their classical editions a world commerce. Painters flocked to Paris from everywhere because modern art was a going concern there; it made fame and money. Foreign musicians went to France in the 1920s not so much because modern music was prosperous as because it was twentieth-century oriented. There was no pressure for it to be anything else, no weighted emotional ambience. Music was for musicians and for people with brains; it was not for mass consumption. And it was not, as in Germany, big business.

Music in France was organized something like this. The Paris Conservatoire and the two chief opera houses (plus two state-subsidized operetta theaters) were the instruments of a civil service hierarchy. Except for an occasional guest artist at the opera houses and two foreign students a year admitted to the Conservatoire, everybody connected with these institutions was a French citizen. The four subscription orchestras of Paris were less official; but they all received government subsidy, at that time 100,000 francs a year ($4,000) in return for playing one hundred minutes of new French music. The official and semiofficial music world was run by the French for the French, and foreign composers were not much patronized. The idea of encouraging live composers, however, was built into it.

Nonofficial instrumentalities were more open. Among these were three series of modern concerts, the oldest and least radical being the Société Nationale, the moderately radical being the Société Musicale Indépendente, the freshest music being that heard at the Concerts Jean Wiéner. In the thirties another group was to appear, Le Triton, devoted to conserving the dissonant styles. Also a neo-

Romantic series, Les Concerts de la Sérénade. All these were run by private groups, and most of their programs were internationally oriented. So also were two privately administered music schools, the Schola Cantorum and the Ecole Normale de Musique, where foreigners were as welcome as in the private studios. For public performance of their music, however, foreigners were limited to the modernist societies, to the graciousness of string quartets and other chamber music groups, and to the kindness of some friendly virtuoso. Special concerts could be organized by anyone; and remarkably fine musicians were available. For such an occasion one needed, of course, not only funds but also enough friends to fill up the hall.

Private musical entertaining was frequent, since music at this time was fashionable. Previously it had not been so, and it is not so now. But during the lifetime of the Diaghilev ballets several stylish French houses and many foreign ones received musicians, dancers, poets, painters, even actors (the less self-centered ones). The chief go-between for artists and hostesses was Jean Cocteau—poet, playwright, and impeccable theater workman. He could launch a fashion, guide a career, organize its social and financial backing. And his main protectorate in music, the group that he had publicized so powerfully after World War I that they came to share condominium with him in the salons, were four composers out of the well-known Group of Six—Milhaud, Honegger, Auric, and Poulenc. I have always imagined that this quartet, though none of them had been at my concert, put thumbs down at this time regarding me. They seemed to remain as friendly as before, and their agent Cocteau could on occasion be quite generously so; but those particular musicians, who would have been the ones indicated by common friendships—literary, artistic, musical—and by our common commitment to Satie for making a hospitable gesture, did not then nor at any time afterwards make one. Neither did any of them speak out against me.

My concert had taken place on May 30. Gathering the grandeurs of it and enjoying the warmths engendered, which were many, took me a month. On July 1 I went to a Basque village called Ascain, six miles upcountry behind Saint-Jean-de-Luz, and started writing out Acts Three and Four. These I put down not with figured bass, as I had done Acts One and Two, but as a complete voice-and-piano score. That took two weeks. I also tempted myself with Spain. I had not wished to view it in reality while still composing music about it. But after nine months of writing an opera on the subject, naturally I was headed that way.

On July 8 I wrote Gertrude Stein, "Every day I walk nearer to Spain," also that it looked "an extremely God's-country sort of country." Another time, "I saw San Iñacio today. By his real name, just like that. In a chapel on a mountain divide called the Col de St.-Ignace. And he was handsome and thirty-five between thirty-five and forty-five and alive [a quotation from Act Three] and had a black beard and was singing an aria." Then on the nineteenth, "The opera is finished including the Intermezzo and Act IV, that is to say . . . the composing is done. . . . My plan now is to go look and listen to Spain a bit because I've an idea that Spain makes a special kind of noise that will bear imitation orchestrally. Her tunes and her rhythms are too good to be of much use, but I think her *timbre* may have possibilities." (I had heard Spanish high-squealing laughter on the beach at Saint-Jean-de-Luz.) On the twenty-fourth, in company with an American army officer and his wife with whom I had made friends at the hotel, I set off by car for a week in the northern parts.

We went first to near-by San Sebastián and from there took the spectacular hairpin-turn, mountainside road by way of Zarauz, luxurious and residential, to Castro-Urdiales, a humble beach resort and humbler fishing town. There we spent the night; and there, before sleeping, I sketched a whole fourth movement for my Symphony on a Hymn Tune, which had been awaiting that for two years and a half. We had made a side trip into the mountains for visiting the Renaissance granite palace of the Loyola family, birthplace of my operatic hero Saint Ignatius. Every room of the edifice is now a chapel and each more jeweled than the last—one of them covered with scenes from the Passion done in silver high relief, another completely lined with gold-framed foot-square plaques of lapis lazuli. We stayed a night in Santander, where what seemed the entire Spanish navy, most of the French, and a large part of the American were at anchor, beflagged for welcoming the arrivals in a New York-to-Spain yacht race. We saw the yachts arriving, swam in the cold Atlantic (out of bathing-machines on wheels), and saw a bullfight (I loved it). Then via Palencia over high Castile to Valladolid, where I had my first adventure with a bed-bug, and where I spent absorbed hot midday hours in a museum devoted entirely to polychrome religious sculpture. To Burgos too we went, and to Logroño, and to Pamplona, which is spirally approached, and lies at the center of a huge green saucer.

Returned to Ascain, I wrote Hildegarde Watson that the opera was finished and that there were "a ballet and an intermezzo and an appearance . . . of the Holy Ghost and a procession and a great many fine arias for everybody and in general just about one of everything and the whole . . . makes a composition." Also that Spain was "very grand. And very much like Texas. And the Spaniards are all enclosed like Americans and very sad though not about anything in particular and they are sweet and gentle and they like you. They are really very tender. Yes, very tender in their bashful way. I think they love the bull which they kill with such a loving gesture."

Having written earlier to Gertrude's Chicago millionairess, who had given me $1,000 toward completing the opera, that this was finished and the money also, I received a letter from her saying, "I regret that I am not able to help any further, but I was chiefly interested in what you were doing for Miss Stein." Since this seemed final, I wrote her what I termed to Gertrude "a polite and gentle thanks for past assistance." "There remains," I went on, to Gertrude, "Mrs. L's 3,000 francs a month. In the fall I shall give up my flat and either go to a hotel or find a cheaper one. But for the present, status quo and who knows God may provide more luxury to His needy ones."

Then I went to Brittany, to a tiny port called Loctudy, where I visited Madame Langlois and her Russian friend, made fifty pages of orchestral score on my Hymn Tune Symphony. From there to Saint-Malo, joining Georges Hugnet, and with him in a car badly driven over bad roads by Théophile Briant (swimmer, poet, publisher, and art dealer), we went to be with Cliquet-Pleyel and Marthe-Marthine at Bagnoles-de-l'Orne, a Normandy watering place where Cliquet was engaged at the casino. Our hilarious visit eventually got described in a poem by Georges, which I set to music and which Marthe sang in a concert that November. Writing to Gertrude, I said I had

done a great deal of sleeping and cracked my nose wide open on the bottom of the swimming pool and made a portrait of

Marthe for the fiddle. I also played on the piano Acts III and
IV because I have worked all summer without a piano and I
hadn't heard any of it and wasn't I surprised it is . . . full of
inspiration and variety and I can only hope it isn't as bad as
my contentment with it would maybe indicate.

When I returned to Paris around the first of September after
a two-month absence, I had been in the Basque lands, in Spain, in
Brittany, in Normandy; and I had brought home a completed
opera, a symphony finally finished and mostly orchestrated, and
two essays in what was for me a new genre, that of the portrait
in music. The first of these had been composed at Ascain, where
a young Spanishwoman who played the violin had asked me to
write her something. She had a way of entering the hotel's dining-
arbor with assurance, her equally self-assured mother one step behind, that pleased me because this granting of priority to youth,
in Europe uniquely Spanish, was also our American way. Otherwise the mother and daughter were not of American pattern; they
were almost like sisters, happy together, discussing but not chattering, alert in repose, occupying themselves while waiting for the
evening, and not surprised that a particular evening should bring
no mating male, though when it did they would be ready, for
Spain is a timeless image of eternity. All this plus some gesture
(Spanish gesture) I endeavored to depict in music; and although
the piece was written to be played without piano, I called it
a *Portrait of Señorita Juanita de Medina Accompanied by Her
Mother*. As a matter of fact, the mother later asked permission to
compose an accompaniment for it.

At Bagnoles-de-l'Orne I made another violin portrait, this time of
Marthe-Marthine; and I wrote to Gertrude that "my portrait trick is
developing nicely and seems to be quite new. That is, for music,
since the idea of it comes obviously out of you." And since with
Marthe and Cliquet and Hugnet a concert was being planned for
November, I went on making portraits that early fall in Paris. I
sketched *Miss Gertrude Stein as a Young Girl, Cliquet-Pleyel in F,
Georges Hugnet, Poet and Man of Letters,* and *Mrs. C.W.L.*
[Jessie Lasell], all from memory. Then I did *Sauguet, from Life,*
after which I never again made a musical portrait (and I have
made upwards of 150) except in the subject's presence.

Two years before, at Thonon on Lake Geneva, an enlightenment had come to me that made portrait writing possible. This was the very simple discovery that the classic masters, in terms of logic and syntax, did not always quite make sense. My sudden awareness of their liberties in this regard so firmly forced me to take up my own freedom that never again was I to feel that I must necessarily "know what I was doing." This meant that I could write almost automatically, cultivate the discipline of spontaneity, let it flow.

Now the value of spontaneous work is often zero, especially when it merely follows reflexes, as in pianoforte improvisation. But spontaneity can be original also, if it wells up from a state of self-containment. And it was through practicing my spontaneities, at first in a primitive way, and through questioning Gertrude Stein about this method of work, which was her own, that I grew expert at tapping my resources. Making portraits of people was just beginning to serve me, as it had long served Gertrude, as an exercise not only in objectivity but also in avoiding the premeditated. My associates at this time were many of them fine draftsmen, and I had often watched them finish each drawing in one sitting. Gertrude had long before applied their way to writing. And it was from her success with this (in my view) that I was led to try it in music. My first efforts came out so well, both as likenesses and as compositions, that I was sure I had discovered something. But exploring it could wait. Opera and symphony were my preoccupations right then.

In Paris I took my Symphony on a Hymn Tune to a copyist, so that I could have a clean score to show in America; and the pianist John Kirkpatrick (remarkable for his devotion to American composers) made a four-hand transcription of it. I also, while waiting for Gertrude to return, which was late that year, played and sang Acts Three and Four for the closer friends—for Sauguet and Bérard and Tonny and Bravig Imbs (American minor novelist and minor poet) and Georges Maratier (French picture merchant) and Kirkpatrick, of course, and Hitchcock and Madame Langlois and my American composer-colleague Roy Harris (who kept exclaiming over and over, "Living! Living!"). I also wrote a vocal piece entitled *Commentaire sur Saint Jérome* on a text by the Marquis de Sade for a young literary group in Lille, about to publish a magazine called *Les Cahiers Sade*.

On November 14 our concert took place in the ornate ballroom of the Hôtel Majestic. The program included piano music by Cliquet-Pleyel and by myself played by ourselves, poems by Georges Hugnet set to music by Cliquet and myself and sung by Marthe-Marthine, and two extended poems by Hugnet read by the actor Marcel Herrand. There were in addition six of my portraits for solo violin, played by Lucien Schwartz, and *The Death of Socrates,* from Satie, which I played for Marthe to sing. Among the other vocal pieces were my *Commentaire sur Saint Jérome* and *Les Soirées bagnolaises,* to poems of Hugnet that memorialized our hilarious visit to the Cliquets at Bagnoles-de-l'Orne, where

> *une chanteuse blonde*
> *qui chante en ce moment*
> *nous montra du bras*
> *notre nouvelle maison.*

This text, all innocence and camaraderie, shocked more than did the frankly outrageous passage from Sade. Bérard remarked that Georges and I seemed to think we were Goethe and Schiller. Everybody was there, of course. And we had shown our newest work, which is always a pleasure (or used to be) to both shower and shown. Alice Toklas, thinking to please me, said of Cliquet, "He's your Matisse," referring to a time when Matisse and Picasso had shown together at the Salon des Indépendents and where it had seemed, at least to her and Gertrude, that Matisse's facility and brilliance were no match for Picasso's brains. I did not relish the remark, because I was not out to kill off a colleague. My thought was rather that we should stand together while young and still capable of loyalties. At least that is what we had all thought we were doing in this concert of communal admiration.

Two weeks later I took the brand-new *Ile-de-France,* third class; and Madame Langlois accompanied me to Le Havre, where as sister of an admiral she presented me to the captain, who, I wrote to Gertrude,

> has since done me all the best honors and invited me to the bridge and showed me all the beautiful electrical devices for steering which never work and had me shown engine-rooms by 1st lieutenant and invited to aperitifs and officers' messes and so I don't really go back much to third class except to

dress or sleep or be sick which I was most awfully for 1½ days. . . . There are *primeurs* at table and quails in jelly and *foie gras à volonté*. Raymond Mortimer turned up and we eat together and my Lanvin holds up with the best England can offer. The added swank of my third-class cabin gives me an edge on Britain of which all concerned are conscious and which I try not to accent.

I have a nice cabinmate too, a husky, an aviator in Canada winter postal service between Montreal and Nova Scotia where airplanes wear skis and icicles and he shows me his tattoos and his war wounds and only sleeps four hours and combs his hair over a bald spot and uses Coty's face-powder and eats with officers and dances second-class because he doesn't like dress clothes and really all around a *chic type*.

Regarding a translation into French of excerpts from *The Making of Americans,* which I had begun with Hugnet that fall, then left for him to finish with Gertrude (it was for publication in Georges's Editions de la Montagne), she wrote me on December 3,

. . . god bless our native land and how are you liking our templed hills, we are peacefully and completely translating [,] it goes, I go alone and then Alice goes over me and then we all do it with Georges and then he goes alone and really it all goes faster than anyone would think. I guess we will get it done on time. Otherwise life is peaceful that is with the usual gentle xplosions. . . .

American Interlude

IN FRANCE MY SUBJECT MATTER, my nourishing nostalgia, had been the middle-South farm landscapes of my forebears, the half-hick Arcadias of my growing up. Set down now in another America, that of a Massachusetts manufacturing family, there came over me again the sense of displacement which I had experienced earlier in New England, as if that were where I did not belong, did not want to belong, could not bring myself to accept to belong. Paris was both warmhearted and harsh, like Kansas City; Whitinsville was neither of these. It tried to be friendly but could not give itself. I tried to be friendly too, but could not open. It was like being starved and stifled at once—starved for lack of spontaneity, buried alive in a useless luxury.

Jessie Lasell's house, large, wide, and wandering was a post-Richardsonian manor with wide hallway, a vast dining room, parlors of all sizes, a ballroom, a billiard room, a sun room, a gun room, two pantries, two kitchens, and a great many very large bedrooms with very large baths. None of these bedrooms received furnace heat. There were fireplaces everywhere and Franklin stoves always laid for lighting; but unless one planned to spend the morning alone it seemed not worthwhile to strike the foot-long match. It was simpler to jump from warm bed to warm dressing room to warm bath and preheated towels. This meant that once dressed, one drifted to the downstairs rooms, which being all wide open to one another gave to everything one did a country-club tone, further expressed, if one looked out the windows, by tennis courts, shooting-targets, and stables housing both trotters and saddle horses.

For Chester Whitin Lasell was a sportsman. He had bred, trained, and driven world-champion trotting-racers; at seventy he still rode to hounds, stalked deer, and shot. He had a box in Virginia for quail, a refuge for duck just off Rhode Island, and a place in Maine where the whole family could kill salmon and deer in the fall and from which they brought back pheasant by the brace. He did not pretend to work at business, never had done; he merely practiced the skills of a country squire, and well. So well that his table, from early fall till Christmas, held game in abundance, all of it hung just the right length of time, cooked just the right amount, and served with just the right accompaniments according to classical cuisine, including wines of the best years and vineyards, conserved in a cool cellar since before Prohibition.

Jessie Lasell, from San Francisco, loved forever having company and serving food. A naturally smiling woman midst tight-mouthed New Englanders, I think she found her expansiveness a bit walled in there. In any case, together we laughed and made jokes and gossiped as if breathing a Western air; and we exchanged cooking advice too, for she was wise about ways and knew the right ones, as well as how to engineer a large occasion. She could read aloud too and would oblige, when asked, with Milton's *Lycidas,* Shelley's *Adonais,* or selections from Marianne Moore and e. e. cummings. Everything she read gave pleasure because she spoke in the good San Francisco way, which is to articulate all the consonants and all the vowels.

Others around the house were mostly family—Hildegarde and Sibley Watson (temporarily near by on their farm), divers grandchildren of divers ages, a young architect and his widowed mother, Philip Lasell's parents and brothers and sisters from across the road, Jessie's brother and his Whitin wife, and a small selection of other relations, all named Whitin or Lasell. Family gatherings were inevitable at the approaches to Christmas; but I did miss e. e. cummings, with whom I had so often been there in the earlier time and to whose ironic sallies Sibley Watson, spitting image of Abraham Lincoln, would play straight man. There were large dinners too with guests from Worcester County, Republicans of quiet manners and correct tastes. I remember once Judge Thayer came, who had presided at the trial of Sacco and Vanzetti. He spoke lucidly of the case, showed no feeling.

We dressed for dinner, of course; and the younger ones all day long kept changing their costumes, as if something were about to happen. The monotony of life among these charming people came, I think, from their having been trained to intellectual self-effacement. Their good brains and excellent educations, their experience of the world and basic decency were not to be shown off, or used outside the channels of convention. They read, but not advanced books or unknown ones; they owned pictures and art objects but not distinguished ones, nothing they could not explain to Worcester County; they backed causes, but not dangerous ones; they risked their lives, but only in wars, private airplanes, or polo. Many among them were beautiful; all were gentle, some tending toward the neurotic; not one of them was passionate or mystical or scholarly or aflame. Temperament, among the males, had for generations fled to Europe. I was later to observe, as the girls grew up, a sizable proportion of mating failures, as if, brought up to every privilege, and film-fed, they had imagined that good clothes, good looks, and a trust fund entitled them without further effort to success in love.

An exception was Jessie's son-in-law Sibley Watson, who had always been for sticking his neck out. From a mercantile family in Rochester, New York, aspiring to excellence in medicine, he had teamed up after college days with Scofield Thayer, another with intellectual leanings, to start a literary magazine. The revival of *The Dial* resulted, by far the most distinguished, I should say, among American advanced magazines during the 1920s. The careers of e. e. cummings, Marianne Moore, and T. S. Eliot had been largely launched by it, also that of many another high-quality writer. But Watson believed that an editor should resign at thirty. "Before that he understands everything; after he has chosen his own way he is less open." And Watson had already started on a way of his own, which was to make movies. In his own barn he had completed *The House of Usher* and was preparing *Lot in Sodom,* both of which are now historic films. In the summer of 1930 Hildegarde wrote, "Sibley is putting in by gradual stages, to alleviate expense, a sound-apparatus. We'll have it by fall. Wishes you were here and willing to do a sound-picture of you singing your opera." The new equipment served for making a sound picture out of *Lot* and for adding music to *Usher*. Then he abandoned the experimental cinema, returning to experimental medicine.

During December of 1928 Jessie and I would sometimes be driven to Boston for symphony concerts and for seeing people (she loved the social). On these visits I arranged for concerts that were to take place later and had some music copying done (very expensive, very poor, compared to Paris). The Flute Players' Club, having announced my Sonata da Chiesa for March, now regretted that there was no money for the musicians. I had already come across this maneuver that same year, when the Société Musicale Indépendente in Paris had programmed my Song of Solomon, then let me know I must provide performers. There I had declined to do so. Here, since I thought the performance important, I paid the $100 required (or rather Jessie did). I made an engagement near that time in March for a program of my works at the Harvard Musical Club, and I promised the Harvard Glee Club a male-voice transcription of the Procession scene from *Four Saints*. Aaron Copland had already set a February date for *Capital Capitals* in New York, and Hildegarde had asked me to give a lecture and musical program in Rochester whenever I should be coming that way. It seemed indicated, therefore, to go West in January, running off my Eastern music dates later. I could then be back in France by April.

Meanwhile there was Christmas, the last affluent one America was to see for twenty years. Such a hanging of holly and tying of ribbons, such a dressing of trees and all that and all that! Impatient with attaching the shiny balls one by one, I tied them into bunches and hung them like grapes (much prettier). There were jewels arriving every day from Tiffany and from Cartier (on approval), emeralds rejected, a bracelet of square diamonds chosen. And then it was Christmas, with blue sky and snow, and the routines all working as they should. (Trust Jessie for that.) There was dinner Christmas Eve for twelve or sixteen, with—I can't remember which—wild duck or venison, preceded by Jessie's hot mousse of bay scallops. Afterwards drop-in callers had the Dickens punch, made by pouring warm beer and mulled claret over cinnamon sticks and hot baked apples. For breakfast Christmas day there were quails, strawberries, and champagne. At eleven the servants came to the ballroom for their presents, drank something (champagne, I think), and then to recorded music were danced with by family and friends. Later there must have been the statutory Christmas feast with turkey or goose or roast pig, appropriate wines, and ceremonial libations. If so, I went through it like a man. I was a skillful guest in those days.

After Christmas, my visit over, I went for a few days to Boston, where I showed Koussevitzky my *Symphony on a Hymn Tune,* which he had asked to see. At his house in Jamaica Plain I played it to him while he read the score. After one movement he said, "Good!" After two he said, "Very good!" After three he said, "Wonderful!" After the fourth, he threw up his hands and said, "I could never play my audience that." He was not articulate about his troubles with the fourth movement, but he seemed to find it not serious enough for a Boston public. He besought me to salvage the work by writing another last movement. I thanked him for his graciousness and left.

From Kansas City, in January, I wrote the story to Gertrude. She replied with my portrait:

> I am awfully sorry about the symphony but then how could the Russian like it, . . . we believe in you a lot as you can see from the profundity of inclosed portrait, it has a new rhythm with sense . . . I am pleased about the glee club, I hope they will sing it, give it my love I mean the glee club they were so romantic in my youth when in the moon-light they sang Here's a health to King Charles, I like to think of their singing us instead . . . we had a beautiful reunion dinner at the Hugnets in honor of the first outbreak of the edition, it looks as if it were going to be quite alright, we all spoke of you very tenderly, you are as our dear Nellie would say not forgotten by your little friends.

I had expected to stay a month in Kansas City, but when Henwar Rodakiewicz (of the Harvard house party) invited me to Santa Fe (with ticket paid) I did not decline. To see my beloved Southwest again, and in a version far grander than the Oklahoma I had known in wartime, was precious for that replunging into Western things that I was finding so much more tonic than the Northeast.

Henwar had married, just out of college, a New England woman thirty years older with brains, heart, high temperament, and wealth. He too made films privately. The ranch near Santa Fe, only one of their several residences (including a yacht), was wide and full of warmth. I stayed a week, maybe two, saw sights and scenery from a Rolls-Royce runabout, observed the social tensions of Taos and Santa Fe. Taos held the richer hostesses and the more conservative painters; Santa Fe, a refuge for tuberculars, was more violent in its drinking, more promiscuous about love, and more experimental in art. Today it is no longer an outpost of bohemia. With four museums, a symphony orchestra, and an opera company it is a culture town, with everybody older and quieter. And lungers don't go West any more. A jolly group they were, as I remember, mostly young, many gifted, all excited (since they ran a temperature), and ready for anything. They gave a lively tone to any place, many of them staying on after their malady was arrested to furnish doctors, writers, intellectual workers, and even statesmen to the Southwest and Colorado, people all the more humane in later years for having faced death when young.

From Kansas City I sent Alice Toklas some Missouri recipes, along with that for Jessie's scallop mousse. As for Missouri weather, "oceans of slush froze last week and everything is now solid ice (motors waltzing)." Of Missouri speech,

> It is curious and interesting. In its provincial condition it is incredibly low. And yet it seems to lose all its horrid quality with only a very little training and to become quite beautiful when properly educated. Unlike Kansas or Illinois, which are difficult to train and almost never lose their harsh intonation. And there are marked differences [in Missouri] between male and female speech.

To Gertrude,

> The portrait is very beautiful and serious and like me too. Yes very serious and with a quite gratuitous beauty an extra beauty *par dessus le marché*. . . . I am on my way to lecture on us at Rochester. I arranged the *Saints' Procession* and wrote a *Conversation for Four Clarinets*. [This at the request of Gaston Hamelin, my Franco-Bostonian admirer]. . . . It was nice visiting my grandfather, who at ninety-seven was full of wise po-

litical comment and people comment and questions about French life and agriculture.

And later, "I reread my portrait twice and find it has a very fine texture especially the long middle paragraphs and great variety of sentences and a really concentrated progress . . . which is I suppose what we mean by profundity . . . anyway."

Gertrude in return kept me up on Paris news, about Hugnet's

> beautiful fight Christmas eve at the Select with [Roger] Vitrac purely on the subject of how they that is Hugnet did not like his play and it all ended with their being put out with contusions and [taken to] our *commissariat* around the corner. . . . Poor Gody [Godiva, the car] has lost her stability owing to too many poems and music [a reference to *Le Berceau*] she took to dropping little pieces of herself and groaning distressfully and once had to be disgracefully rocked in front of the Senate and now I am having a new Ford car and with the unfaithfulness characteristic of us all I am violently . . . devoted to the new. . . . Alice is making tapestry in our leisure moments, I am making sentences in my leisure moments and darn good sentences, otherwise as we were . . . do remember me most kindly to Mrs. Lasell.

Hildegarde and Sibley Watson lived in Rochester, New York, in an Edwardian house on Sibley Place, right next to downtown. On my way East I gave a talk there to invited guests (I remember Howard Hanson, newly director of the Eastman School of Music) in which I explained a little of what our group in Paris thought it was up to. With Philip Lasell, also visiting, I played them Satie's piano duets *Three Pieces in the Shape of a Pear*. I also sang parts of my opera. And as so often happens in some regional center or university, everybody seemed to understand everything and to like it (or almost everybody; I was not sure about Hanson). This can occur only before New York has told them what to think; afterwards they are more reserved. But so far, in Whitinsville, in Kansas City, in Santa Fe my solo performances of *Four Saints in Three Acts* had never failed to please. I gave a similar talk in the Rochester Art Museum. And I watched Sibley's films achieving their form, slowly (as films always do) and with a great rightness (as they almost never do).

Sibley worked at cutting; Hildegarde practiced singing and sometimes painted. The University, the Eastman School of Music, and the Art School provided the bulk of our visitors. There were rich people around and one saw them, but only those who were also workers, aiders, abettors, in some way participants in a world of intellectual exercise. Such an ambience was the only one Sibley Watson would be part of (he never owned a dinner jacket, rarely went even so far as blue serge); and such was the tone of Hildegarde's house in Rochester, bare downstairs of carpets and bric-a-brac, with only some recent paintings and a pianoforte, a large dining room, and an excellent cook whom Hildegarde had never laid eyes on, though she had been in residence for two years.

Her New York house, where I lived for the next two months, was more suited to a woman of elegance, though that too showed interest in contemporary art, what with a bronze nude by Gaston Lachaise in the ground-floor two-story drawing room and expressionist canvases by e. e. cummings all over the staircase walls and upper landings. This luxuriously appointed four-story town house with garden, on Nineteenth Street just south of Gramercy Park, was kept ready for residence, though the Watsons had not lived there for several years, by a caretaker, who made breakfasts for me and for a woman vocal teacher (permanent guest), also for Philip Lasell, who used the house as his hotel. I occasionally had guests of my own in the drawing room, where a full-size grand piano enabled me to make quite an effect demonstrating my music.

My most effective number was the singing of *Four Saints* complete, which by this time I could do from memory. And it was for the purpose of my doing this that Gertrude's friend from olden times Carl Van Vechten gave me an evening party at his flat in Fifty-fifth Street. Twelve people were there, all of them chosen by Carl for their possible usefulness toward producing the opera, toward publishing it or spreading the word about it. The music publisher was Alma Morgenthau Wertheim, who sustained a small press called Cos Cob, publishing chiefly music by Aaron Copland. The other ladies were of literary allegiance—Mabel Dodge Luhan, Emily Clark, Muriel Draper, possibly Blanche Knopf, Fania Marinoff of course (Carl's actress wife), and Ettie Stettheimer. Not one of the men can I recall, though in addition to Carl and myself there must have been four. Men do tend toward self-effacement in a New York drawing room.

After the party we went to a "drag," or travesty ball, in Harlem. At some point an amiable square joined our group (we called them "butter and egg men" in those days); and on our way back downtown in the square's Rolls-Royce Carl recounted what Mabel Dodge had said of *Four Saints*—that this work would do to the Metropolitan Opera "what Picasso did to Kenyon Cox" (an American painter earlier much admired). His reply, no less naïve, was "Then what will I do on Thursday nights?"

The evening had introduced me to several key persons in the New York worlds of opinion-forming and of distributing advanced work, but only one of these acquaintanceships bore fruit directly. Ettie Stettheimer invited me to meet her sisters, and it was with sets and costumes by one of them that the opera came to be produced in 1934. The sisters were three—Ettie, Florine, and Carrie— all of uncertain age; and they lived with their invalid mother in the most ornate apartment house I have ever seen—a florid Gothic structure called Alwyn Court, at Fifty-eighth Street and Seventh Avenue. Their own flat was ornate too but nowhere Gothic, being laid out rather in the marble and gold and red velvet German-royalty style with a fluffy overlay of modern Baroque. There were crystal pendants everywhere and gold fringes and lace and silk curtains so much longer than the windows that they stood out in planned puffs and lay no less than two feet on the waxed floors. Throughout the house were pictures by Florine, a painter of such high wit and bright colorings as to make Matisse and Dufy seem by comparison somber. Ettie, the youngest, a Ph.D. from Heidelberg, had published two novels about intellectualized love; and Carrie, the eldest and usually the hostess, had spent twenty years on a doll's house (now in the Museum of the City of New York). Their associates were all working artists—writers, painters, theater people (plus a film-producing nephew, Walter Wanger)—and these were received at rich teas and sumptuous dinners. One never saw the invalid mother. One felt, however, her presence in the house and knew her appearance (white hair and black lace) from paintings by Florine. The three sisters never went out all at the same time, each in turn staying home so that their mother should never be left alone. This was a discipline of devotion, of course, since the good German servants were always there; and it had gone on since at least 1915, only to end with the mother's death in 1935.

Carrie had a small apartment near by for working on her doll's house and Florine a studio at the Beaux Arts Building on Fortieth Street facing Bryant Park. Ettie, short and a little dumpy, tended in the evening to wear red taffeta, puffy as to skirt and tightly closed around each ankle. Carrie, tall, stately, and sad, was for gold and white. Florine liked black velvet. In the daytime they all wore black.

As soon as I had seen Florine's pictures, especially the very large ones now in the Metropolitan Museum, I knew we shared a view about the stage. So I besought her, should there be an American production of *Four Saints,* to consider designing its costumes and scenery; and would she listen to the work, me singing, with that in view? So I did sing it for her one afternoon, and she did accept designing it as a possibility, and she did start finding ideas right away for making it look like the Cathedral façade in Avila executed in crystal and ostrich feathers and red velvet and gold fringe. She actually, one year later (it is dated 1930), painted a picture (with silvered frame) in which an evocation of me is playing and singing midst the attributes of Saint Teresa and Saint Ignatius, along with some imagined ones appropriate to "St. Virgil," "St. Gertrude," and "Florine St."

Copland had found for singing my *Capital Capitals* a group of four men called appropriately the Ionian Quartet, and these I rehearsed daily for the mid-February performance. This came off as very lively indeed, with the audience hilarious, so much so in fact that at one point, to prevent the laughter from getting out of hand, from the piano I held up my right arm, palm out traffic-cop-wise, and stopped the fun from stopping the show. At the end there were bravos. There is no question that the performance constituted a success in terms of pleasure given, press space devoted to it, and intellectual excitement created. And a pattern in that excitement was established at this time which I have come since to expect whenever any work by Gertrude Stein and myself is given in America. The literary consensus is always that the music is lovely but the poetry absurd; whereas the music world, at least nine tenths of it, takes the view that Stein's words are great literature but that my music is infantile. The musical press on this occasion mostly took the latter view, though certain reviewers found it "merry" and "a bright spot on the program." But even the most deeply outraged among them found it less "nondescript," "aimless," and "dreary" than the other pieces, which were a Violin Sonata by Alexander Lipsky, a set of songs by Vladimir Dukelsky, and a Piano Sonata by Roy Harris. As Copland reminded me only recently, "In those days our music always got terrible reviews."

During that same February (we are still in '29) a bright and worldly woman wishing to pay me honor and also to give a stylish party, arranged for the same singers to perform the *Capitals,* with me playing, at the house of her banker, other works of mine filling out the program. I think I played some of my piano pieces; I know Aaron Copland played with me a four-hand work called *Synthetic Waltzes;* there were probably forty-five minutes of music all told. The party took place in a flat newly decorated by the lady who had organized it, with real marble wittily juxtaposed against plaster painted to imitate marble (ever so much more expensive). There was a delicious supper too with vintage champagne (bought at Prohibition prices). The singers received a fee. When I informed our host sometime later that he owed me five dollars for music stands hired, he sent me a check for exactly that amount, saying he did not think I "should be out of pocket at all," adding, "A number of my guests commented very favorably on Sunday evening and since then, so that I think you can feel very well satisfied."

I was still living at Hildegarde's Nineteenth Street house when Emily Clark Balch, a Virginia writer married to a Philadelphian, phoned to ask if she could give me a dinner party of twelve or more, which I accepted. Then she wondered whether perhaps I might consent to play and sing my opera, which she had heard at Van Vechten's. "I haven't lived in New York before, and I don't know how far one can go with musicians." Understanding from this that she did not choose to go as far as an honorarium, and not caring myself to be the season's free party-singer, I replied that I thought the evening at Carl's house should remain unique. She understood my answer, accepted it, produced a fine evening (as to food and drink and people); and we became friends. At table, being asked by an actress how everything had gone off at the banker's party, I said, "Just fine! Everybody was paid but the composer." The actress squealed, "I never heard of paying the composer!" "Not even when he has played the piano," I said, "and conducted and brought in another composer to play too?" This set off an animated discussion that must have lasted all of four minutes and in which everybody agreed I was wrong. Not one among all those prosperous professionals of art would admit my assumption that to provide music for a *soirée* given by a man one hardly knows is a professional service worth at least a gift. (Mozart's father used to say, "My God! Another watch!")

Other essays made in my behalf turned out even less well. The League of Composers, alerted early to my impending presence (probably by Copland), had asked to see scores in view of performance that spring. I sent first instrumental ones and then vocal; none was accepted. And Alma Wertheim, who had a press for publishing music and who had asked for manuscripts, returned them on the grounds that there was "no money for publishing them." Both the Cos Cob Press and the League of Composers were by the carefully neutral tone of their rejections letting me know I was no part of their power-group. And it was always to be that way. When they wanted a favor from me, they asked for it, usually got it. Virtually nothing was ever to be done about my music at any needful moment. Alma Wertheim's press printed four years later, in 1933, one five-minute work. The League of Composers gave me in 1934 and 1949 two of their less remunerative commissions. They performed the five-minute piece (*Stabat Mater,* for soprano and string quartet) after it was already familiar; and at their twenty-fifth anniversary concert, in 1948, they gave my Sonata for Violin and Piano (already in the repertory of the artists playing it, who were available free), a work they had refused in 1931, when it was new, shocking by its use of curvilinear melody and suave harmonic textures, and badly needing the blessing of some establishment.

As to how it came about that for all my musical abilities I was consistently excluded from the musical power-groups, it was plain to me then; I was too terrifyingly frank. Bérard had said of me that "Virgil speaks the truth." And indeed I was forever blurting things out. Among my intellectual equals the habit was stimulating; but in a group of musicians banded together chiefly for capturing patronage, I was bound to be disruptive. Thus it was that in New York in 1928 and '29, just as it had come about already in Paris, those who kept me out of their musical politics did so from sound impulse or wise reasoning. I have never been a joiner or much of an operator. And the League of Composers, for all that it worked hard for other composers, was not likely, I judged, to be doing much for me.

New York was a delight, all the same, in nonmusical ways. It was nourishing to be again with Briggs Buchanan and Maurice Grosser, to visit Jere Abbott, at this time a graduate student in Princeton, and "Cuffbutton," my sister's former painting teacher, just home from seven years in China and living in a New Jersey forest. And there was an absorbing new friendship with a dark and handsome tall girl (much too tall). Her name was Dorothy Speare; and she seemed to have sung opera in Italy and to have had lessons there, especially to know well the Milan music world. She had in fact written a novel about Milan studio life that had been published in a women's magazine. Just then it was being made into a play, and Dorothy was convinced that my personality had "just the flair and fillip required" for an important role in it, "that of a young operatic tenor (American student in Milan) who sings and plays." I was reserved about my acting powers but happy to spend hours with her on any subject. So we met often, either at her flat in New York, where she lived with a husband named Christmas, or in Boston, where she visited parents in Newton Center. And sometimes I played for her to sing Italian arias or tried coaching her in Mozart, though she knew more about coloratura style than I did. Nothing ever came of any project beyond our happiness in being together, but we went on meeting whenever we were in the same town. Her novel became eventually a highly successful film, *One Night of Love,* with the opera star Grace Moore in it; and Dorothy, though quite well to do after that, continued to write scripts in Hollywood. The last time I saw her, in 1934, we dined at Twenty-One on caviar and champagne, then went off to the Forty-fourth Street Theatre to see *Four Saints in Three Acts.* Dorothy Speare had beauty, also a certain radiance that must have been the afterglow of her student days. For she was opera-struck, and fatally. She had one story; she had told it; she still could not accept that it was over.

Another whom I saw with pleasure was Van Vechten's friend (and formerly Gertrude's) Mabel Dodge Luhan. I had expected of so legendary a hostess and a muse a personality more inclined toward the showy. To my surprise she was a quiet one; she let you talk. Now a woman who will listen without interrupting is obviously someone to be valued. And when Mabel herself spoke, however briefly, in a voice soft, sweet, and young, you understood her attractiveness to men. I did not see Mabel often that winter, nor ever again later. Nor could I do for her what I think she had hoped, restore to her Gertrude Stein from their estrangement. The causes of that, which went back to Florence before World War I, were unknown to me; and neither Gertrude nor Alice, though they often spoke of her, ever told me the reasons for it.

Less rewarding was a younger hostess, the still handsome and never heartless Muriel Draper, widow of Paul, a singer, mother of another Paul (later to dance), and at this time an author of best-selling memoirs called *Music at Midnight,* all about giving musical parties in London. She was leading now in a Fortieth Street stable a life of resplendent poverty, still party-giving, and receiving the arts and letters every Tuesday for tea. The tea, a gift, was always excellent; the cookies, from Schrafft's, were likely to be twelve for forty people. She had asked me to come half an hour before the others so that we could "really talk." Really talking seemed to mean that I must listen, and that I must accept her opinion as final on everything regarding art. (Later she was to add Marxist politics.)

Actually Muriel was aspiring to dominate through her natural warmth and kindness an artistic and intellectual world of which she was just the playmate. I realized her lack of intellectual continuity when in the middle of an address to me about my music (pronounced with the warmest intimacy and from her gilded stage-throne, as if I were the only courtier that mattered), other callers began to arrive. Instantly she dropped the subject and with it all special treatment; from then on I was just another guest. As a hostess, I must say, she was expert. Her divers domiciles remained for several years among the best New York had to offer as salons of arts and letters, and Muriel could till her death be no less commanding as a guest. Mabel Luhan, who had known her in prewar Florence days, drew a portrait of her in one of the memoir volumes that is both warm and perspicacious.

If New York had received me as a possibly acceptable invader, Boston and Cambridge took me as one of their own. The Sonata da Chiesa, which I conducted at a public concert of the Flute

Players' Club, was performed in splendor of sound by first-chair men from the Boston Symphony; and although it shocked some (always has, still does), the society's director expressed in a letter his admiration and that of his colleagues for the work, adding that he would like in the very near future to play me again, "this time without obligation" on my part. I have never taken him up on the offer.

The Harvard Musical Club evening was informal, companionable, and as to repertory comprehensive. My merrier works were received with jollity, selections from *Four Saints* with awe (no reserves), my Symphony on a Hymn Tune, played in four-hand piano version, with frankly expressed bewilderment. (Walter Piston still considers absurd an unaccompanied canon for bass tuba and piccolo.) E. B. Hill, my teacher and good friend, though not bothered by its orchestral textures, was doubtful, as Koussevitzky had been, whether the work would communicate in performance, or as musicians say, "come off." About the opera, on the other hand, he was quite sure. "A good musical idea," he called it. "You've got something there."

Back in New York for leaving, I wrote Gertrude that in Boston everyone was taking my work "very seriously and nobody there thinks any more that I am a bad boy." New York was still dining me and interviewing me and writing Sunday articles about my work. No music publisher, however, no opera house, no conductor was showing interest. Even the League of Composers had given me, through three different representatives, what I took for a planned brush-off. From Paris Gertrude was writing, "Delighted at the success perhaps we will get on the radio and the gramophone yet and have royalties and buy a prize Bedlington terrier and [put in] a telephone and pay for my new Ford car, perhaps, but anyway I am most awfully pleased." And Russell Hitchcock wrote that Madame Langlois would meet me in Le Harve, he in Paris; Cliquet-Pleyel, that the lament he had composed would now be answered:

Ah, que revienne avril
et avec lui, Virgil!
En avril
ne quitte plus Virgil.

So before March was over, I was back on the *Ile-de-France,* third class as before and with the same special privileges, plus from a dozen demonstrative New York friends baskets of fruit, boxes of candy, tins of caviar, splits of champagne, flowers, books, and from others letters of loving farewell and the ubiquitous telegram. It all made my cabin, shared with some three or five, a trifle crowded.

An Epoch Ends

DURING MY FOUR MONTHS' ABSENCE I had sublet the quai Voltaire studio to two American girls. These had turned out, as usual, to be three. And all three had boy friends in and out, actually more in than out, according to Madame Jeanne. The wear on carpets, curtains, and wallpaper had been intense. My amiable landlord, Dr. Ovize, placing no blame on me, agreed that all these must be replaced. The renewals took over a month, during which time the pianist George Copeland, whose acquaintance I had renewed on shipboard, used to like coming there of an evening and sitting among the ladders. Sometimes too he would sit at the piano and play Spanish music or Bach. My favorite was his version of Chabrier's *España*, incredibly busy as to finger and powerful as to volume. Copeland played it as if it were real Spanish music. The Spanish themselves have in my time mostly played Spanish music as if they had learned it in Germany, forgetting its origins in the dance and mooning over it. Copeland also played Debussy well, had begun his career that way; but his Debussy renderings were more subtle for color than tightly structured. It was almost as if he were improvising them. Spontaneity was there, as were also lovely sound, the power of poetic evocation, and a temperament for grandeur, all these qualities showing at their best, probably, in just such an informal circumstance.

On my American tour I had been able, thanks to Christian Bérard, to leave handsome gifts with all the persons who had been especially useful to me or generous with hospitality. Bérard, who was a draftsman of vast fecundity and like many another artist of that time prodigal with his product, had given me twenty or thirty wash drawings before I left, knowing that I would lodge them where they might be loved; and I had done just that. Now he proposed that I sit for my portrait, which he had got interested in doing from having made a series of ink sketches of me for the Ten Portraits by Gertrude Stein that Hugnet was to publish. I posed afternoons at the small private house in the villa Spontini where Bébé lived with his widowed father, an architect. He used the former drawing room for a studio; and this he kept dark, because he as often painted late at night as during the day, using at all hours blue bulbs for light.

Bébé was blond and plump, with a sharply defined small beak of a nose and a carved mouth. The blue eyes, indeed the whole being, radiated intelligence, jollity, and good humor. He was self-indulgent in every way, however, and quite without self-discipline. At this time his grooming, though careless, was not yet willfully negligent. Later he stopped shaving and even washing much; but by that time no one minded, since he had become the playmate of the richest ladies. He was also to smoke opium and drink a great deal. This was after his fashion drawings in *Vogue* were being imitated everywhere and he had become the most admired stage designer in the world. But at twenty-five, Bébé was frequenting his own generation, which considered him their most gifted painter and possibly the one who would lead his art into paths of humane awareness, as Goya had done.

The reasons why Bébé did not do this are all part of his self-indulgence, of his inability to face the travail, the certainties of public refusal and the probabilities of private persecution, the whole painful progress of an artist who wishes to be a great one, who knows he has to be a great one, and who cannot turn back. Bébé did what he could; he was not self-deceived. But he did not, he could not persist as in France Degas had persisted, and Renoir and Monet and Bonnard. So he made stage designs. These were beautiful and appropriate. But all who were touched by his painting, especially his painting of people, came to regret, as he did too, that

he had not been able to live up to his genius—for his talent, intelligence, and depth of directly expressed feeling did amount, I
think, to that.

At the time he undertook my portrait he had already painted the
large dark ones with candlewax under-modeling, and he was not to
do these again. Later he was to paint waifs and fashionable women
in light bright colorings and some remarkable multifigured
murals in private houses, still later a series of self-portraits by the
sea. But just then he was more interested in studying me as a model
than he was ready for painting a new kind of portrait. I sat exactly
twice, I think; and he made a beginning of a head that was like
me. I am not sure whether he added a stroke or two later or
whether in the course of time the picture may have seemed to him
finished enough. In any case, though given to me, it was never delivered. I think Christian Dior had bought it, for it did turn up in
a Paris exhibit of Bérard's work held at a gallery where Dior was
a partner, still later in a New York gallery, where it was bought by
friends of mine who had been touched by its resemblance.

At these same sittings I made a portrait in music which I called
Christian Bérard, prisonnier. I wrote of both efforts to Gertrude,
"Bébé did me again as portrait very good and I did him but very
bad." Nevertheless, I later found I liked mine and composed others
to go with it. I had already that winter, in Kansas City, written for
a quartet of clarinets (at the request of Gaston Hamelin) a piece
which I called *Portrait of Ladies.* This was a sound-picture of the
way my four Stuyvesant ladies (friends from the New York wartime and from visits in Maine) used to tell a story, all talking at
once, in counterpoint rather than in rivalry. Bébé's portrait was for
the same four instruments. Later in the summer, at Villefranche, I
made two more, one called *Bébé Soldat,* to picture him on his
twenty-eight days of reservist's duty, and another called *En per-
sonne (chair et os),* evoking the personal presence. Then one day
when Maurice Grosser had a cold, I sketched him as *A Young
Man in Good Health.* Together these all made up a suite which I
called Five Portraits for Four Clarinets, and which I sent off to
Hamelin, who had them played in Boston. At a music camp in
Michigan they were later performed by 150 youngsters. And after
World War II Hamelin produced them for the Paris radio. Other
performances have been brought to my notice, and I am often asked

to lend out score and parts. Until the fall of 1963, when they were run up in my honor at a college in Pennsylvania, I had never heard them.

In June, Aaron Copland arrived, with money from a New York patroness for giving a concert of works by young Americans. There were to be his own *Vitebsk* trio and Two Pieces for String Quartet, also a Sextet by Roy Harris. Of lesser weightiness were a short piano sonata by Carlos Chávez and various vocal works. The latter consisted of three James Joyce songs by Israel Citkowitz (then a pupil of Boulanger) and of five by me (three in French, two by Stein). Marthe-Marthine sang them all, pronouncing phonetically. According to the press, the show was mine, with the Harris piece "also attracting favorable attention," a result not wholly satisfying, I think, to Nadia Boulanger, who had helped with arranging the program and with mobilizing an international modern-music audience. At that time she was viewing my musical development with some reserve.

To Gertrude Stein, in the country, I wrote that

the concert went off with much success to us you and me, and Joyce came & liked us and so did Adrienne [Monnier] who said sweet things next day to Mme. Langlois about *"fine et spirituel et de l'ironie dedans,"* etc. which I suppose means that Antheil isn't *"civilisation française"* any more since he has moved to Germany and written an opera in German and so . . . maybe I'm it [,] anyway Tonny said it was like an arrived *maître* who loaned his *concours* to a concert of aspiring young ones and the Gide faction it seems was also there and has passed around the word that I am the berries . . . and really it is surprising how much glory seems to accrue from a concert that cost nothing in fact was given with any intention but that of popularizing me who was supposed I guess to be just comic relief.

The last remark was aimed at Boulanger. I knew better than to ascribe such a motive to Copland, who had always behaved frankly toward me. Actually he admired my vocal music more than my instrumental, just as, contrariwise, he held in especial respect the instrumental works of Chávez and Roy Harris. And as for my music, vocal or instrumental, attracting more attention than his, Aaron knew how to bide his time. Anyway, he believed, as I did, that the good ones in our generation must stick together; and we were each of us sure the other was a good one. I had written that of him (in *Vanity Fair*) when his First Symphony was played. And he had written of me just then in *Modern Music:*

> Virgil Thomson can teach us all how to set English to music.
> . . . In the opera *Four Saints in Three Acts,* in *Capital Capitals,* in his numerous songs he has caught the [amazing variety of] rhythms and inflections that make the English language different from any other. . . . It would be impossible to translate these compositions into any other language.

I was about to receive, nevertheless, from the Hessisches Landestheater in Darmstadt a request for the score of *Four Saints,* in prospect of its possible production in German. The letter was in English, written by the poet Edwin Denby (dancer and assistant *régisseur*) in the name of "Messrs. Rabenalt and Reinking . . . respectively, a young operatic *régisseur* of great promise and reputation in Germany and a young stage designer of genius." They wished to consider my opera for the coming season, and Denby assured me it would receive "a quite exceptionally careful and at the same time brilliant production." Also that "their reputation [and] the great interest in Germany in novel forms of opera would bring the production wide publicity. Besides," he added, "the theater . . . is one of the best in Germany." Denby himself, "almost bilingual," would be of help "in verifying a translation."

My score was in no condition for such a trip. It existed in one pencil copy, and that incomplete as to piano accompaniment and the choral passages. Of orchestral score there was not one page. I did not even have an extra copy of the libretto—about to be printed, however, in *transition.* But even before the Darmstadt group had seen this, it had been suggested that I come there in September to play and sing the opera for them and to offer whatever ideas I might have for "action, stage directions and so on." Once he had read the libretto, Denby expressed himself as "enthusiastic over the possibilities for production which it offers" and "the more eager to see the music." Also, "Mr. Reinking [the designer], who glanced at my copy, was much interested in it." And again he repeated his insistence that as soon as possible I send "at least a piano score."

But I was not to have one available till late September. The

Paris concert had kept me in town through June. In July I had gone with Mrs. Lasell to Madrid, where she became ill. Then two weeks in Savoy with Madame Langlois and her Russian companion and Maurice Grosser, who had left New York to be in France again. There it was, I think, that he wrote out his scenario for the opera, a clear plan of action that allowed it to be staged. I did not, till September in Villefranche, have the time to complete a voice-and-piano score in ink. But between Flumet and the south coast I did stop for spending a day or two at Gertrude's newly hired manorial property in the village of Bilignin, near Bellay. There I proposed accepting the invitation to give an audition of my opera in Darmstadt, and since that trip would have been aimed at our mutual advantage, I inquired whether Gertrude would care to share its cost. She declined on the ground that "the libretto had already been accepted." Though this was not quite true, for it had merely been read by an assistant *régisseur* and "glanced at" by a designer, I did not argue the matter. I did not, however, undertake the trip. I went on South, finished the score and mailed it to Darmstadt.

Seven months later, on May 1, 1930, Denby wrote, "The chances are pretty black. The music director can't be prevailed on, and the rest of us interested are the more enthusiastic the better we come to know the opera; still a production is dependent on the [musical] director." Later that year, when I made Denby's acquaintance, he told me the explosion my opera had caused. Darmstadt's bright history in producing left-wing or far-out operas and ballets had been the work of a house-team with progressive ideas, encouraged and protected by the *Generalintendant* Carl Ebert. Ballets by Satie, Milhaud, and Florent Schmitt, operas by Falla, Křenek, and Hindemith had all attracted artistic attention to the city; but these productions had also been costly, losses being only partly recuperated through works of standard repertory needing little rehearsal and no new scenery. Someone in authority, presumably the *Generalmusikdirecktor* Dr. Karl Boehm, had decided to begin tapering off on modernism by taking a firm stand against *Four Saints*.

Had my opera been produced around 1930 in Darmstadt, it would be today a different work from what it became under the conditions of its American première in 1934. Its text would have acquired for twin a German version, and the whole work would have taken on the mood of the German art-theater. I would have scored it, moreover, for a much larger number of musicians; and its future life, in consequence, would have been led in middle-to-large-size repertory houses. Its American production, had there come to be one, would not therefore have been a possibility for the museum director in Hartford who allowed me eventually to give it a Negro cast, an English choreographer, and cellophane scenery designed by an American painter, and where the exiguous theater-pit led me to score it for a very small and special-sounding group. The repertory houses might or might not have taken it on, but its whole Hartford and Broadway adventure and its production as choreographic theater in the Diaghilev tradition would most likely never have taken place. Of the translation project I remember just one line, Saint Teresa's Christmas carol, "There can be no peace on earth with calm with calm," which came out in German not at all unattractively: "*Es kann sein kein Fried' auf Erd' mit Ruh' mit Ruh'*.

The spring and summer of 1929 had been full of movements and projects. Hugnet's film *La Perle,* which our Belgian friend the Comte d'Ursel had been supervising in a professional studio, got slowly finished. This was a mixture of detective story with amorous episodes and photographic fantasy (such as a friendly cow in a bedroom and a rue de la Paix jewel shop giving directly on to sylvan fields). It was sweetly poetical and lived for a season. Then it became an antique, like all the other films without sound tracks. The Cocteau morality-film *Blood of a Poet* and Luis Buñuel's exercises in horror and shock, *Un Chien andalou* and *L'Age d'or,* were to have more relation, anyway, to the cruelties of the decade that was beginning. *La Perle* remains a charm piece with all the innocence of the 1920s. When d'Ursel's financial resources for making art films had come to an end, the subsidizing of this field was undertaken by a richer patron, the Vicomte de Noailles. This benefactor in turn renounced film making when as a result of an irreligious passage in *L'Age d'or* (the Holy Sacrament being thrown into a gutter) he was threatened with excommunication from the Church and, what to many seemed graver, expulsion from the Jockey Club.

That same spring, the Misses Stein and Toklas, who had been spending their summers at a gastronomic hotel in Bellay, took lease on a seventeenth-century manor house near by, at Bilignin—a move that furnished Gertrude with a geographic center, turned Alice into an ardent cook and gardener. My own landlord, after doing over my studio on my return from America, had begun construction work that was to change my life also. A whole cluster of furnished studios, all with views of historic Paris, came into being at the top of the house; an elevator was added to the main stair well; and my apartment acquired on its upper level a small kitchen. As a result of these additions, various acquaintances came to live in the new studios and I myself started cooking in. For by the next year, when the changes were complete, Mrs. Lasell had discontinued my allowance, so that eating at home became a necessary economy, as well as a possible hospitality formula. Actually I started cooking that fall, using a gas ring that sat on the floor of my bathroom and a single large pot. After the kitchen became available, my concierge Madame Elise made dinners for me at a charge (besides the groceries) of five francs, or twenty-five cents.

But all this was to be part of the 1930s. For the present the 1920s were getting themselves ended without quite knowing they were doing so. The Vicomte and Vicomtesse de Noailles (to the new bohemia "Charles" and "Marie-Laure") gave in June of 1929 their celebrated *bal des matières,* for which everyone was asked to dress in plastics, glass, metal, straw, whatever might suggest only modern times. And the Duchesse de Clermont-Tonnerre, hoping to repeat the success of *Capital Capitals,* had requested for next season a miniature opera, to be written in collaboration with Georges Hugnet.

As I mentioned earlier, there had been laid down in the middle twenties a line of expressivity that was to be all of tenderness, compassion, sweetness of the heart. With the surrealists insisting loudly on a contrasting line of cruelty, subversion, and hysteria, this opposition was to produce in discussions about art a bitterness almost matching that which would accompany the decade's social and political changes. The visible signs of a new time did not, moreover, await the American stock-market collapse in late 1929 but followed hard on the 1928 Franco-German commercial accord. It was in immediate reaction to that event that the long evening dress, floor-length and wide, came into fashion and that for daytime women began to wear the trench coat. For five years or more, in spite of dressmakers' efforts (subsidized by cloth-makers) toward

In Paris, 1926, V.T., Walter Piston, Herbert Elwell, and Aaron Copland at Nadia Boulanger's before a concert of works by six young Americans. Absent from this picture, George Antheil and Theodore Chanler.

Emmanuel Faÿ, gifted French painter. When he died in New York, 1923, his pictures disappeared and were never found.

René Crevel—tubercular novelist, polemicist, surrealist—wrote ten memorable and violent books (one called *La Mort difficile*). He killed himself in 1935.

Nadia Boulanger was thirty-four, I twenty-four, when I went to her in 1921.

Bernard Faÿ, for circa fifteen years (till the end of World War II) professor of American civilization at the Collège de France.

Darius Milhaud and Jean Cocteau, whom I first knew in 1921.

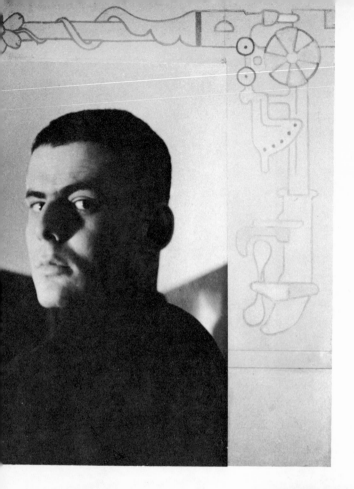

Above: Lincoln Kirstein, editor, impresario, and poet, who in the late 1920s painted mechanistic murals in the dining room of the Harvard Liberal Club.

Right: Sherry Mangan, earlier a poet, a printer, and the publisher of an advanced magazine, became in the 1930s a revolutionist of the Trotsky line.

Right: V.T., ink wash by Christian
Bérard, 1930.

Below: V.T., a monoprint by Kristians Tonny, 1928, depicting character and attributes. These include dancing, public appearance, lovemaking, sadness (*"le pessimisme américain"*), piano-playing, a church, church bells, other bells, wine bottles, food, a tomahawk, and several birds or insects. Ideas and remarks are represented as stones. Inspiration comes in waves, lies around in coils.

James Joyce as I knew him in 1925.

George Antheil arriving in New York, 1927, for the performance of his *Ballet méchanique*.

Janet Flanner in 1924, dressed as Uncle Sam for a costume party at Nancy Cunard's and wearing Nancy's father's gray top hat.

Pablo Picasso dressed as a matador, somewhere near the time I knew him first, which was 1921.

Gertrude Stein and Alice B. Toklas in the middle 1920s.

getting women to consume more yardage, their clothing had not changed. Then suddenly they did accept a change—two changes, in fact—the symbolizations, equally urgent it would seem, of military duty in the daytime and of femaleness at night. And these were to remain the dominant themes of women's dressing, at least in Europe, throughout the 1930s, with the constant military actions (in Italy, Spain, and Germany) and the constant threats of paramilitary revolution (in France, in Czechoslovakia) that led up to the five-year militarization of all Europe.

The twenties had been a peaceful and busy time, with lots of parties and dancing and casual sex-lives, and with minor new movements in music, art, and poetry every year. These were essentially a continuation under easy success conditions, of the modernist efforts that before the first World War had blossomed in far tougher weather. The radical art, music, and poetry of before that war were already the classics of our century (indeed still are), and the 1920s had been further enriched by the subsequent produce of the prewar masters, as well as of their pupils and their progeny. And with the formerly subservient ethnic groups no longer just contributors, culturally, to Berlin or Saint Petersburg or Vienna, but national entities with capitals of their own and seats at the League of Nations, a musical league of nations had come into being in which ethnic integrities and international conformities were neatly balanced. Vienna, Berlin, and Paris remained the centers of advance, as well as of musical publication. But one could still have said of Europe that from Bucharest to Lisbon "all God's chillun got modern music." Even the United States, slower to ripen in music than in letters or in visual art, had its modern-music societies and its up-to-date composers. Among these Aaron Copland, Roy Harris, and myself (plus the lone-wolf experimenter Henry Cowell) were the most active and since Antheil's virtual disappearance the most visible internationally.

This in the modern-music sense, of course. George Gershwin, whose *Rhapsody in Blue* was already in the "pop" concerts, none of us ever could compete with for distribution, nor he with us for intellectual prestige. And Brazil, which had already in the nineteenth century produced an international figure, Antonio Gomes (composer of *Il Guarany*), sent to Europe in 1924 Heitor Villa-Lobos, a fountain, a volcano of colorful music, most of it folklorically inspired and all of it as lively as a Carioca carnival. Villa-Lobos told me later of his arrival in Paris and of going to call, with introductions, on all the French composers old and young. Every one of them, he said, after glancing at his music, began to say how charming it was but how much more so it could become if he would compose in their way instead of his. After about the tenth experience he answered, "But I have not come for lessons, only to show you what I have done." Which silenced them. As a result, he became a part of modern music's establishment, with all its intellectual privileges.

Music's evolution in the twenties was still governed by the pre-war masters Stravinsky and Schoenberg. Debussy was dead, Ravel no longer an influence. In France Milhaud, Honegger, Poulenc, and Auric, Hindemith and Křenek in Germany, were minor masters, material for the immortality machines. So were Berg and Webern in Austria; so was Falla in Spain; and so were a few Italians, English, Poles, and Soviet Russians. Music's league of nations, except for Stravinsky and Schoenberg, was a consortium of profit-sharing minorities. And if the epoch seems now to have been a vigorous one, let us say rather that it was active, that lots of music got written and performed, and that modern-music audiences were friendly.

Poetry was similarly geared to the prewar giants—Yeats, Pound, and Stein—with T. S. Eliot as a rising power and with excellent minor masters available in William Carlos Williams, e. e. cummings, Wallace Stevens, Hart Crane (are there more?). French poetry still stemmed from Rimbaud and Mallarmé, coming to contemporary flower in St.-John Perse, Paul Valéry, and Paul Claudel, none of them young. The novel meant Proust (dead in '22) and Joyce; nobody else was doing comparable work. And neither had the minor painters yet become influential. Braque and Picasso reigned; Matisse still functioned. And Picasso himself was wiggling, struggling, twisting to get free of the cubistical trap he had helped to invent. This is not to say that beautiful work was not done in the twenties. It is merely to remind those who look on those years as a golden age that perhaps they were just that, a time when money, caviar, and diamonds; intelligence, amiability, and good looks; talent, imagination, and wit; ambition, success, and charm were available everywhere.

These came together in certain theater spectacles still unmatched. In France and the West the most impressive of these were the Ballets Russes of Serge de Diaghilev. In Germany and central Europe there were the fabulously successful productions of Max Reinhardt, who personally owned over thirty theaters (as well as the historic archiepiscopal palace of Leopoldskron in Salzburg, where he kept his prompt-books in the sacristy safe). Diaghilev and Reinhardt seem to have kept up from the early 1920s an agreement not to invade each other's territory. In any case, we in Paris never saw the Reinhardt shows (though New York did have *The Miracle*); and central Europe remained for the most part ignorant of the Stravinsky ballet scores, the Picasso stage-sets, and all those striking collaborations between advanced composers and advanced painters which gave to the Diaghilev spectacles (already impeccable for dancing) one glory of the time's finest artwork, another, out front, of a mundane firmament, a dynamo-audience generating its own light from the magnetic proximities of talent, vast worldly experience, known sexual prowess, and beauty aflame.

It was not just the presence of Picasso and Joyce and Stravinsky that gave to the Paris twenties an opulent tone, for these were quiet men who worried and worked and for the most part went to bed o' nights. It was the choreographic stage that made the epoch shine. The splendor of this had led other theaters toward high-level collaborative artwork. And it had at the same time opened the doors of the great Paris houses (the London ones too) to artists and writers, to musicians and dancers. Certain patrons were thereby led to furnish money for opera and ballet seasons in a climate of artistic (and sexual) cooperation that caused class barriers for a little time to disappear. After Diaghilev's death these barriers came right up again, save in a very few houses where sex parties or opium had become ingrained. And one can take the date of his death, I think, as significant, because with it the Ballets Russes, which had lit up the West since 1909, overnight went dark. I have suggested that the kinds of painting and music which were to be influential in the thirties (including surrealism and dodeca-phony) had all come into being by 1925. I have suggested also that a new temper, not necessarily peaceful, was created in 1928 through the Franco-German commercial accords. And certainly after 1929 grave economic events followed our Wall Street disaster. In a historical change marked by hidden steps as well as headlines, it is not easy to pick out the point, like a continental divide, where the thirties began their downward tragic course. But it might be possible to imagine that the twenties, that lively and legendary time which had preserved all that was ever to be preserved of the even grander epoch in the arts that had come to flower just before World War I, expired on August 19, 1929, with the death in Venice of Serge de Diaghilev.

The New Romanticism

IN ALL THE SHOWY LIVING that went on throughout the twenties, the Americans, though not the biggest spenders (leave that to the Indian princes), were certainly in France the most numerous. Wherever there were Ritzes and races, champagne night clubs and gambling casinos, they made up the bulk of the trade, seasoned with a dollop of bejeweled Argentines, a few well-dressed and amorous Brazilians, some impressively casual English and Scots (terrifying gamblers these last), and two or three vastly visible maharajahs. Except for the Greek syndicate that owned the bank at Monte Carlo, all these had come to France because that was where clothes were prettiest, the gambling highest, the really good gems and jewelry cheapest, and the hotels best administered for year-round luxury. Only a few played the game of getting into French society; the best way for that was to be Catholic and do it through marriage. But here and there in the world of hard-driven pleasure one would come on a token Frenchman acting as guide or a French family looking to sell their château. The solvent French went mostly to resorts not internationally fashionable, such as La Baule on the west coast, San Raphael on the south, and beach places on the north that were not Deauville.

Within less than a year after the stock-market tumble began, virtually all the foreign spenders had gone home. The Argentines had turned in their diamonds, the British sold their yachts, the Americans packed up their furs and children, left mistresses behind; only the Oriental potentates remained, and a few foreigners who owned their houses. Mary Garden, ruined by the collapse of the Insull enterprises in Chicago, sold for debts her seaside villa at Beaulieu and shortly afterwards (or so she said) left by accident all her remaining jewelry (uninsurable, since she was a star) in a Monte Carlo taxicab. In the grander hotels of Paris, only half filled in summer, the wintertime became a time of desolation, with tips almost cut off and room clerks, porters, waiters, night men all down to a take-home pay of genuine poverty.

Among the artists and writers too exodus went on, those vowed to preserving the gay twenties being first to leave, since it was clear by the end of 1929 that the postwar time was over. To those of us no longer living in that aftermath no shock came with its demise. We had long since lost taste for its bar-stool discussions of courage, its pride in banal misbehaviors, and had moved into a range of sentiment that seemed to us far fresher. Our new romanticism was no nostalgia for the warmths of World War I or for the gone-forever prewar youth of Stravinsky and Picasso, but an immersion complete in what any day might bring. *Mystère* was our word, tenderness our way, unreasoning compassion our aim.

We did not need to go away, or want to. A small group following a path discovered only a short time earlier (and by Christian Bérard, for certain), we should have found elsewhere few comrades prepared for aiding or abetting us. Our ways of life and art belonged in Europe anyway; they were not ripe for being submitted to home-front pressmen, pedagogical organizers, or price manipulators. And hardly any Americans besides myself were involved.

Our novelty—and I am speaking of less than a dozen poets, painters, and musicians—consisted in the use of our personal sentiments as subject matter. Modern artists of the prewar time had mostly refrained from doing this—Debussy, Ravel, Stravinsky; Matisse, Picasso, Braque; Bernard Shaw and Yeats; Mallarmé and Valéry. For them the theme had always been outside themselves, however secretive or eloquent the statement. And those whose chief careers came after World War I, though their forming had taken place earlier—Pound and Eliot, Joyce and Stein—had scrupulously maintained an objective method. Of all the large-size twentieth-century artists only Proust had pointed up a private feeling; and even with him the search for a particular recall was little more than a pretext for painting a panorama. But in poetry, a century earlier, Wordsworth, Blake, and Byron; in music Chopin and Schumann; in painting, Goya, at least, had all been unafraid to speak their sentiments. In our time the Austrian composers Schoenberg and Berg had spoken of sentiment too, pouring out in their grandly hospitable way the secrets of the soul, of any soul, like May wine for visitors. Perhaps we in Paris, few and young, were only a trickle beside their vast Danubian vats; indeed they seemed to think of us (if at all) as just that, though we believed ourselves of better vintage. It matters not. In an age that kept insistently looking backward—and Vienna most of all—an awareness of the daily present had become our way of life, and in spite of wars and cataclysms was to remain so throughout the 1930s.

I have said we were young; we would have had to be, for constant vibrancy is hard to sustain after thirty-five. But we did have mentors among the older artists. The poets Max Jacob, Jean Cocteau, and Gertrude Stein admired our work. So did the fiction writer Marcel Jouhandeau. The painters among us had no older ones at all to whom they looked for praise. But the composer Charles Koechlin, ever curious about novelty and warm toward youth, followed our music from a distance; and Darius Milhaud was more than tolerant.

Milhaud was in fact the keystone of French music's power structure in so far as it controlled the distribution of contemporary work. And a more devoted chief could scarcely be imagined, self-sacrificing of his time and far-flung as to influence. My own acquaintance with him, a long one, has borne no marks of tension. And if he at no time aided my career, as he did that of so many others, indeed of almost all the others with whom I shared affinity, I have long thought that probably the fault was mine. If I had submitted my music to his judgment, as the others did, and frankly asked for tutelage, I might well have become in those early 1930s as clearly a part of the School of Paris as did Nicolas Nabokov, Vittorio Rieti, and Igor Markevitch, all of them later arrivals than I. But I could no more submit myself to Milhaud, invited or not, than I had been able to submit myself to Ravel when in 1926 he offered friendship. Some unconquerable rebelliousness had made it so. It was for them, discovering me, to make the move; and even then I did not always follow. So it was with all the French to whom I became attached, including Madame Langlois, though there were always to be some nearly-exact contemporaries (Sauguet, for instance, and Cliquet-Pleyel) with whom no such question of protocol arose. With Milhaud, and with Francis Poulenc too, there may have remained a wariness from ten years earlier, when in my Boulanger and fresh-from-Harvard days I had very likely impressed them as a shade uppish.

As for the neo-Romantic upsurge itself, to which Milhaud bore a benevolent and avuncular relation, its identification as a movement was yet to come. Neo-Romanticism in painting was defined twenty years later as "the personality of the painter reflected in the character of the thing seen." This from Maurice Grosser's book *The Painter's Eye,* where he also states that "by reintroducing humanity and personal feelings into an art that had become dehumanized, the Neo-Romantic painters made, I am convinced, the most important contribution to painting since the innovations of the great Moderns, and one which will have much influence in forming the painting of the second half of our century."

Of its musical aspects I wrote in 1933 for *Modern Music* that

around the personality of Sauguet the present epoch has begun to crystalize. Neo-Romanticism is the journalistic term for it. Spontaneity of sentiment is the thing sought. Internationalism is the temper. Elegance is the real preoccupation. Nobody expects further technical research to supply its own corrective . . . [and] grand passion . . . hasn't recovered from Wagner yet. What about well-bred salon music? That was tried in 1920 and called neo-classicism. (The idea of being well-bred is behind all neo-classicism: Vergil, Racine, and Pope, for example.) It turned out [to need] the same corrective that the late eighteenth century needed [and got from Romanticism], an infusion of warm personal feeling. Sentimental love, spontaneous sympathy, faithful comradeship, playful libertinage, domesticity, tolerant rivalry, and affectionate bickering, these are modes of living still at hand, . . . usable in art. . . . The first twenty years [of our century] occupied themselves with technic. The present age is concerned about feeling. [Only] when these elements [shall] have been . . . coordinated . . . [will there] be a way of living, of contemplating, and of writing grandiose tragedy.

This statement presents a Paris-based view, of course. Music in central Europe had long since adopted an introverted pathos. If our hope in the West was rather to diminish than to augment the anxiety content of art and thus possibly to preserve the whole of modernism from scleroses already developing through success, no such danger existed in the Germanic regions. On the contrary, the danger there after 1933 was total extinction; and even before that time the great migration had begun that was to furnish the United States, Mexico, Brazil, and Argentina with scholars and skilled workers, France's rapidly maturing film art with directors and cameramen. (The French film also benefited from French stage actors, once the sound track had given them their language.)

Except for the noticeable number of departures, the early 1930s in Paris did not seem, right off, to be very different from the twenties. The sun still rose; the Seine still lapped its quays; and prices, most conveniently, fell a little. One did not greatly mind there not being so much money around, so long as one had any at all. And with the departure of the sardonic ones, the heart and its ways became more precious to us. As a result of this new sensibility, most of those who had been free lancing as to love now began to pair off, move into flats, and cook. My first *bœuf à la mode en gelée* came off with beginner's luck simply because Madame Elise, who had told me how to make it, had failed to warn me that it is far from easy. However, along with cooking's delights and mating's conveniences came, of course, mating's frictions. And quarreling, which in the Arcadian twenties had seldom seemed worthwhile, became in the emptiness of the beginning thirties a refuge from boredom, a diversion, the darker side of friendship and of love. Warfare, in fact, though just now chiefly personal, was later to involve class bitterness and national envies and thence to become by 1932 in China, by 1933 in Germany, '34 in France, '35 in America, '36 in Spain, the decade's dominant theme. It was not to be for long a peaceful time, the period that began in 1930; after the financial panic of 1929 the growth was gradual and steady toward the wider holocausts of ten years later.

Nevertheless, with masses of the foreign moving out, the French themselves turned individually sweeter; and those of us who had remained came to be warmly adopted. After 1933 there were refugees from Germany, and from 1936 many Spanish; but as the thirties began we were mostly just Americans alone with the

French. And very glad they were to have us too, for a French family feels most secure when it privately owns at least one American. The French need foreigners to admire them. Also, unless there is a peppering of likable outsiders available to whom they can explain France, the French can start explaining it to one another—an urge that throughout their history has led to civil war. It came almost to that in 1934 and '35. Then the next year, with thousands of republican Spanish to take care of, they turned euphoric and stayed so right up to World War II, even through the first year of that, though their beloved Americans had thinned out. Americans remain always, in spite of politics, their favorite foreigners, because though we are firmly a part of the Judeo-Christian fellowship (a necessity for brotherly loving and brotherly quarreling), we never bore them by acting like Europeans.

The English-language literary giants of the 1930s were to be the same as those already gigantic before—Joyce, Stein, Yeats, and Pound, with Eliot, though less of an influence in poetry than these, becoming a power in publication. The magazines previously devoted to these authors, however, showed a high mortality. *The Dial* ceased in 1929, *The Little Review* not long after. Sherry Mangan's *larus the celestial visitor* (hand set in Lutetia type on special paper), which had begun to appear early in 1927, had expired in 1928 after seven issues, largely because he persisted in paying for manuscripts. His American contributors had included the largely unknown Hart Crane, Yvor Winters, R. P. Blackmur, and George Davis. As his "European editor" I had procured for him poetry and prose from Gertrude Stein, Mary Butts, Bernard Faÿ, Robert McAlmon, Pierre de Massot, and Henry de Montherlant. A year later he transferred his unexpired subscriptions to "a young friend with money"; and the result was *Pagany,* edited in Boston by Richard Johns[on]. This quarterly began in January of 1930 and went on, according to the copies I own, for at least three years. Since Mangan was an advisory editor, I continued helping him to secure European contributions, though I never met Johns.

Pagany ran to 150 octavo pages of still good reading, including work by such already famous writers as Ezra Pound, William Carlos Williams, Erskine Caldwell, Cocteau, e. e. cummings, and Dos Passos, as well as by others who would be known later, Paul Bowles, for example, and Harold Rosenberg. It printed a handful of remarkable poems by Mary Butts and some of her best stories.

The second number contained, by Sherry Mangan, one of the funniest polemical pieces I have ever read, *A "Note" on the Somewhat Premature Apotheosis of the Late Lamented Thomas Stearns Eliot.* (Gertrude, no lover of Eliot, found it "Jesuit" but not jesuitical.) And in the winter issue of 1931 there appeared on facing pages a confrontation of George Hugnet's *Enfances,* a suite of thirty poems, with Gertrude Stein's English version of them.

To the opening number Hugnet had contributed (in French) the first of his regular Paris letters, also a two-page article about my music. French poets are less hesitant than American poets to speak up for music; and we know the self-assumed authority with which for fifty years they have backed modern art. Thus Hugnet could without embarrassment think of himself as spokesman for the whole intellectual world when he exposed a point of view that was coming to be a credo. He discerned in my music, as Bérard had done some time before, two qualities much admired just then, "simplicity" and "purity," which he relates in my case to "the singing of Negroes . . . blended with the rigamarole rhythms of Sunday School songs and children's games." He finds my music generally "joyous" and "its effect on the skin beneficial . . . a sort of heliotherapy." He considers my Sonata da Chiesa to embody "a manner of writing that needs to be renounced, a 'modern music' of which the high dissonance content has lost its charm." My *Capital Capitals,* however, is a "torrent resplendently clear" and my vocal music in general "a truly novel contribution . . . an Elysian field in which the air is neighbor to that which one breathes in the garden of Satie."

In Europe the literary twenties had proliferated an armful of English-language magazines—Harold Loeb's *Broom,* Ford Madox Ford's *Transatlantic Review,* Ernest Walsh's *This Quarter,* and several less impressive. The transition from that decade to the next was mirrored after 1926 in a quarterly named exactly that, *transition,* edited by Eugene Jolas, trilingual poet (French-Alsatian-American), and sometimes by Eliot Paul. Almost every number, as I remember, contained a chunk of Joyce's *Work in Progress;* but every number seemed also to indicate increasing involvement between Jolas and the surrealists. Early in 1930 I wrote Gertrude,

Our friend C[ary] Ross presented translations of poems by our equally friend G. Hugnet to our more or less friend E. Jolas

latter remarking in re same (but not reading poems) that pub-
lication was impossible because Hugnet belonged to the wrong
French group. Does this means *transition* gets money from
Surrealists? (Who in turn ditto from Russia says Bernard.)

The idea that Russian gold could be supporting surrealism, from
its beginnings admiring of Trotsky and after 1928 openly anti-
Stalinist, was a fantasy that only the Catholic and royalist Bernard
Faÿ could have entertained. My correspondence of the time constantly reports wide misses of this sort, also misunderstandings,
frustrations, projects initiated only to be abandoned, quarrels threatened, some pacified, some moving in like an Oklahoma twister.

Hugnet kept trying all one summer to make a poem to which
I could write a short opera, commissioned by our admirer the
Duchesse de Clermont-Tonnerre. He finally produced *L'Invention
de la rose,* which he called a *mélo[drama].* Then came another,
Pléthore et pénurie (surely a 1930s theme). Eventually I renounced
the collaboration on grounds that Hugnet was a purely lyric poet
without stage instinct. But the duchesse still wanted a piece for her
next spring's party; and when I naïvely proposed my just-finished
Funeral Oration by Bossuet (for Henriette-Marie de France widow
of England's Charles I), she listened to it with interest but found
it (naturally!) not quite right for her costume ball. I also played
and sang it for Alfredo Casella, then a conductor of influence in
both Italy and France. His comment was, "The best I can say is
that it is not a bore." The very idea of turning a Bossuet funeral
oration into a solo cantata seemed as outlandish to him as a musical
treatment of the Communist Manifesto might to a Russian or that
of a sermon by Jonathan Edwards to an American. A few ultra-
Catholics were receptive, scenting in it possible propaganda for the
faith. Virtually everyone else found it lacking a *raison d'être.* Except, of course, my own courtiers, who admired its declamatory
melodies and high-arched Baroque curves, some of them pages
long and all built to match Bossuet's long, florid, loose-hung, and
as often as not quite illogical Baroque sentences. I mention the
Bossuet piece merely to show how detached I was at this time from
career calculations and how concentrated on purely musical problems, in spite of my impending loss of income.

Gertrude Stein, at the same time, was trying to move everybody
she could for my sake and for the sake of our opera. She ceased
communication with the Chicago millionairess who had failed to

continue her support of me. She tried to stimulate English interest in *Four Saints* through writing to a London music critic her sister-in-law was said to know; and I wrote myself, at somebody's insistence, to Charles B. Cochran, London's most enterprising producer of music shows. Gertrude even persuaded me to write to Otto Kahn, Maecenas of the Met, proposing that I play and sing it for him. And she got Muriel Draper and Carl Van Vechten to mention it to Mary Garden, then powerful at the Chicago Opera. Nothing came of these efforts; the time was not for novelty.

Characteristic of the whole new decade, along with wars and massacres, was to be its preoccupation with the price of paintings. The twenties had shown collectors that no major fresh adventure was to be expected from painting itself and that it was consequently time to solidify the values in prewar modernism, that is to say, in the work of the cubists and their predecessors. Following this line, a group of New York collectors had opened in 1929, under the direction of two modern-art scholars, Jere Abbott and Alfred H. Barr, Jr., a Museum of Modern Art that was to become the world model for similar operations. In a decade of declining receipts from stocks and bonds, the buying of Modern Old Masters (Picasso, Braque, Matisse) and of the still inexpensive younger masters (Miró, Ernst, Arp, Dalí) was to be a source of rising wealth for the well advised, and a fascination to the public. In neither New York nor Paris was there to be much movement in art itself, only a great activity in the market. Even the time's most influential movements, the neo-Romantic and the surrealist, were both of them a heritage from the twenties. And if certain ripenings among poets and painters, and the withering away of others, gave drama to inner councils, no basic change took place in either viewpoint. Nor indeed did any change take place in the power structure of contemporary music; those in command were to remain the same.

Surrealism, born out of Dada's demise in the early 1920s, was not concerned with music at all, only with poetry and painting, both of which it essayed to govern through disciplines of spontaneity. In poetry the discipline was that of automatic writing, in painting, the transcribing of dreams, preferably in color and with *léché* (or "tongue-licked") brushwork. "Directed spontaneity" one might call its operation, since no writer or artist was allowed to remain in the group unless his spontaneities conformed to the particular blend of Marx-cum-Freud that constituted the philosophy of its poet-dictator André Breton. As an independent Marxist, Breton favored the intellectual freedoms nurtured by Trotsky; but politically he was nonparticipant, breaking in 1928 with those of his colleagues who accepted the demand of the French Communist party that the surrealists prove their allegiance to Stalin-directed Marxism by joining up and carrying out an anti-Trotsky line. The surrealists from that time on remained (as a group) politically uncommitted, though they still talked about revolution and aspired toward a generalized subversiveness.

They spoke for neither labor nor capital but rather as petit-bourgeois intellectuals. And throughout the 1930s, though politically ineffective, they were to contribute the valuable stubborness of their class to the dialogue that went on throughout the *bourgeoisie* (both the *petite* and the *grande*) regarding wealth, poverty, civil rights, privilege, class solidarity, private loyalties, and national honor. They were also, like everybody else, to play games, when they could, with art prices. For surrealism, though originally a literary movement, had inherited from Dada the sculptor Arp and the painter Max Ernst and had acquired during the later twenties the painters Joan Miró and Yves Tanguy. Around 1930 Salvador Dalí, an obviously rising value, joined the group; and from then on the names of Pablo Picasso and Marcel Duchamp were also connected with many of their public statements.

The other side of the street, the neo-Romantic—as represented by Bérard, Tchelitcheff, and Leonid and Eugene Berman—was also enjoying prestige and some prosperity. And just as the surrealists for their themes sought out the irrational, the subversive, and the cruel, the subjects of the neo-Romantics were predominantly humane and tender, the feelings you have when you let your mind alone. They spoke, moreover, both to and for the *grande bourgeoisie;* and if their politics were conservative, in some cases even royalist, their avoidance of political action was as strict as that of their surrealist opponents. Their chief defenders also were poets—Jean Cocteau, Max Jacob, and Gertrude Stein. And though their collectors in France were on the whole quite well-to-do (Paris millionaire bohemia), in America their work was bought only by intellectuals, chiefly the friends of Russell Hitchcock, who had been their earliest announcer. Edith Sitwell, who had formed with Tchelitcheff (over portrait sittings) a friendship of iron, managed to make a certain success for him in England. In 1935 he left both France and England for America; in 1938 Eugene Berman moved to New York; during 1939 and '40 Leonid Berman was in the French army, passing the Occupation underground; by 1937 or '38 Bérard, the leader of them all, had wholly given up painting in oil for fashion drawing and stage design. And so their side of the street lost its last contact with the European picture market. Today, with Picasso and his contemporaries having inherited the customers from both sides, the modern-art market, in spite of a prosperous American younger school and a world-wide boom, has remained for basic investment a Modern Old Master market.

It is worthy of note, moreover, that both of the chief contemporary movements, neo-Romanticism and surrealism, were concerned almost exclusively with figurative painting. Abstraction was still a note in sculpture (and in sculpturesque painting, such as that of Tanguy); but the newer painting of the time was generally concentrated on images. In this sense, it was all of it romantic, though surrealism spoke more directly to the mind, neo-Romanticism to the sensibilities. It was only at the end of the decade, after the neo-Romantics (whom the French elegant world had begun to invest in, especially Bérard, who seemed possibly a new classical French painter) had either given up France or given up painting, that the French collectors, as the Americans had done already, settled for the abstract and the nonobjective. The subversive content of surrealism, they had learned in the early 1930s, was of no help to either social or business standing; and the grand return to painting nature and people that the neo-Romantics dreamed of bringing about had failed for lack of a personnel sufficiently tough to face, as artists, a lifetime of persecution from the collectors of pre-World-War-I modern art—in other words, from the Picasso marketeers. Hermetic art became therefore the only safe investment.

In the summer of 1930 I went to Spain again, this time with two painters, Maurice Grosser and the Catalonian Ramón Senabre. The three of us hired on the island of Mallorca a roomy flat in the fishing village of Puerto de Soller, from where we did a great deal of walking and mountain climbing. After a month of that, I moved to a hotel near Palma that had both rocks and a beach. From there I could go by tramcar to the bullfights, or shopping to order shirts and shoes, beautifully made and absurdly inexpensive. I also stayed a great deal in my room, writing music in bed under a mosquito net. Grosser eventually left Soller too, for Senabre's daily distress when the postman failed to bring the check owed to him by his Paris dealer had become too depressing to bear. So the two of us did more mountain climbing; and then he went off to Barcelona, where he took a dismal room near a noisy beach and beside the railway tracks. From this self-punishment I rescued him; and we made our way by third-class trains to Villefranche on the Côte d'Azur, where I wrote more music and he painted still life. I also went back to Ascain on the West coast for some rainy fall days with Madame Langlois.

In 1931 we went to Mallorca again, Grosser and I, both staying in my previous summer's hotel at Calamayor and going out from there on trips. Once we walked from one coast village to another clean round the island. Another time we motored with a young German couple, fraternizing in a wine cellar at Inca with farmers, who gave us all the wines of the island to taste but who would allow no paying. At Valdemosa, we saw Chopin's apartment in the monastery, which seemed to have been moved three times over the last century and to contain no furniture even vaguely authentic, except for an upright piano that might or might not have been the one sent out to him from Paris by Pleyel. Then again to Villefranche by September, relieved to be back in cheerful France. Spain is for me an intense experience always, even when the intensity is that of a deep dissatisfaction not unlike the irretrievable boredom that seems to be endemic among male Spaniards over thirty.

My monthly checks from Mrs. Lasell, which had been announced as stopping, did keep on arriving through 1930 and halfway through the next year. Also, at about that time the United States government essayed to relieve poverty by offering a bonus to the veterans of World War I. My length of service entitled me to $1,094 one half of this to be paid right off. So I decided that rather than merely live it up, I would spend it on a concert of my works. For program I had a String Quartet, the Max Jacob *Stabat Mater,* the Bossuet Funeral Oration (all brand-new), a Violin Sonata, an *Air de Phèdre* out of Racine (which had been given but not yet in a stylish hall), and a set of Inventions for piano that were five years old but that somehow had not yet been played. As locale I engaged for June 15, 1931, the Salle Chopin, recital hall of the new Maison Pleyel. And for performers I engaged the best—the Quatuor Krettly to play my String Quartet; a tenor from the opera, José de Trévi, for the Bossuet; a dramatic soprano from the Opéra-Comique,

Madeleine Leymo, to sing the *Phèdre* aria and (with string quartet) the *Stabat*. The American pianist Gertrude Bonime played my Inventions. And an excellent French violinist, Yvonne Giraud (in private life Marquise de Casa Fuerte), who had been ten years absent from the concert stage, took this occasion for returning to it.

Sauguet's review of the concert in *L'Europe nouvelle* mentioned that my music had "singularities capable of disconcerting on first approach. Voluntarily [Thomson] uses a language of extreme purity that could easily be inexpressive, white, and savorless. But he uses it with such intelligence, such tact, and his musical sensitivity is so alert, that this surprising idiom actually gives depth." And far from being shocked, as others were, by my having subverted to musical purposes texts from French literary classics, he drew a parallel between my Bossuet and Racine settings and Erik Satie's of Plato.

This concert also won me the attention of the powerful editor Henri Prunières, who reviewed it both in his own magazine, *La Revue Musicale,* and in *The New York Times*. He complimented my "remarkable feeling for musical declamation," deplored my use of piano tremolo at the end of the Bossuet, opined that I was "destined for the opera." In the same article, reviewing two concerts of American music recently conducted in Paris by Nicolas Slonimsky, he paid honor to *Intégrales* by Edgard Varèse, estimating it as far superior to the works by Cowell, Ruggles, Riegger, Chávez, Weiss, Sanjuan, and Caturla. But he did grant that Charles Ives, composer of *Three Places in New England,* was "manifestly a musician."

There had been other concerts in 1931 involving my music. I still have the program of one given with Cliquet-Pleyel on January 10, in a series called "The Parthenon," where we played my *Synthetic Waltzes* duet, where Marthe-Marthine sang songs of Gertrude Stein and the *Phèdre* aria, and where I gave a first performance, with Lucien Schwartz, of my Violin Sonata. To this concert came, looking for evidence, the new boy-genius Igor Markevitch. This Russian of barely twenty had been discovered some three years earlier, in 1928, by Diaghilev, then launched by Cocteau, taken up as a cause by Nadia Boulanger, blessed by Henri Prunières, patronized by the Princesse de Polignac, and endowed by the Vicomtesse de Noailles. He needed evidence regarding me because he seemed to be planning for us to become enemies. My not wholly adoring reactions to his music being already known to him (in the Paris of those days everything got to be known), he found my Violin Sonata a work he could easily dismiss as "just César Franck." My reply to this opening of hostilities was made two years later in *Modern Music*, where I remarked that, as with George Antheil, "the career is more interesting than the music." He never forgave me for that, and I am not sure that his career as a composer (he now conducts only) ever really recovered from the wide distribution my article received when reprinted in a New York Sunday paper. It was even believed to have influenced Koussevitzky to postpone playing the new young Russian. I had not meant to hit so hard. But in the 1930s no one pulled his punches. Indeed the whole decade was to be marked by such intensities, by violent loyalties and passionate betrayals, by idyllic loves and out-of-joint ones, by friendships indivisible and by threats relentless, by panoramas of poverty and shocking displays of wealth.

It may have been for feigning prosperity (or was it out of bravado) that the dressmaker Gabrielle Chanel in one of the decade's early years staged in her own sumptuous house, rue du faubourg Saint-Honoré, a show of diamonds. There must have been fifty pieces, all of modernistic design and all involving masses of gems. I remember a flat cigarette case made of square stones held together by almost invisible platinum lines. Another was a limp tiara to be worn in reverse, lying on the forehead like bangs.

Grandeurs like this and miseries walked side by side, as in Louis-Philippe days. And if my own existence illustrated neither, it was no example of rising fortune. At one time I ran clean out of money. Then I learned that my tradesmen would trust me for two and three months. So I began to eat in; and the credit of my butchers, bakers, grocers, and wine merchants, along with the cooking counsels of Madame Elise and my landlord's tolerance of rent delays, made it possible for me to enjoy in my far-too-expensive quai Voltaire studio an unworried life of working and of having company. Actually, during the years of 1930, '31, and '32 I was happier in France than I had ever been anywhere, felt snugger there and calmer, working away at my music writing and cocooned by friendships, loves, and tasty cooking against the nervous anxieties of America, the despairs of England, the disasters that were surely on the march in Germany.

A Portrait
of Gertrude Stein

GERTRUDE STEIN IN HER YOUNGER DAYS had liked to write all night and sleep all day. She also, it seems, ate copiously, drank wine, and smoked cigars. By the time I knew her, at fifty-two, she ate abstemiously; she neither drank nor smoked; and she was likely to wake, as people do in middle life, by nine. Her volume had been diminished too. Her appearance, nevertheless, on account of low stature (five feet, two), remained monumental, like that of some saint or sybil sculpted three-fourths life size. Her working powers also were intact, remained so, indeed, until her death at seventy-two.

Actually a whole domestic routine had been worked out for encouraging those powers to function daily. In the morning she would read, write letters, play with the dog, eventually bathe, dress, and have her lunch. In the afternoon she drove in the car, walked, window-shopped, spent a little money. She did nothing by arrangement till after four. At some point in her day she always wrote; and since she waited always for the moment when she would be full of readiness to write, what she wrote came out of fullness as an overflowing.

Year round, these routines varied little, except that in the country, if there were house guests, excursions by car might be a little longer, tea or lunch taken out instead of at home. When alone and not at work, Gertrude would walk, read, or meditate. She loved to walk; and she consumed books by the dozen, sent to her when away from home by the American Library in Paris. She read English and American history, memoirs, minor literature from the nineteenth century, and crime fiction, rarely modern art-writing, and never the commercial magazines. When people were around she would talk and listen, ask questions. She talked with anybody and everybody. When exchanging news and views with neighbors, concierges, policemen, shop people, garage men, hotel servants, she was thoroughly interested in them all. Gertrude not only liked people, she needed them. They were grist for her poetry, a relief from the solitudes of a mind essentially introspective.

Alice Toklas neither took life easy nor fraternized casually. She got up at six and cleaned the drawing room herself, because she did not wish things broken. (Porcelain and other fragile objects were her delight, just as pictures were Gertrude's; and she could imagine using violence toward a servant who might break one.) She liked being occupied, anyway, and did not need repose, ever content to serve Gertrude or be near her. She ran the house, ordered the meals, cooked on occasion, and typed out everything that got written into the blue copybooks that Gertrude had adopted from French school children. From 1927 or '28 she also worked petit point, matching in silk the colors and shades of designs made especially for her by Picasso. These tapestries were eventually applied to a pair of Louis XV small armchairs (*chauffeuses*) that Gertrude had bought for her. She was likely, any night, to go to bed by eleven, while Miss Stein would sit up late if there were someone to talk with.

Way back before World War I, in 1910 or so, in Granada Gertrude had experienced the delights of writing directly in the landscape. This does not mean just working out of doors; it means being surrounded by the thing one is writing about at the time one is writing about it. Later, in 1924, staying at Saint-Rémy in Provence, and sitting in fields beside the irrigation ditches, she found the same sound of running water as in Granada to soothe her while she wrote or while she simply sat, imbuing herself with the landscape's sight and sound. In the country around Belley, where she began to summer only a few years later, she wrote *Lucy Church Amiably* wholly to the sound of streams and waterfalls.

Bravig Imbs, an American poet and novelist who knew her in the late twenties, once came upon her doing this. The scene took place in a field, its enactors being Gertrude, Alice, and a cow. Alice, by means of a stick, would drive the cow around the field. Then, at a sign from Gertrude, the cow would be stopped; and Gertrude would write in her copybook. After a bit, she would pick up her folding stool and progress to another spot, whereupon Alice would again start the cow moving around the field till Gertrude signaled she was ready to write again. Though Alice now says that Gertrude drove the cow, she waiting in the car, the incident, whatever its choreography, reveals not only Gertrude's working intimacy with landscape but also the concentration of two friends on an act of composition by one of them that typifies and reveals their daily life for forty years. Alice had decided long before that "Gertrude was always right," that she was to have whatever she wanted when she wanted it, and that the way to keep herself always wanted was to keep Gertrude's writing always and forever unhindered, unopposed.

Gertrude's preoccupation with painting and painters was not shared by Alice except in so far as certain of Gertrude's painter friends touched her heart, and Picasso was almost the only one of these. Juan Gris was another, and Christian Bérard a very little bit. But Matisse I know she had not cared for, nor Braque. If it had not been for Gertrude, I doubt that Alice would ever have had much to do with the world of painting. She loved objects and furniture, practiced cooking and gardening, understood music. Of music, indeed, she had a long experience, having once, as a young girl, played a piano concerto in public. But painting was less absorbing to her than to Gertrude.

Gertrude's life with pictures seems to have begun as a preoccupation shared with her brothers, Michael and Leo. The sculptor Jacques Lipschitz once remarked to me the miraculous gift of perception by which these young Californians, in Paris of the 1900s, had gone straight to the cardinal values. Virtually without technical experience (since only Leo, among them, had painted at all) and without advice (for there were no modern-art scholars then), they bought Cézanne, Matisse, and Picasso. In quantity and, of course, for almost nothing. But also, according to Lipschitz, the Steins' taste was strongest when they bought together. Gertrude and Leo did this as long as they lived together, which was till about

1911. Michael, who had started quite early buying Matisses, kept that up till World War I. After Gertrude and Leo separated, she made fewer purchases and no major ones at all, save some Juan Gris canvases that represented a continuing commitment to Spanish cubism and to friendship. She could no longer buy Picasso or Cézanne after their prices got high, or after she owned a car. But throughout the twenties and thirties she was always looking for new painters, without being able to commit herself to any of them till she discovered about 1929 Sir Francis Rose. From him she quickly acquired nearly a hundred pictures, and she insisted till her death that he was a great painter. No other collector, no museum, no international dealer has yet gone so far.

Looking at painting had been for Gertrude Stein a nourishment throughout the late twenties and thirties of her own life. She never ceased to state her debt to Cézanne, for it was from constantly gazing on a portrait by him that she had found her way into and through the vast maze of motivations and proclivities that make up the patterns of people and types of people in *Three Lives* and in *The Making of Americans*. "The wonderful thing about Cézanne," she would say, "is that he was never tempted." Gertrude Stein's biographers have stated that Picasso also was a source for her and that in *Tender Buttons* she was endeavoring to reproduce with words the characteristic devices of cubist painting. There may even be in existence a quotation from Gertrude herself to this effect. But she certainly did not repeat it in the way she loved to repeat her allegiance to Cézanne. I myself have long doubted the validity, or at any rate the depth, of such a statement. An influence of poetry on painting is quite usual, a literary theme being illustrated by images. But any mechanism by which this procedure might be reversed and painting come to influence literature (beyond serving as subject for a review) is so rare a concept that the mere statement of Gertrude Stein's intent to receive such an influence surely requires fuller explanation. Let us try.

First of all, *Tender Buttons,* subtitled *Objects.˙.Food.˙.Rooms,* is an essay in description, of which the subjects are those commonly employed by painters of still life. And cubist painting too was concerned with still life. Cubism's characteristic device in representing still life was to eliminate the spatially fixed viewpoint, to see around corners, so to speak, to reduce its subject to essentials of form and profile and then to reassemble these as a summary or digest of its model. Resemblance was not forbidden; on the contrary, clues were offered to help the viewer recognize the image; and cubist painters (from the beginning, according to Gertrude) had been disdainful of viewers who could not "read" their canvases. (Today's "abstract" painters, on the other hand, maintain that in their work resemblances are purely accidental.)

According to Alice Toklas, the author's aim in *Tender Buttons* was "to describe something without mentioning it." Sometimes the name of the object is given in a title, sometimes not; but each description is full of clues, some of them easy to follow up, others put there for throwing you off the scent. All are legitimately there, however, since in Blake's words, "everything possible to be believed is an image of truth," and since in Gertrude Stein's method anything that comes to one in a moment of concentrated working is properly a part of the poem. Nevertheless, unveiling the concealed image is somewhat more difficult to a reader of *Tender Buttons* than to the viewer of a cubist still life. For a still life is static; nothing moves in it; time is arrested. In literature, on the other hand, one word comes after another and the whole runs forward. To have produced static pictures in spite of a non-fixed eye-point was cubism's triumph, just as giving the illusion of movement within a framed picture was the excitement of vorticism, as in Marcel Duchamp's "Nude Descending a Staircase." To have described objects, food, and rooms both statically and dynamically, with both a painter's eye and a poet's continuity, gives to *Tender Buttons* its particular brilliance, its way of both standing still and moving forward.

Now the carrier of that motion, make no mistake, is a rolling eloquence in no way connected with cubism. This eloquence, in fact, both carries forward the description and defeats it, just as in cubist painting description was eventually defeated by the freedom of the painter (with perspective making no demands) merely to create a composition. Cubism was always, therefore, in danger of going decorative (hence flat); and the kind of writing I describe here could just as easily turn into mere wit and oratory. That cubism was something of an impasse its short life, from 1909 to 1915, would seem to indicate; and there were never more than two possible exits from it. One was complete concealment of the image, hence in effect its elimination; the other was retreat into naturalism. Both paths have been followed in our time, though not by Picasso, who has avoided abstraction as just another trap leading to the decorative, and who could never bring himself, for mere depiction, to renounce the ironic attitudes involved in voluntary stylization.

Gertrude, faced with two similar paths, chose both. During the years between 1927 and '31, she entered into an involvement with naturalism that produced at the end of her life *Yes Is for a Very Young Man, Brewsie and Willie,* and *The Mother of Us All,* each completely clear and in no way mannered. She was also during those same years pushing abstraction farther than it had ever gone before, not only in certain short pieces still completely hermetic (even to Alice Toklas), but in extended studies of both writing and feeling in which virtually everything remains obscure but the mood, works such as *As a Wife Has a Cow, a Love Story; Patriarchal Poetry;* and *Stanzas in Meditation.*

Her last operas and plays are in the humane tradition of letters, while her monumental abstractions of the late 1920s and early 1930s are so intensely aware of both structure and emotion that they may well be the origin of a kind of painting that came later to be known as "abstract expressionism." If this be true, then Gertrude Stein, after borrowing from cubism a painting premise, that of the nonfixed viewpoint, returned that premise to its origins, transformed. Whether the transformation could have been operated within painting itself, without the help of a literary example, we shall never know, because the literary example was there. We do know, however, that no single painter either led that transformation or followed it through as a completed progress in his own work.

Gertrude had been worried about painting ever since cubism had ceased to evolve. She did not trust abstraction in art, which she found constricted between flat color schemes and pornography. Surrealism, for her taste, was too arbitrary as to theme and too poor as painting. And she could not give her faith to the neo-Romantics either, though she found Bérard "alive" and "the best" of them. She actually decided in 1928 that "painting [had] become a minor art again," meaning without nourishment for her. Then within the year, she had found Francise Rose. What nourishment she got from him I cannot dream; nor did she ever speak of him save as a gifted one destined to lead his art—an English leader this time, instead of Spanish.

In her own work, during these late twenties, while still developing ideas received from Picasso, she was also moving into new fields opened by her friendship with me. I do not wish to pretend that her ventures into romantic feeling, into naturalism, autobiography, and the opera came wholly through me, though her discovery of the opera as a poetic form certainly did. Georges Hugnet, whom I had brought to her, was at least equally a stimulation, as proved by her "translation" of one of his extended works. She had not previously accepted, since youth, the influence of any professional writer. Her early admiration for Henry James and Mark Twain had long since become a reflex. She still remembered Shakespeare of the sonnets, as *Stanzas in Meditation* will show; and she considered Richardson's *Clarissa Harlowe* (along with *The Making of Americans*) to be "the other great novel in English." But for "movements" and their organizers in contemporary poetry she had the greatest disdain—for Pound, Eliot, Yeats, and their volunteer militiamen. She admitted Joyce to be "a good writer," disclaimed any influence on her from his work, and believed, with some evidence, that she had influenced him.

She knew that in the cases of Sherwood Anderson and Ernest Hemingway her influence had gone to them, not theirs to her. I do not know the real cause of her break with Hemingway, only that after a friendship of several years she did not see him any more and declared forever after that he was "yellow." Anderson remained a friend always, though I do not think she ever took him seriously as a writer. The poet Hart Crane she did take seriously. And there were French young men, René Crevel, for one, whom she felt tender about and whom Alice adored. Cocteau amused her as a wit and as a dandy, less so as an organizer of epochs, a role she had come to hold in little respect from having known in prewar times Guillaume Apollinaire, whom she esteemed low as a poet, even lower as a profiteer of cubism. Pierre de Massot she respected as a prose master; but he was too French, too violent, to touch her deeply. Gide and Jouhandeau, making fiction out of sex, she found as banal as any titillater of chambermaids. Max Jacob she had disliked personally from the time of his early friendship with Picasso. I never heard her express any opinion of him as a writer, though Alice says now that she admired him.

In middle life she had come at last to feel about her own work that it "could be compared to the great poetry of the past." And if she was nearly alone during her lifetime in holding this view (along with Alice Toklas, myself, and perhaps a very few more), she was equally alone in having almost no visible poetic parents or progeny. Her writing seemed to come from nowhere and to influence, at that time, none but reporters and novelists. She herself, considering the painter Cézanne her chief master, believed that under his silent tutelage a major message had jumped like an electric arc from painting to poetry. And she also suspected that its high tension was in process of short-circuiting again, from her through me, this time to music. I do not offer this theory as my own, merely as a thought thrown out by Gertrude Stein to justify, perhaps, by one more case the passing of an artistic truth or method. which she felt strongly to have occurred for her, across one of those distances that lie between sight, sound, and words.

There was nevertheless, in Alice Toklas, literary influence from a nonprofessional source. As early as 1910, in a narrative called *Ada,* later published in *Geography and Plays,* a piece which recounts Miss Toklas's early life, Gertrude imitated Alice's way of telling a story. This sentence is typical: "He had a pleasant life while he was living and after he was dead his wife and children remembered him." Condensation in this degree was not Gertrude's way; expansion through repetition (what she called her "garrulity") was more natural to her. But she could always work from an auditory model, later in *Brewsie and Willie* transcribing almost literally the usage and syntax of World War II American soldiers. And having mastered a new manner by imitating Alice Toklas in *Ada,* she next mixed it with her repetitive manner in a story called *Miss Furr and Miss Skeen.* Then she set aside the new narrative style for nearly thirty years.

In 1933 she took it up again for writing *The Autobiography of Alice B. Toklas,* which is the story of her own life told in Miss Toklas's words. This book is in every way except actual authorship Alice Toklas's book; it reflects her mind, her language, her private view of Gertrude, also her unique narrative powers. Every story in it is told as Alice herself had always told it. And when in 1961 Miss Toklas herself wrote *What Is Remembered,* she told her stories with an even greater brevity. There is nothing comparable to this compactness elsewhere in English, nor to my knowledge in any other literature, save possibly in Julius Caesar's *De Bello Gal-*

lico. Gertrude imitated it three times with striking success. She could not use it often, because its way was not hers.

Her own way with narrative was ever elliptical, going into slow orbit around her theme. Alice's memory and interests were visual; she could recall forever the exact costumes people had worn, where they had stood or sat, the décor of a room, the choreography of an occasion. Gertrude's memory was more for the sound of a voice, for accent, grammar, and vocabulary. And even these tended to grow vague in one day, because her sustained curiosity about what had happened lay largely in the possibilities of any incident for revealing character.

How often have I heard her begin some tale, a recent one or a far-away one, and then as she went on with it get first repetitive and then uncertain till Alice would look up over the tapestry frame and say, "I'm sorry, Lovey; it wasn't like that at all." "All right, Pussy," Gertrude would say. "You tell it." Every story that ever came into the house eventually got told in Alice's way, and this was its definitive version. The accounts of life in the country between 1942 and 1945 that make up *Wars I Have Seen* seem to me, on the other hand, Gertrude's own; I find little of Alice in them. Then how are they so vivid? Simply from the fact, or at least so I imagine, that she would write in the evening about what she had seen that day, describe events while their memory was still fresh.

Gertrude's artistic output has the quality, rare in our century, of continuous growth. Picasso had evolved rapidly through one discovery after another until the cubist time was over. At that point, in 1915, he was only thirty-three and with a long life to be got through. He has got through it on sheer professionalism—by inventing tricks and using them up (tricks mostly recalling the history of art or evoking historic Spanish art), by watching the market very carefully (collecting his own pictures), and by keeping himself advised about trends in literary content and current-events content. But his major painting was all done early. Igor Stravinsky followed a similar pattern. After giving to the world between 1909 and 1913 three proofs of colossally expanding power—*The Firebird, Petrouchka,* and *The Rite of Spring*—he found himself at thirty-one unable to expand farther. And since, like Picasso, he was still to go on living, and since he could not imagine living without making music, he too was faced with an unhappy choice. He could either make music out of his own past (which he disdained to do) or out of music's past (which he is still doing). For both men, when expansion ceased, working methods became their subject.

One could follow this design through many careers in music, painting, and poetry. Pound, I think, continued to develop; Eliot, I should say, did not. Arnold Schoenberg was in constant evolution; his chief pupils, Alban Berg and Anton Webern, were more static. The last two were saved by early death from possible decline of inspiration, just as James Joyce's approaching blindness concentrated and extended his high period for twenty years, till he had finished two major works, *Ulysses* and *Finnegans Wake*. He died fulfilled, exhausted, but lucky in the sense that constant growth had not been expected of him. Indeed, for all that the second of these two works is more complex than the first, both in concept and in language, it does not represent a growth in anything but mastery. Joyce was a virtuoso type, like Picasso, of whom Max Jacob, Picasso's friend from earliest youth, had said, "Always he escapes by acrobatics." And virtuosos do not grow; they merely become more skillful. At least they do not grow like vital organisms, but rather, like crystals, reproduce their characteristic forms.

Gertrude Stein's maturation was more like that of Arnold Schoenberg. She ripened steadily, advanced slowly from each stage to the next. She had started late, after college and medical school. From *Three Lives,* begun in 1904 at thirty, through *The Making of Americans,* finished in 1911, her preoccupation is character analysis. From *Tender Buttons* (1912) to *Patriarchal Poetry* (1927) a quite different kind of writing is presented (not, of course, without having been prefigured). This is hermetic to the last degree, progressing within its fifteen-year duration from picture-words and rolling rhetoric to syntactical complexity and neutral words. From 1927 to 1934 two things go on at once. There are long hermetic works (*Four Saints, Lucy Church Amiably,* and *Stanzas in Meditation*) but also straightforward ones like *The Autobiography of Alice B. Toklas* and the lectures on writing. After her return in 1935 from the American lecture tour, hermetic writing gradually withers and the sound of spoken English becomes her theme, giving in *Yes Is for a Very Young Man,* in *The Mother of Us All,* and in *Brewsie and Willie* vernacular portraits of remarkable veracity.

Her development had not been aided or arrested by public success, of which there had in fact been very little. The publication of *Three Lives* in 1909 she had subsidized herself, as she did in 1922 that of the miscellany *Geography and Plays*. *The Making of Americans*, published by McAlmon's Contact Editions in 1925, was her first book-size book to be issued without her paying for it; and she was over fifty. She had her first bookstore success at fifty-nine with the *Autobiography*. When she died in 1946, at seventy-two, she had been working till only a few months before without any diminution of power. Her study of technical problems never ceased; never had she felt obliged to fabricate an inspiration; and she never lost her ability to speak from the heart.

Gertrude lived by the heart, indeed; and domesticity was her theme. Not for her the matings and rematings that went on among the amazons. An early story from 1903, published after her death, *Things as They Are,* told of one such intrigue in post-Radcliffe days. But after 1907 her love life was serene, and it was Alice Toklas who made it so. Indeed, it was this tranquil life that offered to Gertrude a fertile soil of sentiment-security in which other friendships great and small could come to flower, wither away, be watered, cut off, or preserved in a book. Her life was like that of a child, to whom danger can come only from the outside, never from home, and whose sole urgency is growth. It was also that of an adult who demanded all the rights of a man along with the privileges of a woman.

Just as Gertrude kept up friendships among the amazons, though she did not share their lives, she held certain Jews in attachment for their family-like warmth, though she felt no solidarity with Jewry. Tristan Tzara—French-language poet from Romania, Dada pioneer, early surrealist, and battler for the Communist party—she said was "like a cousin." Miss Etta and Dr. Claribel Cone, picture buyers and friends from Baltimore days, she handled almost as if they were her sisters. The sculptors Jo Davidson and Jacques Lipschitz, the painter Man Ray she accepted as though they had a second cousin's right to be part of her life. About men or goyim, even about her oldest man friend, Picasso, she could feel unsure; but a woman or a Jew she could size up quickly. She accepted without cavil, indeed, all the conditionings of her Jewish background. And if, as she would boast, she was "a bad Jew," she at least did not think of herself as Christian. Of heaven and salvation and all that she would say, "When a Jew dies he's dead." We used to talk a great deal, in fact, about our very different religious conditionings, the subject having come up through my remarking the frequency with which my Jewish friends would break with certain of theirs and then never make up. Gertrude's life had contained many people that she still spoke of (Mabel Dodge, for instance) but from whom she refused all communication. The Stettheimers' conversation was also full of references to people they had known well but did not wish to know any more. And I began to imagine this definitiveness about separations as possibly a Jewish trait. I was especially struck by Gertrude's rupture with her brother Leo, with whom she had lived for many years in intellectual and no doubt affectionate communion, but to whom she never spoke again after they had divided their pictures and furniture, taken up separate domiciles.

The explanation I offered for such independent behavior was that the Jewish religion, though it sets aside a day for private Atonement, offers no mechanics for forgiveness save for offenses against one's own patriarch, and even he is not obliged to pardon. When a Christian, on the other hand, knows he has done wrong to anyone, he is obliged in all honesty to attempt restitution; and the person he has wronged must thereupon forgive. So that if Jews seem readier to quarrel than to make up, that fact seems possibly to be the result of their having no confession-and-forgiveness formula, whereas Christians, who experience none of the embarrassment that Jews find in admitting misdeeds, arrange their lives, in consequence, with greater flexibility, though possibly, to a non-Christian view, with less dignity.

Gertrude liked this explanation, and for nearly twenty years it remained our convention. It was not till after her death that Alice said one day,

> You and Gertrude had it settled between you as to why Jews don't make up their quarrels, and I went along with you. But now I've found a better reason for it. Gertrude was right, of course, to believe that "when a Jew dies he's dead." And that's exactly why Jews don't need to make up. When we've had enough of someone we can get rid of him. You Christians can't, because you've got to spend eternity together.

Gertrude and the
Young French Poet

NEITHER GERTRUDE NOR I had ever wished to quarrel. Our way
was to back off when trouble threatened. For after all we
were a sort of team, needing to face the French with a calm front
and not be led on to explode at them, for in that case they could
win by talking faster. Our partnership involved, moreover, business
affairs such as translations, publications, and musical performances.
Also, we liked sharing pleasant feelings, our memories of World
War I, of Harvard, and of the West. We shared friends too, and
that helps to avoid quarreling. She had brought me Carl Van
Vechten, Jo Davidson, Natalie Barney, and the Duchesse de Clermont-Tonnerre, more casually the sculptor Janet Scudder and the
Sitwells, and ever so practically Mrs. Emily Chadbourne Crane. To
her I had brought for inspection Madame Langlois, Mary Butts,
Maurice Grosser, Russell Hitchcock, and Pierre de Massot, all of
whom she accepted, and two more whom she had adopted with all
her heart, the poet Georges Hugnet and the historian Bernard
Faÿ. The painter Pavel Tchelitcheff we held no common front
about, since my friendship with him was only beginning, while
hers was drawing toward its end.

It was in fact over Pavlik, as we called him, that our first un-
pleasantness occurred. Dropping in one evening in October of '27,
I had found Gertrude in a teasing mood; she had that day aborted

a cold and was trying to get her mind off her symptoms. "We were just saying," she began, "that you were like the little girl who had a little curl right in the middle of her forehead." Now my proclivity for being either very very good or quite quite horrid was a trait of character long since known, and the quip was all the more apt since my hairline had begun to imitate Napoleon's forelock. Nor was the personal remark in any way offensive, though I should have been warned by it to mind my manners, since Gertrude, who rarely opened with an attack, was surely looking for trouble.

Trouble came with the arrival, also just calling, of Pavlik and Choura, his sister, a well-mannered young woman unquestionably a lady. As the conversation rose and languished, Pavlik seemed consistently reserved toward me, which was not his way unless something was wrong. Thinking to eradicate misunderstanding, should it lie in the only direction I could imagine, I mentioned an American young woman, a singer, who had asked me to coach her through Satie's *Socrate* and then never returned for her appointment. I mentioned her because a member of his household was her regular accompanist; but at her name Pavlik's long face froze, and I realized that his household suspected me of trying to win away a paying customer. This was not true, but I could not argue the matter; I could only, when Pavlik denied knowledge of the incident, drop the subject.

But Gertrude would not let it be dropped. She began to ask irrelevantly and repetitively, "Where did you meet her? How did you come to know her?" Pestered, confused, embarrassed by the whole scene, and feeling set upon, I blurted out, "Through her having slept with one of my friends."

In the silence that followed, Alice observed gently, "One doesn't say that." Whereupon I murmured regret and was allowed to remain quiet. Pavlik and Choura stayed just long enough to make with our hostesses several remarks on several subjects. As they took leave, Choura wished me good-night graciously; but Pavlik, to make clear I had offended, said icily, unsmiling, and without handshake, "*Bon soir, monsieur.*"

As soon as they were gone, both ladies wanted to know details. I furnished them; and they furnished, in return, facts about the financial situation at Pavlik's house which could have made my seeming intrusion, no matter how purely musical, a cause for alarm.

We also noted the impropriety of my using before his sister so crude a verb as *coucher avec*. And Gertrude remarked that though I had a perfect right to quarrel with Pavlik, I should not have used her house for doing so.

I was in Coventry for exactly a week. Then I sent her yellow roses, for which she had a liking, with a note that read: "Dear Gertrude/love/Virgil." She replied, "My dear Virgil, thanks for the very beautiful flowers, we may look upon them as a pleasure and a necessity." And that same day, when I met the two ladies on the rue des Saints-Pères, and Gertrude said something about seeing me sometime, Alice added specifically, "Come soon," and nodded as if in complicity.

But though my quarrel was over, Pavlik's had just begun, for from that time he came gradually to be removed from Gertrude's circle. Bravig Imbs thought Alice responsible for the severance, that she had already become unfriendly somewhat earlier, on his having painted a portrait of her that she found disobliging, and that she had been biding her time till Gertrude, becoming one day impatient with him, could be maneuvered into a break. Others—Georges Maratier, for instance—believed that Alice, as an *éminence grise,* was prone to hasten the excommunication of those she had no taste for (or whose wives bored her). Myself, I never saw her act toward anyone with open malice, but she did not conceal her satisfaction at Tchelitcheff's being no longer received. Gertrude at the same time let me know by inference that she found it intolerable of Pavlik to have first suspected me of an intrigue against him and then to have initiated one against me by asking her, in effect, to choose between us. And though she did not exactly offer me his head, it came off in the spring of '28.

Bravig Imbs was to lose his three years later. He had been devoted for half a decade, serviceable as an extra young man, good at errands, and pleasing in the home. In the summer of '28, visiting in Latvia, he had made off with his young host's fiancée and wired Gertrude, as his mentor, for permission to marry her. And Gertrude had wired back, says Alice, "Bravig, you can't do that." He did, however; and Valeska turned out to be a Russo-Baltic countess in her own right, economical, a good cook, and far from ugly. When she became pregnant early in '31, Bravig had to arrange carefully for the coming months, as he had for source of income only his job at an advertising agency. And it was natural for him, as a close friend, to announce his plans to Gertrude. His downfall came from doing this in front of Valeska.

The plan was for his wife to move in early summer to a country boardinghouse some twenty kilometers from Belley, where Bravig had often spent vacations himself, and for him to join her there for two weeks in late summer, just before the baby was to be born. He did not know that Gertrude, who had in medical school walked out on obstetrics, had an intense distaste for the procedures of childbirth. With the prospect of having a pregnant woman on her hands all summer, for she could not forego some obligation to Bravig, she went all nervous about it but could not say no in front of Valeska. It was Alice who resolved the emergency next day by announcing to Bravig that the friendship was terminated. Their newly installed telephone was the instrument of this one-way communication as she told him at his office, "Gertrude asks me to say that she considers you to have been of a colossal impertinence and that she does not wish to see either of you again." And she did not see Valeska again, as Bravig removed his family to New York in the middle thirties. When he came back with the armies of liberation in 1944, Gertrude's arms and house were open to him, though unfortunately not for long. He became briefly, as "Monsieur Bobby," France's most beloved radio news-announcer. Then he felt that a successful man should learn to drive. Going South in a jeep, he skidded on a rainy curve and died against a tree. My concierge wept as she told me the tragic story. Gertrude, when she heard it, went immediately to his place of residence, which was Francis Rose's flat on the Ile Saint-Louis, taking with her a hardware man and having the locks changed, to discourage theft not only of Bravig's property but also of Sir Francis's.

Georges Hugnet's quarrel with Gertrude came in the fall of 1930 over a matter of publication. His own Editions de la Montagne had already put out two books by her—*Dix Portraits*, in English and French, and *Morceaux Choisis de "La Fabrication des Americains,"* in French, with a preface by Pierre de Massot and a portrait by Bérard. She had written me to America the year before, "The french I think are going to like me in translation all thanks to you." For indeed the whole matter of translating her had been initiated through me and mostly done by me, first with Madame Langlois and then with Hugnet. Selections from *The Making of*

Americans had been begun by Hugnet with me and finished with Gertrude. They also translated together *Composition as Explanation*. Several years later there was published a longer French edition of *The Making*, translated by Bernard Faÿ and the Baronne Sellière; and Gertrude's autobiographical works, her lectures, and her early stories have been rendered into many languages. I do not know of the more hermetic works appearing in translation anywhere, except for those made with my help into French.

Though she read and spoke French comfortably, Gertrude did not aspire to write in it, beyond the necessities of social correspondence. And she had never used her literary powers for translating works that she admired. For Georges Hugnet, however, who had possibilities, after *La Perle*, for making another film, she wrote a scenario in French that tells how she acquired a poodle. The title of this, *Deux Soeurs qui sont pas soeurs*, contains a grammatical error of which she was perfectly aware but which she declined to correct, as I remember, when her text was published in *La Revue européene*, though it did get changed for *Operas and Plays*. Her other concession to French was to make, in the summer of 1930, a rendering into Stein English of Hugnet's suite of poems entitled *Enfances*. This work was the cause of a quarrel with Hugnet, Alice intervening firmly lest it end. Also of one with me. And since the young Frenchman's poetry had set off Gertrude Stein's in a new direction, it is no wonder that she went all emotional about him.

Hugnet wrote me on learning of the translation, "Really I have friends too strong for me." When Gertrude sent it to him, he had replied from Brittany that it was "more than a translation." To me she wrote of it as her "version" or her "thing," again as "a mirroring of it rather than anything else[,] a reflection of each little poem. . . . I would read each poem and then immediately make its reflection." And as she went on with the paraphrase, she too was overwhelmed by it, needed praise of it from others, which Bernard Faÿ furnished her, along with praise for Hugnet's work.

She wrote:

> My very dear George[s]
> *La traduction qui est plutôt reflet, c'est un vrai reflet et de moment à l'autre je suis là-dedans tellement contente de vous et de moi, et quelque fois j'ai un peu peur mais quand même je*

*suis contente de vous et de moi. C'etait pour moi une experience
riche et intriguante et les resultat[s] enfin il y a un resultat et
nous sommes je suis sûr vraiment pas mecontente de vous et de
moi. Mon cher George[s] toute mon amitié et mon confiance
et plaisir en vous est toute là-dedans.*

(The translation is more like a reflection, a true reflection
and from each moment to the next I am so pleased with you
and with me, and sometimes I am a little afraid but all the
same I am pleased with you and with myself. It was for me
a rich and fascinating experience and the results after all there
is a result and we are I am sure truly not displeased with you
and with me. My dear George all my friendship and my confidence and pleasure in you are all in it.)

Her excitement came from having opened up a new vein of
poetry. For in her need to catch an English lilt comparable to that
of Hugnet's in French, she had caught the cool temperature and
running-water sound of her beloved Shakespeare Sonnets, even to
the presence of pentameters, rhymes, and iambs. As a testimonial of
involvement with another poet, another language, these versions are
unique in Gertrude Stein's work. Three samples will suffice, the first
not far from literal.

I

*Enfances, aux cent coins de ma mémoire
si ma mémoire est l'oeuvre de la passion,
enfances décimées par les nuits
si les nuits ne sont qu'une maladie du sommeil,
je vous poursuis avant de dormir, sans hâte.*

*Sans hâte, mais plié sous des tâches ingrates,
tête nue et transpirant de fièvre,
je vous mesure au trajet de la vie
et vos insoumissions, enfances, sont muettes,
enfances si l'enfance est ce silence
où gravement déjà s'installe la mort
et si ma main n'a pas retrouvé sa solitude,
et c'est avouer que je vous laisse libres
hors de mon destin que d'autres voulurent court,
à vos robes d'indienne, à vos plaisirs sanguins.*

1

In the one hundred small places of myself my youth,
And myself in if it is the use of passion,
In this in it and in the nights alone
If in the next to night which is indeed not well
I follow you without it having slept and went.
Without the pressure of a place with which to come unfolded
    folds are a pressure and an abusive stain
A head if uncovered can be as hot, as heated,
to please to take a distance to make life,
and if resisting, little, they have no thought,
a little one which was a little which was as all as still,
Or with or without fear or with it all,
And if in feeling all it will be placed alone beside
and it is with with which and not beside not beside may,
Outside with much which is without with me, and not an Indian
    shawl, which could it be but with my blood.

By poem 14 the versions are farther apart.

14

Que me disent amour et ses tourelles?
J'ai perdu la plus belle en ouvrant la main,
en changeant de pas j'ai trompé la silencieuse,
rira l'éternelle en tuant la plus belle,
la morte a su garder son domaine,
en refermant les bras j'ai tué l'éternelle,
l'enfance a renié, renié la souveraine
et c'est ainsi que vont les semaines.

14

It could be seen very nicely
That doves have each a heart.
Each one is always seeing that they could not be apart,
A little lake makes fountains
And fountains have no flow,
And a dove has need of flying
And water can be low,

Let me go.
Any week is what they seek
When they have to halve a beak.
I like a painting on a wall of doves
And what they do.
They have hearts
They are apart
Little doves are winsome
But not when they are little and left.

As the finale approaches they get together again.

26

Embarquons, partons aux Indes,
vanille, vanille,
toutes les nourritures se valent.
Marie, trio de neige,
Eugénie, Irène, l'ordre
a changé son courant d'amour,
l'ordre des mots dans ta bouche,
enfance réveillée par mes désordres.
Sous la pluie sérieuse
quand tournait le vent,
quand remontait le vent
du phare au rocher de la Jument,
en cachant ta tête
tu prenais ce vent
pour ma pensée et sans mal
tu tendais ton bras
vers la croisée où mon absence
a mis le silence au rang de la lumière,
ton absence dans ma solitude,
ce don que la lumière avait fait à ma mémoire.

26

Little by little two go if two go three go if three go four go if
four go they go. It is known as does he go he goes if they go they
go and they know they know best and most of whether he will
go. He is to go. They will not have vanilla and say so. To go Jenny

go, Ivy go Gaby go any come and go is go and come and go and leave to go. Who has to hold it while they go who has to who has had it held and have them come to go. He went and came and had to go. No one has had to say he had to go come here to go go there to go go go to come to come to go to go and come and go.

Stanzas in Meditation, begun at this time, take off from the poems written on *Enfances,* preserving their Shakespearian lilt along with Hugnet's suite-of-poems form and his frankness of introspection. Its last number, completed in 1935, reads:

Stanza LXXXIII
Why am I if I am uncertain reasons may inclose.
Remain remain propose repose chose.
I call carelessly that the door is open
Which if they can refuse to open
No one can rush to close.
Let them be mine therefor.
Everybody knows that I chose.
Therefor if therefor before I close.
I will therefor offer therefor I offer this.
Which if I refuse to miss can be miss is mine.
I will be well welcome when I come.
Because I am coming.
Certainly I come having come.

These stanzas are done.

The "two *Enfances,*" as Gertrude had begun to call them, were submitted to *Pagany,* which accepted them for publication on facing pages. Hugnet also arranged for their Paris issue as a book to be illustrated by Picasso, Tchelitcheff, Marcoussis, and Kristians Tonny. This was in the fall of 1930. Now let me go back to the spring.

Gertrude had stayed in Paris till the end of April, signed the sheets with Hugnet and myself for the special-paper edition of *Ten Portraits,* then gone off to Bilignin, already late for garden planting. She had also published that spring, at her own expense, her novel *Lucy Church Amiably,* a neo-Romantic landscape piece. In the country she made her English version of *Enfances,* spent much of the summer having company—Bernard Faÿ, the Picassos, Carl Van Vechten.

I spent June and July in Majorca, wrote there the last three movements of my Violin Sonata, the *Phèdre* aria, and a piece in five short movements which I called Sonata No. 3, "for Gertrude Stein to improvise at the pianoforte." She enjoyed the piano she had found in the house at Bilignin, used for her improvising only the white keys. My Sonata was therefore composed for only those.

In late August I spent ten days at Bilignin, and it was near there (waiting in Aix-les-Bains while the ladies did an errand) that I set Gertrude's French film scenario to music, adding to its narrative vocal line a pianoforte accompaniment that is a portrait of the dog Basket (her first of the name), a character in the film. In September I returned briefly to Villefranche, wrote more music, then paid a visit to Madame Langlois in the Basque country, returning to Paris in late September.

All this moving around cost little, as I traveled third-class and either visited friends or stayed in modest lodgings. Also my allowance, which had been announced to end in May, was being inexplicably extended for a few more months. Gertrude, sympathetic as always about my money troubles, wrote,

> Emily C[hadbourne] has opened communications again, via Ellen [Lamotte] I said back that I was peeved and thought she had been millionairish the message will probably not be transmitted so there we are, I am happy that supplies have recommenced, I was that sad about it that it was disturbing, I was about to suffer as much as you although as the small boy remarked to an admonishing father not in the same place.

She spent a large part of that fall on my affairs, plotting by mail with Carl Van Vechten about how to attract for our *Four Saints* the attention of Mary Garden and definitely arranging with Hugnet, who came to Bilignin in September, a project for publishing a volume of my music.

His Editions de la Montagne, which were breaking even, had already got into print a half-dozen works of rare prose and modernistic poetry. A musical volume, though more costly to issue, might well recuperate its costs if capital could be found for guaranteeing them. This Gertrude offered to advance in part, and Georges Hugnet's father accepted to furnish 5,000 francs ($200). Gertrude's offer, even more generous, was to provide the remaining needed sums for a project which might run, all told, as high as $800. The book was to be printed by inexpensive methods on very good paper and with illustrations by advanced artists, just as Georges's other books had been issued. And it was to contain vocal works only, since these were the field of my budding reputation and also since the distribution of vocal music could be more easily envisaged under the imprint of a literary publisher than could that of an instrumental volume.

Four Saints in Three Acts was thought of for inclusion but rejected on account of its length. And Carl Van Vechten was proposed for writing a preface, since he enjoyed credit in America as a critic of music. But when he wrote from New York that he might find a publisher there for the opera, we decided to use him for prefacing that, should publication occur, and to combine a selection of other poetico-vocal works with an essay by myself on words and music. A further decision had to be made about including English texts, and the final advisability seemed to be that one language only, French, would be more suitable for selling the book in Paris.

The first plan—a hundred pages that would include *Capital Capitals* (Stein), *La Valse grégorienne* (Hugnet), *Five Phrases from the Song of Solomon,* and the Boussuet *Funeral Oration*—proved cumbersome in every way. So I wrote to Gertrude that

I had imagined Trois Tableaux de Paris: *La Seine* (Duchesse de Rohan), *Le Berceau de Gertrude Stein* (Hugnet), and *Film* (Stein). But Georges objects to appearing between two ladies and really feels very deeply [opposed] anyway on subject of [the] D[u]chesse de Rohan. And he prefers Racine but that makes a funny mixture and so we settled for the present on four pieces: Fable de La Fontaine (*Le Singe et le léopard*), *Phèdre* of Racine, *Valse grégorienne* of Georges, and Film (Stein).

Gertrude replied to this,

I am being quite thoughtful you see I want this book to do for you something like *Geography and Plays* did for me, make something definite and representative . . . and now this is a feasible idea . . . *Capitals,* Bossuet, and *Gregorian Waltzes* of Georges, that is all on the same more or less idea, and represents three distinct periods and would be saleable, and would show you at your heights, think this over very carefully you see I want you shown at your best and want you saleable to those who are your natural audience, and so far this is the only combination that seems to me to have raison d'être, I don't mind being with two gentlemen, it may of course be too long, that is another matter anyway think about it . . . lots of love my dear, yours, Gtrde.

She kept holding out for *Capital Capitals,* not wishing to be represented by only a French text. But Georges kept insisting that we should not use any English. So that by the time Gertrude came back to Paris in late November I was not certain, in spite of all her sweet-seeming reasonableness, that she would go through with the project.

Georges, moreover, was being difficult. He had had too much success that year. His Editions de la Montagne were gloriously distinguished; in the spring he had won a prize of 20,000 francs ($800) for a short story; he had been put into English by Gertrude Stein and was to be published beside her in both America and France; now he was about to appear with both her and me in a musical volume subsidized largely by her; and besides all that, he had just entered into housekeeping arrangements with a young woman who made him feel continuously successful and happy. Perhaps it was for showing off to her that he began pushing us around. Anyway, before Gertrude was to have her big quarrel with him, I had a small one.

This had to do with a book by Pierre de Massot, *Prolégomènes á une éthique sans métaphysique ou Billy, bull-dog et philosophe.* I had usually subscribed to Georges's publications, and occasionally he had given me an extra copy, copiously inscribed. In the case of Massot—a writer of fine classical reflexes and a friend from earlier days who had fallen into bad times and worse health—I had brought him back into circulation and had even got out of him a much-appreciated preface to *The Making of Americans.* When I did not subscribe for his book, Georges knew I expected one; and when he did not offer one, I angrily demanded one and got it. On December 6 I wrote Gertrude, "I'm afraid I have a *cœur sensible* after all. I thought I had won the little incident with Georges about Pierre's book and was proud of myself but I came home and went to bed of a grippe and so I guess I didn't after all."

Gertrude wrote back,

Sorry about the grippe but look here I am not awfully anxious to mix in but you must not be too schoolgirlish about Georges and also after all he is putting down his 5,000 francs of his father's credit for your book and hell it is a gamble and he could do things with it that would be surer and after all he is doing it and after all nobody else is, its alright but nobody else is so remember the Maine and even if there is a minority report you must not overlook this thing, and besides why the hell should not Pierre give you the book as well as Georges but anyway that is another matter, this is only to cure the grippe, anyway I love you all very much but I always do a little fail to see that anyone is such a lot nobler than anyone else we are all reasonably noble and very sweet love to you . . . Gtrde.

In a very few days, however, she was thoroughly upset herself. The arrangements for publishing in book form the two *Enfances* had been left to Georges, so that Gertrude did not see the subscription blank till it was printed. It read:

GEORGES HUGNET

ENFANCES

SUIVI PAR LA TRADUCTION DE

GERTRUDE STEIN

And in another place it referred to "*Enfances,* by Georges Hugnet."

Gertrude viewed this layout as disloyal, with her name in smaller type than his; and neither did she like the word "translation." As she pointed out by letter, he had said himself it was "not really a translation but something more." Furthermore, their joint work, she felt, should be presented as a collaboration. Georges, on the other hand, worried lest subscribers mistake his poem for a translation by him of an original work by her, held ferociously to the word "translation" and to a superior type face for his name, quoting precedents from the French Authors' League and mobilizing for indignation against the "greedy" American many writers and painters who already harbored ill will toward her. So that very quickly sides began to be taken.

Pushed into a defensive position, Gertrude refused to defend herself in words, simply withheld her text from the publisher, Jeanne Bucher. Then at Madame Bucher's art gallery she met Georges; and since they were in a public place, where quarreling is rude to no host, she ceremoniously refused his proffered hand.

From this moment the break was formal. As Gertrude informed me by letter, "The last act of the drama was played this aft. you have been very sweet about not saying I told you don't imagine I don't appreciate it." She also wired *Pagany*, hoping to forestall their face-to-face publication of *Enfances*. The time was too late for that, though not for changing a title. So she sent hers as "Poem Pritten on Pfances of Georges Hugnet," and in reply to Boston's telegraphic query Paris confirmed this spelling of the message.

Georges, regretting the break, besought me to arrange the matter in any way I could, in order to save the book's publication and to save everybody's face too. Gertrude, being informed of his wish, replied that a solution could no doubt be arrived at and requested that I "act as [her] agent." She considered as fair any layout in which the two names were of equal size and no reference was made to "translation." I actually worked out such a title page, first showing it to her, then negotiating step by step with Georges till he agreed. The authors' names were to be printed at top and bottom (his at top), with the title centered and equidistant from both.

Alice had in the meantime sent me a *pneumatique* asking that I phone her without delay; and when I did so, she specified that whatever proposal was arrived at, it must be "distinctly understood that it comes from Georges." I replied that I would do what I could about that, but could guarantee nothing. Getting Georges's agreement to a layout that I knew to be satisfactory to Gertrude and then persuading him in front of his own Muse (a stubborn Alsatian) that he must not only accept it but submit it as his own, all this was more than anybody's agent could expect to accomplish. So when Georges wrote on the model of the page, "I accept," I was aware, warned by Alice's message, that Gertrude might still refuse it.

It was Alice Toklas who stated the refusal, as she had previously stated the conditions for acceptance. The scene was the big studio drawing room of 27 rue de Fleurus, the time Christmas Eve. I had been asked for dinner, along with Maurice Grosser, toward whom Gertrude had been feeling especially warm, in gratitude for the scenario he had devised for *Four Saints*. ("Maurice understands my work," she would say.) And I knew there would be gifts. So I had prepared one too, a picture for the country house, not an expensive gift but amusing, a Victorian lithograph (in a white frame of the period) representing two ladies in a swing. I was depressed in advance about the evening and exasperated toward the end of one of those dark, wet, winter days; also, on my way to the house, I had dropped the wrapped picture, breaking its glass.

But our hostesses were cheerful; a crèche with small statues from Provence had been set up beside the fireplace; in the tiny dining room, which with its octagonal Florentine table and equally massive Florentine chairs could seat just four, there was venison for dinner; and afterwards, back in the studio, there were neckties and silk scarves from Charvet. When all the ceremonies had been accomplished and well-being established (for nobody had a power like Gertrude's for radiating repose), I brought out the paper. Gertrude looked at it, did not bridle or seem to be suspicious. She merely said in a wholly relaxed manner, like a businessman signing a contract already negotiated, "This seems to be all right." Then she passed it to Alice, saying, "What do you think, Pussy?" And Alice, after seeing the two words written on it, said, "It isn't what was asked for."

I have no further memory of the evening. I know that we all got through it by talking of many things and that we spoke no more of Georges or of *Enfances* and that we wished one another "Merry Christmas" at midnight. Then I went home and by morning had my usual frustration-grippe.

My pocket calendar of 1930 indicates an engagement with Gertrude on the twenty-seventh, and a note from her mailed the day before asks that I bring with me three manuscripts she had lent me. I do not know whether I went or whether, being ill, I sent her the typescripts (one of which was *Enfances*). I do remember that sometime around the New Year Madame Langlois became ill and that though surrounded, as always, by stars of the Medical Faculty, she received attentions from me also, including the regular making and taking to her of strong vegetable broth, a product her hotel could not provide. I was also practicing for a concert in which I was to play my own music. So it must have been two weeks before I made any attempt to continue my visits with Gertrude and Alice. Then one evening, when I rang the bell, Gertrude herself came to the door and said, "Did you want something?" I replied, "Merely to report on my absence," and she replied, "We're very busy now." But I still owed her an announcement of the concert, since certain works with texts by her were on the program. So I sent it with a note saying that both Marthe-Marthine and I hoped she might care to come. Her reply was a largish calling card in matching envelope with, under the engraved name *Miss Stein,* a handwritten "declines further acquaintance with Mr. Thomson."

If she expected flowers, as after my former moment of offensiveness, she did not receive them, for I was aware of no wrongdoing, unless my failure to discipline Georges for her advantage might be so viewed. In any case, I took her at her word. Two years later, with an American production of *Four Saints* being contracted for, her literary agent, William Aspenwall Bradley, transmitted her suggestion that I write directly regarding certain details. I did so, and she replied at great length warmly. We continued to correspond, on matters regarding our joint enterprises and with increasing warmth. When she came to lecture in America in the fall of 1934, freshly famous for her *Autobiography of Alice B. Toklas,* which had been published the preceding year, and also for *Four Saints,* which had been produced on Broadway just that spring, we embraced at Carl Van Vechten's party for her. There was no point in keeping up in New York a quarrel so purely Parisian and one which for both of us had long since lost its savor. We did not attempt to excuse or to explain; we simply did not mention it.

Gertrude has told this story her way in a narrative called *Left to Right,* written not long after the events and published three years later in *Story,* November 1933. This version does not vary from mine, except that it reveals a certain suspicion on her part that I might have been trying to work for Georges's benefit. She does not mention having asked me to negotiate a settlement "as [her] agent." She might have forgotten that already. And she might have meant by "agent" a personal representative charged with no interests but hers. I am more inclined to think of her as terrified by

Georges's rapid mobilization of the French intellectuals and as feeling herself not at all adequate to fighting a war with them and that my failure to fight it for her was a disappointment that she could not bear.

In December of 1963 I read my present account to Alice Toklas, who found no error in it. She said that Gertrude had believed Bravig Imbs to have influenced me in my discussions with Georges, an idea wholly without foundation. And to my question as to how she had come to interfere after Gertrude and Georges were finally in agreement, she answered, "I was only trying to protect Gertrude." Could Gertrude's affection for Georges, almost schoolgirlish in her letters, have seemed to Alice an intensity warranting protection? She added that the friendship with Hugnet was "never a permanent attachment—a youthful thing." On the other hand, she assured me that in my case Gertrude had been "very disturbed by the separation" and "deeply relieved by the reconciliation." I see no reason to doubt her on any of these matters.

Neighborhoods and Portraits

On my arrival in 1921 I had become a Parisian instantaneously, and by 1931 the patina was ingrained. Kansas City, Cambridge, New York were still my core, my structure; but Paris was where I felt most at home. Remembering what it looked like then and earlier, I find little alteration in its forms. Paris does not change much anyway. Its skyline evolves but slowly, over centuries; and only surface varies with the time. Its color, for instance, after World War I, was a thousand shades of gray from bone to violet. Then gradually, between the wars, repaintings turned its weathered stone to cream. By the end of World War II the whole was blanched. Today, all freshly scrubbed with soap and water, the city has become a golden blond running in shades from pumpkin to camembert. But she will turn gray again, no doubt about it, for that is the way with Paris building stone.

In the Paris of 1921, the inside of hotels and restaurants was a riot of huge flattened flowers and jumpy stripes inspired by the painting of Henri Matisse. By 1925 the major source was cubist painting; and the colorings had turned quite pale. In the thirties one was to see all-white rooms in private houses, but for redecorating a public place there was no choice save between the strictly modern as we know it—a composition of oblongs—and the convention known in France as "*style auberge*" (called in America

"French provincial"), all chintzes and checks with copper warming pans and wooden chandeliers. These were what any decorator had to sell, all that any customer could buy.

The intellectual center for Americans and the English had remained since World War I Montparnasse. And if its sidewalk cafés by 1930 seemed less crowded, that was simply because there were more of them, the original Café du Dôme and La Rotonde having bred bars, nightclubs, and restaurants of every variety. There were the all-Dutch "Falstaff," the Swedish "Stryx," the Anglo-American "Dingo" and "Select," the diversified but Germanically vast "Coupole." During the late thirties a move took place toward Saint-Germain-des-Prés, where "Les Deux Magots" and Lipp's had long been frequented by French authors and their left-bank publishers.

The Café de Flore, just opposite Lipp's, was a dreary place till bought by a progressive management and done over to look less nineteenth-century. Offering toast, ham and eggs, and surprisingly good coffee, it came to be frequented by many of the better-off late risers. And as the war approached one saw there of an evening the painters Picasso and Derain, the sculptors Zadkine and Giacometti, the surrealist general staff (headed by poets Breton and Eluard), the loyal-to-Stalin ex-surrealists Tristan Tzara and Louis Aragon, the royalist historians Bernard Faÿ and Pierre Gaxotte, and a dozen dealers in contemporary art, such as Pierre Colle from the faubourg Saint-Honoré and Pierre Loeb of the nearby rue de Seine. Sylvia Beach's bookstore in the 1930s, though still a daytime rendezvous of writers, was less glamorous than before, with Hemingway and Antheil gone, Joyce rarely about.

Montmartre, briefly a painting center before World War I, had from Louis-Philippe times been the neighborhood of musicians. Milhaud and Honegger, Nadia Boulanger, and many another established one lived on its middle and lower slopes. Its top, the former home of Gustave Charpentier and the locale of his *Louise,* was occupied largely by restaurants and by a semiunemployed bohemia that called itself a Free Commune and elected every year a Communist "mayor." Lower down there were night clubs—the impeccable Zelli's and Brick Top's, the fashionable "Grand Ecart" (a branch of Le Bœuf sur le Toit) all black and crystal, and the Bal Tabarin, where a cancan still ended the floor show. It was to this lower Montmartre that even left-bankers went for a night on the town or for observing French low life in the Place Pigalle and Place Blanche, where pimps and *souteneurs* as stylized as anything out of Jean Genet played cards in cafés while their girls worked the sidewalks. Also, in the boulevards de Clichy and Batignolles ambulant street fairs with rides and rifle ranges seemed to linger on all fall, moving along just a few blocks every week or so, but always turning back when they got to the Plaine Monceau, a rich, gloomy quarter inhabited by vocal teachers and successful singers.

Henri Sauguet had moved in 1929 to the northwestern Batignolles district, where he lived in a small hotel, the Nollet, named after its street. Max Jacob lived there too, and the Italian composer Vittorio Rieti, as did also a laughing young scoutmaster named Gaétan Fouquet, who was to become a professional traveler (he once hitchhiked to India). Also came to live there the violinist Yvonne de Casa Fuerte, and all these made a companionable house full of working and of laughter. Sauguet, a lean and liverish *bordelais* with damp hands, had already composed ballets and chamber music lovely for lyrical spontaneity. And he had begun work on *La Chartreuse de Parme,* which was to occupy him for the next ten years, being produced at last in 1939 by the Paris Opéra. I had felt happy with his music always, and he with mine. And the same people who would find mine light-minded usually mistook his for insufficiently learned. It was not so, however, though wonderfully fresh and pure in heart.

Léon Kochnitzky, who sought from all modern art that which could remind him most intensely of past masters, would reproach me for my devotion to Sauguet and my intolerance toward fabricated masterpieces (toward *"le style chef-d'œuvre"* of Honegger, for example), assuring me that I was inveterately a follower of "false values." I, on the contrary, judged all those who mistook for high quality a mere resemblance to the past to be not gourmets of music but rather its addicts, conditioned to blind pursuit and to repeating patterns. Sauguet and I shared faith in "the emotions you really have" and in their authentic transcript, however thin. And I must say that I still find his music (sometimes frugal, sometimes overflowing) ever a clear source, just as I have ever found his friendship frank, loyal, and without guile.

Max Jacob was another whom Kochnitzky considered a "false

value." Eric de Haulleville, following Kochnitzky's malice, would even declare him false clean through—as a poet and as a painter, as a Catholic and as a Jew, as a Frenchman, as a Breton, as a friend. And certainly Max could be hard to take, for meanness and perfidy were as strong in him as generosity of spirit. But even his malice was mercurial. With a volubility uncontrollable he would pour out praise and sarcasm, insults, jokes, apologies, tirades, and rigamaroles at once rhythmical, compassionate, penetrating, poetic, and funny. His verbal virtuosities were not planned nor his harshest words ever less than instantaneously come by. Moreover, he could prophesy, tell fortunes, speak as an oracle. Regarding proletarian demands he announced that there would be no real trouble from the Left in France before 1980, since all that the workers wanted now was the right to live like bourgeois (or as he put it, *"le port ultérieur de la redingote"*). Of Maurice Grosser he said success as a painter would come surely but very late. I was destined, he predicted, to glory, to appearing on great stages, and to friendships with royalty. "But not," he added, "until after forty."

Though his volume of stories in epistolary form called *Le Cabinet Noir* remains a devastating prose picture of French family life, Max was primarily a poet and to my ear a fine one. He made his living during all the time I knew him by painting in gouache and drawing in ink, the results being bought largely by friends and curiosity collectors. His gouaches of French monuments and historic interiors, according to Grosser, were drawn from postcards by ruled enlargement, a method that seemed to make their forms a little flat. Their color, however, had vivacity and depth, a good deal of spit and cigarette ash getting added as the picture progressed. Max's ink drawings were vibrant as to line and invariably religious in theme.

A middle-class youth from Quimper, Max had in Paris sought out intense experiences—through poverty (real), through poetry, and through drugs. At thirty-three there came to him the most intense of all, a vision of Jesus Christ. Overwhelmed, he ran to a parish priest and asked to be baptized, but was refused. When five years later the vision recurred, he knew what to do. This time he consulted the Fathers of Zion, whose specific assignment is to convert the Jews. His godfather at baptism was Picasso. Then for thirty years he wrestled with sin and the devil, as well as with his poetry and painting. "When the sins of the flesh grow fewer," he would say, "those of the spirit increase." In his middle fifties he would pass summers near the monastery at Saint-Benoît-sur-Loire, and after 1936 he lived there always. During the Occupation the monks gave him partial sanctuary under a false name. But toward the end, the Germans, always looking for Jews to persecute, learned of his presence in the town and arrested him. Left outdoors for two days in freezing weather at the railway station of Orléans, he caught pneumonia there and died at the prison of Drancy, his martyrdom preceding by only a short time the Germans' exodus. Today, though twenty years have passed, there is no French edition of all his prose and poetry; nor has any of it at all, so far as I know, appeared in English.

Sauguet and Cliquet-Pleyel set Max to music often. My *Stabat Mater,* to his text, has been performed for over thirty years. On the flyleaf of a gift, *Bourgeois de France et d'ailleurs,* he wrote in 1932 (I translate), "to Virgil Thomson, brilliant and courageous spirit, delightful in friendship, terrible in combat, learned musician and grand innovator, tree of which the root is genius itself, his admirer and his friend Max Jacob."

Was he pulling my leg? Perhaps. Was he caught up in a rodomontade that he could not stop? Everything was possible with Max, including sincerity. Or was he asking pardon for an earlier moment when at my Salle Chopin concert our *Stabat Mater* had been shiningly delivered and where, ever the buffoon, he had remarked, though not to me, that obviously the music was negligible but that his poem, *n'est-ce pas,* was a masterpiece.

I used to tease Roy Harris for writing "masterpieces." Roy had come abroad in 1926, already twenty-eight years old and needing to acquire a technique of composition that could sustain the pouring out that was his urgency. Farmer from Oklahoma and California, he spoke with dry humor and a bonhomie not unlike those of the comedian Will Rogers, then popular as a cowboy commentator. His Western ways were winning; and his musical vocation, only lately clear to him, was serious. He had come to France for help in building mastery, and in order to avoid wasting time had gone to live outside of Paris. After one winter spent on the banks of the Seine at Chatou, he found that neither the dampness nor his wife, a worried reader of intellectual magazines, was good for his work. So he renounced them both and went to live alone on higher ground, near Gargenville, where his teacher, Nadia Boulanger, lived much of the year. There, surrounded by year-round gardening, by wheat fields and ripening fruits, he wrote many of the early chamber works that are still his glory. And my teasing him about his hope of creating masterpieces by remembering the past may well have been unjust, since that was exactly what Brahms had essayed, and also since Roy's own singing line possessed a breadth related to that of the Romantic masters.

Boulanger was impressed by Roy's expressive powers and pleased by his masculine personality. He taught her to drive a car; and she plotted to get him another wife, this time a musician who could help him with his harmony and whose family had some wealth. Roy almost went through with the arrangement and actually did, I think, allow the family to pay for his divorce. But eventually he balked at being "taken over," as he put it, and found for himself a young woman less demanding about marriage but equally amenable to copying music. And so his quiet life of composing and of learning to compose and of being a future great man (for Roy always carried about with him a bit of that) went on for a few more years; and he would come to Paris every week; and almost always we saw each other; and always, just as it had been with Copland and with Sauguet, we showed each other with confidence all our music.

Then one day Roy fell down a staircase and broke his coccyx, which would not heal. And women came from far and close to be with him—his mother and his sister from California, his ex-wife from New York, his copyist-companion from the village. Maurice Grosser said that unlike Saint Teresa, who in my opera was described as "seated and not surrounded," Roy was "surrounded but not seated." Eventually the Guggenheim Foundation and Alma Wertheim, clubbing together, shipped him in plaster to New York, where an operation cleared up the injury.

A letter from the *Mauretania*, mailed in Plymouth, was as breezy as Oklahoma itself. "O thou great Bard of sunny climes and all that," was his address.

I want to thank you for your last and latest farewell in pure post-Satie vernacular and say that altho all present indications deny that I shall ever walk up your damnably long stairs and eat your good Digestives and drink your good Italian Vermouth and refresh my masterpiece psychology (with its Russian mood flavor) in the gentle breezes of your Dadaistic wise-cracks (some damned wise and some somewhat abortive) that altho all present indications deny the above I'm not done writing masterpieces and you've not told me about it for the last time.

Marcel Duchamp's painting career had come to an end through his creation of a real masterpiece, a picture even today little known in Europe but famous in America since 1913. *Nude Descending a Staircase* had certainly not been planned to remind art lovers of earlier painting, though neither had its perfection been arrived at without study. It is simply that the artist, at twenty-five, was shocked to the depths of his own idealism on learning how successful he had become. By 1912, only three years after cubism's inception, there were already in Paris thirty dealers selling only that; and his Nude had been bought on second sale for $30,000. Wishing no truck with any business so inflated or with any success so quickly come by, he renounced painting altogether, created in the next few years at least two sculptural constructions now classical and a half-dozen pieces of perfect "pop" art, then after thirty never worked again. At least he imagined he did not, though he could not tie a string or drive a nail without beauty resulting.

Slender, erect, red-headed, Norman, son of a Rouen *notaire*, brother of a sculptor killed in World War I and of the painter Jacques Villon, he spent his patrimony early, lived virtually without funds, was adored by women. During my Paris years his most adoring woman was an American named Mary Reynolds, a war widow out of Minneapolis (by way of Vassar and Greenwich Village) who received her sustenance from a well-off but grudging father who considered sinful her gracious way of life. Like Marcel, Mary did not pretend to work; but since her friends were mostly artists and poets, and since at various times they had all given her drawings, engravings, and books, she began in the 1930s to learn the art of binding for the preservation of these. Her books and bindings are in a special collection now at the Art Institute of Chicago, given by her brother and itemized in a catalog by Marcel Duchamp, *Surrealism and Its Affinities.*

Straight, well-dressed, and clearly a lady (though she did love roistering and bars), she had formed with Madame Langlois, also straight and proud (though not a barfly), a friendship that involved once every week or two our all three dining together with Marcel or with Maurice Grosser and then playing bridge (the French kind, known as *plafond,* in which you score the extra tricks you take). And at these evenings we would forever discuss, by means of gossip, the ethics of behavior and of art. None could be more approving than they of misbehaviors committed with style, or more intolerant of grubby deportment. And I would sometimes ask Marcel questions aimed at making it clear to me how he had come to renounce being an artist. On one occasion he answered, "There is never room for more than two at the top; and Picasso and Braque were already there."

From his serene retirement, Duchamp seemed not to be involved any more with schools or styles in art, save as an observer. He was the friend of many artists, from Brancusi to Grosser; but never, saving only once, did I hear him speak of any with disdain. He did observe, that time, that Picasso's large and somewhat indiscriminate production came from the fact that "he gets sexually excited by the smell of turpentine and works every day." Another time, discussing the survival of workmanship over the centuries and the inevitable disappearance of stylistic distinctions, "In seventy-five years nobody will be able to tell a Picasso from a Corot." And of Manhattan as viewed from New York harbor, "Its beauty comes from the fact that nothing you see was built before 1900."

Marcel had been, during the first World War, an intellectual flirt with Ettie Stettheimer and an admiring colleague with Florine. I own Florine's portrait of him, painted in the early twenties, and a large drawing of her, made by him around that time, completely classical as to resemblance and style. After Mary Reynolds's death in 1955 he gave me a realistic leaf made of gold-colored metal, a 1900 piece that had been a present to her from Madame Langlois.

For the late fall of 1931 Aaron Copland had organized a concert of American music to take place in London under the auspices of a British contemporary music society, and he had asked me to participate by rehearsing and accompanying *Capital Capitals.* That same fall he had sent me a young composer, glimpsed the preceding spring at Bernard Faÿ's, his pupil Paul Bowles, who arrived in my studio with a traveling companion on a morning of dazzling sunlight. Was it really the light that dazzled, for I did sometimes receive sun through my northeast window; or was it the radiance that they brought with them, both nineteen, both in camel's hair overcoats, both with yellow hair and yellow cashmere scarfs. They had just taken, or rather Harry Dunham, the wealthy one, had taken, the largest of the new studio apartments at the top of 17 quai Voltaire; and Harry's sister would be coming from Cincinnati to live with them. They too were going to London for the December concert, since a work of Bowles's was to be played. Meanwhile they were off to Morocco for sight-seeing, had been there already during the summer with Copland. At some point Harry got sent on from Morocco, just as his grandfather had once done, a young Arab servant. This child of twelve turned out to be no helper, but he did have entertainment value from the scrapes he could get into. These continued till Harry's sister Amelia took an occasion of her brother's absence to send the Muslim Tom Sawyer back to Africa, providing money for his travel and a Vuitton suitcase. Since he had no clothes to speak of, he packed up all of Paul's and left with them. The dramas of the irrepressible Abdelkader, of Paul's dainty and devoted sweetheart (a French girl surnamed Miracle), and of the jealous Amelia, intriguing to remove anyone who came close to her brother, provided farce-comedy for a season. Then Harry went back to Princeton, still surrounded by the white light he seemed always to give off; and Paul stayed on to learn to be a composer.

Bowles had thought of himself as first of all a poet, having already during his short stay at the University of Virginia published verse in the advanced magazines, even in *transition*. Neither Gertrude Stein nor Bernard Faÿ nor I nor indeed any of the Parisians to whom he showed his poems could find their quality. His music, on the other hand, Ravel-like piano improvisations, charmed us all, as it had already charmed Copland. And Copland had tried in New York teaching him harmony but had found him a stubborn pupil. In Paris he approached Boulanger for lessons; I had recommended Paul Dukas. He ended by working with neither. Beyond a few meetings with Vittorio Rieti, he actually never succeeded in following any musical instruction, though he tried, persuaded by Aaron and myself that there was no other way to become a composer. Actually he did become a self-taught composer; and later in New York I inducted him into the practice of writing incidental music for plays, which he did (and still does) with imagination. I also, to replace an absent colleague during World War II, caused him to be engaged as a music reviewer on my staff at the New York *Herald Tribune*. This work he did perfectly, because he wrote clearly and because he had the gift of judgment. After the war, returning to Morocco, he practiced both music and letters, gradually renouncing major involvement with the former and becoming instead a novelist and story writer of international repute. He has not gone back to poetry. When I spoke only recently of my wish that he had been asked to take over my critic's post when I resigned it in 1954, he said, "I don't think I could have handled it, any more than I could have followed a career in composition. I lacked the musical training that you and Aaron had."

It was before the London concert that Aaron wrote to ask whether I would write an essay about him for a series of composer's portraits to appear in *Modern Music*. Since 1925 I had declined all requests for writing. But for Copland, who insisted I was not to look upon the essay as a favor and that "if [I] should decide to do it, nothing but [my] honest judgment would please [him]," I did accept. I wrote the article, received $20 for it, and during the next ten years contributed many pieces to that quarterly. Minna Lederman was a first-class editor. She never changed my copy; but she questioned many a time my angle of judgment, made me aware that in so partisan a paper (originally devoted to the entire League of Composers, it had already become by 1931 largely the personal organ of Aaron Copland) I must keep before my mind the differences between New York musical politics and Parisian.

Appearing in print again did me no harm. For just then there seemed to be a chance that something like an American career might be imminent. Since Russell Hitchcock had far and wide been praising my opera, his friend and neighbor A. Everett Austin, Jr. (or "Chick," as he was known) had got interested in doing something about it. Chick was director of the art museum in Hartford, Connecticut, a man of substance, young, my own classmate, an entrepreneur of unrestrained imagination. In that particular moment he was building for himself and family a neoclassical-

and-Baroque house that remains to this day bold and beautiful. In fact, from behind all the art activities of Chick Austin peer constantly the learning of Russell Hitchcock and his insatiable taste for grandeur. This influence, plus a restlessness in Chick which amounted to a major drive, caused him to decide, in full time of depression, to build a modern wing to his museum. And because he wanted to produce my opera (for he loved giving every kind of show), he was planning to build into the new wing a fully equipped theater.

My English interlude had been a delight, rehearsing and performing with singers of good speech, and walking again after ten years through Victorian red and earlier black-and-white London, even though in December the days were dark till noon and dark again after three—delightful also despite a supercilious press, for we were all so used in those days to scornful reviews that we scarcely noticed them. The program itself would today stand handsomely—a Chávez Sonatina, a Bowles Sonata for Oboe and Clarinet, Copland's Piano Variations, the Citkowitz songs from James Joyce, Roger Sessions's Piano Sonata [No. 1], and my *Capitals* to end with. At Aaron's suggestion I had held off writing my portrait of his music till I should have heard the new Piano Variations. I found these grandly expansive, only regretting that he played them too loud (as composers will do their own music) and missing in this loudness "the singing of a certain still, small voice that seems to me . . . clearly implied on the written page." It was through Aaron also, who was coming to be a power in New York, that Alma Wertheim's Cos Cob Press engaged shortly afterwards to publish my *Stabat Mater*. This was my first musical publication of any kind; and back in Paris I corrected the proofs with pride, though not with complete accuracy.

But as it began to seem that my American career might be pointing upward, my French professional relations were lowering. It was in that same December of 1931 that the violinist Yvonne de Casa Fuerte (with whom I had struck up friendship playing my Violin Sonata a half-year earlier) began a new series of contemporary concerts. My music was not programed in this series, was not ever to be programed there. But I had wanted it to be, and I am sure Yvonne too had hoped for that. It was a disappointment to be omitted from the group, because my chief musical associates were all included—Henri Sauguet, the Russian Nicolas Nabokov, the Italians Leone Massimo and Vittorio Rieti, and naturally the arrived composers Milhaud and Poulenc. As I reread now the programs of La Sérénade, I realize that Igor Markevitch's music was regularly exposed and that two of his patronesses—the Princesse Edmond de Polignac and the Vicomtesse de Noailles—were among the backers of the series. I also know that its organizer, Yvonne de Casa Fuerte, made efforts throughout 1932 to get my Second String Quartet accepted into her programs. I know too that the group governing these consisted besides herself of only Milhaud, Poulenc, and Rieti. She admired the new quartet; Rieti was reserved about it. Poulenc tried to like it, but after reading it twice still could not. What Darius Milhaud thought, I do not know. When the work was decidely not to be played, in spite of Yvonne's support, I knew I was being refused admittance to neo-Romanticism's musical Establishment, though I did not fully understand why. Bérard found the exclusion unfair and told me so. Georges Maratier, though not involved himself, mentioned some years later that there had been, to his knowledge, a move to throw me overboard (*on débarque Virgil*); and Jean Ozenne, who had had the inside story from Sauguet, tried, also much later, to tell me why Yvonne had not been able to influence her committee. I seemed to understand from him, as I had suspected all along, that Markevitch, though not a member of the committee, had maneuvered the rejection. I still do not know whether this is true; the strong opposer may have been Rieti, ever jealous of my friendship with Yvonne. Today both Yvonne and Sauguet have conveniently mislaid their memories.

In 1930 I had begun writing string pieces and piano sonatas. Three of the latter had poured out right off, then a sonata for violin and piano, divers portraits for the same ensemble, a string quartet, and the Max Jacob *Stabat Mater*. All these, save the portraits, had been performed during that year and the following one. I had also composed a Serenade for Flute and Violin, which I had hoped would be played at the opening concert of *La Sérénade*. I had written songs too, their words out of a poetry cycle by Georges Hugnet called *La Belle en dormant*. And I had transformed the first and most extensive of my piano sonatas into a fully orchestrated symphony. My last and most ambitious effort of this period—which had been one of steady progress from the mosaiclike structure of *Four Saints* to the long-line nonrepeating continuity of the Violin Sonata and the First String Quartet—had been the String Quartet No. 2, in which all my now considerable experience had been applied to creating a sonata-structure amply modulatory and cyclically thematic. I considered this four-movement piece to be authentic as inspiration, solidly built, and for all its classical architecture, a modern work. My surprise had been considerable when the Sérénade group failed to recognize its quality publicly. I was even tempted to think of it as possibly disquieting to the established ones. Whether I was right time has not told, for the piece, though still played, seems neither deeply to offend nor in any other way to attract special notice. My Second Symphony, also of this period, begins now to excite certain hearers; perhaps the Second Quartet will eventually. All I can be sure of now is that it marks a stage in my musical maturing, and I knew in fact in 1932 that I had either broken new ground or brought something to term.

I was so confident of this that I actually paused in my headlong composing and began to look around for other outlets and adventures. An American production of *Four Saints* would offer both; and I was already trying to help that out by organizing, as Chick and Russell and Alfred Barr kept suggesting by letter, a voyage of exploration. They needed me there in order to learn how much financial support some informal auditions of the opera could inspire and how low its costs could be kept down. Marga Barr wrote that she was "dividing acquaintances into two new categories—those who could be useful to Virgil and those who couldn't." I wrote to Harvard, Rochester, and Cleveland, hoping that friends there could help with lecture dates. None could, though Smith College promised one. The Alfred Barrs could offer "a shakedown on arrival," Jere Abbott, lodging for a week. And a kind crippled woman from Wisconsin whom I knew briefly in Juan-les-Pins as a friend of Georges Maratier's American wife asked if she could be allowed to subsidize my trip. So I took this for settled, turned my thoughts to other things.

The thoughts of us all, that spring, had been full of the Ballets Russes de Monte Carlo, where the director, René Blum, brother of Léon, had assembled a whole new generation of ballerinas and turned them over to the young choreographer George Balanchine. New ballets had been ordered too, and new sets, including one by Bérard for a piece called *Cotillon*, with music by Chabrier. Here the neo-Romantic youth-centered view was fully matured and Bébé come full-blown to stage design, his earlier décor for the Comédie Française of Cocteau's *La Voix humaine* having shown him still obsessed by easel-painting. And Lincoln Kirstein, not completely preoccupied any longer with his Cambridge-published magazine *Hound and Horn,* was deeply stirred by it all. He used to stay at the Hôtel du Quai Voltaire and come to my studio every morning for talking about it and to try out, with me as audience, ballet scenarios he had thought up during the night. I could find things wrong with almost all of them, but Lincoln's supply was inexhaustible.

With summer coming on and with no money for going away, I used to walk in the country by the Seine with Eugene Berman, making musical sketches while he filled notebooks with things seen, these to be worked up later into paintings and formal drawings. And I would wonder why he always had to amplify them, when the freshly noted forms were of such beauty. And he would say, "But, Virgil, you must understand that these notebooks are my capital. I do not sell them; I make my pictures out of them."

Then in July the widow of Lucien Herr lent me a country farmhouse for one month. It was at the edge of Grosrouvre, a village near the small city of Montfort-l'Amaury, home of Maurice Ravel, a church town with sixteenth-century stained glass and a pastry shop, just off the Plaine de la Beauce, where wheat is grown, and the Fôret de Rambouillet, where gnomes stack wood in piles. One got to know both these landscapes completely, because one walked. There was money for food but none for bicycles. So every day with Maurice Grosser, who shared the house and the living expenses, and for a time with Marga Barr, who came for a week and whose portrait was painted in a yellow suède jacket, one walked the countryside, explored the forest and its hidden villages— Gambais, with thatched cottages straight out of Hogarth, and Gambasais, where Landru had burned his wives and where, in the garden of his two-story brick-and-rubblestone *villa coquète,* one could have cakes and tea.

It must have been in late summer, when Jeanne Herr's farmhouse was no longer available, that I went to the Côte d'Azur, for it was there I met Rena Frazier, Florence Maratier's Wisconsin friend, who offered to pay for my trip to America saying, "Write me what you will need." I do not know how I got to the South just then, having no money. But I was there; and in Villefranche Lady Rose, Francis's mother, who was clairvoyant, told my fortune prophetically; and at Francis's house in Mougins, above Cannes, I was rude without wishing to be so to Mrs. Patrick Campbell, giant twin to her Pekingese lap dog, both of them drenched in Chanel No. 5. I spoke of having seen her unforgettably in Shaw's *Pygmalion* and asked when she was going to act again. "Never," she answered. "I'm too old and too ugly; nobody would come to see me." "But they advertised Polaire," I said, "as the ugliest woman in the world; and everybody went to see her."

I was also tactless with Rena Frazier when from Paris I wrote her what I thought I should need for the American trip, a sum much larger than just the fare. She replied from Wisconsin that hard times had diminished her resources and asked me to excuse her from the project. It was already October; and I knew no means of getting to America. Then Philip Johnson, on his way home from examining modern architecture in Germany, said not to worry, that he would be glad to lend me $200, price of a round-trip third-class passage, and that in New York I could stay at his flat. So once again I advertised my studio, let it to somebody not now remembered, lent my large black-blue Bérard to Philip Lasell, who had always loved it, and once again took off on the *Ile-de-France,* this time with Mary Reynolds, going home to visit her ailing and ungenerous father, leaving behind on a cold and windy quay Madame Langlois, who had ridden with us to Le Havre, and heading into a December North Atlantic.

Adopted by the
Modern-Art Distributors

I WAS MET AT THE FRENCH LINE PIER by Jere Abbott and taken
to Philip Johnson's flat on Forty-ninth Street, it having been
arranged between Philip and the Kirk Askews that I was to be
passed back and forth between them. There was also sleeping space
at Russell Hitchcock's in Middletown, Connecticut, at Jere Abbott's in Northampton, Massachusetts, and at Chick Austin's in
Hartford. At some point I would go to Kansas City, stopping,
should I come back by bus, at Cleveland, Ohio, where Harry
Francis was a curator of painting, and at Sibley Watson's in Rochester, New York. I should probably not be going to Boston and
Cambridge, because my early friend and protector E. B. Hill had
written that a lecture-recital was not to be thought of, since "the
depression has struck the Harvard Music Department." Nor did I
expect performance by the Boston Symphony Orchestra, after the
run-in with Serge Koussevitzky four years earlier over my *Symphony on a Hymn Tune*. He and I were still on courteous terms,
even affectionate ones viva voce; and I had another symphony all
complete that I could have shown him. But it was even sassier than
the first, and I saw no reason to embarrass either of us.

Actually, though my errand in America was musical—getting my
opera performed—I was not to be moving mainly among musicians,
but rather among the avant-garde art distributors. Philip Johnson,

originally a classical scholar, had through Russell Hitchcock become interested in contemporary building design; and they had written a book together, *The International Style,* which served as catalog for a photographic show of new architecture that they had assembled for the Museum of Modern Art. Alfred Barr, sole director, since Jere Abbott's retirement to Smith College, of this three-year-old enterprise, was the most powerfully placed among a rising group of modern-art promoters. In modern-art scholarship (a new profession) he was considered impeccable, and his tactful manipulation of trustees with names such as Rockefeller, Ford, Chrysler, Goodyear, Bliss, Crane, Clarke, Whitney, and the like was keeping the museum's rapidly expanding influence on collectors oriented as well toward academic prestige. Russell Hitchcock, as the most knowledgeable historian anywhere of modern building, was being invaluable to the architectural department; and Philip Johnson, Hitchcock's pupil in taste, as he was Barr's in the professional operation, was to become in time the museum's architectural curator. Iris Barry, English and thoroughly intelligent, had invented there for herself a librarian's post and was working in it so well that within another short span, five years, she was to establish at the museum the first Film Library in the world. Both architecture and films, however, were side issues; the museum's major line was painting. For showing that (still strictly on loan) Barr was the guide of policy as well as of selection and of hanging, and the shows that took place under his direction were remarkably successful. Scholarship, showmanship, and the tact of a Presbyterian minister's son were fused in him to produce a leadership of taste that was to influence collectors for thirty years.

Close to Barr and to the museum, but no part of it, were a half-dozen young art historians, some of them already curators, all of them oriented toward the modern. These included, besides Hitchcock at Wesleyan and Abbott at Smith, Agnes Rindge and John McAndrew at Vassar, Agnes Mongan, believed hopefully a modernistic influence at Harvard, and most spectacular of all, Chick Austin, a professor at Trinity College and director of the Wadsworth Atheneum in Hartford, Connecticut. All these had been trained at Harvard's Fogg Museum by Paul Sachs and Edward Forbes; and they all bore allegiance to a common ideal, that of administering collections of art as if these consisted of intellectual capital and of guiding the young, many of them future millionaires, into viewing art collecting as itself an art to be practiced by professional standards. Also they visited one another constantly, constantly, constantly, driving by night and by day up and down the Connecticut Valley, over the hills to Vassar, cross-country to Boston or New York.

In New York their centers of fraternity were the house of Kirk and Constance Askew on Sixty-first Street, the sales-galleries of Kirk Askew on Fifty-seventh (Durlacher Brothers), where Baroque painting was a specialty, and of Julien Levy (importer of neo-Romantic and surrealist painting), and a little bit that of Pierre Matisse (who sold Modern Old Masters, including his father). The back offices of these galleries were open for gossiping every day, and the Askews were at home at six on Sundays. Also every day at five, when one could drop in on the hostess for tea and be given cocktails later by the host.

Kirk Askew was a child of Kansas City, though I had not known him there. Our Harvard ways had crossed through Philip Lasell, whose butterfly brightness, flickering over modern art and music, had brought to my notice the especial flamboyance in both intellect and character of the art history group that centered around Chick Austin. On leaving Harvard, Askew had gone to work in New York and London for a firm of Bond Street art dealers, to whose collector-and-museum trade he was introducing his own generation's faith in the Baroque. His wife was a New England woman of means, of broad cultural experience, and of striking beauty.

Kirk was slight of frame with curvaceous facial forms that gave him a carved-in-mahogany aspect which accorded well with his Victorian house. Constance was curvaceous too, and generous as to bosom. And just as her figure was "advanced" for the decade when breasts were just beginning to emerge, her facial carriage was also of a novel kind. In a time when eyes still were tightly squinted and smiles were grins, Constance Askew's relaxed visage, as calm as that of Garbo, was deeply exciting to the young men of her generation.

The people one saw at the Askews' high brownstone on East Sixty-first Street were a wider world than just the modern-art-distributing in-group. There were story writers (John Mosher and Emily Hahn), musicians (Eva Gauthier, Aaron Copland), stage

directors (John Houseman, Joseph Losey), some actors, many literary critics, all the poets (e. e. cummings to Lincoln Kirstein),
distinguished Negroes (Taylor Gordon, Edna Thomas), curators
from the Metropolitan Museum (Harry Wehle, Preston Reming-
ton, Alan Priest), Muriel Draper, of course, and Esther Murphy
Strachey (ever literate and talkers both), and as often as not a
painter in the flesh (Alexander Brook, Florine Stettheimer), and by
1935 whole bunches of them—Massimo Campigli, Pavel Tchelitcheff, Eugene Berman, Kristians Tonny, Maurice Grosser. Sometimes the novelist Elizabeth Bowen would come from London to
stay a month. I myself for the next three years moved in and out
of the guest room almost at will.

The drink, till Prohibition went, was homemade gin. Evenings it
was diluted with ginger ale or soda. For cocktails it was shaken
up with a nonalcoholic vermouth that produced a flocculation in
the glass not unlike that which snows around Eiffel's Tower or
New York's *Liberty* when rotated in their filled-with-liquid globes.
The furniture was splendidly Victorian, with carpets, seats, and
curtains richly colored. In the early thirties all pictures there were
modern, but by the decade's end some Italian Old Masters had
been inherited. Perhaps the happy years of the Askew salon were
ending anyway; I only know we never laughed again there, though
the drink had by that time turned to proper Scotch and once in a
while, as on Christmas night, champagne.

The Askews' schedule was a firm routine. Both came downstairs
for breakfast in street clothes; houseguests, if they preferred, could
have a tray. Kirk walked to his office; that was his exercise. Unless a child was in need of watching over, Constance would read
in the library till noon. At twelve she drank some sherry while she
read. At one she lunched with someone, usually at a speak-easy
called Michel's. After lunch she looked at art shows, shopped a
little, took a nap. At five came tea, cocktails at six, dinner at seven-
thirty, for which one dressed. And every night, except when dining
out, the Askews had guests. Then after dinner others came; more
drink was served; and talk went on, sharp and hilarious, but more
about art than politics or travel. Europe, though a constant theme,
could scarcely count as travel, what with Kirk working in London
half the year, with me a resident of Paris, and Marga Barr's own
mother long a Roman. Besides, all those young and mobile art

historians spent their years-off and their summers moving round and round in Europe, just as in winter they circulated constantly up and down the northeastern seaboard.

Often, toward midnight, some would decide for Harlem; but the Askews seldom went along, though Constance might be itching to. Russell, however, and Chick, always in town for just a day or so, loved making a night of it. It was on one of these trips uptown, at a small joint where Jimmy Daniels was just starting out as host and entertainer, that I turned to Russell, realizing the impeccable enunciation of Jimmy's speech-in-song, and said, "I think I'll have my opera sung by Negroes." The idea seemed to me a brilliant one; Russell, less impressed, suggested I sleep on it. But next morning I was sure, remembering how proudly the Negroes enunciate and how the whites just hate to move their lips.

From the time of my arrival in America it had been assumed that *Four Saints in Three Acts* was to be produced. Chick's new museum wing, the Avery Memorial, would be finished the following winter; and he wanted to open it in gala style with a retrospective show of Picasso's work (the first in America), an exhibit of original sketches for Diaghilev's ballets (the Serge Lifar collection, which he was buying for the museum), and a world *première* of the Stein-Thomson opera in sets and costumes by Florine Stettheimer. I had early invited Alexander Smallens to conduct the work. And I had persuaded Florine to go on with her plans for decorating it, though her sisters, fearful of a public failure, were insisting that she give the project up. I had looked around too for a stage director; but none of the old and famous ones was interested, and the young ones seemed to have no prescience about opera. There were no opera workshops then, no ballet companies training choreographers, no ballet companies at all, in fact, only a modern-dance studio here and there, consecrated, sectarian, barefoot. When I went back to Paris in April, I knew my décors and my music were in good hands; but I still had no idea what director or choreographer would add movement.

The intellectual leaders of the group I have described—Barr, Hitchcock, and Austin—were desirous that my opera be produced, because they had as yet no outposts for modernist prestige beyond the visual arts. They dreamed of support through letters and through music, but not much was available in these domains not already tied down to other epochs or occupied by other power groups. Lincoln Kirstein's quarterly magazine *Hound and Horn* had never been, though lively enough, an organ of literary distinction comparable to *The Dial,* now defunct, or to the magazines from Paris, London, Rome that had given off such bright light in the twenties. The thirties, though destined to move radically in the theater, were still, in 1932, holding on to their hats (old hats). And the modern music of the twenties had all been heard.

All except mine, that is; and Stein's poetry was on that shelf too. We both had been much heard about, but our larger works were unknown. Since 1929 there had not been a single performance, to my knowledge, in either New York or Boston of any piece by me until my *Stabat Mater* was given at Yaddo, Saratoga Springs, in May of '32. As late as November of that year, almost as I was sailing for America, the editor of *Modern Music* was warning me by letter not to hope for even a lecture date. My reputation, all the same, was after Yaddo not malodorous; and my opera *Four Saints,* though a product of the twenties, was still new. Actually it had been kept new by the League of Composers' constant refusal of all my suggestions about performing in New York anybody's neo-Romantic music. It was therefore no less apt for exploitation than Stein's still largely unaccepted poetry.

Hitchcock and Barr and Abbott knew my opera from Paris; Chick had accepted it on faith. So had those New York and other friends who were accustomed to respect Hitchcock's insistences, especially when Barr proposed no veto. But their final adoption of it had been brought about by my singing it and playing it on everybody's piano till all could recognize it as something possible for them to admire without intellectual shame. And they could admire it all the more as a property about to be launched by their world rather than by some group mainly musical or literary.

Moreover, it was through their support that Chick knew he could find the money for producing it. Certain friends of mine would gladly contribute (though not one of Gertrude's did); and his art dealers, from the smallest up to Lord Duveen, would feel obliged to. But the Museum of Modern Art trustees could stop many a contribution by turning cold shoulder to Chick's planned gala. It had been my assignment from Abbott to make friends with certain of these and not to offend any. Nor was I offensive to Chick's insurance-magnate trustees, many of whom called Mr. Pierpont

Morgan "Cousin Jack." So Chick went ahead with the opera plan in the same way that he accomplished other things, not by seeing his way through from the beginning but merely by finding out, through talking of his plan in front of everyone, whether any person or group would try to stop him. Then once inside a project, he would rely entirely on instinct and improvisation. For he considered, and said so, that a museum's purpose was to entertain its director. And come to think of it, if it does not do that, God help us all!

Production details were left to me. The cast was to be rehearsed in New York, then moved to Hartford for a final week with orchestra, sets, costumes, and lights. Meanwhile, my scoring, luckily not yet begun, could be designed for the size of the theater; and so could Florine Stettheimer's scenery. Decision had been made to produce a work already refused in Germany and not tempting to any professional group in America. Nobody knew yet what it would cost, but I knew something of what it would look like and sound like. And I was not to be stuck with the banalities of professional stage design, the poor enunciation of professional opera singers. I was to have the ultimate in dream fulfillment, a production backed by enlightened amateurs and executed by whatever professional standards I chose to follow.

How I contrived my living for those four months, outside free lodging and free meals, I do not remember. I gave lectures at $100 each in Hartford, in Northampton, possibly in Rochester. One snowy night at Muriel Draper's frame house in East Fifty-third Street I spoke on musical prosody, singing from my own works in English and in French. Russell Hitchcock had provided a grand piano from Steinway's. Admission was charged, $2. I had not done much lecturing except informally. When I asked how I had done, Russell answered tactfully that I seemed to be more at home in writing than in speaking.

In January I went to Missouri for a month, visiting my parents in Kansas City and in Slater my jovial grandfather, just one hundred. I have no other memories of this Western trip beyond attending with George Phillips the weekly meetings of a small and hilarious lunch club of highly intellectual businessmen ·and professionals. I may have done some writing in Kansas City, words or music; but I am certain I earned no money on the spot.

In New York, especially when staying at Philip Johnson's elegantly bare Turtle Bay apartment, I also wrote articles, though I think not any music. I tried to renew my connection at *Vanity Fair,* but the new managing editor, Clare Boothe Luce (then Brokaw), did not answer me. Also from Philip's flat I led a social life with friends not of the art world and with certain rich trustees not previously of mine. In January the League of Composers, pressed by Aaron Copland, produced a performance of my *Stabat Mater* duplicate to that of Yaddo. I did not hear it, being in Missouri. I did hear a performance of the work in Philadelphia, given in late March at Smallens's recommendation by The Society for Contemporary Music.

Copland had written me after its Yaddo performance that it was my "first real success in America," meaning by "real success," I think, acceptance without prejudice or *parti pris.* This five-minute work, as a matter of fact, has never failed to communicate, in spite of its French text. It is a perfect work in the sense that I have never felt an urge to tamper with it; it has nothing to ask of me, leads its own life. It must have been the simon-purity of Max Jacob's religious inspiration that held me in line while writing it. I remember starting out to compose music in the twelve-tone convention; then feeling constricted by the method, I let the piece write itself. When it was finished, I went for a walk in the Bois de Vincennes; and there, suddenly, lying on a bluegrass hillside near the empty race track, I had felt all trembly, joyfully tired, and emptied, as by a visitation. But I knew for sure only what I had already known, that visitations did occur to Max.

At some time after I got back from Missouri, Philip Johnson's young sister Theodate arrived to visit him. Was it from Cleveland, their parental place, she came, or from Wellesley, where she had earlier, at college, found a Boston vocal teacher? Anyway, she was getting set to be a singer; and as a brunette with blazing eyes and a jacket of leopard skin, she was looking operatic absolutely. Her soprano voice was warm, her presence commanding, her musicianship carefully acquired. And she was about to move her studies to New York. Wanting to be of help to her, to me as well, Philip proposed a musical evening at his flat to which museum trustees would be asked. And he suggested we give my Second String Quartet, still unheard anywhere.

And so I built a program around that. There was no question

of compromising the glorious nudity of his living room with a grand piano. But my *Stabat Mater* with string quartet accompaniment seemed just right. I thereupon engaged a group of young players from the Philharmonic who had been several years together as a quartet. And since a fine Haydn D major was in the repertory, I chose that for leading up to my pieces. ("You set yourself high standards," said Ettie Stettheimer.) Theodate sounded lovely, sang beautiful French, repeated the *Stabat* after the concert was over.

The party, which took place mid-April, accomplished exactly what had been desired. Theodate gave a preview of her singing which was sure to be of advantage later. I heard my quartet and, as I had hoped to do, found it in all ways satisfying, so much so that I overdrank champagne punch and was sick. Philip's friends, too, seemed to find it solid enough to have been paired with Haydn. Philip in fact was vastly content all round. I had been strikingly performed and handsomely received; Theodate had been heard to advantage and admired; and, to the benefit of his own projects, not only had divers influential trustees of the museum climbed his stairs, but Mrs. John D. Rockefeller, Jr., the most important of them, had left still smiling. He proposed that we consider the $200 lent me for my trip as no longer due him, but as a fee paid for my services.

Four days later I sailed at midnight on the *Paris*. The Askews had given a dinner party for twelve, with low-cut dresses, white ties, and champagne. And all eleven took me to the ship, where my fourth of a third-class cabin was found to be crowded with gifts, as on the preceding time, including, from Constance for taking to Paris in the ship's cook's icebox, a cheesecake from Reuben's fourteen inches wide.

I 9

Orchestrations and
Contracts

ALSO TRAVELING THIRD CLASS on the *Paris* were some seventy-five
Americans of the communist faith, pilgrims to Soviet Russia.
I had not previously known the rank and file. Intellectual communists, yes, both Trotskyists and loyalists, even rich ones who
dreamed of a tax-free socialist nirvana, all government "withered
away." And in the late twenties one had in Paris joined working-
men's cinema clubs for seeing *The Cruiser Potemkin* and similar
films in halls filled to the last seat, save for a few art-curious, by
laborer families of the Marxist line. But not since college days in
Kansas City, where one boy knew real "wobblies," had I shared as
with these gentle tourists a view from below of the modern working world.

On their way to spend three weeks in the Soviet Union, in England they would transfer to a ship for Leningrad. There they would
visit the palace and the museums, travel to Moscow, see the sacred
sites, taste a new world. Some had relations they hoped to visit;
some, knowing that good tools were scarce in Russia, had brought
boxes of these to leave behind. Sweet people they were, soft spoken
and believing, many of them Jewish, though not all, since the Marxist faith has always held appeal for Protestant Americans dispos-
sessed. For those reduced in social pride it can supply, as with the
Jewish-born, a belief to organize their lives around, in case religion

has somehow got lost. In fact it was through talking of their Marxist faith with many of the Jews among them (and speaking to communists in those days was no crime) that it came to me that for these kindly men and their gentle wives Lenin was Moses and Russia the Promised Land. And since belief was stronger in them than any reasoning, I knew I must not hurt them by pointing out the Biblical origins of their new theology, any more than I would have teased my Southern Baptist father about his sources of integrity.

I did, though, repay them for their comradeship. The *Paris*, delayed by loading, was to arrive in England late, which meant the group would miss their ship for Russia; and the French Line representative on board proposed to substitute rail transport overland from France. The travelers were resigned to losing one or more precious days but not to the added expense of buying food, and the agent could not agree that his company's responsibility involved more than the railway fares. Nor did he speak English, and not one of them spoke French. So a meeting was held for ironing the matter out, at which I offered to serve my fellow travelers as both interpreter and advocate. As moral backing for our side, I asked Agnes de Mille to be there too. We won; the French Line settled for box lunches. And at Le Havre our partings were fraternal.

In Paris I had errands to perform, such as negotiating with Miss Stein's agent contracts for Chick to sign and some kind of agreement between Gertrude and myself, as parents of a work that was about to leave home. I also had to orchestrate the opera; and to save time in doing that I had a professional copyist write out the words and vocal parts and rule the measure bars for all six hundred pages. Chick was to pay the cost of preparing orchestral score and parts; I was to bring them with me on my return. Florine Stettheimer had promised to work at designing sets and costumes as fast as ideas came, and they were coming fast.

But before I could lay out the score, I had to decide what instruments to use. According to Smallens, I could with careful seating get nineteen men into the theater's pit, fewer if I used up space on kettle drums, pianoforte, or harp. After taking thought, I decided on ten strings, one flute-piccolo player, one oboe-English horn, one bassoon, two saxophones (one doubling on clarinet, the other on bass clarinet), one trumpet, one trombone, one percussion player, and an accordion. This combination was designed to provide for four-part woodwind chords, four-part brass chords (by using the saxophones), complete string chords, and full harmonic support for tutti passages. It turned out to give a strange sound indeed, largely on account of the dominating accordion, but also from the presence of the saxes imbedded among straight symphonic timbres. That strangeness I was not to know until the first rehearsal. When I did hear it I was shocked, then got used to it. In the theater it gave the work a color like that of no other, though this color had been created not through any search for novelty but by trying to achieve with a minimum number of players a maximum number of classical sound combinations.

Paris that spring was busy with ballets; and I went to the new ones, which were many, reviewing them that fall for *Modern Music*. I also gave with Cliquet-Pleyel a concert of works by both of us; but I do not remember playing either alone or with Marthe-Marthine, who sang, anything that had not been heard before. I also posed for an English sculptor, Winifred Molyneux-Seel, who modeled my head. And I recounted to Bérard exactly how Florine was going to decorate *Four Saints* and listened to him describe his new ballet *Mozartiana;* and I admired his picture by Maurice Grosser, which he had already written me was a *"portrait charmant . . . que j'aime."* And again there were daily morning visits from Lincoln Kirstein, deeply excited by the ballets and looking for a way to work with them. He had been urging Chick that they must next year in the museum's new theater stage a "ballet demonstration." And I had taken him to Bérard, who passed him on, I think, to Diaghilev's former secretary, Boris Kochno, though it was actually through Tchelitcheff that he came to speak with Balanchine. Within that year, in consequence, came Balanchine's removal to New York and the founding of The American School of the Ballet.

The year before, ballet in the Diaghilev style had been revived in Monte Carlo and in Paris, with four young Russian ballerinas (all out of the Paris studios), with one young decorator (Bérard), and with the chief heirs of Diaghilev's distinction in command—the choreographer George Balanchine and the scenarist, general taste-director, Boris Kochno. Then Kochno and Monte Carlo had disagreed; and an English poet, Edward James, had staked Kochno to seasons in Paris and London (called Les Ballets '33). Monte

Carlo had kept de Basil as organizer, Massine as choreographer, and most of the better dancers. Kochno and Balanchine, using Tamara Toumanova as chief star and Tilly Losch, James's wife, as a modern-dance novelty, produced at the Théâtre des Champs-Elysées seven new works, among them two in the German taste—*Errante* (Schubert's *Wanderer-Fantasie* orchestrated by Koechlin, with décor by Tchelitcheff) and *Les Septs Péchés capitaux,* called in London *Anna-Anna,* a mimed cantata by Bertolt Brecht and Kurt Weill danced by Losch and sung by Lotte Lenya with a male quartet in a set by Caspar Neher. Others were by Milhaud, Sauguet, and Nabokov, plus Tchaikovsky's *Mozartiana* and some Beethoven Waltzes. Les Ballets Russes de Monte Carlo repeated at the Théâtre du Chatelet their last year's novelties plus standard Diaghilev repertory, adding to these a new work by Jean Françaix, selections from Boccherini, and Tchaikovsky's Fifth Symphony. At this house were to be found the connoisseurs of fine dancing and the lovers of ballet tradition, at the other all the city's youth and elegance; and both were filled.

Kirstein's capture of Balanchine was later to make dance history in America. Just then, we who had grown up with the Diaghilev tradition were pleased at seeing it so ardently revived. And we were moved by Lenya's singing, at a concert of La Sérénade, in the Weill-Brecht *Rise and Fall of the City of Mahagonny* (a forty-minute version, made for Paris, that seems now to be lost). And diverted by a Markevitch concert containing his finest orchestral work, *La Chute d'Icare.* And impressed by an all-German *Tristan und Isolde* at the Opéra, with Furtwängler conducting and seats at $10 each. What a season! And all the more a joy to me since my own project was simmering nicely.

For keeping down the labor of writing out in score six hundred pages, I had not only had the measures ruled and voice parts written in; I had also made a deal with Maurice Grosser for inking over what I would do in pencil. Through several years of practice, Maurice had become, for helping me out, a music copyist of good calligraphy. And I did not choose to give up pencil scoring, being ineradicably American about that. Europeans more often than not work directly in ink. They write poetry that way; they compose that way. The powers of quick situation-analysis developed from childhood by a pen-and-ink culture may be responsible for Europe's voluminous musical production over the last four centuries; and I am sure that voluminous production is with any art a necessity for excellence. But Americans are slow to make up their minds—in art, in business, in diplomacy; and this propensity toward putting off decision has made us a pencil-and-eraser civilization. Even on the typewriter we are addicted to many drafts. And by telephone, when a European would say yes or no, our characteristic reply is, "Call you back."

In those days, when you had lots of work to do, you went somewhere, for life away from Paris was a saving, and third-class train fare very cheap. My usual work place was the southern coast; but I did not care to go that far so soon, having been asked, with ticket paid, to spend a week in London with the Askews. So first I went with Grosser to Honfleur, ancient small port town on the Seine opposite Le Havre, where my landlord, Doctor Ovize, knew a country boarding house. This turned out to be a haven of sweet smells and of silence under apple trees, except on Saturday nights and all day Sunday, when youth danced on an outdoor concrete floor to fox trots and javas stentoriously amplified. And after having scored a hundred pages there, I knew the time the whole of the job would take. I had only to average ten pages a day to be through in two months, and this would leave time for a copyist to extract the parts before I left for New York in late October.

In London I stayed longer than was planned, because Captain Peter Eckersley and his wife were giving a ball. Dolly Eckersley, former wife of the conductor Edward Clark, was a tall woman of soft figure and relentless drive. Indeed, she urged her men toward greater zeal than England likes. Clark, as a result, after combing the world for music of the utmost far-outness, had been demoted by the B.B.C. Captain Eckersley was at this time vigorously promoting an invention, a patent for the wired transmission of radio. Such a method would furnish to receiving sets only such programs as were wired into it; the listener could hear no others. Though the device was economical and efficient, the British government had for political reasons declined to adopt it. The German government, on the other hand, was about to settle with Eckersley and his associates for installing it throughout the Reich.

Cooperation between British business firms and Hitler's government was already active; and England had its fascist mood in politics as well, represented by Sir Oswald Mosely's Blue Shirts.

And the scientific interests of her husband were leading Dolly toward involvements with Germany that were to become definitive. Being there in 1939 with her fifteen-year-old son by her previous husband, Edward Clark, instead of returning home while she could still have done so or accepting incarceration as an enemy alien, she denied her country, both for herself and in her son's name, and spent the war in Germany. After the war was over she was tried for treason (she had broadcast anti-British matter, as I recall) and did time in prison. The son, a minor, was not held responsible. And Peter Eckersley, honorable, of good family, and well-to-do, managed to keep out of sight by reducing his engineering career to somewhere near zero. When Dolly, finally out of jail, wrote me that she was destitute, I sent her a food package but did not answer otherwise.

It was after my return from London in the summer of '33 that Dolly, writing for herself and for Edward Clark, besought me to be kind to Arnold Schoenberg, then a refugee in Paris. I used to call for him at his hotel and take him walking, since he did not know Paris well or speak much French. Milhaud, it seems, had invited him to the ballets—not a pleasure, since he could not bear the music of Kurt Weill. "Franz Lehar, yes; Weill, no," he said. "His is the only music in the world in which I find no quality at all." He also did not relish, he would say, being a martyr, for he had not previously thought of himself as Jewish. But since this status was now pressed upon him, he went to a synagogue and embraced it formally. Together with his wife and baby daughter, we all three went to New York in late October on the *Ile-de-France*. Years later, when I gave two lectures in Los Angeles, Schoenberg, though weak, came to both and embraced me warmly. At the time of his seventieth birthday he wrote me regarding an article of mine written to honor it, "I wanted already long time ago to write you that I am very pleased with the manner in which you write about my works. It raises hope that one day in the future there will be an understanding of my music. Thank you!"

It was at the Askews' house in Chelsea that I encountered that summer Frederick Ashton, and friendship flourished as I played and sang my opera for him. Freddy had danced in Ida Rubinstein's Paris troupe, but he was not ever going to be a dancing star. With his taste and brains, however, he could move into choreography;

and that is what he was beginning to do at the small dance-theater in Sadler's Wells. "Could you imagine staging my opera?" I asked. "O yes, and with delight," was the reply.

The Eckersleys' party had revealed to me the length to which personal quarrels can be carried in English social life. Though cards had been sent out, well over a hundred, everybody asked had also to be telephoned, because anyone who might find himself at the same party with someone he was not speaking to would be certain to create a "situation" by leaving. I also learned how inconsiderate, in those days, English cuisine could be. Gossip had promised that the food and wines at the house of the essayist Cyril Connolly would be unusually fine. Was his menu a practical joke, or merely a summer solution by his American wife? Dinner consisted of three "cold shapes"—mixed vegetables in gelatin, cold meat in gelatin, cut-up canned fruit in gelatin—and the wine was sparkling Burgundy.

While I was still in America, Georges Hugnet had written, "I am disgusted with what is going on everywhere: the politics in France, Hitler, Japan.... What a bouillabaisse to make you vomit!" In Paris I had found that others of my acquaintance, especially those who favored royal government (yearning young men, for the most part, who lived by Proust) had joined up with a protofascist group led by a deputy named Doriot; they actually went to drill meetings once a week. In the south, on the island of Porquerolle, where I had gone with Grosser to finish my score, I met a deputy who declared France in a state for civil war and he himself unsure which side to take, the Third Republic's comfortable corruption or the hazardous adventure of armed uprising.

I encountered him again in late September, back in Paris, where the presence of a stubborn proletariat and ready troops had made him hesitate about taking the latter chance. I never knew whether he did, but the civil war then threatening to boil did come to scalding point the following winter. The Comédie Française, directed by the playwright Edouard Bourdet, had produced Shakespeare's *Coriolanus,* accenting all its inferences about a country's need at certain times for dictatorship. This fanning of fires already lit provoked mob protests in front of the Chamber of Deputies till on the sixth of February the mounted Garde Républicaine fired without trumpet's warning, killing several. (A young man I knew, brother of the poet Edouard Roditi, crossing the Place de la Concorde, was crippled by a bullet in the spine.) But the Republic had won. The next day Edouard Bourdet was replaced as director of the Comédie Française by the director of the Sureté Générale, François Thomé (son of the composer of *Simple Aveu*), who remained in office just one day, removing *Coriolanus* from the repertory—an action that only the theater's director could take—and then resigned.

A Paris literary agent, William Aspenwall Bradley, had written as early as January that Miss Stein had "learned indirectly" of the Hartford project regarding our opera and that she "would be happy to have further particulars concerning the production itself, your arrangements with the director Mr. Austin, etc., etc." These particulars being eventually transmitted through him, I proposed that contracts be drawn between Miss Stein and myself, to define our respective rights and obligations, and between Austin and us both, governing the production. I proposed for Miss Stein and myself, since I knew well her pride in authorship, equal sharing in all the opera's benefits. Later I argued that I had been overgenerous. Here is the correspondence about that and about the production plans:

[To Gertrude Stein]

17 quai Voltaire
30 May [1933]

Dear Gertrude,

Mr. Bradley has communicated to me a passage from one of your letters to him in which you express some reserves about the opera-mounting as I described it. . . .

Before I go on about the mounting, however, I am taking the liberty of mentioning a business matter which I have already spoken of to Mr. Bradley. . . .

At the beginning of my conversations with him I mentioned that although the usual practise was otherwise, I preferred, in view of the closeness of our collaboration and of the importance given to the text in my score, to offer you a 50–50 division of all profits. It has since been called to my attention by the Société des Droit d'Auteurs that such an arrangement defeats its own end and that the contract commonly made in France allowing two-thirds to the composer and one to the author is designed to establish that very equality;

1) because the manual labor involved in musical composition is so much greater than that of writing words that half the proceeds is an insufficient return for the composer, considering him as a joint worker,

2) because a literary work is perfectly saleable separate from the music and thus brings further profit to its author, whereas the music is rarely saleable in any way separated from the text it was designed to accompany. . . .

In view of these considerations would you consider it just on my part to ask that our projected contracts (and any eventual publication of the score) be based on the 2–1 rather than the 1–1 division of profits, a proportion which, as I said above, is the one used in France to secure an equable division of benefits? . . .

About the mounting, we are all in accord that the idea of a parochial entertainment must remain. Miss Stettheimer suggested, however, that since any interior is less joyful than an outdoor scene, and since Sunday-school rooms and chapels have been done in so many religious plays (black and white), perhaps the same entertainment might take place on the steps of a church, in this case the cathedral of Avila itself, although represented in a far from literal imitation. Spring at Avila could thus be expressed doubly. Also the general atmosphere somewhat lightened. The colors and materials she suggests are merely an amplification of the dazzling fairy-tale effect ordinarily aimed at in the construction of religious images out of tin and tinsel and painted plaster and gilding and artificial flowers. Her idea seems to me to be more efficacious than our original one in expressing the same thing, especially in view of the enormous heightening of every effect that is necessary in order to get a dramatic idea across the barrier of foot-lights and music. I must admit I am rather taken by the whole proposal, having seen the extraordinary grandeur and elegance which Miss Stettheimer has produced in her own rooms with exactly those colors and materials. We are all, however, open to persuasion and to suggestions, and no maquettes have been made.

The idea for the May-pole dance in Act II is even less definite than the other. That also is Miss Stettheimer's. The negro bodies, if seen at all, would only be divined vaguely through long dresses. The movements would be sedate and prim, and the transparence is aimed . . . not at titillating the audience with the sight of a leg but at keeping the texture of the stage as light as possible. This end is important to keep in view when there are as many things and people on a stage as this opera requires and all frequently in movement. Naturally, if the transparent clothes turned out in rehearsal to be a stronger effect than we intended, petticoats would be ordered immediately for everybody. I think the idea is worth trying, however. If it can be realized inoffensively, the bodies would merely add to our spectacle the same magnificence they give to classic religious painting and sculpture. One could not easily use this effect with white bodies, but I think one might with brown.

My negro singers, after all, are a purely musical desideratum, because of their rhythm, their style and especially their diction. Any further use of their racial qualities must be incidental and not of a nature to distract attention from the subject-matter. . . .

Very faithfully yours,
Virgil

[To Virgil Thomson]

Belley, Ain, 5 June 1933
[Postmarked Paris, 6 June 1933]

My dear Virgil,

Have just received your letter. I think, in fact, I wish to keep to the original terms of our agreement, half share of profits. It is quite true that upon you falls all the burden of seeing the production through but on the other hand, the commercial value of my name is very considerable and therefore we will keep it 50–50. The only other point in the agreement between [us] is the one referring to the phrase, unreasonably withheld, Bradley will have told you that I think that we should take for granted one another's reasonableness. . . .

I am entirely agreed that the stage setting of out of door scenery would be the best, and I hope there will be the ox-carts, with the donkey, and the river and the landscape. Would it not be possible to have something in the nature of their out of door processions, with daylight and candle light and overhead canvas stretched between the houses. It altogether makes a beautiful light. I supposed one of the reasons for using negroes was the diction, it all sounds very hopeful and about all these things I am quite ready to accept what seems best to those who are doing it. The best of luck to us all.

Always,
Gtrde

[To Gertrude Stein]

17 quai Voltaire
9 June [1933]

Dear Gertrude,

Thank you for your kind and frank letter. If the only reason, however, for holding to a 50–50 division, aside from the natural enough desire to obtain as favorable an arrangement as possible, is the commercial value of your name, I should like to protest that although your name has a very great publicity value as representing the highest quality of artistic achievement, its purely commercial value, especially in connection with a work as hermetic in style as the *Four Saints,* is somewhat less, as I have found in seeking a publisher for our various joint works. . . . Moreover, it is not the value of your name or the devotion of your admirers (I except Mrs. Chadbourne, who began very practically indeed but didn't continue very long) that is getting this opera produced, but my friends and admirers, Mr. Austin . . . and Mr. Smallens and Florine and Maurice, who are all giving their services at considerable expense to themselves, and a dozen other friends who are contributing $100 or more each to Mr. Austin's costly and absolutely disinterested enterprise. The value of your name has never produced any gesture from these people, whereas every one of them has on other occasions manifested his interest in my work by creating commercial engagements for me and by offering me further collaborations with himself. And dear Gertrude, if you knew the resistance I have encountered in connection with that text and overcome, the amount of reading it and singing it and praising it and commenting it I have done, the articles, the lectures, the private propaganda that has been necessary in Hartford and in New York to silence the opposition that thought it wasn't having any Gertrude Stein, you wouldn't talk to me about the commercial advantages of your name. Well, they *are* having it and they are going to *like* it and it isn't your name or your lieutenants that are giving it to them. If you hadn't put your finger on a sensitive spot by mentioning this to me, I should never have done so to you. However, I've got it off my chest now and the fact remains that even were the situation reversed, a 50–50 contract would be, so far as I know, absolutely without precedent. . . .

I am glad you approve of the scenic plans. The second act in-

cludes just such a night scene as you have described. I don't
know whether a river can be got on the stage too, but I hope
so. . . .

Best of greetings.

Always faithfully,
Virgil

[To Virgil Thomson]

Bilignin par Belley, Ain
[Postmarked 11 June 1933]

My dear Virgil,

Yes yes yes, but nous avons changé tout cela [referring to
her recent success with *The Autobiography of Alice B. Toklas*],
however the important thing is this, the opera was a collaboration, and the proposition made to me in the agreement was in
the spirit of that collaboration, 50–50, and the proposition that
I accepted was in the spirit of that collaboration 50–50 and the
proposition that I continue to accept is the same. When in the
future you write operas and have texts from various writers it
will be as you and the precedents arrange, but our opera was a
collaboration, we own it together and we divide the proceeds 50–
50, and we hope that the proceeds will be abundant and we
wish each other every possible good luck.

Always,
Gtrde Stein

[To Gertrude Stein]

17 quai Voltaire
22 June [1933]

Dear Gertrude,

Everything is arranged now, at least for the duration of our
present contract and I have signed it and Mr. Bradley is sending it to you. The copy of score is ready (or will be tomorrow). It
is in the original form plus Maurice's stage directions. I suggest
(since they are neither your nor my invention and though they
will be used in the production are not the only ones that are
possible) that I cross them out of the copyrighted work. . . .

I find on working over the opera and orchestrating it that I
should very much like to make a few simple cuts. You offered
me that privilege at the beginning of our collaboration and I
didn't care to avail myself of it, preferring to set everything and
wait for a later time to make any such cuts in view of actual

performance. I find now that there is a little too much singing and not enough instrumental relief. I should like to eliminate for example a few of the stage-directions as sung, especially where they are repeated frequently. I don't mean systematically to remove them, just a few repetitions now and then, in every case (or nearly) to replace them with an instrumental passage of the same length and tune. This makes a rather amusing effect and is as if an instrument were saying the words that somebody has just sung. There are also a few passages that I should like to eliminate for the purposes of this performance, substituting in one or two cases a short instrumental passage, in others nothing at all. This in view of tightening the structure musically and making a more simple and effective musical continuity. The aria in Act III about roses smell very well, for instance, comes right after another aria for tenor and rather impedes the advance of the spectacle toward the ballet. I should like to cut it out.

The cuts I propose are only for the purposes of my score for this performance. The copyright score would include everything. I mention the cuts because I don't want to avail myself of a permission offered so long ago without its being renewed. I hope you will allow me to do this. I assure you the theatrical effectiveness of the work will be enhanced.

Many thanks for your gracious acceptance of the consent clause in our agreement. We now have, I think, a simple way of settling any differences that may arise without bitterness. As a matter of fact, we understand each other so well and our interests lie for the most part so close together that I am sure we shall always be mostly reasonable with each other anyway.

Best of greetings.

Always devotedly yours,
Virgil

[To Virgil Thomson]

Bilignin par Belley, Ain
[Postmarked 25 June 1933]

My dear Virgil,

Yes of course you are to make the cuts, the burden of making it a successful performance lies upon you. . . . I am very pleased that everything is arranged, Bradley will be sending me the agreement and I will sign it, and I hope it will all be as successful as possible, we certainly deserve it, do we not. . . . You are quite right about not using Maurice's suggestions in the copy for copyrighting, I am glad he is to be in the show, he certainly helped a lot.

Always,
Gtrde

Four Saints in Three Cities

At Porquerolle I did my stint of ten score-pages a day; and Maurice kept up with me, respacing the notes, inking them in, and erasing the pencil marks. Every day I proofread my work as well as I could with the eye alone (having no piano); and I did this very badly, it turned out, hundreds of faults surviving in the score and consequently in the orchestral parts. And since I had no time for checking these materials before I sailed, my orchestral rehearsals were to cause Smallens untold trouble and me no end of shame. But I did get through my chore, thanks to Maurice, who vowed he would not ever copy music again; and by mid-September I was back to Paris, where I delivered the pages for extraction and for binding, ordered new dress clothes from Lanvin (on credit), and packed up for moving from the quai Voltaire. I could not afford to go on paying rent during an absence I could not calculate; and there were not likely to be subtenants for my studio, since the French had always found it a bit dear, and American money, now gone off gold, had lost two fifths of its worth.

Chick Austin had written in July that a project "about the Russian Ballet in Hartford" had gone through, and that it was "under the auspices of the American Ballet, Inc. that [he hoped] to produce [my] opera, since money is more easily raised for a continuous plan like that." This plan was of Lincoln Kirstein's undertaking, based on founding under Balanchine's direction a school for ballet dancers and a ballet company. The young Edward M. M. Warburg had given money to get this project started; and Chick had offered it a home in his museum. He assured me at the same time that the opera "comes first" and added:

> I think that it will be a winter of fun for all, as I hope that you can spend it mostly in Hartford . . . first with the opera—later orchestrating things for the new American ballets, writing some new scores perhaps and possibly conducting a permanent orchestra which will serve all sorts of purposes. I am hoping to raise extra money to pay you some sort of salary. Balanchine can do the ballet for your opera and I don't see why we can't all together do something of interest if not of importance. . . .
> When can you come over and how much money is it going to take? (Minimum please.)
> Please forgive my stinginess—I am not a rich art patron. I'm just a poor boy trying my damndest to get that opera produced. Come soon please. We have so much to discuss and plan. . . . The building seems to be coming along well and the builders still insist that the theater will be finished on December fifteenth.

By the time I arrived, on October 31, and moved into the Askews' spare room, it had been decided that only New York could furnish enough students for a ballet school. So Chick, lacking the ballet's "continuous plan," transferred the producing of my opera to a concert-giving group he had formed some five years earlier, called The Friends and Enemies of Modern Music. He still had no money for the production beyond small gifts of $100 each that a half-dozen friends had paid toward my travel and for the copying. And a budget could not be arrived at till a director had been found. But professional ones showed little faith in the work; it resembled nothing they knew. And I was not entrusting it to amateurs.

It was Lewis Galantière who brought me John Houseman, with whom he had written a play. And Houseman, to my delight, turned out to be a European, a product of French lycées and an English public school. And when I had played and sung the opera for him, he said, "This could have been for Etienne de Beaumont's Soirées de Paris" (the series of spectacles for which in 1924 Satie and Picasso had produced *Mercure*). Then I told him of my wish for a Negro cast and about Miss Stettheimer, who had already built a toy stage and was filling it with dolls, lace, and feathers, crystal, and cellophane. Did he think the work would interest him to stage? "It would be fun to try," he answered. "There is no fee involved," said I, "not for Smallens nor Florine nor anyone except the cast and orchestra." I knew that he had not directed previously; neither, for that matter, had Florine ever worked in show business; nor had I, since my early movie days in Kansas City. He would have to see his own play through its opening, of course; and he would always have to be working at translations from French and German, for that was how he earned his livelihood. But he would see me through, if I wanted him to. I did. And we began an association that has lasted thirty years—in operas and plays, in radio and films, in television, even in dance and vaudeville numbers, as such moments occur in other dramatic forms.

Houseman took us over, organized us, secured Kate Drain Lawson, working free, to see that sets and costumes got made right, secured also an ace press agent, Nathan Zatkin, and Lee Miller, the most stylish photographer in town, to take our pictures. Houseman drew up a budget right away. And he hired us a rehearsal hall in Harlem, the basement of Saint Philip's Episcopal Church. Aided by a Negro talent scout, I had held soloist auditions in the Askew drawing room; for hearing choristers I moved uptown, engaging there, for access to these, a Negro woman who had the best of them under contract. In return for program-credit as our choral director, she furnished me singers musically literate.

Houseman was more effective in the producer's role than bold in his concepts about *mise en scène*. I felt he would welcome help from a choreographer. There was no possibility of using Balanchine, new to America and busy with his school. So I wished in front of Chick and to the Askews that there were a way of getting Freddy Ashton over. He had never directed opera, but he understood *Four Saints*. We could pay his fare third class, and the Askew household could provide a bed. If he were willing to work free, like the rest, Constance would send a telegram inviting him. So it was sent; and he did accept; and he arrived on December 12, along with Maurice Grosser.

Freddy was a godsend both to Houseman and to me, as well as

a joy forever to the cast. Maurice, knowing the opera by heart, helped me to cut it for a smooth trajectory. But for all his inside knowledge of the work, he turned out to be a trouble at rehearsals. He would get nervously excited, which he was prone to do at any time, and communicate impatience to the cast. Deeply upset about the omission of a storm, I think it was, he could not be consoled. Eventually I induced him to stay away from St. Philip's. His excellent observations could not be offered calmly enough to be of use, though he it was, among us all, who really understood the text and who had devised, with Stein's acceptance, a scenario that was bedrock to our production.

That production grew as naturally as a tree. I took the vocal rehearsals; and I kept the tempos firm and the words clear while Ashton choreographed the action, standing, as choreographers like to do, in center-stage and moving the singers round him, at first with their music scripts in hand, so that movements and music and words all came to be learned together. Stein's sentences, set to music, were easy to memorize; to recall them intact one had only to think of their tunes. And Houseman surveyed us all as if unworried, watched over us like some motherly top sergeant, wisely kept the bookkeeping vague, met financial emergencies dead pan.

The Negroes proved in every way rewarding. Not only could they enunciate and sing; they seemed to understand because they sang. They resisted not at all Stein's obscure language, adopted it for theirs, conversed in quotations from it. They moved, sang, spoke with grace and with alacrity, took on roles without self-consciousness, as if they were the saints they said they were. I often marveled at the miracle whereby slavery (and some cross-breeding) had turned them into Christians of an earlier stamp than ours, not analytical or self-pitying or romantic in the nineteenth-century sense, but robust, outgoing, and even in disaster sustained by inner joy, very much as Saint Teresa had been by what she took for true contact with Jesus, Saint Ignatius by dictates from the Holy Ghost. If Beatrice Robinson-Wayne and Edward Matthews, who played these roles, seemed less intensely Spanish and self-tortured than their prototypes, they were, as Baroque saints, in every way as grandly simple and convincing.

The Negroes gave meaning to both words and music by making the Stein text easy to accept. And every day visitors from downtown—playwrights like Maxwell Anderson, reporters like Joseph Alsop, colporteurs of news like Mrs. Ira Gershwin—would come to watch the miracle take place. Eventually a Broadway producer arrived for tasting the show—Harry Moses, a retired manufacturer of underwear, avid of distinction in the theater and not without a nose for it, a flair. The previous year, with *The Warrior's Husband,* he had made a star out of Katharine Hepburn; and in the following one his production of *The Old Maid,* by Zoë Akins from a tale by Edith Wharton, was to receive a Pulitzer. Moses scented prestige in *Four Saints,* also a bargain, since our production was being made at off-Broadway prices. He realized that the work was not a commercial venture but an art piece, and that if it could be made to pay its way, or nearly, both he and Broadway would gain intellectual credit.

We moved to Hartford the first of February for a week of rehearsals with orchestra, sets, costumes, and lights. The cast stayed in hotels and houses listed by a Negro committee; the staff, for economy, mostly in the guest rooms of Mrs. James Goodwin, Helen Austin's mother. For the last three days of rehearsal Florine Stettheimer and her sister Ettie were at the old-fashioned, still gastronomic Hotel Heublein, as also were Carl Van Vechten, his wife Fania Marinoff, and the art reviewer Henry McBride, who sent almost hourly dispatches to *The New York Sun.* Weather was unbearable out-of-doors (sixteen below), but we scarcely noticed it.

On February seventh and eighth the New Haven Railroad put on extra parlor cars for New York fashionables and for the international museum-and-dealer world arriving to honor the new wing's opening and to see the Picasso show. Serge Koussevitsky had written that regretfully he could not come on any night that week. There did come from Boston, however, the composer George Foote, our only guest, I think, to arrive by air. And there were stylish parties, of course, every night, the finest to my taste being that offered to the cast by the Negro Chamber of Commerce. It was not showy and there was nothing strong to drink, only a pale rum punch in paper cups; but there was Southern-style jazz in a big bare hall. I remember climbing its stairs at midnight and dancing for what seemed about a minute. Then it was five o'clock; the jazz band went home; our week was over.

In a letter of December 6 to Gertrude I had given her a foretaste of its grandeurs.

Hotel Leonori
Madison Avenue at 63rd Street
New York

6th December [1933]

Dear Gertrude,
. . . The cast of the opera is hired and rehearsals [have]
begun. I have a chorus of 32 and six soloists, very, very fine
ones indeed. Miss Stettheimer's sets are of a beauty incredible,
with trees made out of feathers and a sea-wall at Barcelona
made out of shells and for the procession a baldachino of black
chiffon and bunches of black ostrich plumes just like [for] a
Spanish funeral. St. Teresa comes to the picnic in the 2nd Act
in a cart drawn by a real white donkey [eventually omitted]
and brings her tent with her and sets it up and sits in the door-
way of it. It is made of white gauze with gold fringe and has
a most elegant shape. My singers, as I have wanted, are Negroes, and you can't imagine how beautifully they sing. Frederick Ashton is arriving from London this week to make choreography for us. Not only for the dance-numbers, but for the
whole show, so that all the movements will be regulated to the
music, measure by measure, and all our complicated stage-action
made into a controllable spectacle. Houseman is a playwright,
friend and collaborator of Lewis Galantière. He "understands"
the opera too, if you know what I mean by that word. Everything about the opera is shaping up so beautifully, even the
raising of money (It's going to cost $10,000), that the press is
champing at the bit and the New York ladies already ordering
dresses and engaging hotel rooms. Carl's niece has taken a
Hartford house for the opera-week. . . .

The Stettheimer décors and costumes have been commented on in
many books. The Stein text and my music have also received both
praise and blame. The elements that never have been questioned
are the Negro casting and the choreography, though their examples have been very little followed. Negroes had not been much
used for playing non-Negro roles. Today, though they are so used,
even in opera, they are not used for their characteristic qualities,
but in spite of them rather, as if one was not supposed to recognize their race. And operas, a few of them, have been choreographed. But they have been choreographed for white dancers, who
tend always to look arch in the presence of song, and for white
singers, who do not walk well and who stand around like lumps,

rather than for Negroes, who can move boldly and who stand with style. It was thanks to the choreography, indeed, and to our cast that the production's major quality shone out—a unity of concept and performance that no one had seen before in opera.

We gave six shows in Hartford, including a preview, charging $10 a seat for that and also for opening night. We then moved to New York and rehearsed for a week, adding more singers to the chorus, a harmonium and strings to the orchestra. We also relit the show to Florine's taste. Since her stage colors were all bright and all clean, never muddy, she had insisted from the start on white light. Now the custom of that time was to produce white light by mixing colored lights; even so skilled a lighting technician as our Abe Feder believed that the only way. But Florine persisted, told him where white bulbs, strong ones, could be bought; and he got her a dazzling effect for the opening scene. She also insisted that Moses buy gloves for all the cast; the ungloved hand she found inelegant. And she made herself, for St. Ignatius in the first act to offer St. Teresa, a multicolored heart-shaped floral piece, also a large gold sunburst with orange clouds for the last act, both out of cellophane.

Her use of net-backed cellophane has remained unique. On the afternoon of our New York opening the Fire Department required us to spray with waterglass our draped and tufted sky-blue shining backdrop, as well as the pink tarletan palm trees. As soon as the inspectors left, Kate Lawson replaced on these the hopelessly wilted leaves; at eight that night she was ironing out still others so they would stand perky again. It was luck we had been allowed to open at all, for the Fire Department that same week adopted on our account a rule forbidding cellophane ever again to be used on a New York stage. In the 1952 revival of *Four Saints,* in New York and Paris, a woven plastic substitute material was employed; but neither in texture nor in color was it pleasing; and instead of standing out like crystal rock, it drooped in gathers like a window drape.

On our 1934 New York opening night the February cold was still intense, the streets were icy, and there was a taxi strike. But everybody came, from George Gershwin to Toscanini—a showy full house at $6.60 top, though $4.40 was the standard then. The press was excited and voluminous. *Modern Music,* as if hesitant to take sides, sent two reviewers—Gilbert Seldes, who thought it a lovely show, and Theodore Chanler, who found my music, compared with the rest of the spectacle, "a sow's ear." In 1948 Chanler confessed to my biographer Kathleen Hoover that he had wished to write otherwise but that a composer he deeply respected, encountered that same evening at a reception, had "simply pulverized [him] with scorn and indignation for having *dared* to like it." "I was intimidated," he said.

Copland, as always, spoke frankly, in this case glowingly. "I didn't know one could write an opera," he said. (He was to compose one shortly, *The Second Hurricane*.) And of the orchestral sound, "It's so fresh! When the bassoon plays, it's as if one had never heard a bassoon before." Roger Sessions, on the other hand, told me he thought I had "not made maximum use of [my] orchestral resources."

Whether or not one found the work acceptable, its notoriety was unparalleled since that of Marcel Duchamp's *Nude*. For six months and more the show was named at least once every week in every New York paper and in some paper somewhere in the United States every day. There were constant editorials, cartoons, and jokes about it; all the music and drama critics in the East reviewed it. H. T. Parker came from Boston to hear and see it, caught cold, died with the unfinished article on his desk.

But for all the publicity, Ashton got no offers to do other work in America, none, at least, that he found worthy. Nor did celebrity do me any good, though as Van Vechten had said, I was certainly at that moment "the most famous [meaning "talked-of"] composer in the world." A former English teacher of mine did procure me a lecture date, and for that I paid a short visit to Kansas City. And Lawrence Langner, of the New York Theatre Guild, did propose a possible composing of music for a possible production of a Molière comedy. The project, as I remember it, seemed tentative and not, as planned for staging, a very good idea. Aside from this, there were any number of librettos offered, invariably low-grade comic scripts. No music publisher wished to issue the *Four Saints* in score. No lecture agent cared to take me on. And colleges were as silent as the clubs.

The only paying customer my fame attracted was the ever-watchful League of Composers. They who had declined my instrumental music seemed to have acquired some confidence in my vocal skills. In any case, a commission was awarded me to compose a choral piece for female voices, the cash value of it their smallest fee, $300.

And Lincoln Kirstein proposed a ballet for which e. e. cummings was to write the scenario. For subject, cummings leaned toward *Uncle Tom's Cabin;* and though I thought the choice a bit Yankee of him, I did not discourage it. When he gave me the text that autumn, called simply *Tom,* I pointed out that it was not a ballet scenario, but a poem about one. I saw no way of getting it on a stage, much less of dancing it; nor has it to this day, I think, been choreographed, though David Diamond did compose a score.

By the time my opera opened at the Forty-fourth Street Theatre, all our staff, excepting Miss Stettheimer and Maurice Grosser, had been put on salary. The $10,000 budgeted for the Hartford production (and overspent) had been obtained through gifts and from the sale of seats. An additional $2,000 (one fourth of this required for an extra rehearsal of the orchestra on account of time-consuming errors in my score and parts) had been lent by Houseman, by Constance Askew, and by Chick himself, all of whom needed to be paid back. The paying of this debt, plus royalties due the author and composer for the Hartford run, was all the compensation Chick expected from Harry Moses in return for his gift of the production. Moses did pay the New York royalties, of course; but those due from Hartford never did get paid. When Gertrude inquired about these, through her agent, I replied we must not pester Chick just now. I also raised the question of paying Grosser, whose royalties, though unforeseen in any contract, were properly a charge against the librettist. But on this matter she was firm, giving no reason, simply saying no—surely, I thought, a case of consent "unreasonably withheld."

We played a month at the Forty-fourth Street Theatre, then moved to the Empire for a fortnight. Smallens, who had not believed the opera would last so long, was obliged to leave at the end of five weeks. So for the final week I took it over, a privilege for the experience it offered, in view of our coming engagement in Chicago. For a concert manager there, Grace Denton, had offered to subsidize the opera for a week in November at the Auditorium, Louis Sullivan's monumental opera house, still favorable to the sound of music and to voices. And since Smallens would not be available, I was to conduct.

A new backdrop was run up for Chicago, our old one being by then too stiff to fold. By what means Miss Denton cleared cellophane with the Chicago Fire Department I do not know; but it was used. Before I went there to rehearse the orchestra, Smallens had reviewed the score with me, explaining certain ways of beating time and how I must mark my beats into my score, then never change them. The orchestra men, all better than my New York group, contained among the violins three former concertmasters of the Chicago Symphony Orchestra. Only the accordion player, unused to orchestral routines, needed special watching. When he made a false entrance on opening night, I resolved the emergency, which might have led to chaos, by stopping the orchestra, looking at Saint Teresa, then beginnig her aria without his interference.

Though the Auditorium stage was twice the width of Hartford's, we did not change at all our set's proportions, kept them the same as for Chick's tiny theater, merely masking the proscenium down to size. And I used my New York number of orchestral players, twenty-six, seating them closely massed for resonance against the pit's back wall. Ashton, long since gone back to England, was not there to rehearse the cast; but one of our singers, Thomas Anderson, who had kept a prompt-book, knew every movement. The performances were as lively as in New York, the press reports just as excited. And there were the usual parties, the last of these being given by a Negro group way out on the tough South Side, where one of our dancers got into an argument and, trying to pull a pistol from his pocket, shot himself in the leg.

My father, now over seventy, retired and motorized, drove from Kansas City with my mother. Jessie Lasell and Hildegarde Watson turned up too. As did also Russell Hitchcock, on a lecture tour, and Joseph Brewer, formerly a New York publisher, just then president of a small college in Olivet, Michigan. Chicago was jolly, hospitable, culture-aware. The Arts Club gave me a luncheon, and the local branch of the American Opera Society bestowed on me its David Bispham Medal. Unused to awards, and feeling a bit ashamed, as if I were being blest by some Establishment, I gave it to my adolescent niece.

Gertrude Stein, newly arrived in America for a lecture tour, had flown from New York with Alice Toklas and Carl Van Vechten. After the first act, still deaf from her first airplane ride and wishing to hear her own words, Gertrude left her seat of honor in Harold McCormick's center box and moved to an orchestra seat down front. After the performance, when photographers backstage were posing her with local potentates, it was McCormick who courteously suggested that I join the group. Otherwise, no one was much aware of me. The party that night was at "Bobsie" (Mrs. Barney) Goodspeed's, a sit-down supper with champagne, twenty at table. Houseman later remarked that Miss Stein's lips showed dark spots such as his father's had when he was ill of Addison's disease. Gertrude, then sixty-two, lived twelve more years. She may, though, have been cancerous already.

When the contracts for Chicago were being drawn, I had told Harry Moses I would not conduct unless Grosser, so far unpaid, was put on royalty for a small percentage. Also that this was not to come from my share. He could either deduct it from Miss Stein's or pay it himself. Grosser was not being insistent; but I was out to win the point from Gertrude. The producer, however, did not wish to pay for Miss Stein's stubbornness; and her agent could do nothing with her. Moses tried simply omitting Grosser from the contracts, then sending them to my hotel by an assistant, who tried to secure my signature through confusion. But I was unconfused, and the assistant gave up. "You make out the contract as you want it," he said at last.

For doing this, I telephoned a Wall Street law firm, which sent me that same night a young man just from Yale, wearing a revolver in a leather holster. "Collecting rent in the slums," he allowed, "is tough these days." He made out a contract from my dictation, Grosser to be paid half of one per cent of the receipts, and charged me $50 for the service.

Next morning Alfred Barr was on the phone. One of his trustees, a woman in the advertising business, needed to make a present to a client who collected autographs. She would love to have something nice by Gertrude Stein. Did I have a letter I would consent to sell?

"Yes," I said quickly, "and the price is $50."

I had, in fact, a fairly recent one about our opera. I had not sold letters before; nor have I since. But selling one of hers to reimburse the cost to me of enforcing payment on a production charge I believed to be owed by her seemed poetic justice. I did not mind that it was Moses who really paid, since he owed me a favor from the New York run, when I had secured Gertrude's consent to a diminution of both our royalties. I did not tell her what I had done; I did not care to risk another quarrel. For Gertrude, about money, did not joke.

Communists All Around
and High Life Too

BACK IN THE TWENTIES, both Sauguet and I had been regularly
under attack for writing simply, as if straightforwardness in
music were an outrage. So naturally *Four Saints,* when given in
New York, had shocked many by the plainness of its harmony.
Nevertheless it seemed to be pointing a way, and for composers the
way it pointed was toward the stage. Now for invading the theater, baggage needed to be light. To encumber the social-content
stage (for that was where in the 1930s many of us came to be
working) with all the impedimenta of modernism was to hinder
communication. And communication, after the middle thirties, had
become urgent. Noble subjects, moreover, taboo in the twenties,
were suddenly available to art. And for treating all such themes—
in America sociological, in Russia historical, in Spain patriotic, in
France humanitarian—self-consciousness of manner was ineffectual.

It came about therefore that during the 1930s, especially their
highly productive last half, music could be contemporary without
being hermetic. Obscurity, long the hallmark of modernism, remained a trademark for masters over fifty—for Picasso, Schoenberg, Stravinsky, Joyce—for all but Gertrude Stein. After her return from America in 1935 she more and more transcribed just
"outer realities." Likewise, and especially in America, composers
moved with the times toward lofty themes and plain speaking

about them, as first I, then Copland, Piston, Blitzstein, Antheil, and Douglas Moore began to work for the stage and for documentary films.

My first job in the speaking theater came in 1934 from Joseph Losey, engaged by the Harvard Dramatic Club to direct Denis Johnston's *A Bride for the Unicorn.* To this I added male choruses and percussion, went to Cambridge for fitting them in, stayed through its opening in Brattle Hall on May 2.

My next commission was from John Houseman, planning an off-Broadway season of off-Broadway plays, the first to be Euripides's *Medea* in verse translation by the Negro poet Countee Cullen, using for star the Negro tragedienne Rose McClendon. Awed in *Four Saints* by the dignity of Negroes' stage presence, Houseman was all for finding out whether this could be used to comparable advantage in poetic tragedy. He wished to mount (in English) not only an ancient Greek play but also a French modern classic, *Le Cocu Magnifique* by the Belgian Fernand Crommelynck, believing its story of violence through jealousy, like that of *Medea,* a natural for Negro interpretation. Neither play came to production, though two years later we produced a Negro *Macbeth.* And I did, in Paris that summer of '34, compose the *Medea* choruses.

I also composed there, for my League of Composers commission, a Mass for Women's Voices and Percussion, using a severe manner, derived from the medieval, that I esteemed no less appropriate for modern music societies than for nuns. When the work was performed the next April in Town Hall the press gave copious coverage (for after *Four Saints* I was news) but found it no show of force on my part, since I had got through in less than fifteen minutes a text that Bach had made to last out three whole hours.

It was that same summer of 1934 that I declined regretfully James Joyce's invitation to write a ballet for the Paris Opéra after the chapter on children's games from *Finnegans Wake.* I was to reject cummings's *Tom* that fall. A third subject, suggested by Florine Stettheimer and acceptable to Kirstein, was Pocahontas at the court of James the First. Eventually I renounced that too, because I could find no way to give it urgency. For décor it was splendid, but it lacked drama. Even reenacting the John Smith episode would not have saved it, I felt, since plays within plays, unless interrupted, are merely a rite.

In New York, with my last $20, I bought a secondhand piano and in my rooftop hotel room (oh, the crushing September heat that year and the crashing storms!) auditioned replacements for Chicago in the *Four Saints* chorus. In October, for Theodate Johnson's Town Hall recital, I accompanied my percussive Song of Solomon. My new dinner jacket from Lanvin, double-breasted, as was about to be the style, had an extra pair of buttons that would click most unexpectedly when I damped the cymbals edgewise on my chest.

Back from Chicago in mid-November, I returned to composing portraits of my friends—some for a modest fee, some for none. In all cases I would give a manuscript. The Friends and Enemies of Modern Music continued to produce concerts in Hartford, all of which I organized and in most of which I performed. In December, at Chick's theater in the Wadsworth Atheneum, we offered a new kind of concert—new, at least, for the twentieth century, though it would have seemed normal to the eighteenth—namely, one with especially designed stage-sets.

We had already experimented the April before with dramatic cantatas framed in décors planned out by Chick himself. I remember Theodate in the *Lucrezia* of Handel, melodramatic in an ominous light-effect, singing dramatic coloratura in black beside a black piano. This time I was to conduct two scenes out of Avery Claflin's *Hester Prynne,* an opera based on Hawthorne's *The Scarlet Letter,* with scenery and costumes designed by the painter Victor White and by Roy Requa, John Houseman directing the stage. Preceding this there were to be played two string quartets. And Chick, fearing both auditory and visual imbalance with regard to the opera's massive stage-effects, had asked Tchelitcheff, just arrived from Europe, to design a décor for the quartets. He did, and it was ravishing.

The theater's sky-blue cyclorama was its background. A low black platform large enough to seat four players was backed by a three-panel screen and framed by a simulated forged-iron arch draped in white tulle. The arch, made out of rubber hose suspended by invisible wires, was like a stroke of penmanship. The screen, painted by Maurice Grosser, bore the first three pages of my Quartet Number Two, drawn in white on black, like an engraver's proofs. Maurice also copied out the cello part in black on twenty yards of pure white tulle. All white and black against ethereal blue, as insubstantial as the sound of music, the set gave visual presence to the musicians and picked up the red brown of their instruments. Maurice, in helping Tchelitcheff, had broken his vow never again to copy music; but thanks to his help the screen became musically legible. And thanks to Tchelitcheff the whole effect was in just that spirit of fluffy Baroque that Chick loved and that was Florine's private kingdom even more than it was Pavlik's.

At another concert of the Friends and Enemies, this time in Chick's Venetian drawing room, four composers performed their own and one another's music. Aaron Copland played pieces of mine and also his Piano Variations. I played portraits of a half-dozen people present and sang songs by Paul Bowles (one made from a letter of Gertrude Stein) and by Antheil (out of *Alice in Wonderland*). George Antheil played duets with me and by himself a Suite. Bowles offered portraits of the other three composers, plus a Piano Sonatina.

It must have been during that same season that I organized a concert of old music played on old instruments for opening a show of eighteenth-century French art at the Metropolitan Museum, where it turned out that our historic viola bastarda was actually depicted in one of the paintings. The curator was delighted with the whole occasion until he learned that I expected to be paid.

Dates of this kind, some public, some private, kept small sums coming into my bank account. At one time I went to Providence to play and sing for a party given by Charles Brackett, fiction writer and Hollywood film director. At another I went to the Taconic hills for lecturing on my music in a fine house where the hostess, about to take off for Portugal, asked me whether Capri also was "unspoiled." Impertinent as usual, I answered that the word "unspoiled" was scarcely applicable to an island that since Roman times had been a rendezvous for every kind of vice.

It was also in 1935, I think, that efforts began to be made toward organizing the serious composers. Concert and opera soloists had already formed, for collecting fees and strengthening their contracts, The American Guild of Musical Artists (AGMA). And concert managements had been merged into two main trusts. It was the lawyer who had formed one of these, the Columbia Concerts Corporation, itself tied up to recording and broadcasting, who first brought together the composers. The American Society of Composers and Publishers (ASCAP) was not then so hospitable to classical musicians as it is now; and virtually no such composer, consequently, was receiving payment for performances or broadcasts of his music. So that when about a hundred of us were asked to dinner by Milton Diamond and given applications to sign for membership in a projected society, many saw the dawn of a new day.

But I figured that Diamond and his associates were probably moved less by our interests than by theirs and that their proposals had better be examined. So when my colleagues elected me, along with several others, to meet with Mr. Diamond for drawing up bylaws, I went to every meeting, asked embarrassing questions, and confused the lawyer, who knew lots about mergers but very little about authors' rights, into revealing that he was not completely on our side. When these negotiations failed, as I had been determined that they should, the desirability of a composers' society remained. Over the next three years the plans for this were worked out, partly by me, who had in my European years learned something about authors' rights, and partly by Copland, who could mold them into forms acceptable to others. The result of our work was the American Composers Alliance, incorporated in 1938. The eventual outcome of Milton Diamond's project was Broadcast Music, Incorporated, of which the main commerce was selling to the broadcasters, who themselves owned BMI, performing rights controlled by its publisher members.

In the summer of '35 I visited Constance Askew in Stonington, Connecticut, then Grosser in Huntsville, Alabama, then Chick in Castine, Maine. Nothing was accomplished through all this bus travel beyond the delights of friendship and a dozen or so portraits in music. Also, as always when with Chick, lots of planning. This time it was for a festival of the arts, to be held the next February. There would be films, selected by Iris Barry, ballets danced by Balanchine's new troupe, concerts of music selected by me to be performed in stage sets by Alexander Calder and Eugene Berman, and a costume ball designed by Tchelitcheff.

That fall I teamed up with John Houseman for sharing flats; and from October through March we lived in four, some rented, some lent by friends. And Houseman was a joy for living with; he never scolded, and he was away all day. Like a proper Englishman, he got up at eight, bathed, washed in his bath the previous day's wool socks, cooked coffee and eggs, ate, and left. We always break-fasted in French, settling matters that regarded books and plays and actors in that best of all languages for making critical dis-tinctions. In November, when Kurt Weill and his wife, Lotte Lenya, arrived, we thought, with Chick, that it would be good to produce in Hartford Weill's German opera made with Brecht, *Mahagonny*. We took Weill there to see the theater, and I even played through the score with him for setting tempos. But quietly the project was dissolved; and one came to understand that Weill's working association with Bertolt Brecht, as part of a possibly com-munist-tainted past, was to be buried. And buried it remained until his death. He developed on Broadway a new career which made him fame and money. Lenya, who had been identified with the earlier works, was omitted from the new ones. After Weill's death in 1950 she appeared on the stage again, though still chiefly in Ger-many, in revivals and subsequent recordings of the operas composed with Brecht.

And just then (we are in November of '35) Broadway began to be aware of a slender, moon-faced actor, Orson Welles, who was playing a small role with Katherine Cornell in *Romeo and Juliet*. My other close director friend, Jo Losey, could not bear him; but Houseman, scenting brains and temperament, brought him to our flat. That Welles could be so overbearing at eighteen was in his fa-vor; that he had already directed plays in Dublin we did not believe. But Houseman was organizing a theatrical production-unit under the Works Progress Administration; and he had faith in Orson, as he had in me. It was around the three of us, with Feder for light-ing, that he organized the Negro Theatre in Harlem which was to be the first of all the federal theaters to open. In fact, with the turn of 1936 both Houseman and I began to have lots of jobs; and all of these we felt sure were important.

Before that time there had been a series of musical performances that were for me important. Copland, ever adept at attracting subsidy, had been put in charge of five one-composer concerts at the New School for Social Research and had chosen as subjects for these the members of American music's most up-and-at-'em commando unit—himself, myself, Roy Harris, Sessions, and Piston. For my program, November 8, I coached my Second String Quartet, *Stabat Mater,* and Violin Sonata, played portraits and a Piano Sonatina, accompanied Ada MacLeish singing in French poems by George Hugnet.

Eva Goldbeck, Marc Blitzstein's wife, reviewed the concert for *Modern Music.* Less a musician than a polemicist, she wrote almost as if she had been assigned a hatchet job, or in any case permitted the attempt. She spoke of "salon" music with clearly pejorative intent. "Fundamentally sanguine, with a few well-timed sighs," "a slight but graceful voice," "depends on associations[,] as emotional impact is outside Thomson's range or intention," "the relaxed mood of a well-carpeted cocktail hour"—were the phrases with which she must have hoped to kill.

The Federal Music Project, come January of '36, initiated a concert series that still goes on. This invention of Ashley Pettis, called then The Composers' Forum-Laboratory, now The Composers' Forum, has always been a mixture of talk and music, since the public, after the music has been played, is invited to question the composers. I shared the first such program with Roy Harris, Goddard Lieberson, and Isadore Freed; and under the questionings I defended firmly my right to make music after my own aesthetic dictates. I also parried several attempts to invade my political privacy. For the communists, who had turned out in force, were surely hoping that by means of loaded questions they might prove my inveterate trade-unionism and solid colleague relations just a front, as if the *Four Saints* and museum worlds had left me suspect or contaminated. Actually, as that year turned into 1936 I was about to be involved no less with leftist musical politics than with the ultrastylish Hartford Festival.

The latter took place in February of '36, just two years after my opera's opening, The Friends and Enemies of Modern Music still serving as impresario. It comprised five chief events—a showing of historic films, three concerts, and a ball. The films—and this was before such showings were at all common—consisted of the Méliès

A Trip to the Moon, of 1902; two from 1914, Theda Bara, the original "vamp," in *A Fool There Was* and dance sequences from *The Whirl of Life,* with Vernon and Irene Castle; and René Clair's Dada fantasy from 1924, *Cinéma (Entr'acte),* accompanied by the Satie music.

An orchestral concert called "Music of the Connecticut Valley" ran from a Festival Overture of 1896 by John Spencer Camp, through substantial works by Roger Sessions, Frederick Jacobi, Ruth White Smallens, Werner Josten, and Ross Lee Finney, the latter's offering being a set of songs which had won the festival's chamber music prize.

I conducted a program running from the eighteenth-century French *gambiste* Caix d'Hervelois to modern rarities that included works by Henri Sauguet and Paul Bowles, also a seven-instrument paraphrase by Henri Cliquet-Pleyel of *Swing Low, Sweet Chariot.* I had also inserted my own Sonata da Chiesa. The early music was played on early instruments; the set for the concert was the work of Eugene Berman.

Berman had dreamed of theatrical settings all his grown life. When Chick suggested his actually designing one, almost overnight he made thirty-four water-color sketches, all evocative of seventeenth-century Italian ruins and all showing mud puddles in the foreground. When I questioned the practicality of real mud and water, I was assured that the puddles were there in the sketches only for lifelikeness. And when I asked whether he had calculated the effect on his already complex stage-pictures of musicians, chairs, and instruments, he answered, "They will injure it, of course." The young James Soby, who from having already bought roomfuls of Berman canvases was Chick's diplomatic agent for dealing with him, suggested that passages from several sketches might possibly be combined. But Genia would have none of that. "An artist," he would say "can accept only negative criticism. If the first sketches are not satisfactory, I shall be glad to make others. But I will not be told how to solve a problem." I do not remember how the solution was arrived at, but one of the less busy backdrops came to be used. And Berman was happy; I was happy; everybody was.

The most complex of these concerts was one involving three contrasted works and three stage-sets. Stravinsky's *Les Noces,* conducted by Smallens, was sung in Russian in front of a décor painted after the original design of Natalia Gontcharova, which was in the museum's Diaghilev-Lifar Collection. There was no dancing, however, in this presentation. That appeared only in a ballet called *Magic,* which Balanchine, with Tchelitcheff as designer, had imagined after seeing Chick, as "The Great Ozram," do a sleight-of-hand matinee for friends and children. In this ballet, to music by Mozart, Felia Dubrowska made her last public appearance and America's finest classical male dancer, Lew Christensen, his first.

The piece that I held closest to heart was Erik Satie's *Socrate.* For this performance, America's first complete orchestral one (conducted by Smallens from the pit), I had abandoned the Paris tradition of using just one singer and arranged for two, so as to pass the conversations back and forth. These were Eva Gauthier, soprano, and Colin O'More, tenor; and I did not require the latter always to sing the role of Socrates. For an equal distribution of opportunities, I cast him also as Phaedo, who recounts the death scene.

Alexander Calder's set was an arrangement of geometric forms, all capable of motion. They were supposed to be moved mechanically; but the motors Calder had provided were too weak. So our lighting expert—Feder, as usual—with the help of a stagehand manipulated them by ropes. This mobile sculpture, simple to the eye and restrained in movement, was so sweetly in accord with the meaning of the work that it has long remained in my memory as a stage achievement. Its layout was as follows: The singers stood in evening dress before lyre-shaped black music stands, right and left near the proscenium. Upstage and to the viewer's right, against the sky-blue cyclorama, there hung by invisible wires a scarlet disk. Downstage, also on the viewer's right and also hanging in the sky by invisible wires, was the framework of a globe, drawn in space by aluminum tubing as if to represent meridians of longitude. At center-stage and to the left, also invisibly supported, stood two narrow white rectangles unequally tall.

During Alcibiades's praise of Socrates (from *The Banquet*) nothing moved. During the philosopher's walk with Phaedrus along the banks of the Eleusis, the sphere revolved sedately. For Phaedo's narrative of Socrates's death the sphere stood still while all the other forms moved very slowly. The white stele-like rectangles leaned to right, lay down, became invisible, then stood again, now well to right of center, exposing their other face, which was black. And meanwhile, from the beginning of the death scene, the sunlike disk had been descending diagonally across the sky, so that when the movement of the steles had been completed (from left to right and from white to black) the disk was low and on the viewer's left. Attention to words and music had not been troubled, so majestic was the slowness of the moving, so simple were the forms, so plain their meaning.

The final event of the Hartford Festival, a *Bal des Chiffoniers,* or Ragpickers' Ball, was Tchelitcheff's joke for high society about the Depression. He had papered the covered court's three balconies with newspapers, brushed lines on these in black to simulate draped lace, creating in this way boxes for paying guests, themselves got up in paper or in circus rags. For a *Cirque des Chiffoniers,* with Chick and a fashionable hostess as ringmasters, was theme for the prepared entrances. Of these the program listed seventeen, well more than half of them taking place to music especially composed by George Antheil, Nicolas Nabokov, and Vernon Duke and in costumes designed by Calder, Tchelitcheff, Berman, Alice Halicka. One of Berman's most effective was a walking structure entitled *Hartford in Ruins,* A.D. *3095.* Modern art was parodied from Chirico to Brancusi. And there was a ballet, fortunately interrupted by the Fire Department, in which dancers with lighted candelabra on their heads leaped through the paper porticos.

This Hartford Festival, announced as the first, was also the last. And its concerts marked my last service as "musical director" of Chick's Friends and Enemies, for by then I had got involved with plays and films. I was back and forth to Hartford as a visitor; and my ballet *Filling Station* came out there two years later. And Chick went on with his unusual shows of painting and with the producing of rare operas and of classical tragedies such as *'Tis Pity She's a Whore.* He even played the leading role in *Hamlet* to the music I had made for Leslie Howard. But after the war in Europe had begun, and he turned forty, the flame of youth went out of him, though youth's energies were there still when he died in '57. He had not liked not remaining thirty. Also, his team had got dispersed. He had staged an epoch right in his museum, using Baroque art, surrealist art, and the neo-Romantic when all three were exotic to America. He was at home with artists too, loved to admire them, give them comforts and affection, put them to work. One of his finer inspirations, just before his career began to lose momentum, was to commission murals from Kristians Tonny. Completed in 1938, they still light up the side walls of the theater where so many of us worked happily and well.

Show Business
for Uncle Sam

PARE LORENTZ WAS A FILM REVIEWER beginning to make films. And his first essay, a documentary, had just finished being photographed. Looking for a composer, he invited me to lunch. This was in January of '36. I was not the first one he had interviewed; Copland, I know, and Harris, I think, he had already not got on with. Houseman, whom he had consulted, had suggested me as musically straightforward and theatrically wise; and though Lorentz had yet to hear any of my music, he engaged me on the spot. Our conversation went like this. He first explained his film, asked could I imagine writing music for it. My answer was, "How much money have you got?" Said he, "Beyond the costs of orchestra, conductor, and recording, the most I could possibly have left for the composer is five hundred." "Well," said I, "I can't take from any man more than he's got, though if you did have more I would ask for it." My answer delighted him. "All those high-flyers," he said, "talk nothing but aesthetics. You talk about money; you're a professional."

The film was a documentary about cattle raising, wheat growing, and dust storms on the Western plains. Its sponsor was the United States Resettlement Administration, needing to justify its program of aiding refugee families from devastated areas. Lorentz had begun his film by engaging as story writers a trio of photographers who knew the Southwest—Ralph Steiner, Paul Strand, and Leo Hurwitz; and early he had quarreled with them about their wishing to ascribe the grassland's rape not to just human nature, the Great War, and lack of foresight, but to a more conventional villain of the time, capitalist greed. Next he had fought with Hollywood over the right of our government to purchase, as any U.S. citizen could do, stock shots of World War I, of forty-eight-mule-team reaping, of flood-lit harvesting, and similar subjects not available for him to photograph. With the aid of a former Assistant Attorney General, Mabel Walker Willebrandt, he did secure the release of certain footage. He never secured permission to show his film in houses controlled by the industry, as Hollywood called itself. The industry did not hold with documentaries anyway, still less with films made by the government, above all not with anything well done that was not theirs. And *The Plow That Broke the Plains* was powerful storytelling; documentaries so dramatic had not been made before.

When I was hired, the film was in the cutting stage; and composing music before each sequence has found its true length is rarely advisable. So all that I could do while waiting was to grow familiar with the uncut film through frequent viewings and to look up all the books of cowboy songs and settler folklore, since Lorentz's mind was set (and oh, how rightly!) on rendering landscape through the music of its people. When at last he was through with cutting, he wanted me to write twenty-five minutes of music, symphonically scored, inside a week. I told him I could not do that, because I should be away for four days at the Hartford Festival, but that I would have everything ready for recording within the fortnight. To do this I should need, in addition to the usual copyist for extracting the parts, a musical secretary trained to help with score.

The cost of this he did not mind, since he had foreseen that I might require a paid arranger. It was from Antheil, who had the year before made music for *Once in a Blue Moon,* a Jimmy Savo film, that I got the address of a very young Canadian composer, Henry Brant. Working in pencil, I could sketch-orchestrate everything myself, then check his ink score to be sure it had come out my way, which indeed it had, for the most part. And Brant was such a natural orchestrator that I even asked him once to salt up a passage with percussion. I did not, after one essay, depend on him for string chords or for phrasing, for though he could dispose these admirably, I did not like another's personality to color my sound.

Returned from Hartford with a blasting grippe, I composed at night, scored over Brant's shoulder in the daytime, finished my work as promised. It was recorded in New York by thirty men from the Philharmonic and from the Metropolitan Opera, conducted by Smallens, who was accustomed by then to my music and had a lively understanding of its ways. Nor was he surprised when errors turned up in the parts. Delays caused by correcting these in full recording session ran up the costs, according to Lorentz's stop watch, by something like $500. Teaching a guitarist to play in three-four time against a six-eight beat cost plenty too. But Smallens could work fast; and the Philharmonic boys, used to one another and to achieving balanced sound, produced a symphonic richness not at all common in films.

Then Lorentz disappeared with the sound track into the cutting room, was gone a week. When he emerged, he had recut his film. Some of the recutting had been required by my war music's not being as heavily scored as it should have been. To compensate for phrases of light texture he had rearranged the order of the views, also added cannons and bomb-sounds and tank-noises. All the other adjustments he had made were for illustrating passages in the music. For Pare was musically sensitive to the last degree. He would have preferred, before he cut his film at all, to have a full recording of the music, because details, especially of orchestration, would make him want to match them visually. But since a visual narrative cannot be based on auditory timings, a film must be cut before any score is made. Then after the music track has been recorded, only the sight track can still be manipulated. And it was within this limited flexibility that Pare created, working to the very sound of music, a music-stimulated intensity within each sequence. As a result, photography, words, and music in *The Plow* seem not to be at war with one another but to be telling, all at the same time, the same story.

We were living at this period, Houseman and I, in a furnished apartment on Central Park South; and it was from there that I did all my work for the Negro Theatre. This enterprise, a unit of the Federal Theatre, operated a large Harlem playhouse from prewar times, the Lafayette. Houseman was its director, Orson

Welles his assistant, Feder his lighting and technical man, myself in charge of music. I think we were the only whites, save our scene designer, Nat Karson, and a secretary. Ninety percent of all who worked there had to be drawn from the city's relief rolls. And all were paid the same, $23.86 weekly. Establishing such units all over the United States not only for theater workers but also for artists, writers, and musicians was the W.P.A. assignment; and it was urgent because the relief of poverty was urgent. That our unit was the first of all these theaters to open was due to Welles's brilliant planning and to Houseman's administrative tact.

The plan involved, as any repertory project must, preparing two plays at once, the second to be ready in case the first should fail. Our opening spectacle, a play by a Negro on a theme from Negro life, required no written music. Our second, Houseman's dream but Orson's child, was *Macbeth*. And in this Orson showed himself, still just eighteen, as imaginative, foresighted, patient, above all with a knack for making actors act.

The production idea that was to make *Macbeth* seem suitable for Negro performers was that of moving its locale to Haiti, where a Negro usurper could be believable, at least in Napoleonic times, along with his overthrow by revolution. This transfer gave us, instead of Scottish witches, real voodoo, also some most becoming Empire costumes. I say real voodoo because it was provided by a Congolese who had already produced dance spectacles with African instruments constructed by himself and songs remembered from his mission childhood. Asadota Dafora Horton was authentic, all right; we had checked on that. (In the 1960s he was to become Minister of Culture in the Republic of Sierra Leone.) And he could produce with black Americans music and drumming and dance to put the chill up anybody's spine. I once, for the second witches' scene, asked for more chill. "This sounds a little tame," I said. "Is it real voodoo you're giving me?" "Oh, yes, that's voodoo. Yes, that's real all right." "What kind of voodoo is it?" I insisted. "Real voodoo. Yes, real voodoo," was his answer. And it remained his answer till I broke him down. He finally admitted that it was not *evil* voodoo but only charms against the beri-beri. Anything stronger in that black atmosphere, stirred up by rhythm and poetry, might work; indeed it might. I said no more.

Our Lady Macbeth was Edna Thomas, our first Macbeth Jack

Carter. When he grew undependable, Maurice Ellis took on the role. Canada Lee was permanently Banquo. There was a sizable pit orchestra, which I conducted at the opening. Also there was a percussion group backstage made up of bass drums, kettledrums, a thunder drum, a thunder sheet, a wind machine—all these not only for simulating storms but also, played by musicians and conducted, for accompanying some of the grander speeches. In this way, on a pretext of rough weather, I could support an actor's voice and even build it to twice life size. This device (really Welles's) requires accurate operation, for with all the percussion rattling, players backstage cannot hear lines but must depend on light-cues; nor can an actor so accompanied change his reading much from one night to another.

The whole production, with its voodoo dancing, its ball scene (for there was waltzing at the banquet), its storms, its battle trumpets, and its marching trees, was melodramatic to the utmost. When late that summer Jean Cocteau turned up, circling the globe in eighty days for a Paris paper, I took him to *Macbeth*. And he savored each ingenious violation of the straightforward, excepting only one: he did not understand the constant lighting changes. His classical theater mind found them distracting till he had seized their function in the spectacle as contributing to the climate of violence. The only element not in this "Wagnerian" key, as Cocteau called it, was the music, which consisted altogether (outside its voodoo realisms, its offstage storms and battles) of familiar suspense-conventions, of pathos passages almost *Hearts and Flowers,* and, in the ball scene, of Lanner waltzes.

From this production I acquired two musical aides—Hugh Davis, player of kettledrums and percussion, and Leonard de Paur, a choral conductor. Davis remained invaluable until he died in the early 1940s. De Paur is a colleague still, though he is famous now and tours with his own choir. But Harlem then was full of lovely people. So was the WPA. The times were for sweetness and for joy in work.

My next job, all the same, was bittersweet, the bitter of it being the hemlock taste that permeates all things communist. In such an ambience, someone is always handing you the poisoned cup. And the theater that borrowed me that summer, The Living Newspaper, was up to its ears in commies. My director, also on loan, was Joseph Losey, with whom I had worked before. The script, a montage of scenes from the history of union labor in the United States courts, was called *Injunction Granted*. I used an orchestra of sixteen percussion players, with sixteen bass drums, snare drums, cymbals, sixteen of everything, including bronx cheers. I also had lots of bells and chimes and three electric sirens. I punctuated every exit and entrance, almost every remark, with percussive comment and ironic framing. The complete score came to 496 music cues. The show was less pungent, however, than its predecessor, *Triple-A Ploughed Under,* which had set the dramatic form. This form was documentary, editorial, frankly hortatory. I regret its passing. Its television heirs, known as spectaculars, are seldom so convincing.

Injunction Granted had been made in summer's heat, high up in a house that received hot winds (and greasy soot) from the East River. There too I helped Paul Bowles through his first theater-piece. The apartment was Alfred Barr's, lent for the summer—a large living room, two bedrooms, and two baths. For several weeks I shared it with the lyricist John Latouche, then impecunious and convalescent; but before I got to working on my next show, he had gone to e. e. cummings in New Hampshire. During the August heat I worked on another show with Welles, who with Houseman and their team—which still included the scene designer Nat Karson—had left the Negro unit, forever playing *Macbeth,* and formed one of their own, called Project 891, at the Maxine Elliott on Forty-first Street. Here I joined them for putting on—at my insistence, as I remember—a nineteenth-century French farce by Eugène Labiche, *Un Chapeau de paille d'Italie,* newly translated by Edwin Denby and Welles together and retitled *Horse Eats Hat.*

Welles directed it, of course; he even played at the opening a character bit and sang a song, though his ear was not for music. The other parts were played by Joseph Cotten, Hiram Sherman, Arlene Francis, Sarah Burton, and Paula Laurence. And if *Macbeth* had in Orson's hands turned Negroid and Wagnerian, this classical French vaudeville became a circus. There was a seven-door set "in one," admirable for hide-and-seek; there was furniture by Bil Baird designed to come apart; there was a ball room with crystal chandelier and a functioning fountain. When at the end of Act One, with guests waltzing and waiters coming in with champagne, our harassed hero, Joe Cotten, jumped to the chandelier, which swung with him, and the fountain below began to spout on him, and then in the pandemonium stagehands began to carry off the scenery and a blank curtain came down as if to end the disaster but itself fell clean to the floor, and the house curtain finally descended, Muriel Draper was overheard to cry, "It's wonderful! They should keep this in the show!"

The music too was like a circus with side shows, for in addition to that in the pit there were on the stage (where all was in the style of 1910, with hobble skirts and hats with ostrich plumes) two dance bands, one for playing turkey trots and one in red coats for playing gypsy waltzes. At intermission, from one stage-box a mechanical piano pumped out period selections; and in another a lady trumpeter in hussar's uniform rendered *The Carnival of Venice*.

The pit contained no less than thirty-five musicians, and both the lower boxes held grand pianos. The music by Paul Bowles, and there was lots of it—overtures, intermezzos, meditations, marches, even a song or two—had been selected mostly out of works already in existence. In that way one can have varieties and richnesses of texture almost never available in music run up rapidly. And for further amplitude, I scored these numbers as a suite for two pianos and orchestra. I made the score myself because Paul had not yet learned to orchestrate. Receiving help of this kind shocked him deeply. Within the year, as a result, he had composed and scored excellent music for Orson Welles's production of Marlowe's *Doctor Faustus,* a ballet for Kirstein and Balanchine's new company (*Yankee Clipper*), and a Negro opera (*Denmark Vesey* by Charles-Henri Ford).

Only in such an enterprise as the W.P.A. Federal Theatre, where maximum employment was the aim, could one have mobilized effectives as numerous as those used in *Macbeth* and in *Horse Eats Hat* or in *Injunction Granted* or in the sumptuous mounting of T. S. Eliot's *Murder in the Cathedral* (with quantities of music by Lehman Engel). And only in a time of general unemployment could one have had directors, artistic collaborators, and technical assistants of such high quality. None of our *Horse Eats Hat* cast was yet famous, though news of Orson had begun to get around. The fact that he could both direct and act was leading him into a career that rose like a rocket, only to begin before he had turned thirty its slow descent. Welles as actor, for all his fine bass speaking voice, never did quite get into a role; his mind was elsewhere. He discovered many an actor's talent; his own he seemed to throw away. And by the time he weighed 300 pounds his presence on stage destroyed the composition. But working with him in his youth was ever a delight, also a lesson that might be called Abundance in the Theater.

Horse Eats Hat played to an intellectual public. It might have broadened its appeal had not our Washington inspectors been bent on combing its language for indelicacies. Every day or two another telegram arrived, ordering that such and such a line be cut. Shortly we knew that someone "down there" did not like it; moreover, audiences were finding the show's satire of itself confusing. So Welles began on Marlowe's *Doctor Faustus,* a spectacle grand enough and far less difficult. And Houseman was getting involved with *Hamlet;* so was I. We remained on the federal payroll, since being paid between productions was the only way we could make our salaries support us. And Houseman is at his best when overworked; he cannot do just one job at a time; he must have two; fatigue excites him.

Our *Hamlet* was for Leslie Howard, a drawing room actor principally, but one who felt that modern plays, for all his great success in them, were not using fully his abilities. I am not sure that Schuyler Watts, an enthusiast just out of Yale, had not convinced him Hamlet was his role. For with Howard in mind, Watts had cut and rearranged the play with great sagacity. And Houseman, engaged to direct it, had gone along with Watts's scheme for placing it in medieval sets, adding a Welles-like richness everywhere and engaging me to furnish lots of music. My novel additive to *Hamlet,* aside from bagpipes in the funeral march, was making a ballet-opera out of *Gonzaga's Murder.* This play within the play, to set it off from the drama going on around it, I treated as if a medieval troupe, accustomed to representing saints and miracles, were intoning it in medieval poses. Agnes de Mille translated this conception into choreography; and visible musicians accompanied it, using tiny drums and cymbals especially made, bamboo recorders, and a rare sort of horn.

This treatment was thoroughly effective save for one mistake.

My player of recorders, Youry Bilstin, an expert on old instruments, had found somewhere a handsome serpent made of leather. It would not play, but he proposed to use it as a megaphone, singing into it "hoo" to imitate a hunting horn. The sight of it was so delightful that none of us remarked its shaky sound until on opening night at the Boston Opera House a drunk in the gallery hiccoughed and laughed. That was its end. I tried to quarrel with Houseman on the subject, but he was firm; and anyway I knew I had miscalculated; the chanted play remained without its horn. My music was conducted, on stage and off, by Hugh Davis, my percussionist from Harlem. And for Pamela Stanley, who could sing most sweetly, I set every one of the Ophelia songs. The production, after Boston, played three months on Broadway and something like that time on tour. Never so popular as John Gielgud's *Hamlet,* which was running that same season, through its scenery by Stewart Chaney and its direction by Houseman it was probably more distinguished. And though Howard had not Gielgud's vocal power for the great tirades, in the intimate scenes with Ophelia and with Horatio he was more touching. For the last soliloquy, "How all occasions do inform against me," we placed him on a ship's prow, center-stage high up; and I arranged for offstage instruments, evoking North Sea weather, to build up his voice until it filled the house.

At the middle of November I went to Paris for six weeks, not notifying the Federal Theatre of my absence. I was to start work with Pare Lorentz the first of January on another film. Meanwhile, I wanted to be with Madame Langlois, from whom I had been away two years, and to resume, if only for a time, the flow of friendship's dialogue with Hugnet, Cliquet-Pleyel, Sauguet, Bérard, as well as Gertrude Stein and Max Jacob.

I took with me a film-print of *The Plow That Broke the Plains,* engaged a projection-theater, had friends in to see it. Miss Stein was there, of course; and Cocteau came, bringing the ever so fashionable Daisy (the Hon. Mrs. Reginald) Fellows; and Hugnet brought the surrealist poets Paul Eluard and André Breton. Breton and Cocteau, though literary enemies, committed no unfriendly act, as English enemies would have felt obliged to do, but in the good French way ignored each other.

I also gave a concert with Cliquet, a small one in his studio apartment. And although Marthe-Marthine sang Satie's *Socrate*, which had not been done in Paris recently, and Paul Poiret, known better as *couturier* than elocutionist, read charmingly from the fables of La Fontaine, there was such a grubbiness about Marthe's interior, with its six-yard window curtains almost in shreds, that Julien Levy, arriving from New York, felt he must reproach me for appearing in an ambience so slummy.

Paris itself had turned political; the leftist Popular Front was a success. The Spanish were embraced by civil war. The King of England had resigned for love. Hitler had caused henchmen to be shot down. Russia was disciplining Shostakovich. In Italy liberals had joined the Fascist party. From America Harry Dunham, my former neighbor of 17 quai Voltaire, arrived just then, traveling via Russia into China. Once there, by unknown means, and carrying a Communist party card, he made his way to the communist provinces, took films that became a news scoop. He also, loving ever an adventure, gave his American passport to a German youth who had none, declaring to our consulate its loss or theft.

Before I took ship I received from Washington, which had discovered I was absent not only from Maxine Elliott's Theatre but also from the country, a pink slip terminating my employment. Arriving in New York on New Year's Eve, I shortly took a flat again with Houseman, this time on Fifty-fifth Street at First Avenue. From there Houseman, still at the Maxine Elliott, produced Marc Blitzstein's *singspiel, The Cradle Will Rock*. And at the Neighborhood Playhouse, Orson Welles, with Lehman Engel conducting, produced *The Second Hurricane,* a Copland-Denby high school cantata-opera. As for myself, for the next half year I mostly wrestled with Pare Lorentz.

The Theatrical Thirties

LORENTZ AT THIRTY, already getting heavy but still darkly good looking and with an eye that both laughed and calculated, was talkative, ambitious, truculent, ever a battler. He battled with Hollywood and with Washington; he battled with his cameramen and with his cutter. For seven months he battled with me over music, money, aesthetics, every single point of contact that we had. Nor do I think he was not mainly right. I merely note that battling was for Pare a way of life and that even in creating he warred with his teammates. He did not bicker; his tone was gentlemanly; our weekly all-night conferences were warm. But Pare's film was his brainchild not yet born, and he could not be stopped from going on about it. He could not bear that I should have to wait till it was finished to add music. He even seemed to hope that I, by sharing his birthpains, might end by writing music in his person.

At forty I could not write music in anybody's person. Collaborative art, I knew from instinct and experience, can only give a good result when each man offers to the common theme, through his own working methods and at the proper time, his own abundance. An author-director needs to keep all such abundances channelized for nourishing his theme rather than drowning it; of such are his veto rights. But when he suggests textures he is always wrong. These must come out of each man's own technique. An artist cannot be ordered about or hypnotized, but he can be fecundated by another's faith. Here lies the difference between live art and the commercial, that in live work everybody trusts everybody else. But Pare did not trust anybody quite, because from inexperience he did not trust himself.

The music of *The Plow* had poured forth easily. I knew the Great Plains landscape in Kansas, Oklahoma, New Mexico, Texas; and during the War I had lived in a tent with ten-below-zero dust storms. I had come to the theme nostalgic and ready to work; and the film itself, when I first encountered it, was ready to be worked on. The subject, moreover, was highly photogenic—broad grasslands and cattle, mass harvesting, erosion by wind, deserted farms. *The River* was to be different; its theme was soil erosion by water, not by wind. Its landscape of streams and forests was pastoral, static. Its historical narrative covered a century, its geographical perspective half the continent. And floods, though murderous to land and houses, are not at all dramatic to observe. A film explaining how they come about and how they can be controlled by dams demands a far more complex composition, if one wants to make it powerful, than the blowing away of our dry high-lying West.

Pare's subsidizers in the government, pleased by *The Plow* but aware that *The River*'s theme would be harder to elaborate, were granting him a slightly larger budget for the new film. And Pare, grateful for my underpaid work on the earlier one, was wishing to overpay me a bit on this. So he put me on salary from February first at $25 a day, the wages of a union cameraman. The only trouble with this ingenious solution was that no checks came; I imagine paper work had held them up. Then new floods, grand ones, appeared in the Midwest; and Pare flew out with cameramen to photograph them. But still I had no money, and Pare's office had no news. So I wired him that if he were wishing to fire me by not paying my salary, I should feel free, even obliged, to seek other employment. His answer was telegraphic:

REPLYING TO YOUR LETTER CATEGORICALLY STOP SAID TO YOU COULD
NOT PUT YOU ON FULL SALARY UNTIL CAMERA MEN DISMISSED STOP
AM PAYING YOU EVERY CENT POSSIBLE RIGHT NOW AND MORE THAN
BUDGET ALLOWS AND AM STRAINING TO MEET EMERGENCY PAYROLLS

STOP DID NOT FORSEE FLOODS OR WOULD HAVE BEEN CUTTING PIC-
TURE LONG AGO STOP YOU WERE EMPLOYED TO COMPOSE A MUSICAL
SCORE STOP THERE IS NO MOVIE FOR YOU TO COMPOSE FOR BECAUSE
OF A MEMORANDUM STOP I AM STRAINING TO PAY YOU FOR RESEARCH
DURING PERIOD I CARRY CAMERAMEN ON SALARY STOP CAN PAY YOU
FULL PERIOD FOR FEBRUARY BUT CONSIDER THAT ONLY UNPROFES-
SIONAL THING ABOUT DEAL STOP SINCE WHEN DID SHOW HAVE TO
BE WRITTEN TO SUIT COMPOSER STOP WITH ARMY WEATHER AND
CAMERAS TO WORRY OVER CONSIDER YOUR LETTER UNFAIR AND UN-
CALLED FOR

LORENTZ

My checks, as promised, did start coming soon. And Pare came
back and showed me his new footage. And we went on sitting up
nights, drinking together and trying to solve problems by talk that
cried out to be solved by work—by visual work on Pare's part, such
as cutting his film, on mine by study of regional music sources.
This I began to do, actually; and in the course of that, I came
upon the gold mine of hymns known as "white spirituals."

The identification of this material as authentic folklore had been
made by Dr. George Pullen Jackson, a New Englander from
Maine teaching at Vanderbilt University; but only the beginning
of his work had yet reached print. When I wrote him for access to
the hymnbooks that were his sources, he procured for me the chief
ones and on his way to Europe came to see me with recordings of
these hymns as actually sung. Maurice Grosser, painting in Tennessee, went out to the hills to look for more such books and found
a plowing clergyman willing to lend, since it was "for educational
purposes," his precious copy of the century-old *Southern Harmony*.
And when Maurice came back to New York, I engaged him on
federal payroll, with Pare's complicity, to copy for me all the tunes,
their counterpoints and words, that I did not have already in *The
Sacred Harp,* the other chief available source for folk hymns.

By this time spring was on; our lease was up; and Houseman
had moved out to Rockland County (for sleeping only, since he
was in town all day). I had gone to the Chelsea Hotel on West
Twenty-third Street, where I was to stay for the next full year.
And Pare, who also lived in Rockland County, would come there;
and I would sing and play for him my newly-come-upon Americana. He was skeptical, I think, of its value to the film, but he did

not battle with me over it. We merely wrestled, testing our defenses. My own absorption in these tunes, though passionate, was not exclusive, since I had just received by gift another gold mine, a collection sent to me by Foster Damon. This was a reprint in facsimile, with learned notes, of one hundred American popular songs running from roughly 1800 to 1850. These filled out my ancient hymn-lore with vaudeville ditties, parlor ballads, and levee hoedowns until, along with what I knew already, I had the Old South richly repertoried. I even went to Washington, spending an afternoon there with old John Lomax, song hunter extraordinary, and making free with the vast materials, in so far as catalogued, that he had brought back to the Library of Congress.

As Pare, who was a slow worker but persistent, little by little got his film down to thirty-six minutes (four reels) and perfected his accompanying text, a Whitmanesque prose poem about America's rivers, I little by little would sketch music that seemed to me to suit the sequences. But Pare was worried, I think, lest my involvement with white spirituals get out of his control; and he kept on trying to arrest my pregnancy. I quoted to him Eugene Berman's protests against directive criticism. I also pointed out that he did not have a completed film. How could I be guided about what I had not seen? But Pare, though amused by the old commercial ditties, remained unsure about backcountry hymns and worried lest I overuse them in his film. So in June I resigned again, writing him that since he was not finding my work satisfactory, continuing it would do his film no good, and that I was going off to bask with friends in Rensselaerville.

At the end of a week he telephoned to say that he was ready for me now and would I please return. I said, "Pare, I am on strike. If you want me back at all, you must hear my conditions." He waited a moment, then said, "I'll expect you tomorrow." So I went back.

My main condition was that he was not to give me any more musical directions, though he could veto any music I proposed. My second was that I wished, and rather for his sake than mine, to be present in the cutting room, at least a little bit, so that I might possibly be able to discern what his film needs were, which I had so consistently failed to grasp from explanation. He agreed to both, gave me a near-completed timing sheet, and said I was to finish up my score. From then on he liked everything I wrote; and when I played it all in front of the screened picture, he found no alterations needed. So again I called in Henry Brant, and within a week the score was finished. In late July it was recorded in Astoria by Smallens and some forty Philharmonic men, along with Hugh Davis, who played all the percussion and received at the end a standing cheer from his colleagues. Lorentz disappeared then into the cutting room, said he would let me know when I might join him.

For all Pare's constant talk to me about film problems, at no time had I tried to guide his work, though I had offered him full access to mine. I had no wish, God knows, to interfere; nor was I at all experienced in cutting. But since he had submitted many of his problems as if they might be apt for musical solution, I knew the only place to test this was the cutting room. And besides, my fresh eye might just possibly be helpful; in the theater Welles, Losey, Houseman, all had found it so. This is why at the last I came to insist that Lorentz stop lecturing me and let me help him cut the film. He never did. But he did just once invite me to the cutting room during the week he was holed up there with the music track. He summoned me for sometime before midnight, and with the union cutter we stayed till morning. Through the movie-ola I checked their progress as they labored at recutting the whole film to my music. Pare asked for no comment; I uttered none. He made it clear that my being asked there was a courtesy; I made sure to offer no encumbrance. We went home at eight, Pare pleased, I thought, to have outmaneuvered me and infinitely pleased—that I could tell—with the music track.

For composing the last half reel I had had no cue sheets. "Write me a five-minute finale," he had said, "and I'll cut to that." So I used the finale of my *Symphony on a Hymn Tune,* the theme of which, a white spiritual anyway (though I had not known that when I wrote the piece), had been employed earlier in the film. And for this Pare composed his visual peroration to point up every detail of my scoring. I cannot imagine cutting a whole film that way; but the whole film, this time, did not seem to suffer gravely. In fact, when shown, and it was shown widely in spite of Holly-wood, audiences would applaud, a thing they almost never do for movies. Despite the film's intractable material and despite Lorentz's constant wars and wrestlings, *The River* seems now, seemed then indeed, to have achieved a higher integration of filmed narrative with spoken poetry and with music than had existed since the sound track's coming into use some eight years earlier. Even when the film was cut by one fourth its length (to twenty-seven minutes, for use in schools) the music remained, through Pare's ingenious clippings and refittings of it, surprisingly apt, and almost as closely integrated to the words and scenes as if it had been composed for the compact version.

I worked also on a full-length film that summer, a documentary called *The Spanish Earth*. This was a view of the Spanish civil war from the republican side and of an irrigation project completed in Castile during the siege of Madrid. The script was by Ernest Hemingway, John Dos Passos, and Archibald MacLeish; and I think Lillian Hellman also did some work on it, though her name does not appear among the credits. The film was photographed under fire by Joris Ivens, with Hemingway overseeing; and the verbal text for it was both written and recorded by Hemingway. When the film was being readied for showing, in August of 1937, the absence of a music track became as noticeable as the fact that there was neither time nor money for composing one. Marc Blitzstein and I, being consulted, offered to assemble a music track out of Spanish recordings available in private collections, chiefly those of Gerald Murphy and Paul Bowles. These contained choral numbers sung by Galician and Basque miners, woodwind *coblas* from Barcelona, and naturally lots of flamenco from Seville. Actually we used flamenco only once, for accompanying a view of the rightists; it did not seem sincere enough for dour Castilian farmers or for republican soldiers. The transfer of these recordings to music track and the matching of this in fragments to the sight track was the work of Helen Van Dongen, remarkably skilled and subtle in film cutting. The result is a film completely documentary, since its views of Spain's patient people and high-lying farmland are accompanied throughout by the real music of that land and people. There may be other filmed narratives as authentic; I do not know them. Certainly there are few of such distinguished authorship.

My other work of 1937, almost wholly for me a year of theater, consisted of a ballet and a Shakespeare play. The dance piece, commissioned by Lincoln Kirstein for his Ballet Caravan, was a slice-of-life called *Filling Station*. George Balanchine, essaying to develop both dancers and dance designers, had found his male wing readier for professional appearance than the female. Dance scores already furnished by Robert McBride (*Show Piece*) and by Paul Bowles (*Yankee Clipper*) had been choreographed by Erick Hawkins and Eugene Loring. That midsummer I had found in Lew Christensen a dancer and director I knew I could deal with, and in the subject offered us by Kirstein a theme I thought I could at least take hold of. Aaron Copland had also been invited to compose for the Caravan's formal opening that winter in Hartford, but he was hesitant. He had in 1934, for Ruth Page in Chicago, composed a ballet, *Hear Ye, Hear Ye!* But it was not till he had heard the scores we three had done and watched the new troupe in action that he undertook the medium again, this time to compose for Loring, who would both choreograph and dance, the remarkable ballet-Western, *Billy the Kid*.

For *Filling Station* Christensen and I worked out a suite of "numbers" and "recitatives" to tell the story in appropriate timings. And I wrote a score made up of waltzes, tangos, a fugue, a Big Apple, a holdup, a chase, and a funeral, all aimed to evoke roadside America as pop art. The painter Paul Cadmus designed clothes and a setting for it inspired by comic strips. Christensen, as a filling-station attendant in white translucent coverall, filled the stage with his in-the-air cartwheels and held us breathless with his twelve-turn pirouettes. At the Hartford opening on January 6, 1938, my music was played on a piano by Trudi Rittmann, as was also that of the other ballets. Six weeks later the New York W.P.A., with Edgar Schenckman conducting, performed all three with orchestra.

My Shakespeare play was *Antony and Cleopatra*, the star Tallulah Bankhead. The production was a sumptuous one, the cast full of good names, the cost impressive. As I had done for Leslie Howard's *Hamlet*, I engaged Hugh Davis to conduct the music cues; and as always he was perfect. Tallulah too was fine in comedy scenes such as that with the messenger from Rome, but a tragic stance she could not quite assume. She would die outside the pool of light put there for her to fall in; and she could not get the hang of my offstage sound effects, designed to build up her voice. We opened October 13 in Rochester, played Buffalo a week, then Pittsburgh two. In New York the show closed after four performances. Its flaw was a misreading of the play. "What this show needs is female sex," would say Miss Bankhead, using a single word for it, "and that's what I've got." But *Cleopatra* cannot use overt sex appeal; there is not a love scene in it. It is a political tragedy and can only succeed as that. Played for love, it is all build-up and no showdown.

My concert outlets in America had been mainly vocal. Chamber music groups, modern music groups, and symphony orchestras were all of them resistant to my instrumental music. So firmly so, indeed, that had it not been for the art world of Philip Johnson, Russell Hitchcock, and Chick Austin (plus Alfred Barr's sincere and powerful blessing), my chamber music might have remained as unavailable as my symphonies. Nor had music publication, save for one piece, yet tapped me on the shoulder. Nor recording. For that matter, even the rising and well-protected Copland was not recorded till 1935, though he had won the Victor Company's prize ten years before that. But my opera *Four Saints in Three Acts*, and especially my guidance of its production, had opened the theater to me, including films. The ballet I might have penetrated anyway through Lincoln Kirstein's interest; but my situation in 1938 was that of a vocal composer none too successful save in show business.

In that business I had become a leader, not only for my own generation but also for younger musicians. And this position had been maintained by treating show business as communication, never as glamour, religion, or ideology. Every artist in those days was considered by the communists—who were far more impressive intellectually then than now—as a possible convert. I had learned from the tourists to Russia on the *Paris* that I could without deception be their friend, but also, since all beliefs are tailored to one's needs, that I was not likely to become a convert. I hoped not to be thought their enemy, since socialism is a Christian concept. But I had long since made my peace with Christianity (as heir to it but noncommunicant), and my hopes in socialism were of that same order. I could no more, having avoided Baptist conversion, embrace the Marxists than I could the Catholics. Perhaps less, for the Jewish group within the party, though happy to be making use of me, would never, could never, since my needs were different, allow me even in socialist fellowship to share their Jewishness. Moreover, since their Jewishness, I felt, was half the reason for their membership, I did not need to join a club whose communion, either as Jew or Christian, could not nourish me.

In public matters, especially those involving union membership and fair employment, I took action, signed manifestos, asked for and offered guidance without respect to religion or party membership. In Hartford no such emergencies arose; or if they did, Chick solved them. In film making for my government I followed union practices. In Harlem neither communists nor union men were numerous. When the all-white stagehands' union refused our Negroes, then threatened to picket us if we did not hire their members, Houseman replied, "Go right ahead, if you think you can picket a Negro theater for giving work to Negro unemployed." And at *The Living Newspaper,* a communist hotbed, I walked the narrow path of modesty. It may be that in such a closed communion the rank and file mistook me for their own.

At Maxine Elliott's Theatre, with Welles and Houseman (all of us indeed) pinwheeling with enthusiasm for a play and presentation that, if not decaying capitalism's flower, was surely no branch of socialist realism, we were all suspect. At one point in the musical rehearsals of *Horse Eats Hat,* of which I was in charge, I got into an argument with the chief of personnel, whose duties were to see that union rulings were observed. But since his resistance to my requests stayed sullen and persistent, I deliberately caused him to explode in anger at me, calling me by the ritual insults, "Rat!" and "Stooge!" For the next day's rehearsal I wore a borrowed button showing hammer and sickle in white on red, above and below them the words, "Vote Communist." That day the rehearsal was frictionless, and at the end my contractor apologized, "I'm sorry for yesterday, Mr. Thomson. If I had only known!" I never let him know he did not know, never had trouble in the house again.

The earlier proposals toward collecting performance fees for classical composers, the plans that I had already helped to scotch, began in 1936 to approach a possibility of reformulation, this time by composers themselves. And I had seen to it that Copland, whatever was done, would be our leader. Neither the League of Composers, which he held in his hand, nor the leftist group, always ready to be organized, had any fear of him. He was then, still is,

American music's natural president; nothing could be done without him, with him everything. For this adventure, he called up his commando unit to spearhead it. That unit, throughout the early thirties, had consisted of himself, myself, Roy Harris, Sessions, and Piston. For the meeting he called in New York on December 17, 1937, a meeting well prepared ahead of time by conferences and by my reports on the collection of performing rights in Europe, Copland had replaced Piston, busy in Boston, with the New Yorker Douglas Moore; and he held it in the sacred halls of the Beethoven Association. At that meeting the American Composers Alliance was formed, "to regularize and collect all fees pertaining to the performance of copyrighted music." Its history as a collection group has been spotty, but its influence has nevertheless been large. Of interest both to art and to the economy are the enormous sums now distributed, as a result, by all the societies representing American composers.

Another cooperative enterprise looked toward the publication of American music. Earlier projects of this sort had either ceased to function or were failing. Henry Cowell's periodical, *New Music,* founded in 1922, was limited in circulation; also it seemed in danger of expiring. Alma Wertheim's Cos Cob Press was diminishing its output. The Society for the Publication of American Music had from its inception been in conservative hands. And the standard publishers would not touch anything advanced. Nevertheless, there was good new music around; orchestras played it; the public was receptive. Moreover, there were new ways for reproducing music less costly than engraving it. Still further, our generation and the next were by no means so poorly off as we had been a decade earlier. What with the growth in number of organizations performing and commissioning us, and with the solid salaries of those who taught or conducted, we were all more prosperous than we had been; the depression had been good for us. We would pay for our own publication.

It was in an Automat on Twenty-third Street near my hotel that Aaron Copland, Lehman Engel, Marc Blitzstein, and I drew up the plans for a cooperative music press open to all composers whose music we should find acceptable; it was to be administered by just us four, receiving no salary. The success of this enterprise is historical; and its catalog—containing many works by Copland, Har-

Others than I made musical portraits. This sketch of V.T., dated May 4, 1930, is by Henri Sauguet.

V.T. in 1927, at thirty-one.

Below: Rogert Désormière, a composer from Erik Satie's *groupe d'Arceuil,* became an excellent conductor.

Above: Roy Harris came to France in 1926 to study composition with Boulanger, stayed four years.

Left: Mary Butts was English, an adept of magic, a smoker of opium, a poet, an author of novels and stories.

Below left: Georges Hugnet, poet, and Eugene Berman, painter, with Gertrude Stein in 1929 at Bilignin.

Above: The painter Christian Bérard around 1925, before he had become fat or famous, grown a beard.

Above left: Sergei Prokofiev and Nicolas Nabokov at Deauville, May–June 1931. *Above right:* V.T. with Gertrude Stein and opera score, circa 1929 or '30. *Below: La Sérénade,* 1932—Vittorio Rieti, Marqués de Casa Fuerte, Milhaud, Prince Leone Massimo, Yvonne de Casa Fuerte, Sauguet, Désormière, and Igor Markevitch.

Painters Eugene and Leonid Berman in the south of France, 1937.

Pierre de Massot, gifted, poor, frail, violent, addicted through weakness to communism and opium. Even a Scottish wife could not unbind him.

Above: The mantel and mirror in my present flat were installed in 1791. *Below:* Next door to No. 17 is the Hôtel du quai Voltaire, where, according to a plaque, *Charles Baudelaire, Richard Wagner, et Oscar Wilde ont honoré Paris de leur séjour. Opposite:* My original studio, above and behind the broad central building (at its right), is visible only from the quai du Louvre.

Above left: Mary Reynolds in 1931, relentlessly bohemian, relentlessly a lady. *Above right:* Louise (Madame Jean-Paul) Langlois, 1856–1939, my friend for thirteen years. *Below:* Max Jacob, poet and painter, perhaps a saint, unquestionably a martyr—gouache by Edouard M. Perrot showing the monastery of Saint-Benoît-sur-Loire.

ris, Piston—came to have high value as a property. Its title, The Arrow Music Press, we had hit upon by hazard, after the principle that the less meaning in a name the better. We simply looked out the window and, seeing a lunchroom opposite named Arrow, decided that would do.

The years of 1936 and '37 saw three generations of American composers, from the elders, Edward B. Hill and Arthur Shepherd, through my own age group to the still-under-thirty Samuel Barber and William Schuman, all in full command of their powers and at work. Ruggles, though no longer working, and Ives were beginning to be played; and Gershwin, who died in '37, was to become a classic. American music was performed across the nation. And in the League of Composers' magazine, *Modern Music,* Edwin Denby was covering the dance; Copland, records and published music; Antheil, from Hollywood, music in films; Goddard Lieberson, radio; Paul Bowles, exotica from Latin America; Colin McPhee and Elliott Carter, the New York premières; myself, the theater, including opera. Also there were sermons by Roger Sessions, whose learning was to the cause of modern music as Alfred Barr's to that of modern art.

The thirties were also memorable for major jazz developments such as the swing beat and the concert band, for blues more powerful than any heard before, for light music that includes the finest of Cole Porter and of Rodgers and Hart, and for an opera that defies dispute, Ira and George Gershwin's world-famous *Porgy and Bess.* The twenties had been a romance because one was young. The thirties were a time of fulfillment for musicians of my age because we were ready for that, and also because our country was ready for us. That readiness was surely in part a result of the depression. During the first half of the 1930s Alfred Barr and Chick Austin had got together wealth not yet immobilized by the depression and scholars not yet captured by fame, developing out of these elements museums that expressed the time. The second half, through federal intervention, saw modern play writing, modern acting and production, and a public ready for noble subject matter all amalgamated. The *Four Saints* audience, part well-to-do, part scholarly and intellectual, all of it lively, experienced, and not easily fooled, was inherited by the ballet. The Federal Theatre audience, poor, part intellectual, part professional, not stylish at all but not easily fooled either, was father to today's off-Broadway public. Together they are the parents of a nation-wide university audience that is no easier to fool than the others and that is our present decade's gift to dramatic art.

By '38 I knew the good time for me was over and that I should be getting back to France. In 1937 Mary Butts had died in England. Her loss was irreparable because it ended the possibility that we might speak again. Another loss was the breakup of a new group, which I called the "Little Friends," all young and a quarter mad. This consisted of Paul Bowles and Harry Dunham, as founding fathers; of John Latouche, an author of light verse; of Marian Chase, who was to marry Harry Dunham, then as his widow to become my closest companion; of Marian's friend Theodora Griffis, whom Latouche was to marry; and of Jane Auer, that very year to become Mrs. Bowles. Also, during 1937, they were abetted in their liveliness by Kristians Tonny, who with his French wife spent that year among us, forever quarreling with Paul about money, and painting Flemish murals in Chick's Hartford theater.

I call these lovely people not quite sane because though not besotted and not corrupted and none of them, God knows, the least bit stupid, all were pursued by fatality, as if the gods would destroy them. Harry, flying a voluntary scouting mission, was shot down in Borneo, 1943. Latouche's wife, divorced, died of an early cancer. Latouche himself, successful, celebrated, died of a massive heart attack at forty. Marian caught bulbar polio in Naples, died coming home. Her mother, friend of them all, was killed in a bus crash. Jane Bowles, after writing one fine novel and one play, suffered a stroke, or a cerebral spasm, that has kept her from writing and may go on doing so. The Tonnys, being European, were not affected by a local curse stemming, as we all knew, from Dunham's white-lighted glamour and his unstated but relentless will to die young. Bowles also has remained immune, but he does not live in America or write much music any more. He writes novels and stories now, chiefly about persons obsessed. Both he and Jane feel safer in Morocco.

The story of the "Little Friends" I insert here because with the Tonnys' departure early in '38, with Dunham's going off to photograph the Spanish civil war, hoping to reproduce his earlier luck in the Chinese one, and with the Bowles-Auer marriage in February '38 and their leaving instantly for Panama and France, the group broke up. I also felt that it was coming to be time to leave; and I looked around for means of doing so. I had received good fees for *The River* and for *Antony and Cleopatra*, but no more than it took for me to live; and I was not a spendthrift. For making money to take me back abroad there were two possibilities: one was doing a show; the other was writing a book. I chose both. The show was for The Mercury Theatre, Houseman's and Welles's private company that had grown out of their federal unit. Welles, who had by this time grown quite fat, felt he should play Falstaff; and for making this role major, he had boiled down to one all of the Shakespeare plays involving him, calling the result *Five Kings*. It was to be a grandiose production in the spring of '38; and I was to furnish lots of music.

Webster's *The Duchess of Malfi* was also being planned, with sets and costumes to be designed by Tchelitcheff. Welles was undecided whether I should write the music, or Marc Blitzstein, with whom he had gone all chummy and political since directing *The Cradle Will Rock* and who had composed him a neat score for The Mercury Theatre's antifascist, modern-dress *Julius Caesar*. I won by taking Orson and his wife to a blowout at Sardi's, with oysters and champagne, red meat and Burgundy, dessert and brandy, before he pulled himself into his canvas corset for playing Brutus. "You win," he said. "The dinner did it. And it's lucky I'm playing tragedy tonight, which needs no timing. Comedy would be difficult." Eventually *The Duchess of Malfi* was renounced; Tchelitcheff went off to Italy and I to France. But I had learned the play; and Edwin Denby, helped by Grosser, had made me a cutting. I thought I could write an opera on the text. In France I spent a summer trying to do that, only to conclude in the end that its turbulent pentameters are not for singing and that the whole is irrevocably what it purports to be, a blank verse melodrama with incidental music.

Up Boston way, Sherry Mangan was getting restless. He had divorced his English wife, taken up with a trained nurse who loved him, was living in isolation near Norwood, where he worked as a book designer. He had also become a follower of Leon Trotsky, a vocation that was to dry up his springs of poetry and substitute a faith that he could live by. For Sherry was a Jesuit at heart, trained to intellection, submissive to authority. He too was in need of going somewhere again; and Paris seemed the chosen destination, with prices low and a Trotskyist group available. So Margarete cashed her life insurance, and I helped out a little; and in the spring they moved their books to France.

Grosser had gone there in January. I stayed behind to compose music for *Five Kings* and to try for an advance from some book publisher. Four of these had been after me, in view of my *Modern Music* articles, to undertake a volume; and I had said, "What about a collection of those articles?" But no; they did not want that; only a through-written book would do. And why should I write a book, laborious enterprise, when I could support myself by writing music? But I could not save up by writing music here enough to keep me writing it in Paris. Besides, I had had enough expansion for the moment. Chick's grandeurs involving music were over; Houseman and Welles, through radio, were rocketing to Mars and Hollywood, no right place then or now for a musician. A period in my life had come to term. Time to go home! And so I called on all four publishers, asking what they could offer as advance. Five hundred dollars, answered three of them. The fourth went to a thousand; I accepted.

Meanwhile, my other home, the Missouri one, needed attention, because my mother had been injured in a car. She did not complain; she merely looked, in bed with her chestnut braids, like a little girl. Like a strong little girl she waited quietly to get well, and like a Kentucky hostess she received. She waited and received for a full year, then aided by a crutch relearned to walk. After three years she left her crutch and for seventeen more, till her death at ninety-two, concealed the signs of stiffness when she moved.

Five Kings had been delayed beyond my contract's deadline, which was April. I had received $200 for waiting. With Pare Lorentz, planning another film, I had no contract; but I offered to come back from France at any time he should be ready for me. Actually, though he once inquired by mail when I planned to be home, he did not go so far as to ask for my return. And when his film *The Fight for Life* was ready, it was Louis Gruenberg who composed the music. *Five Kings,* with its music by Copland, died out of town. Minna Lederman wrote me of the demise. Also that my kind of workmanship was catching on in show business. "Group Theatre," she announced, "is doing incidental music—Bowles's score for a Saroyan piece *My Heart's in the Highlands* and Aaron's for Irwin Shaw's *Quiet City.*" With ballet, films, and theater all in such felicitous hands, I knew I could absent myself a while. Besides, if I was going to turn *The Duchess of Malfi* into an opera, I should need to settle down where life was quiet. I had been busy (and in America) long enough.

Pastoral

As my story now moves back to France, let us relist for 1938 our cast of characters. Madame Langlois, in my life since 1926, will be living for one more year. Meanwhile, she is lively and elegant, relaxed, distinguished. Sherry Mangan and Maurice Grosser are there, both living in studios on pittances. Theodate Johnson will be with us by the autumn, taking vocal lessons. Georges Hugnet is potent in the councils of surrealism; also, he has a new girl. Henri Sauguet's *La Chartreuse de Parme* is being cast at the Opéra; Germaine Lubin and Raoul Jobin will sing the leads, and Jacques Dupont, Christian Bérard's best follower, will design it. Les Concerts de la Sérénade are dead or dying, the only music series in the world to have expressed the thirties. The thirties have begotten yet another group—all very Catholic, calling themselves at their coming out in 1935 "*la jeune France*." They are Olivier Messiaen (an organist and teacher of harmony), André Jolivet (knowledgeable in Hindu music and a pupil of Edgard Varèse), Daniel-Lesur (out of the Schola Cantorum), and Yves Baudrier (largely self-taught).

In painting, the surrealist clan has been strengthened by survivors of Dada such as Arp and Max Ernst and blessed openly by Picasso and Marcel Duchamp. The neo-Romantics look like a lost cause. Tchelitcheff will do one more work for the Paris stage the

next spring, a version of Jean Giraudoux's *Ondine,* laden with ingenuities *à la* Orson Welles and with elaborate dressmaking ob-
tainable only in France. Bérard's last décor before the war will be
for Molière's *L'Ecole des femmes.*

A former collector of Bérard canvases, Christian Dior, a bland
young man we had all known rich, had lost his affluence, his pictures, and his health. The elder Dior, a manufacturer, had been
ruined in 1931. Christian, already partner in a gallery, had sold off
his paintings until none remained. In 1934, when he became tubercular, his close friends subscribed each a small sum per month
for sending him to be treated in the Pyrenees at Font-Romeu; and
in the spring of '35 he came back cured. In '34, the Dior family
house at Granville on the channel coast being unsalable, Leonid
Berman had been offered it to live and work in. I collected in
March of that year from among our New York friends a similar
subscription (each paying $5 a month for half a year, to be repaid
eventually in pictures) so that he could work that summer. He
bought paints on credit, old canvases for pennies at the flea market, lived alone on $30 a month, painted a whole exhibit for Julien
Levy, was reestablished. Christian Dior got reestablished by learning a trade, that of dress design, which Jean Ozenne, a cousin of
Bérard, and Max Kenna, an American, taught him in the winter
of 1935–36. When I came back to France in '38 he was already
working for a *couturier.* After the war, in 1947, he was to have a
dressmaking house of his own. He was also to die ten years later,
unbelievably successful, but ever a gentle and quiet one, just as he
had been when young.

Absent from this cast is Max Jacob, who had gone in '36 to live
beside the ancient Benedictine monastery at Saint-Benoît-sur-Loire,
where he was to remain, praying, serving at Mass, and writing
Méditations religieuses until the Germans took him away in '44.
Half absent are Cliquet-Pleyel and Marthe-Marthine, he occupied
with ill-paid music jobs, she with no jobs, but drinking red wine
all day long in a haunted studio shared with four large dogs. Gertrude Stein too is only part-time there, since she likes to spend six
months at Bilignin. When I saw her in the fall of '38, she asked
me had I left New York for good. I said, "For now, at any rate.
I've been successful in the theater, in films, in ballet; I don't like

that kind of situation." "Well, here," she replied, "we all go on being nicely unsuccessful."

Gertrude had moved in January of '38 to an eighteenth-century flat in the rue Christine. Picasso had already bought a seventeenth-century house near by. Many of the painters and writers, moving down from Montparnasse and into the low, damp district near the Seine, seemed to be huddling together for protection. This region has been magical since medieval times, propitious to sorcery, curses, and Black Masses. The demarcation line for magic seems always to have run along the Seine and up the rue du Cardinal Lemoine, then from there, including a patch on the north slope of the Mont Sainte-Geneviève (but not the Sorbonne), to go west along the north sidewalk of the boulevard Saint-Germain. Carefully skirting the church of Saint-Germain-des-Prés, I think it rejoins the Seine by the rue Bonaparte, though a stricter survey might find its west limit to be the rue de Seine. In any case, this was the neighborhood of alchemy; and this was the quarter chosen as home in the years just before the new war and during the Occupation by Europe's most remarkable assemblage of talent. Today, with Montparnasse intellectually as dead as Montmarte, and with Saint-Germain-des-Prés become a costume ball, the region I have just outlined, though the artists themselves have mostly moved away, is the largest agglomeration of art dealers and book stores in the world, spilling over clean down to the rue du Bac.

I was to be moving again to 17 quai Voltaire, ever for me a locale of protective magic. A large apartment, the whole third floor, or *bel étage,* was being given up; and my landlord, Dr. Ovize, would cut it into small units to be let furnished. But for me he would leave two rooms unfurnished and lease them to me at a yearly rental of $200. I could have them at the October term and, with a month out for arranging them, be in my new flat by November first. So that was settled. The weather was Arcadian. June with its fresh peas and fragrant strawberries was gone. July was for the country, for writing music, gestating a book. For Grosser too, painting in the country was right, provided he liked the country he was painting in. It always turned out that he worked best in hot regions; but he liked to try others, though rarely happy there.

Since railway fares that summer were cut for foreigners by two fifths, and regional buses were for almost nothing, we set off south

without precise intentions beyond wandering eventually into the
Jura Mountains. We stopped at Dijon for gastronomy, where after a
three-wine lunch, a long walk, and a nap we went through a dinner
at Les Trois Faisans which began with a hot mousse of chicken
livers. What followed I do not remember, only that next morning
Maurice complained he could not go on with any more such meals.
So we went to Bourg-en-Bresse, where foods and wines are lighter,
sight-seeing the near-by historic church of Brou, and traveled by
bus upcountry to Nantua. There we took to its black-forested mountain and bottle-green lake, stayed for a week on the shore, swimming and rowing and climbing, dining on quenelles and crayfish
and wild mushrooms, and not getting down to work at all. So we
moved by mountain buses into the Jura, at Saint-Claude ate another gastronomic lunch, this one with *morille* mushrooms of the
Franche-Comté, and took another diligence to the uplands. There
on a high and flowery mountain plain we got off at a village called
Lamoura, deeply grassy in the summer time but redolent of winter
rains, with its thick stone houses weatherproofed by shingles on the
windward side. Grosser found it possible, he thought, to paint there;
and in two days I composed two small portraits. But I was restless and proposed a trip. Taking a bus straight south, we came to
the Sickle Pass, or Col de la Faucille, where below us lay, at the
bottom of a ten-mile slope, the blue half-moon of Lake Geneva and
beyond that, fifty miles or more away and dazzling white against
blue sky, the grandest mass of mountain in the world, Mont Blanc.
I could not turn back; I had to go toward it. But before the long
slope above Geneva became Switzerland, we entered a pink French
city known as Gex.

We lunched there and went back to Lamoura, Maurice having
decided to stay on, I to leave the next day. So I took a bus and
steamer to the French side, and was back at the hotel on the cliffs
of Thonon, where in 1926 I first knew Madame Langlois and also
where I received what had seemed to me then a miraculous enlightenment about music. Absorbed with memories and sculling on
the lake, I do not even know whether I worked. Getting back to
work after America is never easy, because in Europe one's best
work is spontaneous, whereas in America practically all work is
done either on order or out of determination. This is a difference
not to be quickly brushed aside; in Europe one must always wait

till ready—otherwise there is no boldness in the product, nor any ease, nor lightness.

After two weeks Maurice came down to visit me, finding me slim and, so he said, good-tempered. But I felt I should go for a week to Madame Langlois, who had not been well; and she was at Arcachon, on the Atlantic. So Maurice went back to Lamoura, eventually to Villefranche; and I took the Geneva–Bordeaux so-called Express, which pommeled me all night on my sleeping-bench by changing its direction at least twelve times. And at Arcachon, after another bumpy ride, I climbed sand dunes, enor-mous ones, ate the local oysters out of season, and bathed in a shallow bay so thick with infants that we named its salty taste a "broth of babies."

Not wishing to go to Villefranche by another of those trains which have to back and fill all night for getting round the Central Mountain Range, I traveled via Paris, picked up mail, and stopped at Saint-Tropez to be with the Brazilian singer Elsie Houston, working for shekels just then in a night club. In Villefranche, finally I did get down to work, sketching a whole act of opera and making notes toward a book. My room, which gave on a play-ground, was filled by piercing childhood shrieks, also by the sound of hunting horns, as boy scouts learning to be *chasseurs alpins* practiced en masse, accompanied by massed drums. Maurice com-plained from his quieter room that out of a still life carefully arranged and already half painted some chambermaid had eaten a grape, changing the composition.

Describing my summer travels in *Modern Music,* I left out the hunting horns, which are as old as Europe, and tried to indicate what the new France was like. My picture has small resemblance to that of the rich-woman's paradise and poor-man's heaven familiar to us from the 1920s, even less to the motorists' hash house that is France today. I quote from it, abridged:

The French have become a singing people again after a hun-dred and fifty years of not being one. It's like this. The law that guarantees two weeks a year of paid vacation to all salaried employees (it is one of the famous Social Laws voted in 1936 by the first Blum government and includes industrial workers) has set the whole population of France to traveling around its own country. Also the forty-hour week (where still applied, which is in most of the nonmilitary industries) makes the two-day week-end quite general. Hence the low week-end railway-fares, which, when combined with low country prices, make leaving town as cheap as staying home, thus keeping a considerable part of the French population constantly moving around even in winter.

That means that about ninety-five per cent of the tourist business is French, but not rich French. So prices have to be reasonable. (Provincial prices are almost exactly the same, in francs, as in 1925.) And French standards about how beds should be made and food should be cooked must be observed. No longer can Americans push up prices just for the fun of it or English ruin the cooking by demanding that everything be boiled in water and served without seasoning. And so we have pre-war standards of eating and housekeeping plus all the post-war standards of ventilation and sport facilities. There is local fare in peasant pubs. There is *grande cuisine* in court-house towns at twenty-six francs a head. And by *grande cuisine* I mean *la grande cuisine française,* not Swiss hotel-cooking. I mean foie gras and blue trout and Bresse chickens in yellow cream and *morille* mushrooms and crayfish and wild pheasant and venison with chestnut purée and ice cream of wild strawberries or of pistache custard and cakes made only of almond-flour and sweet butter and honey and nothing ever boiled in anything but wine or meat-juice.

Sport-lovers by tens of thousands travel in pairs on tandem bicycles, he in front, she behind, in cycling outfits of identical tweed. Unattached youth goes hob-nailing in bands and sleeps in Youth Hostels. This is the point at which singing comes in. Depression-alcoholism being out of fashion, and the promiscuous love-making of the 1920s even more so, the big family-party that France has become now amuses itself in the old French way by drinking wine, telling stories, and singing songs. They dance too, round dances in peasant styles. The Lambeth Walk, England's first contribution to popular dancing in over three hundred years, is used as a get-together for upper-class occasions. But mostly they just sing the old French nursery rhymes, sea chanties, tragic ballads, ribald medievalries, and always, if the company is anywhere to the left of political center, the great revolutionary songs, the *Crakovienne,* the *Carmagnole* and the *Ça Ira.* On the road they sing, in restaurants, in railway-carriages, in boats, bars, and *bordels.* Always in solo or unison, practically never in harmony. Never either do they vocalize. They sing the French language *as she is spoke,* thin, a little throaty, accurate in vowel and pitch, never muffling a consonant. So far I have not perceived in all this anything that smells of mass-singing-under-a-leader nor any imitation of the choral-society concert-style. It is social music in the same sense that round dancing is social dancing. And a few sprightly vocal teams make up their own topical songs and pay their summer expenses *à la troubadour.*

Mangan, who had arrived with his Margareta toward the end of April, had lived for two months, the two of them, in a thoroughly comfortable Montparnasse flat on $75. When that money was gone, he worried his way through summer by sending off to *Time* reports of art exhibitions, which were paid for with small checks that arrived weeks late. From my various country stations I would advance him cash against these; and M, as she was now called, would help out by doing odd jobs of nursing acquired through the American Hospital. Meanwhile, Sherry labored to get back his poetic facility and to establish himself in the councils of the French Trotskyists. Though the poverty line he walked was quite precarious, his letters of that summer show elation.

I was elated too, and Maurice, and M, all of us as euphoric about France as we were about not being in America. It was not that America was not in the long run rewarding. It was simply that our country was a trap. Earning enough to live there was not impossible, but earning enough *not* to live there was. Income and costs seemed always to come out even; and the results of money spent lacked surplus value. In France the shabbiest secondhand chair or stool could still be sold again. And living, loving, dining would create an afterglow, whereas at home whatever happened seemed to leave either a bad taste or none at all. Which is what led Grosser to discover that "France is a rich country and America a poor one," and indeed that was so in the days when business figures read the other way. In terms of just plain feeling good, France was in those days, even for the poor, the richest life an artist ever knew.

Maurice, at thirty-five, was selling his pictures for small sums; but he was selling them. He also had a pittance from his family. And he had taken a small but habitable studio on the rue Bonaparte. A single square room five flights up with good light, furniture, and carpet, it lacked only water. When his landlord put in a basin with taps, the house architect, misreading old plans and taking a small air vent for a drain, attached the washbowl to it, flooding the apartment just below. The heat was furnished by a hard-coal Franklin stove of the sort known as a *salamandre,* and for a time this also did not work right. But that fact turned out to be a benefit, for when Dewitt Eldridge, whose father, a doctor, was a friend of Grosser's father, wrote home that Maurice was "having trouble with his salamander," the elder Grosser quickly mailed, without comment, a check for $50.

Grosser was in full expansion as a painter, had been so in fact since 1932. He painted over-life-size fruit and bread and vegetables in high bright colors; he also painted very striking portraits. I have one of Theodate Johnson from that year; and I remember many sitters climbing his long stairs, a canon from the church of La Madeleine in High Mass regalia and Mary Garden in a tightly flowered small hat. Maurice had by now taken to bicycling and to racing in the woods outside of Paris. A muscular type, he had always needed exercise. Cycling was a winter-and-summer sport that he kept up daily till he came back to America, where he bought a motorcycle, went everywhere on that. In his forties he crossed and recrossed the continent on it before he finally gave it up and bought a car. I was to see quite a bit of landscape and weather myself, riding behind him up and down New Hampshire in 1941, through California in '45.

In the South I had planned out a whole act of *The Duchess of Malfi* before I discovered that singing the text was bound to diminish its impact. Blank verse is in any circumstance no friend to music; and blank verse of the great dramatic masters has never been successfully intoned. Shakespeare in translation, which is to say, without his poetry, has given the opera repertory *Falstaff, Otello, Hamlet* several times, *Romeo and Juliet* even oftener; he has not yet inspired a first-class opera in English. My mistake was to imagine I could help out Webster's text; it did not need me. And without that text the story seemed just gaudy. Nor were my notes toward writing a book worth keeping. Actually, I had accomplished no proper work at all between my June arrival and my September return to Paris.

Nor was I destined to do so till December was over. At the

Hôtel Jacob, where I awaited delivery of my flat, I did write quite a bit about matters musical; but my outpourings were inchoate. My preoccupation at this time was only the flat; and for two months, beginning in October, I went to see it every day, traversed the city constantly on errands regarding it.

It was thirteen feet high, with two tall windows catching light all day and sunshine till noon from a wide courtyard; but its gem was a mirrored mantelpiece put there in 1791, when the house was built. The floors were oak parquet, the doors and wainscots painted a Trianon gray. Also, I owned a little furniture, mostly good pieces out of Madame Langlois's flat. I had to put in some lighting fixtures, install hot water (electric) and a washbowl, buy draperies, upholster, paper everywhere. I had a plan about colors too; I wanted lots of them. Bérard had just selected for Jean Ozenne materials for chairs, carpets, walls, and hangings that were highly varied, harmonious by contrast rather than in a key. I wanted a similar variety, but by tints I was to take from Florine Stettheimer, who in Act One of *Four Saints* had displayed against a luminous sky-blue all of the primary and secondary colors. My plan was to do the same against sunlight yellow; and eventually these colors came to be pointed up with added notes of bottle green, of Roman violet, of Bordeaux red, and of a gray rayon satin that when hung as floor-to-ceiling curtains shone like silver. After two months of labor and an expense of just $200, the place was very pretty indeed. And with my pictures by Bérard, Grosser, Tonny, and Leonid, and with a grand piano hired, and a new concierge who was also a first-class cook, I went all snug again, began to have people in. My unframed drawings, however, of which I had quite a number, especially by Bérard and by Tonny, had in five years of being stored against a damp stone wall become so mildewed in their portfolio that they fell to powder as I touched them.

At home again in France, back on the quai Voltaire in my own flat, and once more cocooned by friendships, love, and domestic ritual, I started work with the turn of the year on a book that I knew from the first would be moving forward. I knew also that my earlier stammerings would not be needed; I never even looked at them again. Before the end of May *The State of Music* had been copied in ink, revised again, typed out by Sherry Mangan. My

New York publisher had it on June first, as he had hoped. Proofs were to come in August. In July I went off to Italy with Bruce Morrissette, a former classmate of Paul Bowles, a Virginian and a professor of Romance languages.

That winter I had sent musical reports to *Modern Music,* in one of which I described the effects of German refugees, of whom France had harbored many since '33, on French concert life.

The season's chief controversy so far, believe it or not, is the war between the supporters of two rival German conductors. Furtwängler, the official ambassador of Nazi culture, fills the big Salle Pleyel at a 150-franc top. Scherchen, the unofficial ambassador of émigré German culture, plays a 40-franc top at the smaller Salle Gaveau and doesn't always fill it. Bruno Walter, now a French citizen, is completely successful and quite outside the controversy. So is Munch, the new Alsatian conductor at the Société des Concerts du Conservatoire.

The Furtwängler audience is rich and fashionable. Lots of chinchilla. He plays sure-fire stuff and stream-lines à la Toscanini. Beethoven, Brahms (yes, I said Brahms), Wagner, Strauss and Debussy are his oysters. His error was an overture by Pfitzner. The Scherchen audience is mostly intellectual and definitely unfashionable, full of German exiles and the international-minded. He plays Bach, Mozart, Purcell, Lully, and some moderns, sure-fire stuff for the liberals. His error was the Beethoven *Grand Fugue,* opus 133, played by full string orchestra. (It sounded terrible.)

A good deal of the side-taking in this war is factitious, worked up for political reasons. A good deal of the enthusiasm at the Scherchen concerts is due to the presence, in a body, of intellectuals who really think they like that sort of concert. Just as the United States is going to have to absorb a goodly number of German composers in these next years, France is having already to absorb and educate a very considerable body of German listeners. This will be a long job, because there are thousands of them. A tedious job too, because they think they are so right about music, are so proud of their bad taste and so ostentatious in expressing it.

A French audience can get violently controversial about a new piece and it can stage a pitched battle about it and have in the police. It is not, however, the habit here either to get hysterical about the classics or to accept orchestral conducting as a major art. The French public is interested principally in music, only incidentally in presentation. It is the only music-listening public in Europe that knows the difference between one good piece and another and that can distinguish design from execution in any given piece. For fifty years Paris has been the accepted world-capital of first performances. Today her concert halls are invaded by Corybantic troupes of classics-worshippers and seekers after soul-states. It is doubtful if she can do or will be asked to do much about the exiled German composer. Technical complexity unjustified by expression, emotional vagueness, most particularly that air of owning all Musical Truth that German composers so naïvely and so impregnably assume, all get short shrift here. Let America handle the composers if she can and she can probably handle quite a lot of them. France has all she can take on, I fancy, with sixty thousand unrestrained music-lovers to digest.

On April 27 Madame Langlois died of pneumonia. I had believed, from her careful deceptions about dates, that she was approaching seventy. Actually she was nearly eighty-four. Not at all the fragile woman she had so long seemed, she was indeed a very strong one for her age. Her surviving older sister, Mathilde Philibert, lived till her middle nineties. And in the French way, on her sister's death she set out, as surrogate, to be my friend, inviting me to lunch, insisting I come and see her every week, inquiring of my health and my career, telling me the progress of the war, when that came on, in a way I could not have known it from the press or even quite from Mangan's Trotskyist prophets, because she knew the generals and their wives.

Learning Madame Langlois's age, and admiring her for having discarded fourteen years of it, kept me from undue grief about her loss. A life so long, a person so fulfilled gives little wish to alter history. Just like my parents, later to depart, she is as much still with me as if she were a book, a gay book and a sweet one, a sourcebook for the conduct of affection and my reference tome for France and all its ways. Her tomb in the Cimetière de Montparnasse, where she lies with the Philiberts, I do not visit. I carry her around with me instead. In that way we can laugh, tell jokes, and bicker, and share an affection that has never dimmed.

In Italy, at Porto Venere, I swam and walked and wrote a little music. And when the proofs arrived I was at Recco, on the Ligurian coast, with Henry Furst, trilingual man of letters out of Brooklyn, who lived in a round stone tower and owned many dictionaries. He was of great help with my galley proofs; and when they had been corrected, we both went to stay with the poet Eugenio Montale at Bocca di Magra. There, with five other men of letters, we sat for days translating into Italian a novel of Henry James, *The Aspern Papers*. And I learned, for all its subtlety in speech, how stiff-necked, academic, and funereal the Italian language can become when written.

Being so near, I thought it wise to take a look at Florence, which I had never seen, traveling by way of Parma to view that city too. I saw no violets there; it seems there are none; but on a plain outside of town is Stendhal's Carthusian monastery, or *chartreuse;* and inside are two of Europe's nobler opera houses—one from Napoleonic times, still used today, and one from the seventeenth century, the Farnese, with its scenery-flats built of stone.

It was in Florence, waiting for my mail and profiting by that week to visit the museums, that I read in the papers of a German pact with Soviet Russia and then of the beginning war itself, confined for that immediate time to Poland. Political events from 1933 on—the Saar plebiscite of '35; the reoccupation of the Rhineland in '36; the Austrian *Anschluss* (spring of '38), the taking of territories that same year in Czechoslovakia—every year some German predatory move had made it clear that one year there would be war. I had known that before I returned to France, and I did not choose to change my life because of it. Current events, of necessity, involve the people caught up in them. But those who play at refugee when under no attack not only are behaving irresponsibly; they also clutter up the roads. And so I waited calmly for my mail, read all the papers, looked at historic pictures, till I could take a train for Paris without feeling I was in somebody's way. My rule for conduct, taken at this time and ever so serviceable in later war emergencies, was very simple: never stand in line.

The Quiet War

THE MOST SURPRISING CHANGE IN PARIS was how charming the
English had become. All the winter before, they had been
intolerable, either under analysis for diminution of income (and
psychotherapy adds to no one's charm) or simply sitting in bars
and feeling mean. I remember three of them at Le Select simply
by withholding a box of matches exasperating the painter Alvaro
Guevara until he cried (and Chilean ex-diplomats do not cry
easily). But now they were smiling, friendly, and content. Grosser
diagnosed right off that the war was to be thanked. "Last year,
after Munich," he said, "they were ashamed of their country."

I had written September 6 to Gertrude Stein, still at Bilignin,
asking if she was all right and whether I could do anything for her,
adding that I was "staying on for a while, at least." She replied,
"For the first time in my life I have had a radio in the house and
it does discourage one about music, why should there be so much
of it, its going on all the time in the air certainly has something to
do with the world's troubles." It is one of them, of course; of that
I too was sure and am sure still.

Many of France's Americans were undecided about whether to
go home; and our Embassy was advising flight, even chartering
ships to hasten it, since normal berths were scarce and out of
price. Within the first month, most of the nervous ones had been

got off, and by November nearly all were gone. Among those who had chosen not to leave were a number who had jobs in France and some with property, also a few habitués attached to living there, like Mary Reynolds and Sherry Mangan and Gertrude Stein.

Sherry and his Margarete would have stayed in any case, I think; but it happened that for the last year he had been importantly employed by *Time,* which had discovered that his trainings as research scholar and as revolutionist were valuable in news analysis. So he ran their Paris office, was prosperous, traveled back and forth to London. At the beginning of the war he moved to Dampierre, in the valley of Chevreuse, and from there commuted daily, bicycling majestically to and from his trains. After a month or so, judging that Paris was not to be bombed, he took the luxurious Harry Dunham studio-flat (with three high balconies to watch the bombings from) and moved into 17 quai Voltaire.

Theodate Johnson had already taken the next-door flat, with two balconies; and the painter William Einstein a studio with one. In January, Leonid came back from painting in the north and moved into one of the still smaller studios. Peter Rose-Pulham, an English poet (I think) and photographer (I know), also moved in. And so the house became almost a club, with nightly dinings in one another's quarters. There was a beauteous American woman, tall and blonde, who Sherry and I were convinced was a Stalinist spy. At least her communist acquaintance was extensive and her vocabulary almost a giveaway. The French had arrested all Germans, including the sixty thousand refugees, and she was waiting for her Austrian lover to be released from concentration camp so that she could take him to America. Eventually he was released and taken there. Meanwhile, she seemed to be in amorous dalliance with an American newswriter for purposes political, or so we guessed. In any case, delightful as she was to listen to in tales not wise of her to tell, we thought it safer not to tell her anything.

We knew our telephones were being listened to; we could hear the click. And Theodate, who knew someone somehow from the French counterespionage, had learned from him that I, though earlier suspected of unsafe acquaintances, had by Christmas been graded lily white. Our concierge, as well as Madame Jeanne from the other house, would seem also, according to Theodate's informer, to have given to the police regarding every one of us, including the beauteous blonde, credit for innocence.

At the beginning, I worked for the French radio, as did also Sherry, translating texts for broadcasting in English. All radio stations, during that part of the war, were broadcasting news and comment in many languages. And the receiving set I had inherited from Madame Langlois came to be a pleasure for culturally and politically circling Europe—from Ankara and Moscow to Helsinki, from Rabat and Lisbon to Athlone. The translations were well paid, but I found them time-taking. Sherry, however, became something of a star, it having been discovered that his warm bass voice and perfect enunciation made him an incomparable radio speaker.

Grosser went off to America at the end of October. He had no money for staying on, no chance of earning any, no instinct for adventure—anyway, not in wars. I also think that with his gift for being always right ("his tragedy," as Gertrude liked to put it) he had judged this war to have no ending soon and not likely to bring good to anyone. From its beginning, he had said he was not taking part. He stayed in France just long enough to show he was not afraid and to be assured that his French friends, at home or mobilized, had no need of him. Then he went off to New York via Bordeaux. Yves Tanguy sailed with him. I put them on a night train at the darkened Gare d'Austerlitz, both traveling with all their pictures, both thoroughly relieved at being about to leave at last that foolish Europe.

For the English view, the French view, and that of many Americans was that this war, which they had so long seen coming, was essentially silly. For small countries early invaded—Poland, Finland, Czechoslovakia, Norway, Yugoslavia—the war was a tragedy right off. For fleeing Jews, as for the exiled Spaniards, it offered only further desperation. But to England and France, imperial powers both, it looked as if the Germans were just being naughty, dangerously so in fact, and that a declaration of war might stop that naughtiness. And yet we knew that the Germans meant not to be stopped. There was therefore a mood of general impatience with them, as of solid citizens toward delinquent youth; and the citizens, who were slow getting started, profoundly disliked the need for getting started. So the delinquents went on advancing. The situation seemed so void of reason that when the Germans, after success in Poland, simply sat down in the west behind their fortresses and looked across at the French sitting in theirs, it did for a moment seem as if both sides in the war knew it for foolish and might even back away from confrontation, if that could be done without their losing face. That it could not and that the Germans did not want that became clear very slowly. Meanwhile, we waited, as the French army waited, knowing the whole thing irrational but also realizing that it would not stop.

My cast of characters, by midwinter, had changed a bit. Gertrude Stein was gone for the duration, having early come and got her pictures, some of them at least, and taken them to Bilignin. Max Jacob was praying in his monastery. Madame Langlois was dead. Sauguet and Bérard had been mobilized, but not Georges Hugnet. Picasso was almost every night at Saint-Germain-des-Prés. Breton and Eluard were also there, in uniform. Cliquet-Pleyel did guard duty in mobilization halls and factories. Jean Ozenne, Christian Dior, Gaétan Fouquet, Jacques Dupont, almost everybody male not ill was under arms. Even Leonid Berman, at forty-four, was eventually called up, having the year before, after twenty years' waiting, received French citizenship. Paris was empty save for the old, the very young, and a few, a very few, foreigners.

The rich among these outfitted ambulances. The poor worked at supporting themselves. Writers wrote; actors acted; painters painted; dancers danced; musicians did what they could find to do. The Spanish refugees I rarely saw, save for some Catalan Trotsky-faithful whom Sherry would allow me now and then to meet. Without informing me of secret matters, he made no pretense that he was not involved with revolution. The German refugees, though wretched in their concentrations camps (*"Es gibt hier ķein' Ordnung,"* they would complain), were nevertheless fed there and kept in health. As a matter of fact, the French medical services, I was told later, had almost used up their drug supplies in '38 and '39 in preventing epidemics among the Spanish refugees. If none broke out now in the camps for Germans, and if when invasion finally occurred few of the wounds became infected, that fact seems to have been to the credit of America, which sent sulfas and other drugs in quantity.

The State of Music came out in November, bringing me reviews only to be described as raves. Its press, if slightly less voluminous than that of *Four Saints,* was as praise more nearly uniform. But the effect of it on sales was just as mild. By March's end their total was 2,045, about all there was to be. The book, however, was not ineffective. Composers took to heart its exhortation that they give up political politics and take up musical. And not for killing one another off but for assuming power, for directing musical matters instead of being directed. I had given them two instruments for doing that, a composer's alliance for collecting fees and a composers' cooperative for publishing their works. These instruments were in use, both presided over by Aaron Copland. "It's slow going, I admit," he had written in May, "but I think we are getting to be a force gradually. I wish you were here to help on all this!" The book I wrote in 1939 explaining why and how the designers of music should be administering it became instantly a handbook for that operation which has not yet been replaced. It still circulates, indeed, among the knowing ones, nowadays in paperback.

At the time of its appearance I had more letters from outside the music world than from within. The literary found its wit invigorating, and my friends in art circles and in the theater spread news of it. They also took occasion to write me their delight and at the same time to recount the state of my America.

Both Chick Austin and Russell Hitchcock, it seems, were less active, at least came less often to New York. The Ballet Caravan, Lincoln Kirstein's troupe, had brought out successfully Elliott Carter's *Pocahontas* and Copland's *Billy the Kid*. An organization called the American Lyric Theatre had in May spent $160,000 presenting an opera by Douglas Moore about Daniel Webster, one about Stephen Foster by persons unknown to me, and my ballet *Filling Station,* then had shut up shop for lack of further funds. To quote from divers correspondents, Copland's music for the film *Of Mice and Men* was a "great success;" Marc Blitzstein's *No for an Answer,* auditioned privately at the Askews', had "marvelous music" but apparently libretto trouble; Maurice Grosser was showing at a gallery, with an "impressive public" attending. The Bravig Imbses were receiving in a Washington Square flat that had been murally handpainted by a "little friend." Eugene Berman was as usual "gloomy." Shows of Magnasco and of Poussin at Kirk Askew's gallery were both novel and "important." Barr's Picasso retrospective at the Museum of Modern Art was "the circus of the town" and "probably the best show that Alfred has ever pulled off." Marian Chase and Harry Dunham had been married. An invitation forwarded from Mabel Dodge announced that on January 12, at 1 Fifth Avenue, "Thornton Wilder will elucidate eight pages of *Finnegans Wake*."

None of this picture made me homesick, for it represented little more than a working out of patterns long familiar. The most dramatic of those workings out was told in a letter from John Houseman which announced his break with Orson Welles.

The Mercury's career, from the time you left America, has been one of uninterrupted failure—sometimes honorable, sometimes idiotic and ignominious—but absolutely constant and uninterrupted. Looking back on it now, I can see how inevitably and how cruelly we paid the price of success, of big time, of a publicity-inflated personality (both Orson's and the theatre's). We paid it in every department—in the department of personal relations and loyalties—in the department of public relations, where audience-friendliness was replaced by audience-challenge—in the department of aesthetics, where feelings of grandeur and what-is-expected-of-the-Mercury completely supplanted the simple desire to put on a bang-up show. I allowed Orson— (and the fault is mine as much as his, since by failing to control and influence him I was betraying my one useful function in the Mercury set-up) to use the theatre not only as an instrument of personal aggrandisement but as a tilting-ground for a particular, senseless and idle competition with an uninteresting and essentially unimportant theatrical competitor-actor by the name of Maurice Evans. *Five Kings* was never a pure aesthetic conception—it was conditioned in its conception and in its execution by a desire to go Evans one better in Shakespearian production. Therefore it fell on its face (though it contained notable things and was often wonderful to look at and gave Orson a chance to be a magnificent Falstaff) not through any difficulties of time or technical inadequacies, as Orson likes to tell himself, but because it was a half-baked, impure idea, in which size and "notions" took the place of love and thinking. And it smashed the Mercury Theatre. Not because it was a flop—no flop ever smashed a person or an organization—but because the year which I shall always think of as the *Five Kings* year (since *Five Kings* pre-influenced and pre-distorted, or post-influenced and post-distorted every single thought and action of ours that season) found us fertile, successful, happy

... foolish perhaps, but in love with ourselves and each other and the theater and the public . . . it left us tired to a point of sickness, loaded with debts and full of hatred and distrust of each other, of our audience, of our theatre—weary and full of fear and loathing for the whole business of producing plays in the theatre. And it left me, personally, without the excitement and, worst of all, without the faith which was, during its brief, brilliant career, the essential quality of the Mercury and before that 891 [the Maxine Elliott Theatre project] and before that *Macbeth*. . . .

Then I suppose you know that during this whole year we had a radio show, for which I did the scripts (and Benny [Bernard] Herrmann the music). At first it was a tremendous amount of fun, playing with a new medium, a medium to which Orson as an actor-producer and myself as a non-radio-writer author were bringing some very exciting new elements. You heard, of course, of the *War of the Worlds—Men from Mars* broadcast. . . . that was about the high point of our radio endeavor. Shortly after that we were bought by a Soup Company—which meant much money, most of which was drained off into *Five Kings*—alas an end of our fun. The thing became a constant squabble with the soup-maker—a compromise between *Saturday Evening Post* material and material not necessarily high-brow but of some human and aesthetic interest. Occasionally a good show gets on—but radio has become (and it still goes as wearily week after week at $5,000 per week) a drudgery and a pain in the neck. It has however been the main contributing element to a very queer and very sinister but also extremely interesting situation . . . the situation of Orson becoming a great national figure (a figure only less frequently and vastly projected into the news and the National Consciousness than Franklin D. Roosevelt, Adolf Hitler, and maybe N. Chamberlain). This has happened (it had begun, I think, before you left) in almost exactly inverse proportion to the success of his artistic and professional endeavors. . . . It is unrelated to his work (it had its origins in *The Cradle Will Rock* [and in] the first brilliant year of the Mercury, and its great growth came out of the Mars broadcast) in fact, it is just about fatal to his work, as it turns out. It is an appetite that grows as it is fed: it is also, in a creative artist, a compensation and a substitute for creation. Since to a theatrical artist the immediate test of his work is public response—if it is found that public response can be stimulated by various forms of monkeyshines (social and mechanical) then the necessity for, even the interest in, creative work inevitably dwindles. . . . That is why, for seven months now, a Picture (under the most magnificent contract ever granted an artist in Hollywood) has been "about to be made," talked of, speculated over, defended, attacked, announced, postponed, reannounced to the tune of millions of words in thousands of publications—without the picture itself either on paper or even in Orson's own mind, having got beyond the most superficially and vaguely conceived first draft. And no effort being made to progress beyond that first draft (partly because of an artist's very natural fears of a new medium but *mainly* because the instant it becomes definite, it has to be made, and the moment it gets made it enters the realm of tangible-work-to-be-appraised instead of potential-work-of-a-genius-which-can-be-talked-about-conjectured-about-written-about. . . .).

And so (and this is really what all this communication is about) I have, not suddenly, but after a great deal of very painful communion with myself, decided to end my theatrical association with Orson. It is not entirely chance, I think, that makes yours the first long and dispassionate letter that I have written to anyone since the break. You are one of the very few —perhaps the only person capable, since you saw it from the very first, of understanding just how much of a decision, how much of an uprooting of a three years' artistic marriage, this means to me. . . . I have not forgotten, after all, that it was you who gave me my first taste of work-in-the-theater-by-those-who-have-faith-in-each-other; I know that you have regarded the direction I have taken with the Mercury and with Orson—if not with disapproval then certainly with doubts. . . . I knew, for some time before you went abroad, that what we were doing or rather the direction in which we were going had already ceased, if not to interest you, at least to give you any personal pleasure. It turns out, of course, that you were right—right from your point of view, that dislikes the notion of work produced on schedule and under compulsion—compulsion of any kind, either of success or of ambition or of desperation or of real-estate obligations or of anything. . . . And ultimately, I suppose you were right, realizing that neither creative work, nor human relationships nor values of any sort can stand up under the kind of pressure to which we submitted them. It is my great virtue that I can impart terrific initial acceleration to any project to which I am a part; it is my great weakness that I am incapable (and not always desirous) of controlling or moderating its speed once it is under way. Instead, there comes a day when I suddenly find myself disliking the direction in which we are moving and sick of that very inertia which I have helped impose upon the object in which I am traveling. At that instant—being an adventurous amateur rather than a creator, and an operator rather than an artist—having made quite sure right along that there is a safety-door open and working, I hurriedly abandon the ship and that is what I did two weeks ago and that is what I am recovering from here in the desert. I am very fond of Orson still and I retain much of my old admiration for his talent: but the partnership is over for good and with it that chapter of my life that is my association with him. It has been many things—very wonderful and very painful and I am very glad that it is over. . . .

For the future my plans are of necessity and of my own volition extremely vague. I have refused already several obvious offers that grew out of the publicity inevitably attendant at this announcement of our separation. . . . I have agreed to remain a few weeks to hold Orson's hand while he begins his picture, if he does begin it. . . . Otherwise I shall go back East in a leisurely manner. . . . I think I shall do nothing for some months, except vaguely prepare the ground for next season. [He discharged his debt to "Orson's picture" by collaborating anonymously with Herman Mankiewicz on both story and script of *Citizen Kane*.] I have a very fine play that I own— about President Wilson—but there is no hurry about that: I have notions for a semi-documentary film: I would like to keep my finger in the radio-pie, partly because it can be good fun if the game is properly played, and partly because Television, when it comes, is the Art-Form, which must of necessity, both for economic and aesthetic reasons, be the Popular Entertainment of the next generation . . . and Television is likely to be run, if not by the Government, then at any rate by the Interests under very rigid control of the Government. I don't believe the Soup-and-Coffee boys can afford to get into it—and if they do, there is a fight there that it will be fun to be in on!

This all sounds very vague and silly, I know, to you in the middle of your new War. This whole letter is something of a pain in the neck and I would not send it to you if I didn't somehow feel that, when you receive it, you will understand just why it is to *you* that I said it and why, to no one else could I have written just what I have. . . . I think the truth is that I miss you, more perhaps than I know even now: not the very pleasant months we lived together in various apartments in the East-side of New York—though they were very happy for me—but for more than that. . . . I think for three years you were the soil of taste and encouragement and good sense and *esprit* in which the roots to my activities were able to grow. . . . I know now—and I suspect that you have always known— just how essential your judgments (not so much on specifics but on the far more important ground of relative human and artistic values) were to me in these few years—beginning with *Four Saints*—which are the span of my valid theatrical career. I think if I had had the salutary, intelligent deflating influence of our evening and breakfast conversations, even for a few days at a time, I should not today (and Orson would not to-day) be in the mess that we are!

What are you doing over there, in your moribund continent, that is more important than returning here to influence pro-foundly the cultural life of your time? That is what you did for three years. . . . (I mean that very seriously) and it is what you terribly need to do again, for our sakes, (for my sake especially) if not for yours. . . .

Reviens donc—L'Amérique a besoin de toi! Moi aussi et surtout! Je t'embrasse. John

I answered saying I would be available for work whenever he needed me, but that I did not think it wise to return "on spec." Lorentz, moreover, had not summoned me. Copland kept writing he wished "passionately that [I] would come home and help, instead of sending all that good advice from Paris." His letter of February 15 ends, "There is a rumor that you are thinking of coming home this spring. Would God 't were true." Only Marga Barr, a European, seemed to understand that America was under control and not very interesting, while Europe, being out of control, was extremely so. "I think you were so right to stay," she wrote. "Here people are nervous if they think of the war, but mostly they don't and life goes on perhaps even more elaborately than usual."

My life was not elaborate at all. I argued politics with Sherry,

practiced the piano, listened to radio broadcasts from all over
Europe, and gave parties. Every Friday night I held an open house
to which friends brought friends. Once in a while the Mangans
came, but mostly the friends and friends of friends were European
—Hugnet, Eluard, Arp, with their ladies, also Mary Reynolds,
Peggy Guggenheim, and whoever among our soldier acquaintances
happened to be on leave. Sometimes there were more women than
men, but not often, since Paris ladies seemed to find replacements
for mobilized husbands and lovers, then more replacements when
the substitutes were called. In fact, for spending time with their
men on leave, there was a protocol. The husband had first right,
then the main lover, then his substitute, and so on through the
substitutes for substitutes. So mostly the ladies with several loves
would arrive with one love or another, as a last resort with someone
very young not under arms. And there would be hot coffee on
arrival, for the weather was cold, and later foie gras sandwiches and
little almond cakes from Poiré-Blanche and a white wine cup containing wild strawberries, available in Paris all year round.

Food was not short that winter, though coal and firewood were,
because the canals that brought them were frozen all of February.
I eventually acquired some *bois de démolition,* oak beams cut up
that gave a glowing heat. And then I almost quarreled with M,
because she wanted me to share them with her for keeping Sherry's
feet warm while he worked, though they had plenty of coal and
their own central heat. I economized my logs by wearing sweaters,
woolens, and a floor-length dressing gown of camel and vicuña that
I had had made for that purpose. Even so, my fingers would get
cold as I practiced Bach and Mozart on the piano.

Except for the frying-oils, chiefly peanut from Morocco, nothing
was yet missing from the markets; and shot game was more available than usual. War having been declared early in September, the
shooting season was not opened at that time. But three months
later, wild game had so overrun the fields and forests that at a
time when shooting and hunting would ordinarily be over, it was
decided instead to let them begin. So from December on, we had
partridges and pheasants and larks and blackbirds and quails and
wild boar and venison. My concierge, André, who cooked for me,
even served one night when I had dinner guests a fillet of fawn,
tender, pale pink, and no more than an inch across.

Philip Lasell, also a remaining Parisian, had sent me a case of champagne for my birthday; and there was one bottle left when Nonotte Roederer, a young girl to whom I had become attached, and Nicolas Chatelain, a Russian painter whom I did not know, arrived one afternoon to inform me the first that they had just decided to be married. So we drank it and planned a triple wedding with music. There would have to be a civil one at the Mairie; that was French law. Then after drinks at the neighboring café there would be a Protestant ceremony and reception at Nonotte's mother's flat. And the next day, since Nicolas was Russian, a church affair in the rue Daru Cathedral, with crowns and choruses, and with a Russian party after that. My role was to play Bach on the piano before the Protestant occasion, which I did, having practiced up a fine prelude and fugue. I only got through the prelude, however, because the deaf *pasteur,* seeing me lift my hands, began to speak.

But practicing for this appearance had set me off. From then on I played the piano constantly, recovering my lost finger skills and mastering a whole batch of Mozart sonatas. Mozart was a major problem in those days; and restudying his works, forging a new style for playing them which would be convincing to a music world longing to hear them rendered with a grandeur appropriate to their proportions, had replaced the Bach problem of thirty years before. Well into June I kept up my investigations, discovering, I think, something like a method for solving the expressive content of any Mozart piece. At least I made sure that there *is* an expressive content, and never since have I been tolerant toward an "abstract" or "absolute" approach to this composer.

Hugnet had started a magazine in November. Printed on fine paper and devoted to esoteric poetry, *L'Usage de la parole* offered as a gift to those who subscribed for copies on even finer stock a print or etching or handmade lithograph by some artist of unusual repute. For the first issue this gift was a piece of music (my *Valse grégorienne,* to poems of Hugnet), a lithograph of my manuscript in a cover by Picasso. It was Georges who had arranged this with the artist; but knowing Picasso's way of offering just anything as illustration to no matter what, and being also somewhat fearful lest his strength, if willfully deployed, might overpower mine, I asked that the cover bear only calligraphy, nothing but the title and all our names. To my relief, he did not seem to mind. Nor have I ever minded his result. On the contrary, its messy lettering makes me happy in a way that very little of his handwork does; its magic,

A music cover by Picasso, 1940

for once, is my magic, hence a blessing; and I have never held its friendliness in doubt.

Wartime restrictions on lights and subways gave us that winter the most convenient hours for theatergoing that I have ever experienced. Plays beginning at half past five and operas at six produced an audience more alert than after dining. It also meant one got home before the ten o'clock blackout. With Mary Garden I often went to the Opéra-Comique, for she had worked there young and felt attached to it. Also, and most conveniently, she never dined. She liked a good lunch, would often take me to Larue for that. And I would give her tea with toast and jam before we went to hear *Louise* or *Carmen* or Xavier Leroux's *Le Chemineau* (revived that year). She had not sung in opera since 1931, but she was always in search of those who could acquire from her something of the dramatic awareness and musical intelligence that had controlled her performances. She did not want pupils; teaching was not her line. But she did want badly to pass on a certain knowledge nowhere else available since Jean de Reszke's death.

We went to hear a girl just out of the Conservatoire sing *Louise,* knowing from word of mouth that she was exceptional. And afterwards, of course, the Louise of all time went backstage to pay her compliments. She would not criticize an artist in the greenroom; she merely asked the girl to come see her. Then at her own flat in the rue du Bac she told her. "Your voice is beautiful," she said, "and so are you. Also you are an actress. Your first act is good, your second better; your third act, with the love scene, is the best. But in the fourth you let the opera down. I suspect you don't quite understand the character. Why do you think Louise left home?"

"Because she was in love with Julien," said the girl.

"But not at all," said Garden. "Louise was a girl who was going to leave home that year."

For other heroines she had solutions too, as guides to understanding their behavior. Of Mélisande she said, "She always lies. Even dying, her answer is ambiguous." Of Carmen the secret is that she is untamable. She does not fear death, only loss of liberty, as she says to her ex-lover with the knife, "Free I live, and free I shall die." And for her dearest operatic memory she chose no role of musical impressiveness, such as Debussy's Mélisande, or of physical display, such as Massenet's Thaïs or Strauss's Salomé, but that of the governess in Alfano's *Resurrezione,* "because it contains everything that can happen to a woman." When her father, eighty-nine, died in December, she brought me duck-billed brandy jugs from

Aberdeen. From that time on, she never left her mother, then eighty-three, an image of herself, all slenderness and grooming but of no age. When the invasion came, and German armies were almost at the gates of Paris, Mary Garden decided that her mother really should be got back home. So she mobilized the British Embassy for places, and the two flew to London on the last of the passenger planes. Alone, she would have stayed, she said; she had seen France through a war before. France was her home, as it was mine; and save for the safety of an aged parent, she would have felt disloyal leaving then.

That spring I had started again making portraits; and as the weeks advanced I made one nearly every day. I composed one of Picasso at his house while at the same time he made one of me, one that he did not ever show me. He spoke of Gertrude Stein, regretted passages from *Paris, France* that he had heard were over-patriotic. I recognized the judgment of some communist adviser, probably Louis Aragon. But Picasso was displeased with her for writing, as he thought, commercially ("just to have a silver teapot," were his words) and also for not staying in Paris like the rest of us. "Why do you suppose she ran away?" he asked. "Sometimes old ladies are afraid," I answered. "Old men too," he offered, as we slowly climbed the stairs.

That closed the subject. Now he turned to music, remarking that he had only known a few musicians. There was Satie, of course: "He was delicious." And he had been interested in Stravinsky until he found the music "just a bird cage." The idea of musical portraits was new to him; how did I do them? I answered that I drew them just as he would; I took paper, looked at my sitter, then let my pencil move—not doodling, of course, but writing down as fast as possible what came to me. "Ah, yes," he said, "I understand. If you are in the room while I am working, whatever I do is automatically your portrait."

The portrait that I made of the man Picasso, called *Bugles and Birds,* was not at all a portrait of his work, though some suppose that to have been my aim. I do not try evoking visual art; in all my portraits only the sitter's presence is portrayed, not his appearance or his profession. Picasso's presence is also in my portrait of Dora Maar. When she came to pose, he came along, curious, as he said, to see my flat and to watch me at work again. I suspected a bit of Spanish punctilio, as if he felt it not quite right for her to come to my place unaccompanied. But I was honored, of course, and said so. And just as might have been predicted, he came into the portrait; he could not not do so, being in the room. I did not identify the intruder then, but only later came to realize that an assertive bass which makes its entry half way through the piece could only be Picasso, for Dora Maar herself was not like that.

The static war's euphoria that bathed us all continued right on through May 10, when Holland was invaded and France's power of resistance virtually destroyed by bombing, along with most of her airplanes. Some Angel of Mons or Battle of the Marne, it was believed, would surely, miraculously, as in World War I, provide a rescue. Nevertheless, the French authorities did what governments always do when defeat is imminent; they put in charge their most admired commander. General Weygand, who had been in Syria, was recalled and ordered (it could only have been that) to organize the military disaster in such a way that the population would believe it gradual. A surrender at that moment, though the war was already lost, would not have been acceptable in France or in England, perhaps not even to the German government. But only the most inside insiders knew the truth. One of my French Friday-night guests was still insisting as late as June that the invasion was only a trap laid by Weygand. "He is drawing them on," she argued. But Mademoiselle Philibert, who had written to Madame Weygand, felicitating their country on the return of her husband to the chief command, received an answer ending with, "May God preserve France in the trials she is about to undergo!" "Now what do you make of that?" she queried me.

Mozart, One Musician's Best Friend

I N LATE APRIL, on the verge of the invasion, I had written to the editor of *Modern Music:*

My account doesn't make very clear why I have enjoyed my winter so much. I'm not sure I know exactly. I've tried to tell you what it's like here musically; for other matters there are plenty of reports in the weekly press. What I can't describe very well is the state of calm that permeates our whole intellectual life. Not the vegetable calm of a back-water country or the relative and quite electric calm that is supposed to exist at the center of a moving storm. Rather it is the quietude of those from whom have been lifted all the burdens and all the pressures, all the white elephants and all the fears that have sat on us like a nightmare for twenty years. I am not referring to any imminence of German invasion or of its contrary. I am talking about that imminence of general European cultural collapse that has been hanging over us ever since the last war ended. As long as the tension was mounting everybody was unhappy. Fascism in Italy, the Jewish persecutions in Germany, the Civil War in Spain, a hundred other scenes of the heartbreaking drama have kept us jittery and trembling. It has been imagined and hoped that possibly some of the brighter boys might stop the progress of it all by taking thought. Our opinions were demanded on every imaginable variety of incident in power politics and in class warfare, whether we had any access or not to correct information about such incidents (which we usually didn't) or any degree of political education that would make our opinions worth a damn, even if we had had access to the facts. For ten years now all sides have been pressing us to talk; indeed many have talked, and I should say that in consequence a great deal less real work got done in those years than was done in the preceding decade.

That's all over now. We are on the chute. And in spite of the enormous inroads on a man's time and money that being mobilized represents, and in spite of the strictness of both military and political censorship over all sorts of intellectual operations, the intellectual life has picked up distinctly. The lotus-land of whether surrealism is really gratuitous and whether such and such a picture by Picasso is really worth the price asked (for, dear Reader, it was indeed by becoming passionate over such matters that many fled the impossibility of being anything beyond merely passionate over matters like Jewry and Spain, because they knew that mere passion wouldn't get anybody anywhere and that passion was all anybody had to offer on any side, excepting maybe a little quiet opportunism in England and in Russia), anyway, the 1930s, that stormy lotus-land of commercialized high esthetics to which New York's Museum of Modern Art will long remain a monument, have quietly passed away. It is rather surprising and infinitely agreeable to find that poets now are writing poetry again rather than rhymes about current events; that painters paint objects, not ideas; that composers write music to please themselves, there being no longer any Modern Music Concert committees to please. Most surprising and agreeable of all is the fact that the young (with so many of their elders away now and with all their elders' ideas on the shelf) have again become visible as young. They are doing all the things they haven't been allowed to do for some time, such as talking loud in cafés and sleeping with people of their own age. Also, instead of discussing esthetics with intelligence and politics with passion, as their elders did, they are discussing esthetics with passion and politics with intelligence. I find the change a happy one indeed. I also find distinctly agreeable the presence around of young poets and young painters who look us squarely in the eye and say "hooey," who don't even look at us at all if they don't feel like it, who behave toward us, their elders, exactly as we behaved toward ours some twenty-five years ago and as no young people have really been quite able to behave since.

I must admit that young composers are not as visible in the cafés as poets are; they never were. Pianists, however, peep out from every corner. To a man, and at all ages, they are occupied with what seems to be the central esthetic problem in music today, the creation of an acceptable style-convention for performing Mozart. I've spent a good deal of time at that job too this winter, and I have found out some things about Mozart's piano music I shall tell you another time. . . .

I've discovered music all over again. And it turns out to be just as it was when I was seventeen, the daily joy of practicing a beloved instrument and of finding one's whole life filled with order and energy as a result.

But of all that, more another time. Give my best to the fellahs.

Je t'embrasse en camarade.
Virgil

From May 10 till I took a train for the Southwest on June 8, I wrote portraits with accelerating frequency. The Friday nights were kept up too, for, excepting the cafés, my evenings and those at the flat of the poetess Lise Deharme were for our artist kind the only gathering places. My last party took place in the first days of June. On May 22 I had written my family,

As you read in the paper, there is more war just now than there was before. Don't believe too much, however, because newspapers do exaggerate. I have not left Paris and I am not expecting to. I could leave on an hour's notice if I thought it advisable, and I shall leave if I think that. It seems to be better just now for exerybody to go on quietly and not to be frantic. In Paris the people are calm and confident and good-humored, much more so than last September, and none of the shops have closed. I continue to write music and practice the piano just as before and to have my regular Friday evening parties. I am not nervous or worried or unhappy. I have my music (my own music) packed so that by carrying with me one middle-sized music-trunk I could save one copy of everything. My pictures and household things I am not even packing. I shall leave everything in place if I go away and expect to find them all when I come back. And I am not really expecting to have to go away at all. I am still expecting to make a trip to the U.S. in the fall. I am doing physical culture 3 times a week and I have no stomach or hips any more. I can wear all my ten-year-old clothes. You might send this letter to Ruby.

Love & kisses,
Virgil

On May 29, the day of the bombardment of the Renault factory on the Seine, I was lunching with the Chatelains in Passy, having just composed a portrait of Nicolas, when the sirens sounded. As usual, we did not interrupt ourselves but went on eating while the food was hot, until a gigantic voice said, "Mesdames et Messieurs, go to your shelters." On top of that came the sound of many airplanes and then of explosions. And so we did go down. Ten minutes later, with the all-clear, we went back to eat our peaches, the first of the season. And after lunch, the portrait of Nicolas being finished, I began one of Nonotte.

A few days later I consulted Sherry. The Germans should arrive, he told me, in about a week. He would stay on, of course, representing *Time*. (The Germans, not liking the way he reported their Occupation, would request him to leave that fall.) Since our country was not at war with Germany, we were in no danger save of being bombed, which could happen to one anywhere in France. Theodate also, with whom I had lunch on the subject one of those fine sunny days, thought she would stay. She had been working for the Belgian Red Cross, receiving refugees at the Gare du Nord, and would remain at her post until evacuated. (By waiting for that outcome, she added nothing to her usefulness, merely lost her voice and a large part of her luggage.) The Paris doctors, teachers, postal employees, concierges, everyone who had a post would be expected to remain. However, on reflection, I decided that I should leave simply because of money. If I should find myself behind the German lines and be obliged to regain the United States through Switzerland, that might be expensive. That I should be leaving one day for America was inevitable in view of my thin resources; it was proper to see your French friends through a war, but not to impose on them. Nevertheless, I did not wish to clutter up any of the exits so long as persons really in danger, such as political dissidents, Jews from all over Europe, Poles, and the English, were using them. Already all the roads were full of cars. I would take a train. And I would take it to Oloron, in the Pyrenees, where Gertrude Newell, a New York lady, had twice invited me to be a refugee. So I wired her, bought a second-class reserved seat, and packed.

I called on Mademoiselle Philibert to say good-by, arranged with my landlord to preserve my books and furniture in case he found it wise to let my flat, took leave of all friends correctly and without haste. My hired piano was released and called for. And Arp, leaving with his wife for Switzerland, brought me as going-away present on the last of my Fridays a sculpture made especially for me.

My packing took two days because of a wooden case built for my pictures. And by agreement made with Leonid, whose canvases were stored in my flat, I had his pictures packed along with mine. My luggage came, in all, to fourteen pieces. There was no reason not to take my clothes, for I had bought that winter suits and overcoats, had even borrowed money for that purpose, moved by an instinct, I suppose, toward facing disaster, should it come, well dressed. Arriving in America without funds could be coped with; having to buy clothes there would be inconvenient. Music and books in print I did not dream of taking, only my life's work, my manuscripts, filling up five music trunks. I cushioned the Arp sculpture among the clothes, also the old French silver I had from Madame Langlois.

My trunks and cases being ready, the shipper who had boxed my pictures put them (all but the pictures) on a large flat push-cart and walked them to the Gare d'Austerlitz (the near-by Gare d'Orsay having been abandoned in September). I walked too, as there were by then no taxis, only speeding staff cars in the empty streets. At the station I presented my luggage to a checker, waited seven minutes while the man just come on duty slowly changed to his alpaca coat, put on fresh paper cuffs, and wiped his pen. Then he wrote out a slip for fourteen pieces and assured me they would all be on my train.

The picture case, however, had adventures. I had omitted from it an unfinished sketch by Leonid, then thought I should include it after all. I carried it round the corner to my *emballeur* in the rue de Lille, whose monumental wife, herself the carpenter, said that the case had left, she thought; but she would make a small one for the extra picture. Actually the case had not left, was reopened, then wheeled to the station and also checked. But the delay caused it to miss my train, and that train was the last to leave for Oloron. The case remained throughout the war in storage at the station, and the Germans never were allowed to take it. In 1944, receiving in New York a request that it be called for, I sent the baggage check to Leonid, who reclaimed it and found everything intact.

The trip to Oloron was slow, on account of bomb alerts; the train was dark and crowded. But I slept some, free of luggage worries; and my fellow travelers were considerate. Once, during a long wait in the countryside, when we heard a drilling, trilling noise, a man of middle age said, "*Ça y est!* Machine-guns! I recognize them from the other war." But pretty soon it turned out to be crickets.

Miss Newell, a decorator with literary and theatrical connections, had retired to live in a manor house named Planterrose in a village called Moumour. Her other refugees were a writer, Jamie Campbell; and elderly Venezuelan lady, Madame Semenario, sister of the composer Reynaldo Hahn; and her daughter Clarita, Comtesse de Forceville, whose husband was under arms. Others came by, some of them soldiers, friends of Campbell or of mine, and were put up for a night or two while on their way to find their families. For with half of France already more than two weeks on the road— women, children, and grandparents fleeing the German troops, or military units disbanded and in disarray—the armistice was followed by still more traveling as families essayed to reunite.

The armistice, asked for on the twelfth of June, was granted six days later. In the meantime, Italy, joining the German side, invaded the South. On the eighteenth, trains and services began to work. And though my picture case did not arrive, mail did, quantities of it, correctly forwarded by my Paris post office. And in the midst of the huge hegira that was France that June, scholastic examinations took place. In every courthouse town, candidates of every age and for every promotion were handed the secret questions. No less than the railway and postal services, the French bureaucracy of education functioned. Wondering how our own would have held up in such a holocaust, I had to remember that we are less used to fighting wars at home and not at all accustomed to invasion.

At Planterrose, among sweet peas and magnolia blossoms, but

without gasoline, we fretted; and Marshal Pétain's cracked voice on the radio saying, "Frenchmen, I have sad news for you" was of no comfort. Miss Newell, moreover, needed to get her British butler off to England, along with his eighteen-year-old son. His wife, who was French, and the younger child, a girl, could remain; but grown males must not be captured. A scouting trip I made by autobus revealed, indeed, that every night (this was before the eighteenth, when the Germans arrived) ships left for England from Saint-Jean-de-Luz. So we hired (with driver) the communal bus, which had a right to gasoline; and I took Manlow and his son down to the port. I made at least three trips during those six days before a frontier was drawn between us and the coast. On one of them Miss Newell went along. She had thought we might add Spanish visas to our passports, she and I, just in case we should be leaving in a hurry. But no hurry was then visible, only long queues everywhere. And we did not choose to stand in line with all those pushing Belgians.

On one of the other trips I met the one-time editor of Chicago's *Little Review,* Margaret Anderson, hoping to procure somehow an American visa for Georgette Leblanc, ex-companion of Maurice Maeterlinck, ex-singer who was old, ill, and French—conditions, all of them, that Washington's representatives viewed unfavorably. I also came upon Eric de Haulleville, who had hitchhiked from Brussels with his wife and with his daughter, aged two. The child, it seems, had by her winning ways induced truck drivers everywhere to give them lifts. Eric, staying upcountry at Dax, was in Bayonne on passport matters; but finding the queues excessive, he decided to come back later. We spent the day together and thanks to his insistent Belgian ways (bluffing a head waiter, for instance, into believing he had reserved a table) actually had lunch at a table. Long suffering from a circulatory ailment, and not bettered by his long walk across France, he was taking the waters before moving south. I did not see him again, for he died in Vence the next year. Georgette Leblanc died also in the South, Margaret Anderson remaining with her to the end.

Eventually Miss Newell's hospitality turned to scolding. Or was it that she merely missed her butler? In any case, come mid-July, I left. On market days communal buses crossed the line in freedom; and the miller, our local mayor, gave me a pass. So with my fourteen suitcases and music trunks I traveled to Bayonne and on to Biarritz. I had enough French money to last perhaps two weeks. Getting to America could no doubt be improvised. So I picked up clothes at Lanvin's local branch, charging them for payment after the war; and the store was pleased that they should be bought by an old customer rather than by German officers. Man Ray was in Biarritz also, knowing he must leave France but worried to have had to abandon his house and car, his pictures, books, and girl friend, not sure either how he was going to secure money for leaving France. A Quaker lady, picked up at the American vice-consulate, solved that problem. She had been administering relief in Marseille until she found her work interfered with by Vichy officials. About to return to Philadelphia with unspent funds, she offered to lend us dollars for traveling to Lisbon, where we could wire for more. So we went to the Germans for exit-permission, the Spanish and Portuguese for visas—all quickly obtained, since there were no crowds any more—using our last French money for train tickets to Hendaye.

Music in manuscript I knew to be a hazard. The Germans might have held me up for months, searching for coded secrets, had not Mozart rescued me. As we left the train a porter had piled our luggage on a pushcart, explaining that after it had passed examination he would walk us across the frontier bridge to Irun. In the empty customs shed he spread our pieces out and told us to unlock them. Man Ray, who had only two, I think, was quickly passed. The examiner, a German peasant soldier, looked hopeless about all mine, then pointed to a small suitcase, as if to say, "Open that." This happened to contain, right on the top, a last-moment thought in packing, a volume of Mozart piano sonatas in which I had marked fingerings, the only piece of print in all my luggage.

As the soldier, suddenly alert with curiosity, opened the volume, I said in German, "*Sonaten von Mozart.*" At that he smiled in happy comprehension, said "*Ja! Mozart! Ja!*" and put back the volume, looked at nothing more. In Spain we bought tickets for the Sud-Express to Lisbon, had dinner, observed the civil war's still unrepaired destruction, mounted our sleeping car, and went to bed.

In Lisbon we wired for money, received it, were assigned passage on the *Excalibur* for two weeks thence, August 12. The town was full of refugees, mostly well to do, all seeking visas at the consulates or waiting for ships. Lisbon was not exciting; but the wines were tasty and the *fados*, a species of tavern ballad, mildly pleasing. The city's nature is that of all things Portuguese—easy-going, a little tired, not strong in flavor.

The American ship was rude as to service, frozen as to food. We slept, some sixty males, on the library floor, Man Ray with cameras underneath his pillow. Daytimes we made jokes with expert jokesters, the film maker René Clair and the still-surrealist painter Salvador Dalí. My warmest friend on board was a woman lawyer, Suzanne Blum. She knew that her safety lay in leaving France, being Jewish and also prominent. And yet she worried over where her duty lay, to leave or not to leave her aging mother. Being by now a practiced hand, through long experience of Blitzstein, Kirstein, Grosser, and the Stettheimers, at comforting Jewish emotional indecision, sweetly, firmly I assured her she had done right. So friends we became, and friends we have remained. Along with Madame Langlois, Hugnet, Sauguet, not many more, Suzanne is one of my small handful of French with whom misunderstanding has never occurred.

In New York, as if by occult message, I was telephoned by Kathleen (Mrs. O'Donnell) Hoover, whom I did not know, but who was to become later my biographer. The occultness lay in the fact that my arrival there, like my exit from France, seemed still to be under the sign of Mozart. For what she wanted was that I lecture on his music for the Metropolitan Opera Guild and illustrate my new approach to it, helped out by the singer Frieda Hempel, who possessed from three decades back a quite wonderful older approach.

Then I went to Alexander Smallens's at Stamford for a weekend; and he phoned Geoffrey Parsons, saying, "Virgil is here." Now Parsons, in charge at the New York *Herald Tribune* of all matters cultural, had been in search since March of a replacement for the late Lawrence Gilman as music critic. Knowing my articles in *Modern Music* and admiring *The State of Music,* he would already have made me overtures, according to Alex, had I not been, so Alex assured him, firmly determined on not leaving France. Geoffrey came to Alex's on Sunday. I played him Mozart in a way that pleased him mightily. He offered me the post. But I demurred. I said that if I scotched some sacred cow, as Teddy Chanler had, taking over from Philip Hale on the Boston *Herald,* I also would be fired within six weeks. He simply said, "I think you are not familiar with the ways of a metropolitan newspaper."

Eventually, that is to say by October, I had been looked at by the staff and found companionable. And at lunch Mrs. Ogden Reid had asked me, "How does it seem to you, the idea of becoming our music critic?" I replied that the general standard of music reviewing in New York had sunk so far that almost any change might bring improvement. Also I thought perhaps my presence in a post so prominent might stimulate performance of my works.

On the day I was engaged, October 10, Francis Perkins, my music editor, though deeply disappointed that he had not himself been named, became forever my firm aide and ally. That night I covered the New York Philharmonic at their season's opening; and the Philharmonic's management and board, one understood, instantly regretted my appointment. Only a few months earlier, Theodate and Sherry, despairing of my seeming quietude and exasperated that I should practice Mozart while Europe burned, had told each other that indeed it looked as if Virgil were finished. Within an even shorter time, when Sherry reappeared, Theo was paying with split vocal cords for having shouted in refugee receiving halls; and he was being sent to Buenos Aires, a city for which he had as little appetite as for New York. Their dear friend, on the other hand, had thanks to Mozart fallen on his feet.

The Paper

THE NEW YORK *Herald Tribune* was a gentleman's paper, more like a chancellery than a business. During the fourteen years I worked there I was never told to do or not to do anything. From time to time I would be asked what I thought about some proposal regarding my department; and if I did not think favorably of it, it was dropped.

The city room was an open space filled with flat-top desks, the classical stage-set of a newspaper; but what went on there bore no resemblance to the behavior of city staffs in plays and films. I never saw anyone use more than one telephone at a time, and I never heard anyone raise his voice. Exception was the plaintive call of "Copy!" from someone sending a late review down to the typesetters page by page. Self-control was the rule on that floor, just as the avoidance of any haste that might make for error was the style of the linotypers and proofreaders on the floor below.

But if the *Herald Tribune* was a decorous paper, it was also a hard-drinking one. The Artists and Writers Restaurant next door, in Fortieth Street near Seventh Avenue, a former speak-easy run by a Dutchman named Jack Bleeck, received from noon till morning a steady sampling of our staff, of writers from *The New Yorker,* who seemed in general to like drinking with us, of press agents, play producers, and after-theater parties. After the Late City

Edition had been put to bed (in those days around half past midnight), our night staff and the working reviewers would gather there to wait out the next half-hour till freshly printed papers were sent down. Everyone read first his own column and after that those of the others. Then we all complimented one another, as one must before going on to discuss points of judgment or style.

The whole staff was pen-proud, had been so, it would seem, since 1912, when Ogden Reid, inheriting the New York *Tribune* from his father (Ambassador to England Whitelaw Reid), had turned it into a galaxy of stars. And until his death in 1950 it stayed luminous. After that, the care for writing faded and the drinking in Bleeck's bar lacked stamina. I do not insist that drinking and good English go together, though certainly over at the *Times,* in Forty-third Street, the staff seemed neither to roister much nor to write very impressively. In my own case, Geoffrey Parsons had no sooner opened the possibility of my writing for the *Herald Tribune* than a dinner was set up at the Players' Club, with a dozen of the paper's best-drinking old hands to test my sociability. That was in September, and I passed all right.

It was still not known, of course, how I would behave in front of a deadline. And Parsons, naturally worried on my first night, prowled about till I had finished writing, then held his breath in the composing room while I checked my proofs. He suggested in these one change, the omission of a slap at the audience ("undistinguished" had been my word). At Bleeck's, when the papers came down, my piece read clearly as a strong one, though it contained, I knew, any number of faults, including seventeen appearances of the first personal pronoun. I had entitled this review of the concert that opened the Philharmonic's ninety-ninth season *Age Without Honor;* and I had snubbed the orchestra's conductor, John Barbirolli, by publishing with it the photograph of his concertmaster, Michel Piastro. It was unfavorable throughout—"hard-hitting," my admirers at the bar had called it—and it ended with a quote from my companion of the evening (actually Maurice Grosser), "I understand now why the Philharmonic is not a part of New York's intellectual life."

Hired on a Thursday afternoon, I had covered the Philharmonic that night. The next day I reviewed from its home ground the Boston Symphony's opening. The following Tuesday I attended the season's first New York concert of the Philadelphia Orchestra. For the weekend after that, in my first Sunday piece, I compared these groups. And if my first review had been brutal with overstatement, my second set a far more gracious tone ("peaches and cream," Parsons called it).

The quality of this piece was not always to be kept up. Sometimes I would write smoothly, sometimes with a nervous rhythm, darting in short sentences from thought to thought and failing to carry my readers with me. But on the whole I interested them; and almost from the beginning I did observe standards of description and analysis more penetrating and of coverage more comprehensive than those then current in the press. I was aware of this; the music world was aware of it; my colleagues on the paper were immediately aware of the fact that my work had presence. Ettie Stettheimer, neither a musician nor a journalist, compared it to "the take-off of a powerful airplane." My editors, of course, knew the dangers of so showy an ascent. Also that I was heading into a storm.

For from my first review they received, as also did I, reams of protest mail. Mine I answered, every piece of it, and with courtesy. "I thank you for the warmly indignant letter," was one of my beginnings, before going on to some point raised, such as, for instance, that of my own incompetence. Before very long the editors, aware through the secretarial grapevine of how I could win over many an angry one, would send me their own mail for answering, thus making clear no protest could be made behind my back.

But at the beginning they showed me only the favorable letters. It must have been two years before Mrs. Ogden Reid, almost more active at the paper than her husband, admitted that there had been demands for my beheading. What kept the paper firm regarding me, she said, had been the fact that those who wrote to praise me were important novelists like Glenway Wescott, enlightened museum directors like Alfred Barr, art-minded lawyers like Arnold Weissberger, and public-spirited heads of university music departments, such as Douglas Moore—in short, what she called "intellectual leaders"—whereas the protesters were practically all just quarrelsome types without responsibility ("nuts") or, worse, spokesmen for the performing institutions.

The most persistent of these last turned out to be the Metropolitan Opera Association, whose powerful hostesses, bankers, and corporation attorneys seemed to feel that their names on the board of any enterprise should render it immune to criticism. At the slightest *lèse-majesté* they would make truculent embassies to the paper demanding that somebody or other, usually I, be fired. Urged thus to remove my predecessor, Lawrence Gilman, Ogden Reid had twenty years earlier inquired, "Who's running this paper?" Similarly rebuffed regarding me, the ambassadors would remark that with the death of Mr. Gilman music criticism had lost a great prose writer.

The Philharmonic board, though no less disapproving, early gave up direct intervention in favor of a business maneuver. One of them did inquire whether I would accept board membership, but I declined. And several, I believe, "spoke" to Mrs. Reid. But the business threat was early provoked, at the end of my second week, when I diagnosed the soprano Dorothy Maynor as "immature vocally and immature emotionally." From e. e. cummings came, "Congrats on the Maynor review. Eye 2 was there." The Columbia Concerts Corporation, however, of which the Philharmonic's manager, Arthur Judson, was president, held a board meeting over it, and not for determining Miss Maynor's fate, but mine. The decision, one heard, was to withdraw all advertising until my employment at the paper should be ended. This plan might have been troublesome to carry out, since it would have denied our services to all Columbia's artists. But at the time the threat seemed real enough to provoke intervention by another impresario.

Ira Hirschmann, a business executive married to a professional pianist, Hortense Monath, and friend of another, the ever-so-respected Artur Schnabel, had been presenting for several seasons, under the name New Friends of Music, weekly Sunday concerts of the chamber repertory. But weekdays he was advertising manager of Bloomingdale's. So when Hirschmann heard about Columbia's plan, he went to our advertising manager, Bill Robinson, and said, "Mr. Thomson has not yet reviewed my concerts unfavorably, though he well may do so. But whatever happens, I shall match, line for line, any advertising you lose on his account." This incident I also did not know till two years later. But it helps explain the patience of my editors with a reviewer who was plainly a stormy petrel. As a storm bird, I should have preferred to sail above the clouds; but to get there I often had to fly right at them, and bump my beak against their leaden linings.

After twenty years of living inside Europe, I knew well the grandeurs and the flaws of music's past, also that with a big war silencing its present, composition's only rendezvous was with the future. America, for the duration, might keep alive the performing skills. But her strongest composers had shot their bolt in the 1930s and retired, as the phrase goes, into public life, while the younger ones who had not yet done so were getting ready either to be mobilized or to avoid that. The time was not for massive creativity, but rather for taking stock. My program therefore was to look as closely as I could at what was going on, naturally also to describe this to my readers, who constituted, from the first, the whole world of music. The method of my examination and my precepts for progress turned out to be those laid down exactly one year earlier in *The State of Music*.

These principles, as I understood them, engaged me to expose the philanthropic persons in control of our musical institutions for the amateurs they are, to reveal the manipulators of our musical distribution for the culturally retarded profit makers that indeed they are, and to support with all the power of my praise every artist, composer, group, or impresario whose relation to music was straightforward, by which I mean based only on music and the sound it makes. The businessmen and the amateurs, seeing what I was up to, became enemies right off. Those more directly involved with music took me for a friend, though Germans and the German-educated would bristle when I spoke up for French music or French artists. They would even view my taste for these as a somewhat shameful vice acquired in France.

The opposite was true, of course. I had not come to admire the musical workmanship of France from merely living there; I had lived there, at some sacrifice to my career, because I found French musical disciplines favorable to my maturing. Nor did the Germans suspect how deeply I distrusted their arrogance. For French arrogance about music is merely ignorance, like Italian arrogance, or American. But the Germanic kind, based on self-interest, makes an intolerable assumption, namely, its right to judge everything without appeal, as well as to control the traffic—as if past miracles (from Bach through Schubert) were an excuse for greed. And all

those lovely refugees—so sweet, so grateful, and so willing to work
—they were to be a Trojan horse! For today the Germanics are in
control everywhere—in the orchestras, the universities, the critical
posts, the publishing houses, wherever music makes money or is a
power.

I made war on them in the colleges, in the concert halls, and

"Play! Play as you never played before! Here comes Virgil Thomson."

in their offices. I did not hesitate to use the columns of my paper
for exposing their pretensions; and I refused to be put off by sneers
from praising the artists of my choice, many of them foreign to
the Italo-German axis. My editors found this method not unfair,
for they too, through our European Edition, were Paris-oriented.
The Germanics would never admit, however, that distributed attention was not mere Francophilia.

My literary method, then as now, was to seek out the precise
adjective. Nouns are names and can be libelous; the verbs, though
sometimes picturesque, are few in number and tend toward alleging
motivations. It is the specific adjectives that really describe and that
do so neither in sorrow nor in anger. And to describe what one
has heard is the whole art of reviewing. To analyze and compare
are stimulating; to admit preferences and prejudices can be helpful;
to lead one's reader step by step from the familiar to the surprising

is the height of polemical skill. Now certainly musical polemics were my intent, not aiding careers or teaching Appreciation. And why did a daily paper tolerate my polemics for fourteen years? Simply because they were accompanied by musical descriptions more precise than those being used just then by other reviewers. The *Herald Tribune* believed that skill in writing backed up by a talent for judgment made for interesting and trustworthy reviews, also that the recognition of these qualities by New York's journalistic and intellectual elite justified their having engaged me. Moreover, in spite of some protests and many intrigues against me, all of which followed plot-lines long familiar, I caused little trouble. If some business or political combine had caused the paper real embarrassment, either through loss of income or through massive reader protest, I should most likely not have survived, for the Ogden Reids, though enlightened, were not quixotic. As Geoffrey Parsons remarked some two years later, "It is possible to write good music criticism now, because no group is interested in stopping you." Which meant, I presume, that I was not a danger to the war effort.

The *Herald Tribune* represented in politics the liberal right, a position usually favorable to the arts. The know-nothing right and the Catholic right, as well as the Marxist left, are in all such matters, as we know, unduly rigid. And papers of the moderate left tend, in art, to be skimpy of space, the sheets of massive circulation even more so. But papers that are privately owned and individually operated make their address to the educated middle class. The *New York Times* has regularly in its critical columns followed a little belatedly the tastes of this group; the *Herald Tribune* under Ogden Reid aspired to lead them. It did not therefore, as the *Times* has so often done, shy away from novelty or from elegance. So when I took as a principle for my column that "intellectual distinction itself is news," the city desk, though not quite ready to admit so radical a concept, found my results lively, especially my wide-ranging choice of subjects and my indifference to personalities already publicized to saturation, such as Marian Anderson and Arturo Toscanini. In fact, when somewhat later John Crosby, then a staff writer, was asked to start a radio-and-television column, hopefully for syndication, the managing editor warned him against overdoing big-time coverage. "Spread yourself around like Virgil Thomson," he said. "Surprise your readers."

Except for courtesy coverage of opening nights at the Philharmonic and the Metropolitan Opera, I must say that my choice of occasions was by the conventions of the time wildly capricious. My third review was of a woman conductor, Frédérique Petrides, leading thirty players in a piece by David Diamond. In my second week, reviewing two Brazilian programs at the Museum of Modern Art, I poked fun at the public image of that institution, at folklore cults in general, at all music from Latin America, that of Villa-Lobos in particular, and found an error in the museum's translation of a title from the Portuguese. I also discovered, for myself at least, a group of young people called the Nine O'Clock Opera Company, all just out of the Juilliard School, singing in English at the Town Hall to a pianoforte accompaniment Mozart's *The Marriage of Figaro.*

My attack on Dorothy Maynor appeared on October 24, a subsequently much-quoted piece in praise of Artur Rubinstein on October 26. On the twenty-eighth I reported on a W.P.A. orchestra led by Otto Klemperer. On the thirty-first appeared a review of Jascha Heifetz entitled *Silk-Underwear Music,* in which I called his playing "vulgar." The imprecision of this adjective and the shocking nature of my whole attack brought protests on my head from Geoffrey Parsons as well as, through intermediaries, from Heifetz. Tasteless certainly were my adjectives weighted with scorn; but I could not then, cannot now, regret having told what I thought the truth about an artist whom I believed to be overestimated. To all such reputations, in fact, I was sales resistant, like William James, who had boasted, "I am against greatness and bigness in all their forms."

That winter, along with covering a handful of standard soloists —Josef Hofmann, Jan Smeterlin, Kirsten Flagstad, Arturo Toscanini, John Charles Thomas—and with a reasonable attention paid to the orchestras and the opera, I reviewed Maxine Sullivan (singing in a night club), Paul Bowles's music for *Twelfth Night* (on Broadway, with Helen Hayes and Maurice Evans), Walt Disney's *Fantasia,* a score of musical books and magazines, a student orchestra, two youth orchestras, an opera at the Juilliard School, a Bach oratorio in a church, a Broadway musical by Kurt Weill, Marc Blitzstein's far-to-the-left almost-opera *No for an Answer,* Stravinsky's Violin Concerto turned into a ballet, several other dance performances involving modern music, an economics-and-sociology report from Columbia University on the "hit" trade in popular songs, the Harvard Glee Club ("fair but no warmer"), Holy Thursday at Saint Patrick's Cathedral, a Negro preacher in New Jersey who wore frilled white paper wings over his blue serge suit and played swing music on an electric guitar (he was my Easter Sunday piece), some comical press-agentry received, a W.P.A. orchestra in Newark, three other suburban and regional orchestras, a swing concert at the Museum of Modern Art, an opera at Columbia University, a *Southern Harmony* "sing" in Benton, Kentucky, the Boston "Pops" in Boston, and the Goldman Band in Central Park. By the following season's end I had got round to examining the High School of Music and Art and to considering the radio as a serious source. Recordings I did not touch, because another member of my staff had them in charge.

This staff consisted of myself and three assistants—Francis Perkins, who also served as music editor, Jerome D. Bohm, and Robert Lawrence. Bohm, who had conducted opera in his Berlin student days under Leo Blech, was a German-oriented voice teacher and opera coach. Lawrence, already beginning his career as a conductor, was an enthusiast for French music, especially Berlioz. Perkins, though not professionally a musician, was widely read in music's history and devoted to exactitude. Since 1922 he had kept a catalog, with dates and places, of all the orchestral and operatic works performed in New York City. This was the extension of a somewhat less careful listing begun in 1911 by Edward Krehbiel, and it was unique. He also kept well-indexed clipping books containing all the reviews and news relating to music that appeared in the paper. And he had a shelf of reference books, many of them bought by him, for checking instantly the spelling of a name, the title of a work, the facts about almost anything connected with repertory. And until the department acquired a secretary, it was Perkins who kept the catalog and scrapbooks up to date, as well as sorting out the publicity and announcements, which arrived in vast abundance at the music desk.

For doing this he often worked late into the night "mopping up," as he called it, until three or four or five, then attended early Mass, had breakfast, and went home to sleep. A vintage Bostonian and proudly a Harvard man, he allowed himself no weakness or neglect, nursemaiding and housemaiding us all, lest some misstatement or a skimpy coverage make the paper inglorious. He it was who had in the 1920s and '30s widened the coverage from just the Carnegie-and-Town-Hall beat by slipping out in the course of many an event to visit half of another, something modern usually, that was taking place over at Hunter College or downtown at the New School for Social Research. At this time still a bachelor, he was, as our secretary said, "married to the *Herald Tribune*"; and if he did not sleep on the premises (as he sometimes did at concerts), he very often spent the whole night there.

Replying to my mail, to all those "letters fan and furious" that I sometimes published along with my answers in lieu of a Sunday think-piece, had early earned me stenographic aid. So when the managing editor lent me his own secretary for use on Tuesdays, his day off, this unprecedented precedent caused Perkins too to ask for help, which was granted. And eventually, at her own request, my secretarial abettor, Julia Haines, was allowed to work wholly for the music department, a happy arrangement that long survived my tenure.

Julia was a jolly and sharp-tongued Irishwoman who from having been around some twenty years was on girl-to-girl terms with the secretaries of Ogden Reid, Helen Reid, and Geoffrey Parsons. Her discretion was complete, and so was her devotion to me. She told her colleagues all the favorable news, showing them admiring letters from prominent persons and unusually skillful replies of mine to the opposition. In return they kept her informed of good opinions received in their offices. If they let her know of any trouble about me, she did not pass that on. They could hint, however, at some complaint that Parsons or the Reids would not have wished to make directly. And she would pass back my reply, embarrassing no one.

She also, on the paper's time, typed all my private correspondence—answers to inquiries about publication, to engagements offered, even to personal letters. And thanks to her use of the secretarial back fence, my life was completely exposed. I liked it that way, and so did my employers. Thus no tension that might arise risked becoming exaggerated, a situation especially valuable with regard to Helen Reid. For though we shared mutual admiration, I almost invariably rubbed her the wrong way. My impishness and my arrogance were equally distasteful, and something in my own resistance to her dislike of being rubbed the wrong way led me over and over again to the verge of offense.

Nevertheless, in spite of our tendency to draw sparks from each other, we worked together quite without distrust. After I had once procured music for the Herald Tribune Forum, a three-day feast of famous speakers held every year in the Hotel Waldorf-Astoria ballroom, she offered to pay me for doing this every year; and when I declined payment, my salary was raised. She did not interfere in any way with my department's operations, but eventually she came to ask my advice about pressures and complaints received regarding these operations. And when the general manager of the Metropolitan Opera, Rudolf Bing, surely displeased with my reviewing of his policy statements, sought to cultivate her favor through invitations to his box, she showed him where her confidence lay by inviting me, along with my chief supporter, my discoverer indeed, Geoffrey Parsons, to lunch with him at the paper.

With Parsons there was never misunderstanding. He admired me, forgave me, adopted me into his family. Besides, he was committed to making a success of me, since my appointment had been wholly of his doing. When I misbehaved, as in the Heifetz review, he would correct me kindly, clearly, with reasons, and with always a joke at the end. When during one of my contests with the Metropolitan Opera, he found in my answer to their protest a reference to the "ladies" of the Opera Guild, he reminded me that "lady" is an insulting term because of its irony. "Always attack head-on," he said. "Never make sideswipes and never use innuendo. As long as you observe the amenities of controversey, the very first of which is straightforward language, the paper will stand behind you."

Nevertheless, he would send to my office from time to time a letter pained, impatient, and unclear. These, I came to believe, meant he had been asked by someone, probably Mrs. Reid, to "speak to Virgil." The speakings were not, of course, unjustified, merely out of proportion to the visible fault. And they were not phrased in Geoffrey's normal way, which was ever of wit and sweetness. I would acknowledge them with all delicacy of phrase, almost as if Geoffrey were some irate unknown, and then be more careful for a while. These occasions were not frequent, and no enmity seemed to build up through them. After my first two years they happened rarely, and during the last ten almost not at all. I must eventually have learned smoother ways, for in 1946, on my fiftieth birthday, Carleton Sprague Smith could say, "Six years ago Virgil was one of the most feared men in New York; today he is one of the most loved." Imagine that!

My errors, when they occurred, were of two kinds, those which shocked the prejudices of readers and those which caused inconvenience to management. In the first kind of case I was merely cautioned to watch my language, use no slang, explain everything, be persuasive. For indeed, in expository writing, failure to convince is failure *tout court*. Inconvenience to management arriving through complaint from prominent persons was not necessarily unwelcome, however. The Metropolitan Opera, the Philharmonic, the Museum of Modern Art, the radio establishments that presented Toscanini or owned Columbia Concerts, these were familiar opponents; and battling with them was tonic to us all. For that sport, methods of attack and defense were our subjects of gleeful conference, punctilio and courtesy our strategy; getting the facts right was our point of honor, exposing them to readers our way of being interesting.

The orchestras from out of town, such as Boston and Philadelphia, sent us no embassies. And the standard touring soloists one rarely heard from even indirectly. What seemed most to bother Mrs. Reid and Geoffrey was unfavorable comment on a suburban affair. My questioning the civic value to Stamford, Connecticut, of a quite poor symphony orchestra brought two strong letters from Parsons. Conflict with Manhattan millionaires, I could read between the lines, was permitted, but not with country clubs. Suburbia had long supplied the nut of our liberal Republican readership, and the paper's eventual drama of survival came to be played out against the sociological transformation of those neighborhoods. Discouraging suburbia about anything, I understood, was imprudent. For suburbs, like churches, accept only praise.

Geoffrey was right, of course; he always was. My quality as a reviewer came from my ability to identify with the makers of music; and when I spoke both as an insider to music and warmly, my writing, whether favorable or not, was communicative. But I simply could not identify with organizers and promoters, however noble their motives. Going out of one's way to cover something not usually reviewed is a lark, provided you can get a lively piece out of it. If not, wisdom would leave it to the merciful neutrality of the news columns. But when you are new to reviewing and still reacting passionately, you are not always led by wisdom. And later, when you have more control, you are not so passionate. Neither are you quite so interesting. Because the critical performance needs to be based on passion, even when journalism requires that you persuade. And in the early years of my reviewing, Geoffrey was like a guardian angel, an athletic coach, and a parent all in one, hoping, praying, and probably believing that with constant correction and copious praise I could be kept at top form.

I had entered music reviewing in a spirit of adventure; and though I never treated it as just an adventure, I did not view it as just journalism either. I thought of myself as a species of knight-errant attacking dragons single-handedly and rescuing musical virtue in distress. At the same time I ran a surprisingly efficient department, organized a Music Critics' Circle (still in existence), started a guest-column on radio music to be written by B. H. Haggin and a jazz column with Rudi Blesh as star performer. When the war removed two of my staff members, I took on Paul Bowles to substitute for one of them and later employed the composer Arthur Berger; I also caused the engagement of Edwin Denby for a year and a half as ballet reviewer; and I established a panel of music writers from outside the paper who helped us keep the coverage complete. This pool of "stringers" constituted a training corps that comprised my future music editor, Jay Harrison, and the present New York Times staff writers Theodore Strongin and Allen Hughes. At one time or another it included the music historian Herbert Weinstock and the composers Elliott Carter, John Cage, Lou Harrison, William Flanagan, Lester Trimble, and Peggy Glanville-Hicks.

I used no one not trained in music, for my aim was to explain the artist, not to encourage misunderstanding of his work. I discouraged emotional reactions and opinion-mongering on the grounds that they were a waste of space. "Feelings," I would say, "will come through automatically in your choice of words. Description is the valid part of reviewing; spontaneous reactions, if courteously phrased, have some validity; opinions are mostly worthless. If you feel you must express one, put it in the last line, where nothing will be lost if it gets cut for space."

My copy was never cut; neither did it ever make the front page. I wrote in pencil, proofread the manuscript before sending it down, preferring, should errors occur, that they be my own. After the first year I did not go downstairs at all, checking my Sunday proofs at home, sent by messenger. In my first weeks I had asked Francis Perkins how long it would take to get over being unduly elated or depressed at a musical event. "About six years," he had said. And he was right. After that time I could write a review, go off to bed, and wake up in the morning with no memory of where I had been or what I had written. Twice, to my knowledge, I reviewed a contemporary work without remembering I had done so two years earlier. And in both cases my descriptions were virtually identical in thought, though not in words.

I had established my routines very early. During seven months of the year I wrote a Sunday article every week and averaged two reviews. During the summer months I did no reviewing; I also skipped seven or eight Sunday articles. Since these could be sent from anywhere, I toured on musical errands of my own or stayed in some country place writing music. I also wrote music in town, published books, went in and out on lectures and conducting dates. The paper liked all this activity, because it kept my name before the public. Also because I usually came back with a piece about San Francisco or Texas or Pittsburgh (after the war, Europe and Mexico and South America, too), which was good for circulation. To the Herald Tribune Forum I added for musical relief opera singers, Southern hymn singers, Negro choirs, and Robert Shaw's Collegiate Chorale. In all these arrangements, my dealings with Helen Reid were quite without friction or misunderstanding. Indeed, unless I look at my scrapbooks I can hardly remember my last ten years at the paper, so thoroughly satisfactory were they to us all and so little demanding of my time. The dramas had all come in the first four, for those were the years when I was learning my trade while working at it. These were also, of course, the war years, naturally full of emergencies, revelations, excitements, departures, arrivals, surprises, and strange contacts.

Europe in America

I F AMERICA IN THE 1920s exiled its artists, the 1940s, especially their first half, saw a meeting of talent here, both foreign and domestic, that made us for the first time an international center for intellectuals. Central Europeans, notably some brilliant musicologists and art scholars, had been coming throughout the 1930s. In 1940 certain English joined us for the duration. And during that winter and all through '41 those who had reasons (and the means) for leaving France arrived in a steady trickle. The painters Eugene Berman, André Masson, and Yves Tanguy were here already; so was Marcel Duchamp. And the surrealist poet André Breton, arriving after the Occupation had begun, came soon to exercise over poets and painters in New York an authority similar to that which for nearly two decades he had practiced in Paris. He did them good, too, freeing poets from censorship by the hatchet men of T. S. Eliot and setting off a movement in painting that has traveled clean round the world. Also, a scholastic group that included the philosopher Jacques Maritain established here an Ecole de Hautes Etudes Libres, which offered French students in exile university credits valid for after the war.

The standard repertory conductors Toscanini and Bruno Walter had established residence before the war. Wanda Landowska, queen of the harpsichord, arrived on Pearl Harbor day. The composers

Arnold Schoenberg, Kurt Weill, and Hanns Eisler had been here since the mid-thirties. Stravinsky in the late thirties kept coming in and out till the war in Europe decided him, like Bruno Walter, to renounce his recently gained French citizenship and opt for ours. A short listing of other composers who joined us in the years around 1940 will recall perhaps the brilliancy of the time.

From Hungary had come to New York Béla Bartók, to the West Coast Miklos Rosza; from Poland Jerzy Fitelberg, Karol Rathaus, and Alexandre Tansman; from Czechoslovakia Bohuslav Martinu. Arriving Russians, via western Europe, were Arthur Lourié and Nikolai Lopatnikoff; Nicolai Berezowsky, Vladimir Dukelsky (Vernon Duke), and Nicolas Nabokov were already here. From Austria came Jacques de Menasce and Ernst Křenek, from Italy Vittorio Rieti and (to Hollywood) Montemezzi, Castelnuovo-Tedesco, and Amfiteatroff; from Germany via London the pianist Artur Schnabel (also a composer) and via Palestine Stefan Wolpe, via Paris the boy-genius Lukas Foss. Directly from France we had not only Nadia Boulanger, the teacher of us all, but the chief then of all the composing French, Darius Milhaud.

Among my own close friends from France, Yvonne de Casa Fuerte was a welcome helper in the music life. To support herself and her son, aged sixteen, she gave French lessons and violin lessons, also playing in pit orchestras such as that of the New York City Opera and, when this was out of season, in musicals by Kurt Weill and for Billy Rose's Aquacade. She also played in concerts. And in the spring of 1943 we organized together a series of Serenades modeled after her Paris originals.

Our patron was the Marquis de Cuevas, who had given us $5,-000. Active with us in the planning were the flute player René Le Roy and the pianist Prince George Chavchavadze. Though the printed prospectus names two more, Carl Van Vechten and Aaron Copland, it is not in my memory that either of these ever sat with us for program making. My membership on the music committee of the Museum of Modern Art helped toward use of its auditorium.

There were five of these Serenades, all involving rare music, much of it presented by artists so remarkable and so new (Leonard Bernstein, for instance, and Robert Shaw) that our evenings offered a refreshing and particular splendor. Thomas Beecham conducted a concert, Vladimir Golschmann another. And one that was devoted to the memory of García Lorca produced both a *cuadro flamenco* with Argentinita and a stage-work by Paul Bowles. Entitled *The Wind Remains,* this was a partial setting to music (in the manner of a *zarzuela*) of a part of a play by García Lorca called *Así que pasen cinco años,* partly in prose and partly in verse, partly spoken and partly sung, partly in English and partly (the verse parts) left in Spanish. It was also partly acted and partly danced. The whole thing was quite beautiful but in an artistic sense only partly successful; largely, I think, because the free form of the *zarzuela* is unacceptable to English-speaking audiences.

Our final concert contained first New York presentations of the Stravinsky *Danses concertantes* and of the Poulenc *Aubade,* the latter with Robert Casadesus as piano soloist. Neither work, however, pleased the press. Olin Downes found the Poulenc "a series of clichés and dull and bad jokes," the Stravinsky "considerably worse." "The pieces were politely received," he said, "and why not? Could a politer set of platitudes be invented? Music guaranteed to upset no one—not even the refugees of the St. Regis." Nevertheless, these concerts were distinguished; and had not my colleague of the *Times* felt moved to crush them, we might have found funds for their continuance. His paper's chronic fear of any take-off toward style came back to mind only the other day, when Howard Taubman, its drama critic, dismissed a play by the poet Robert Lowell as "a pretentious, arty trifle."

Later, just at the end of the war, I helped to organize more concerts, this time benefitting France Forever. I had become associated with this Free French group through the pianist E. Robert Schmitz, ever a patriot as well as a modern-music defender. And I remember particularly fine performances of a new string quartet by Sauguet and of a work composed in German captivity by Olivier Messiaen, called *Quartet for the End of Time.*

It was in the fall of 1940 that I first encountered, through Suzanne Blum, Hervé Alphand, at that time Economic Secretary to the French Embassy. His wife of the time, Claude, who did not much like Washington and who could not bear at all their Vichy associates, was pressing him to resign, which soon he did, going off to join de Gaulle in London and leaving Claude to stay out the war in New York. Sharing a small flat with her mother, she earned money by singing French chansons in New York night clubs, in Montreal, sometimes in Florida, even in Brazil. She was a 1900-style blonde with commanding beauty, a not large voice, and no knowledge of music at all. Her mother, an excellent musician as well as a first-class cook and hostess, taught her everything; she also ran the house. At public appearances, Rudi Révil, a Parisian song composer, would play for her till toward the close she would sit on the grand piano and sing to her own guitar. Though without the relentless intensity of a Piaf, by nature she had star quality.

Loving both her presence and her singing for making me feel that I was back in France, I helped to start off her career by reviewing its debut. Hervé wrote from London to thank me for that. And Claude sent two bottles of claret, left over from their Embassy days, with a note saying, "*Voici le pot de vin habituel dans l'administration.*" Her light touch and her fearless independence reminded me of Madame Langlois. Women at once so courageous and so beautiful are a sort of masterpiece.

The well-to-do refugees who had so shocked Olin Downes included the American-born Lady Ribblesdale (indeed living at the St. Regis, which was a property of her son, Vincent Astor), the Shakespearean scholar Sir Harley Granville-Barker and his American poet wife (at the simpler Mayfair), and the conductor Sir Thomas Beecham, Bart. (installed at the Ritz Carlton with his longtime Egeria, Lady Cunard). With both these last, my friendship was engaged at first sight. It went on too till their respective deaths, though after 1943 their own tie had been cut by Beecham's marriage.

Born Maud Forbes, in California, and inheriting while still young a quite large fortune, she had married around 1890 Sir Bache Cunard and shortly borne him one child, a daughter. After he had welcomed once her return from an extended absence by building a gate marked "Come into the garden, Maud," she changed her name. Sir Bache himself, with fine estates, was a country man; but Emerald, as she now became, loved town. So she mostly lived in London, cutting a figure as hostess, becoming the close friend of George Moore and after World War I of Thomas Beecham.

Earlier concerned with letters and politics, she had moved into music after Sir Thomas became owner and impresario of the Covent Garden Opera House, mobilizing society, the arts, and even government to help him fill its boxes. Later, under Edward VIII, she had abetted the king in his marriage plans. Under his successor she fell into disfavor, but not too gravely, one gathered, since Beecham and his career were an occupation and since, with the war, society was largely dispersed to its jobs and regiments.

Beecham had informed the British government at the beginning of this war that he could not, as he had done during the other, support England's four chief orchestras out of his income. And since opera was to be closed down for the duration, he decided in the spring of 1940 to make a gift to Anglo-Saxon solidarity by going off to conduct in Australia, later in Canada and in the United States. Lady Cunard, at the same time, gave up her house in Grosvenor Square and came to America, accompanied by her lady's maid, to spend the summer visiting in Newport. Come fall, as Beecham's guest, she moved to the Ritz in New York, where till 1943 was played out the drama of his impending marriage to a much younger woman, he denying that nothing of the sort was planned and she well knowing that it was.

As who did not, indeed? There had been a press scandal in Seattle about his sharing a house with the pretty pianist. Then she took residence in Idaho for divorcing *in absentia* her English clergyman. And wherever Beecham appeared as guest conductor, Betty Humby was likely to appear as soloist. There was no concealing their constant proximity, though there was enormous effort on the part of Beecham to save face for Lady Cunard in the destruction of their twenty-year bond, even though the friendship, as he said, had been "for the last ten years only that."

And he himself required a divorce, also procured in Sun Valley. And then he was married in New York, later being divorced and married all over again in England, just to make the whole thing stick. But well before the marrying began, Lady Cunard had gone back to London and taken rooms in the Hotel Dorchester, where she went on giving dinner parties, with wine from the Chilean Embassy and with bills paid out of the sale of jewelry and divers *objets d'art* that had remained after a lifetime of expenditure. She was dead by 1950, having never ceased to be an inflammatory hostess, a tonic wit, an Egeria indefatigable. And to the end she had young poets in attendance, attached almost like lovers.

Small, roundish though less than plump, with china-blue eyes and yellow slightly mussed-up hair, Emerald Cunard had always been pretty and remained so. She also passed for being hard of heart, and certainly she was as relentless as any other career-hostess. After her daughter's communist and Negro frequentations had caused embarrassment, she never spoke to her again, or of her. All the same, she was faithful, with the novelist George Moore and with Beecham, to long friendships deeply engaged. Ever happy with artists, she gave them jolly times, admiration, and money, read their books, hung their pictures, got them posts and publishers, kept them at work, and abetted their love affairs. As an American she could be demanding, even cruel; as a European she was generous and a comrade. For all her preoccupations with grandeur, she was never banal or in friendship dishonest. Nor was she self-indulgent. She merely lived hard every day, reading long into the night; and men of gifts found knowing her a privilege. She once summed up for me a rule, if not of life, of living: "For a good party have beautiful women and intelligent men; for a bad one, intelligent women and beautiful men." Of Beecham she said, "He is deeply sentimental, but also relentless. When he wants a thing, no one can stop him."

Certainly no one stopped him from the marriage he had set his mind on. The young woman, he told Emerald, had awakened in him feelings he "had long thought dead." Betty Humby, on her part, was equally attached and willing to pay with all her strength for the marriage she had long desired. But she wore out that strength in his service. And after she died, fifteen years later, he married again, this time an even younger woman. At eighty, still conducting concerts and recordings and projecting another tour of Germany, he suffered a fatal stroke. For twenty years we had told each other stories, eaten and drunk together, argued and laughed. I know he loved my music, and I think he understood it; I understood, I think, his approach to music making and loved its results. I loved them for resplendent sound and for good sense. He used a shaping hand with Haydn, a warm one with Mozart, a light one for Wagner, and a poetical one (inspired idea!) for Berlioz. And always the sonorities were what musicians call "musical," as if harmoniousness were a virtue, which it is. He once said of his loyal English public, "They have for music little understanding, but they adore the sound it makes."

From our friendship's first beginnings he played my music across the United States, in Canada, in England. No one else has ever made my Second Symphony sound so glowing, though I do not think he was comfortable with the work. *Filling Station* and *The River* he played with more abandon. My operas he professed to adore (*Four Saints* was for him "the finest vocal music in English since Elizabethan times"), but he never conducted them. (The B.B.C. refused him *The Mother of Us All* when he proposed to broadcast it for his seventieth birthday.) My Cello Concerto he played in Edinburgh, paying for an extra rehearsal to get it right. When I began conducting orchestras myself, he at first made fun of me; but he afterwards invited me to Mexico for preparing and conducting under him Mozart's *The Magic Flute*. I did not go, preferring to compose that summer. And by not grasping the precious opportunity, I proved to both of us the innocence of my conducting ambitions. What I chiefly regretted at not being with him was our conversations. For we stimulated each other; and enlivened by Emerald Cunard's bright presence, we were likely to talk far into the night. She would accuse me of being anti-British and I would reply, "No, only anti-English." Then she would scold me for arrogance, praise both of us intensely, and all the time be guiding us toward themes where we could shine. And he would say afterwards, "Virgil is the only man in the world who can keep me up till four."

Others from England spending the war here were the composers Benjamin Britten, Anthony Arnell, Stanley Bate, and the Australian Peggy Glanville-Hicks. Britten I did not encounter often; but I did review his first opera, *Paul Bunyan,* written to a text by W. H. Auden. By finding its music "eclectic though not without savor," its poetry "flaccid and spineless and without energy," I classified myself as no friend of the Empire.

Arnell would call on me every few months with a brand-new symphony; I found his music mostly pretty thin. Then once there was a different kind, grandly funereal and richly sad; and I think I recommended that piece to Beecham. In any case, he played it. He liked, as I did, its tragical and apocalyptic character, and all the more because the run of British composers was continuing to write as cheerfully as if the Empire called for no lament. Lately Britten has composed a *War Requiem* that makes exception to the general British rule, for though their prose literature has had its angry young ones, and though their older novelists and playwrights have faced society's disaster in the language of Oscar Wilde and Shaw, the basic despair of England seems not yet to have touched deeply either music or poetry.

Stanley Bate wrote optimistic music in a British version of the Boulanger style. He could play the piano poetically, too; and Lady Cunard loved piano concertos. So Beecham presented Bate's; and Emerald found him a paying patron, who bought him a Steinway and set him up in an apartment. But Stanley drank too much and quarreled too much and eventually went back to England. Peggy Glanville-Hicks, his wife, stayed here, supporting herself by writing articles and by copying music, achieved distinction as a composer, and became a citizen. Stanley married a Brazilian consul general, Margareda Guedes Nogueira, who backed him up loyally, just as Peggy had done, in his war against the musical Establishment (chiefly controlled by Britten and his publisher, the latter linked by marriage to the throne). So he wrote less and drank more until eventually, after a heart failure or stroke, he drowned in his bath.

Peggy Glanville-Hicks, thin, passionate, tireless, and insistent (for Australian women can indeed insist) might well have been a burden to us all had she not been so willing to turn her hand to musical odd jobs. She wrote for the *Herald Tribune* and for magazines; she copied music; she managed concerts; she ran everybody's errands; she went on lecture tours by bus in the Dakotas; she composed documentary films for UNICEF; she made musicological trips to India for the Rockefeller Foundation; she saw other people's music (particularly that of Paul Bowles, after his return to Morocco) through the perils of recording. She made her own clothes and dressed charmingly. When alone she did not eat much, but she could be a lively dinner guest. She wrote a great deal of music, got it published and recorded, grew as a composer from modest beginnings (as a none-too-remarkable pupil of Ralph Vaughan Williams) into an opera writer of marked originality, setting first *The Transposed Heads* by Thomas Mann, later collaborating with the poet Robert Graves and with the novelist Lawrence Durrell.

She believed, upon some evidence, that the world was out to

crush women composers; and she was convinced (from no evidence) that my music editor, Jay Harrison, actually her protector, was for getting her fired. She complained; she stormed; she telephoned. And with all this she was an indispensable colleague. Even from Greece, where she now lives (still frugally), she continues to fulminate and to be useful. Her generosity is no more to be stopped than her scolding ways. And she remains a memorable composer.

It was also through music that I knew a real French gangster. He had asked for counsel, just at the end of the war, about bringing a French orchestra to America. With perfect discretion, he omitted to mention that his wife, under another name, had sung sizable works of mine in Town Hall. When later I helped her to secure the hall again, he was grateful in the standard gangster way, could never do me favors enough, it seemed.

He lived at the Waldorf-Astoria with his beautiful wife (much younger) and an elderly French maid. Also at the hotel, as his guest throughout the war, was a famous French trial lawyer, to whom he was grateful for having earlier kept him out of prison on charges of white slavery and of trafficking in drugs. He was the eldest of six brothers, Russian Jewish by origin, who had become powerful after World War I in the Marseille underworld. Large assets had been amassed in Alsace and in the Argentine; and he had shipping connections in Jugoslavia. During the Spanish Civil War, with connivance from the French government, I understood, he had run arms into Republican Spain. After World War II he worked directly for his government, he told me, buying coal and steel on the American black market, for these materials were in principle strictly rationed and the French were needing to rebuild their railways quickly.

In addition to his Waldorf-Astoria apartment, he kept one at the Georges V in Paris, and also, to the north, a chateau for week ends. And if he happened not to be in Paris, through the brother who owned a restaurant I always had access to black-market French francs in any amount. No books were kept; I simply paid later in New York. Then the pretty wife got bored with a singing career, spent more and more time with the Cannes high life; and her devoted husband left off coming to New York. By this time his business was mostly in Europe anyway, "working with the

American Army in Germany," he called it. What products he procured I never asked. But he grew richer and richer, and more and
more wretched at his wife's long absences. I had grown fond of
him; and so had others—Oscar Levant, for instance, who had
taste in gangsters, and Maurice Grosser, who could introduce the
French business associates, if need be, to Negro circles. When a
work of Nicolas Nabokov was given in Berlin, our friend arrived
with cases of the best champagne, brought by air. And when my
landlord requested me to bring him from New York a refrigerator,
a blender, and a washing machine, these were all bought at whole-
sale prices and passed through French customs by the President's
secretary. Did he eventually perish of despair? For die he did. And
did he leave vast fortunes, open or secret? A few years earlier,
tried in Morocco for fraud, found guilty, and assessed three billion
francs, he had remarked, "Nobody pays a $6 million fine." All the
same, he was forever buying rubies and diamonds for his wife.
"You never know," he would say. "Someday she may need money."

I hope she has not come to that; I wish her well. For fifteen
years this Waldorf gangster family were my friends; and if with
their rubies and diamonds hidden away they were less showy as
to bosom than Olin Downes's "refugees of the Saint Regis," their
hearts were open and their ways were warm. After all, no law
says exiles must be poor.

All Roads Lead to Paris

THE *Herald Tribune* WAS NOT ALONE responsible for my reacti-
vated professional life, for this had put forth buds on my
arrival from France. Glenway Wescott had been hopeful that I
might compose a ballet with him. Detroit's Pro Musica had offered
a lecture and concert. The Metropolitan Opera Guild had engaged
me to speak on Mozart, with Frieda Hempel singing arias. And
shortly after, Ludwig Bemelmans had sought me out toward collaborating with him on a dance-spectacle about Ecuador. Neither
of the ballets came to pass; but after my newspaper debut on
October 11, 1940, other proposals started to arrive—for performance
and for publication, for lecturing, for composing, for writing articles, and naturally for recommending applicants to the foundations.

It was clear quite early that if I were to lead a practicing musician's life along with that of a reviewer, I should be needing more
help than just a secretary. I had to get my music into shape. Also,
I needed extra housework. This came to be furnished by one of
my Saints, Leonard Franklin, tenor soloist from 1934, a man of
impeccable charm and gentle ways. He came to cook and serve,
to take care of my clothes, to receive my callers, and to do my
errands. And since the Chelsea Hotel did not at that time house
colored lodgers, my Saint found a flat near by; and I began to
have lots of company.

My musical secretary, Mimi Wallner, a curly-haired athletic blonde just out of Bennington, could copy music, speak French, and play the double bass. She too worked in the apartment, making extra copies of all my unpublished works—which meant virtually all my works—and extracting orchestral parts from my unplayed scores, which meant most of those. With her help my career as a composer could take off.

As long as I had lived abroad, neither conductors nor publishers had shown much interest in my music. Encouraging the composers from near by made better news. And even in the 1930s, when I was a figure in the New York theater, the concert-giving establishments had shown reluctance. My status as an expatriate always going back and forth to France would seem to have dissolved all obligation. They did not even have to read my scores, knowing there would be no pressure here for using them. Then all at once they knew they would be using them. There was no pressure really. But I was in the news; they were aware of me. So they asked which works I wished them to use first and in most cases took them sight unseen. They still, I noted, did not read my scores.

Thus it happened that my works began to travel. And before long I began to travel with them. It was Eugene Ormandy who first found that I could conduct (by letting me show his orchestra how to bounce a rhythm in *Filling Station*). After that, he played a piece almost every year; and I was asked to conduct the Philadelphia Orchestra whenever I liked, in two cases on Columbia recordings. Eventually I conducted almost everywhere, though I was not asked to Boston till after Koussevitsky had retired. I requested no engagement, employed no agent. I merely answered mail and stayed available. Nor did I question any artist's motives. Some may have programed my music to gain good will, though they knew that if they played it in New York, I obviously could not review that concert. Others, taking advice from managements or following private scruples, refrained from seeking favor in this way. Myself, I asked for nothing, held no grudges. But I actually believe that my being alert to a possible conflict of interests kept me more punctilious than most other reviewers about describing each performance truthfully. Certainly my editors found nothing suspect, nor did readers reproach me. When Harl McDonald, manager of the Philadelphia Orchestra, inquired if I thought he should possibly not engage me as guest conductor, I passed his letter on to Geoffrey Parsons; and Geoffrey, after asking at the top, replied that the paper saw no impropriety.

My new works that first winter were theatrical. For a radio program called The Columbia Workshop, John Houseman produced on December 9 *The Trojan Women* of Euripides in a cutting

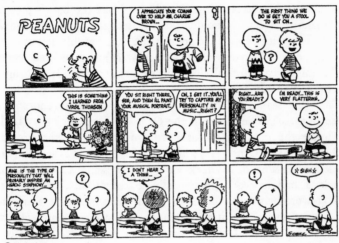

© United Feature
Syndicate, Inc. 1954

of the Edith Hamilton translation; and I made music after a conception that had not, I think, been ever used before. This was to reverse the usual procedure of putting music between the scenes and sound-effects with them. My scheme of separating the scenes by sound-effect interludes and accompanying them with music was designed to help the listener distinguish one character from another in a play spoken almost entirely by women.

Cassandra, Andromache, and Hecuba were cast for speaking voices of high, middle, and low timbre—Zita Johann, Joanna Roos, and Mildred Natwick, as I recall. And for pointing up this contrast, as well as for aiding identification, I accompanied them respectively on a flute, a clarinet, and an English horn, giving to each of these solo lines the expressive content of the speech. Then for separating the scenes I composed sound-effect passages depicting weather, marching men, whatever was needed for making events seem real. Actually my woodwind obbligati were a variant of the percussive accompaniments that I had learned to do from

Orson Welles in the Negro *Macbeth* and later used to build up Leslie Howard's voice in *Hamlet*. They served in *The Trojan Women* for identifying characters, somewhat less for expressivity, since one could not without more rehearsal time train actresses to read less tearfully and leave emotion to the music's line and shading—as when at Cassandra's mention of her child, it took only a tiny tune in the piccolo's low register to evoke the baby's presence and make us weep. I should like to use again this sensitive approach, but with more time to work it out, possibly notating the reading parts for rhythm and for each voice's rise and fall, obtaining in this way a musical elocution suitable both to Greek tragedy and to the English language.

Later that season I did apply it again, this time to choruses intoned in Greek. The play was the *Oedipus Tyrannus* of Sophocles, the locale the library steps at Fordham University, the producer Father William Lynch, S.J., the choreographer Erick Hawkins, himself something of a Greek scholar. Not being a Greek scholar myself, I had to work phonetically. Father Lynch provided me with a word-by-word translation of the choruses, plus a metrical notation of their quantities, cadences, and stresses; and with this help I composed in Greek a monolinear music, accompanied by drums and wind instruments that underlined the modal melodies. It all came off quite well, as I remember; but the really impressive element was Richard Burgi, a boy of seventeen, who played Jocasta with a grand projection. Encountered some years later, he had followed scholarly proclivities; and as I write he is head of the Russian department at Princeton, a constant customer nevertheless at the Metropolitan Opera, where he identifies himself, I am sure, with the singing actors, especially with powerful projectors like Leontyne Price and Maria Callas. I think this because it seems to be roles rather than musical styles that hold his interest.

There was a production of *Four Saints* in the spring of '41, but without staging. Miss Louise Crane, a young woman of means who wished to serve music, had undertaken a series of Coffee Concerts at the Museum of Modern Art, these to include offerings as offbeat as advanced jazz and Yemenite dancing. She esteemed it a cultural service to revive my opera; and in order to broaden the possible audience (since the museum's auditorium could hold only 480), she proposed two performances, one in the museum, to be conducted by me from a piano, and another at Town Hall, with an orchestra conducted by Alexander Smallens. I reassembled my soloists and chorus with the help of my Harlem helper, Leonard de Paur, and prepared the performances. And since it was possible to consider the one at the museum as a rehearsal for the other, the press was asked to skip that and review from Town Hall. It was here that Sir Thomas Beecham, first making acquaintance with the work and identifying it as a child of the Elizabethan masque, came to accept my music as related to his own Britishness. And he loved to tease me about its idiosyncrasies, such as the double bass that would "first play and then not play." The peculiarity he referred to was actually an equivalent of the organist's device for avoiding monotony by now and then taking his feet off the pedals.

Alfred Wallenstein also conducted *Four Saints* in a beautiful performance on station WOR, a broadcast of 1942 aimed at selling war bonds and paid for by the Treasury Department. The original cast was again got together in 1947 and trained by Leonard de Paur for a Columbia broadcast on the Philharmonic hour; and this time I conducted. I also conducted for RCA Victor, with the same cast and orchestra (renamed for the occasion the Victor Symphony Orchestra), a recording of about half the opera. This was the last time the 1934 cast could be used. When the opera was restaged in 1952 for New York and Paris, only Edward Matthews and his wife were still vocally fresh. So a new cast was assembled. But the old one can still be heard, since the 1947 recording, twice reissued, is still in circulation.

Wallenstein had also urged me to excerpt an orchestral suite from *The River;* and it was he, not Beecham, who first played it. The latter became attached to it, however, because of its Protestant hymn content, which carried him back to Lancashire. And Aaron Copland wrote me it was "a lesson in how to treat Americana." Stokowski also took it up, although much later, and gave to its recording a fine buoyancy. I myself have no attachment to it, probably because its pristine inspiration came from an earlier work, the Symphony on a Hymn Tune, a piece for me far more original and more evocative of the South.

Beecham had in 1941 asked for a "major" work that he could play that fall in Philadelphia and elsewhere, and I had proposed my Second Symphony. On his acceptance, I began to reflect as to whether the piece did not require a bit of adjusting, at least oɪ chestrally. A chance for judging that came in the spring, when the Luxembourg conductor Henri Pensis played some of it in Newark. Hearing it for the first time, though it had been in existence for a decade, I concluded that it wanted higher contrasts and a more striking color—in short, that I must reorchestrate. And this I did during the summer months.

Come June, having caught my periodic grippe-cold, I spent a week being cared for at the Askews'. Then I stayed for a fortnight at Woods Hole, Massachusetts, with Mrs. W. Murray Crane, Louise's mother, a friend and patron from my poverty days. In July I joined Mimi Wallner and her parents in Holderness, New Hampshire, where I began to reorchestrate the symphony from sketches I had made while in Woods Hole; and I went on doing this in pencil while Mimi copied out my score in ink. Meanwhile, for my Sunday column, I had read batches of hefty tomes such as Paul Henry Lang's *Music in Western Civilization* and Gustave Reese's *Music in the Middle Ages,* both of which were new that year. Then Maurice Grosser arrived from Alabama on his motorcycle; and on that we toured New Hampshire, visiting at the end the George Footes in stylish Dublin and my beloved teacher Edward Burlingame Hill in Francestown.

Eventually I visited Jessie Lasell too, at her hunting-and-fishing camp in Maine, where I wrote choral music and composed her portrait. Then I joined Grosser again; and we went to Nantucket, this time to be with the Russian-Armenian painter Inna Garsoian. And there I wrote more Sunday articles, covered the island by motorcycle, swam everywhere, and went bluefishing with my colleague Olin Downes. At some point I had been to New York, where I gave the score to Beecham and talked through two full nights with him and Emerald. And with all those changes in air and altitude and with the satisfaction of having done lots of work, I had restored myself from fatigue to vigor after a successful but vastly tiring year.

In 1939 I had received in Paris a letter from John Cage, requesting of me a new work for percussion, to be performed in Seattle. For company on the program there would be a novelty by Henry Cowell, and Lou Harrison's 5th Simfony (*sic*). Being occupied just then writing *The State of Music,* I did not join the concert. Two years later, in New York, Cage phoned to ask if he could play for me the records of a broadcast just made in Chicago of works by Harrison and by himself. He could indeed, I said. And here began a long musical friendship, shortly to be complemented by the arrival East of Lou.

Cage, born in southern California, was half of him Tennessee mountaineer. That is to say that his father had come out of Tennessee and that the lanky and freckled red-haired big-boned son was distilling a clear-as-water musical moonshine without the stamp of any Establishment. At this very moment, having been rebuffed by Aaron Copland, who could not admire a music so abstract, he was organizing a concert of his works to be given at the Museum of Modern Art in collaboration with the League of Composers, Copland's own chief arm of patronage. And Copland did not stop this; few persons, indeed, have ever stopped Cage from anything.

His determination has nothing of Tennessee about it; its relentlessness is of southern California, and only barely hidden by a catlike smile. Already thirty, absolutely confident, and without embarrassment in asking for support, he had become by 1941 the designer of a unique product, its manufacturer, and its sole distributor. And if the abstract character of that product made it easier for him to defend than if it had been a more personal outpouring, the self-assurance with which he would explain it was nonetheless breathtaking. In fact, composers of the hand-work-and-inspiration type have never spoken of their own work so convincingly (for whenever Gluck, Wagner, Schoenberg have done so, we tend to freeze) as have Varèse, Boulez, Messiaen, and Cage, all of whom have practiced an objective method.

With all his rigors, Cage has a wit and breadth of thought that make him a priceless companion. For hours, days, and months with him one would probe music's philosophy. And after Lou Harrison, with his larger reading and more demanding ear, had arrived from the West, the three of us provided for one another, with Europe and the Orient cut off by war, a musical academy of theory and practice that supplied us with definitions which have served us well and which, through the highly divergent nature of our musical products, have given our methods of analysis wide distribution.

Lou Harrison, child of the Pacific Northwest and of San Francisco, was plump and round-faced; and though he smiled less than

Cage, there was joy inside him, both joy and pain. Both of them had been pupils of Henry Cowell and of Schoenberg. Cage's southern California euphoria turned him eventually to Zen Buddhism and to a mushroom-study form of nature cult. A San Francisco sensitivity had first turned Harrison, it seems, toward the not uncommon worship of Mount Shasta, then to Yoga, to nervous breakdown, to the study of Esperanto, to the hospitalization of animals, to the construction of flutes and harpsichords with special tunings, and eventually to a mastery of classical Korean composition methods. In both, the West Coast cultural freedom is dominant, as in Henry Cowell and in Gertrude Stein and in the Northwestern painters Mark Tobey and Morris Graves. And in both, as also in Graves and Tobey, an Asian attraction has balanced the gravitational pull of Europe to keep them solidly anchored over America, though with no limiting local loyalties of the usual kinds, such as to New England, the Midwest, the New or Old South. Spiritually they are not even anchored to the West Coast.

Both, when I first knew them, had produced percussion music. And when Cage, leaving no doorbell unrung in his searches after support, asked for a Guggenheim Fellowship, I wrote unhesitatingly in his favor. He did not receive this aid till 1949, however, when his music had become better known. Moreover, having by that time looked at postwar Europe, I had even greater confidence in his powers. And so I wrote that I considered him "the most original composer in America, if not in the world, . . . also the most 'advanced,' in the professional sense."

For describing Harrison's music the word "original" would be less applicable than the word "personal," for its meaning is intensely his alone. Nor can the concept of "advanced" describe it, since as often as not it embodies a return to some method long since abandoned. Cage's driving ambition and his monorail view of art, by which quality depends solely on innovation, have brought him fame and followers. Lou's work, though known and widely loved, is without influence. The fault is one of temperament, I think; he lacks not quality, merely pushing ways. He stayed in New York till 1953, also teaching part-time in North Carolina, at Black Mountain College. Then fearing the strains of a no-money Eastern life, he returned to California, settling near his family at Aptos, in the Carmel Valley, from which retreat he sends out compositions or sallies forth to Rome (where he won a festival prize in 1954), to Tokyo (where his Esperanto opened doors), and to Korea (where he studied classical Chinese composition). His letters now are calligraphed, sometimes on parchment, their contents no less savory than ever. "I made a Phrygian aulos the other day & can well understand why Plato mistrusted it; ascending 12/11, 11/10, 10/9, 9/8, 8/7, 7/6; what an allure! I wait to hear the Dorian now."

My own first view of California came in 1943. John Houseman, after more than a year at the Office of War Information, was returning that summer to Hollywood for film producing. He was returning, moreover, by car and with a generous gasoline ration. Going along offered a lovely trip; and the paper welcomed it, Helen Reid filling my hands with introductions. On our way we stopped to visit in Kentucky, where we helped to put up hay, thinned out the hemp (and not remembering it was marijuana, threw it away), fed sugar to the thoroughbreds (when allowed), and drank mint juleps out of silver cups. We also stopped in Kansas City briefly and stayed a week in Colorado Springs. In Los Angeles we took an apartment at the Town House, where I was immobilized all day, there being only one car for the two of us. So I would swim in the pool and write piano études in bed till Houseman would come back and drive me to dinner (with Orson Welles and Rita Hayworth, the Joseph Cottens, Bernard Herrmann) or others would come for me and bring me home (George Antheil, who lived there, Aaron Copland, who was scoring a picture, and the people who ran concerts at the Hollywood Bowl). Also I wrote sometimes a Sunday column.

After a while I went to San Francisco and stayed in the Palace Hotel, where the food was lovely. And it was there I met, through Mrs. Reid's letter to the owners of the *Chronicle,* their music and art critic Alfred Frankenstein, a reviewer far more sympathetic to my aims (and I to his) than any of my colleagues in New York. Perkins had said of him, "He knows what it's all about." Also there were E. Robert Schmitz, his boisterously entertaining wife, Germaine, and gentle learned daughter, Monique; and from Paris the indefatigable Milhauds, both teaching in Oakland at Mills College. And they would come to Schmitz's house for playing me on two pianos Milhaud's just-completed opera *Bolivar.* I met society people too, was lionized. And of a Sunday afternoon in the social hall of Harry Bridges's Seamen's Union, I heard Bunk Johnson play New Orleans jazz.

Coming back by train, as I must have done, since planes were not proof against priorities, I stopped again in Kansas City, where in the spring my father had died of pneumonia at eighty-one. Mother was still in her house, my Aunt Lillie Post staying with her. This had been the arrangement since April, when I had gone there for the funeral. My father's end had been a gentle one. When he had felt it near, he said, "I think you should get me to a hospital." And once there, he had died after saying, "I'm all right now."

Certain Europeans wrote me letters, most touchingly Nadia Boulanger, whose mother I had known in life and whose own life was one long service to the dead, and Igor Stravinsky, whose own father, remembered, had become for him a cult. My personal regret (for my father and I were warmly attached, though without the possibility of much ease) was that now I could never let him know my shame for harsh things said in adolescent years. But he must have known and long since forgiven me, for he was a Christian and a loving one; and though the former I was surely not, he had always understood me and spared reproach.

Back East, I went to stay with Briggs Buchanan, then living with wife and children in upper New Jersey in a large white house. I wrote more piano études there, and Maurice Grosser joined us. Then in September, borrowing a cousin's car, I went off with Grosser to Somesville, Maine, facing Mount Desert, where Inna Garsoian was painting landscapes. He painted still life, I think, while I turned piano portraits into orchestral scores for conducting that fall in Philadelphia.

The Marquis de Cuevas, founding a dance company at that time, had invited several composers along with myself—Menotti and Bowles, I remember—to compose ballets. He had proposed for me a subject about a lonely fisherman and a sea gull which becomes a ballerina—a theme I found not fresh but not quite faded. It might do if I wrote a lovely sea piece. And already I knew how to make the trumpets caw quite realistically. So I went to Southwest Harbor, a fishing town, to pick up other points of atmosphere. There men in yellow-and-black waterproofs were unloading codfish and throwing them choreographically from ship to dock, all to the sound of radio full blast. Moreover, on inquiry I was told that the whole trip is so accompanied and that even simple setters of the lobster pot no longer go to sea or skirt the coast without for company their beloved box.

"Well, well!" I thought. "Each lonely fisherman is wired for sound! That lets me out, and the ballerina too." So I wrote no ballet. But I later used the trumpet's downward-smeared glissando in an orchestral work called *Sea Piece with Birds*.

I was driven again to California two years later, this time by Chick Austin, who had resigned from his Hartford Museum and was being a playboy. With Houseman I shared a service flat just off The Strip. He was in romance with Joan Fontaine. And once we gave a sumptuous cocktail party, with Lady Mendl and the Stravinskys and naturally the Hollywood social register, for Houseman was important at M-G-M. And we frequented the Cottens and the Herman Mankiewiczes and the Alfred Wallensteins, who lived near, like the Stravinskys. And the surrealist painter Roberto Matta, with an American rich wife, would take us all out to expensive meals.

And we made a two-reel picture for the government, Houseman and I and Nicholas Ray, whom I had worked with in Federal Theatre days. It was an explication for foreign countries (eventually in some forty languages) of how in America we elect our president. Its title was *Tuesday in November;* and though our government's own films, by treaty with the Hollywood government, can almost never be shown publicly in America, it has long been visible to friends and students at the Film Library of the Museum of Modern Art. It is a fine piece of work, though not so dramatic as the Pare Lorentz films that were its model. I used in the score, for expressing a buoyant euphoria, my portrait of Aaron Copland and, for a sidewalks-of-New-York Americanism, my waltz from *Filling Station*. Out of it, I rescued a fugal treatment of *Yankee Doodle*, to make a children's recording, and a Stephen-Foster-like melody that in the two-piano version called *Walking Song* has long served many a duo-team as encore.

It was in San Francisco, again at the Palace, that I received a telegram from the French Embassy awarding me a "mission" to go to France. Since 1944 I had been looking for ways to get there. But the *Herald Tribune,* having only six travel priorities and needing these for its coverage of news, could not afford to waste one just on music. And though I had drunk with friendly colonels through a Washington week end, and they had all promised to "take a crack at it," nobody had yet been able to get me sent abroad. It was Suzanne Blum, back in Paris and knowing I would want to be there too, who had got the invitation out of Emile Laugier, Cultural Secretary at the Foreign Office, for me to spend two weeks in France as guest of the government, for reestablishing contact with French music.

And all the more urgent did going to France seem since Douglas Moore had written me in San Francisco offering to commission an opera for production at Columbia University, and I had wired Gertrude Stein I had an idea for one, and she had written back her delight.

So I called at the French Consulate for my orders, wired Washington for a new passport, asked the paper to pick up a plane passage, and took myself a bedroom on the train called "City of San Francisco" in a car that went through to New York. Nor do I even remember looking any way but East until my plane began to circle round and round over the pale gray stones of Paris, as if to give each passenger a view of the sacred site and to some a glimpse perhaps of house and home.

France in '45

Y SEAPLANE FROM NEW YORK, after stopping the night in
Botsford Bay, had set down the next afternoon in the River
Shannon. There a small dock, as for motor boats, led to a path,
the path to a cottage surrounded by green fields; and in the cottage's one long, low room, in which at either end a peat fire
smoked, we were refreshed while waiting for our bus. This was
to carry us for an hour up the estuary, through the town, and
back on the estuary's other arm to a dry-land airport, whence a
British military plane, painted a battleship gray inside and out, took
us to London. There I claimed my room at the Savoy that the
Herald Tribune bureau had reserved for me and telephoned to
Emerald Cunard at the Dorchester. I had been on the way for
thirty hours, and it was now nighttime again. And as I fancied
might well be the case, she was giving a dinner party. Having
frequently enough been fed that day, I declined her "Come right
over!" for a half-hour's wash-up and a change of suit.

The guests in her apartment were eight or ten; and carafes of
Chilean wine, both red and white, were on the table. Among those
present were the usual stylish ones, also an attached young poet
and two members of the new Labour government. For hostesses,
however Tory, must be the seeming friends of those in power, if
only to find out which ones are "corruptible." And this exactly was

the subject, after the cabinet members had discreetly left. And then we all left, after somehow a moment had been achieved in another room for Emerald to ask, "Shall you be seeing Thomas?" and for me to promise news of his morale. Also to transmit some nylon stockings (then to be had only in America) without offending the young poet by a gift so intimate.

And the next day there was breakfast in my room, not with real coffee, of course, or with rationed bacon, but with delicious mushrooms on delicious toast. And to the Ritz with Emerald and some others (for she never lunched in public with one man), lunch consisting, after the world's best Martinis, of paper-thin veal cutlets smaller than a playing card. We shopped afterwards, I to see what was in the men's stores, though I could buy nothing without purchase-points, and she to visit a Bond Street jeweler about trading a ruby ring for one less dear. Late afternoon I took a train to Lewes, in Sussex, where at near-by Ringmer Sir Thomas Beecham had bought a house.

I stayed the week end, sleeping away delayed fatigues of travel. And Thomas too seemed to be relaxed in the country air, under the care of his Betty. Naturally he was conducting and recording, though in August not much; and he was planning his next trip to America; and maneuvering financially with the recording companies. Later he was to form a new recording orchestra, the Royal Philharmonic. There is no question that at this time of his life, aged sixty-six, his still vast energies were better nurtured by a young wife-secretary-housekeeper-muse-companion and all-purpose Egeria than they would have been by a driving and driven ex-social leader of his age. For Betty was above all a musician, and save for an only son of twelve (in England not an age that takes much tending) wholly occupied with Beecham and his life. No dinners with cabinet ministers and powerful ladies, no spending of money just for the fun of it. Nothing but work and quietude and gathering his whole career together, as we had so often said he should do, for leaving to posterity a maximum in the form of recordings, books, and edited scores.

Betty's usefulness to Thomas was complete, and Emerald knew that she could never match it. Through a merciful cancer, death came to her five years later. Betty survived in torture nearly fifteen. Till '47 all was bliss unbroken; then began a series of surgical interventions, anemias, and exhaustions. Weighing seventy pounds, she still could not be stopped from traveling everywhere (meaning annually with him clear across America), from attending every long recording session and sitting in at every business conference. Nor could Thomas be stopped from traveling and recording, though increasing attacks of gout would lay him low. He was attentive to Betty and ever patient, but when she died I think he was relieved. The next year he came to New York with just a valet. The following one there was another wife. He was not used to lacking a woman's company; and the new Lady Beecham, surely not yet thirty, was a pretty girl and quietly alert.

In Paris I spent my first night on a day bed in the flat of Suzanne Blum, where with Paul Weill, her husband, they had also their law offices, as is French custom. My own flat I knew to be occupied. And hotels receiving travelers were practically limited to two—the Claridge, on the avenue des Champs-Elysées, and the Ritz. The former gave me a room with carpeting soiled and worn by five years of the military and with one fifteen-watt bulb for light. I stayed there a week, until the Ritz could have me, then moved into a delicious mansard room with balcony on the Place Vendôme. The furniture and carpet were immaculate, the towels and bed linen of the finest. The bath was marble and commodious, the water hot at all the hours permitted. The soap I had brought from New York I kept locked up in my suitcase till I should have time to size up a bit the servants.

Meanwhile, from my window, I used to marvel at the great bronze column that bore on its top Napoleon in Roman toga, while spirally and reading upward were depicted in relief scenes from his glory. At least I fancied this to be their content, though from my distance I could not quite discern. My window, all the same, was on a level with the upper scenes and quite as close as any in the square. I figured therefore that the sculptured story was not intended to be viewed from anywhere; and that even if a closer eye were present, it would need be that of some circling bird, with perhaps a firefly to light up detail.

I stayed at the Ritz till well into November, my expenses paid by our European Edition, rich with French money earned for them during the Occupation by the renting out of offices in their building. And once a week, at least, I sent off an article. These pieces were printed in Europe too and widely read, as was in fact, just then, the whole edition. With paper for printing six or even eight pages, while no other sheet, not even the London *Times,* could manage more than four, our coverage and editorials were more ample. For two years or so they were the best in Europe; and our reader mail, which came from everywhere, was scholarly, punctilious, and thoughtful. Moreover, there was lots to write New York about, with all the state theaters functioning on full repertory, the orchestras revived, and the national radio purged.

Among the radio's musical executives, normally composers, were some I had not known before the war—Henry Barraud, in charge of music, and Manuel Rosenthal, a pupil of Ravel and a conductor of all-embracing curiosity. Roger Désormière was conducting again too, both operas and concerts, also Paul Paray—all those who had been silent for four years. And there were some remarkable performances. I remember a *Pelléas* at the Opéra-Comique with Janine Micheau (Désormière conducting) and a *Phèdre* at the Comédie Française with Marie Bell. I remember these performances, after twenty years, as being grand with a grandeur matching that of the grandest remembered from my early times. And if sentiment a little warms my memory, there are still my reviews, written while the sounds were fresh, to remind me that I was no enchanted adolescent but a man near fifty who had heard everything and was describing for readers, not all of them absent in America, the actual state of music and stage in France.

The orchestral performances, curiously enough, were often better than one had any right to expect, considering the undernourished and irritable state of the personnel, not to mention that many string players were using inferior instruments, having traded their better ones during the Occupation. But Manuel Rosenthal gave a marvelously animated performance of my *Filling Station* suite in a concert of the National Radio Orchestra at the Théâtre des Champs-Elysées; and if Rudolph Dunbar, a Negro war correspondent from Pittsburgh, Pennsylvania, who gave four concerts of American music (all the best of it) in the Salle Pleyel with four different orchestras, did not bring off my Second Symphony anywhere near that perfectly, the fault was surely not that of the orchestra. Nor was it quite mine, who had rehearsed it for him for two hours. Preparing in three rehearsals ninety minutes of foreign music, all of it unknown to the orchestra, is sure to be a hazardous adventure. My work was handsomely applauded and reviewed, all the same. "Paradoxical and poetic" was Sauguet's description of the symphony in *La Bataille*. And *Filling Station* received the honors both of derogatory whistling and of cheers.

The state of French composition I learned from radio colleagues, who had disks, preserved from concerts or rehearsals, covering the whole Occupation. Crude and gritty these were; but they allowed one to hear the pieces, especially when listening with score in hand. Everybody played me everything he had written (Poulenc whole cantatas, also bestowing on me upwards of a hundred newly published songs). And Olivier Messiaen, with Yvonne Loriod, performed a two-hour piece on two pianos.

It was from acetate disks that I reviewed two picturesque works of Manuel Rosenthal with such enthusiasm that cables followed from America asking instantly for scores and parts. Artur Rodzinski, conductor of the New York Philharmonic, wanted the suite about gastronomy called *Musique de table*. And Ormandy desired for Philadelphia the oratorio *Saint François d'Assise*. Both works were played the next season, and Rosenthal himself conducted a bit later at the Philharmonic another picture-piece (his gift was for these), *La Fête du vin*.

The composers brought me all their printed music, and a government office that subsidized recordings bestowed upon me over a hundred disks. These last I gave in New York to the French Culture Office, which had not been able to procure them through French channels. And I acquired all the books, or so it seemed, that had been published since 1940—scholarly books on music, art books, and studies of the cinema. The publisher Gallimard, encountered at a dinner, even sent to my hotel all that had appeared during my absence, at least ten meaty volumes, of crime fiction by my admired Georges Simenon.

Many handsome editions had been brought out since the Germans had left, hand-printed on costly rag. For the French, great lovers of fine paper, had concealed their enormous stocks walled up in cellars, as they had done with wines. So that though newsprint from Norway was rationed and hard to come by, art, literature, and luxury books could now be issued without inconvenience. Thus it was that the most advanced reviews were printing the most advanced authors—Jean Genet, for instance—in editions that made the prewar issues of Georges Hugnet look, except for their art work, almost like pulp.

Revisiting friends was a constant occupation and not at all the easiest of chores. For from the Place Vendôme, which is central, everyone seemed to be living far away. The subways would stop running before midnight, the buses earlier; and taxis were rare. So almost always one walked home from dinner; and if new shoes from America pinched the feet, there was no remedy, since others could not be bought. Or only on the black market and for $200— for $100 if you had black-market francs. This also turned out to be the price of a hat, when in October's cold rain (with no heat in my room, of course) I caught a cold and could not keep my bald head warm or dry. It was also the price of a fair meal for two, with wine, in any of the speak-easy-like black-market restaurants. Unitemized, the total would be jotted on paper scrap, as if it were a telephone number, should police inquire.

At the white-market restaurants, which included all the reputable establishments, prices were regulated; and one gave ration-points as well. The Ritz, where I would have my friends to lunch, served only permitted foods (and in small portions)—poor bread, burned-barley coffee, and saccharine (one tablet offered on a Limoges dinner plate). And with soap a major shortage, there were only paper napkins. The wines, not rationed, still were of the best. And at Larue, where the cellar was historic, one ate, as everywhere, a white fish known as *colin* covered with library paste, while drinking Burgundies of precious years. Once, only once, I caught there a violation, when in the fall oysters became sometimes available, for with these costly delicacies the waiter brought a plate of thin-sliced white bread ever so thinly buttered on the under side.

But when you went to dinner at someone's house, the meal was always copious and rich. For no one would ask a guest to share the vegetable soup and watery boiled potatoes that were standard fare on family nights. But every so often someone would receive from country relations a kilo of butter, a quart of cream, a rabbit, or would simply sell a chair and buy a roast. A feast would then be held and friends invited. Since nobody had an icebox (or any ice), there was no use in keeping meat around.

My urgent matters turned out to be two—recuperating my apartment and getting Gertrude Stein started on the new opera. My gentle landlord, Dr. Ovize, had kept my flat empty for three years, then sometime in 1943, fearing requisition, had sublet it. Later that year he died, leaving the house to his widow and his half brother. The latter, with seeming generosity, offered to liberate the flat in time for my arrival the next year by giving its occupants another in the building. I was not to pay rent on my five-year absence nor expect to be paid for the flat's subletting over the last two. Neither was I to mention the disappearance of minor possessions—a radio and a smallish box of books. The only condition posed by the present occupants was that they take with them the telephone, a sacrifice for me not grave, since the newspaper could get me a priority.

Also, as my landlord explained, I could have it for other reasons. "You are entitled, through your status as a returning Jewish resident, to your apartment and to a priority-B telephone."

"That is all very nice," said I, "but I am not Jewish."

His mouth came open. "But my sister-in-law has always thought that you were like herself." Then, pondering a bit, "Let's leave it that way. I don't have to give you the flat. But I've already spent so much time persuading Madame Ovize of the contrary that I would rather not start all that up again. That is, unless you mind her thinking you a Jew."

"But not the least," said I. "It's a compliment."

And the next year, when I came back in May, I moved into my flat; and with the landlord, who was obliged to go along for my identification, I went to the telephone office and claimed priority. And though I could have done so as a journalist, I chose to do it the other way. So I said yes when the employee asked, "You are an Israelite?" The deception served for nothing, but it amused me.

Gertrude Stein was in love with the GIs. Every day, as she walked her dog, she picked up dozens, asked them questions, took them home, fed them cake and whiskey, observed their language. Its sound and grammar had at this time already been put into a book called *Brewsie and Willie*. And she had also written a play about Occupation life, *Yes Is for a Very Young Man*. When I asked her for an opera about nineteenth-century America, with perhaps the language of the senatorial orators quoted, she hardly thought at all, just started writing. She must have looked into a book or two, just the same, for the political-meeting scene, which she wrote first, has quotes in it (distorted, of course) from the addresses of both Daniel Webster and Susan B. Anthony.

When she chose Susan B. as her protagonist, I could not deny her the feminist approach. When she showed her in a scene of domesticity that might as well have been herself and Alice Toklas conversing about Gertrude's career, I knew that she had got inside the theme and that the work would now be moving rapidly. These two scenes were what she had written by November of '45. She had also exhausted the American Library in Paris, which then began sending to the New York Public for still more nineteenth-century history. She finished *The Mother of Us All* that winter, sent it to me in March of '46. It was her last completed work; she died in July. By that time we had gone over it together. I did not begin composing till October of that year. I finished all but the final scene within two months. In January I wrote the end and began to orchestrate. It opened on May 9, 1947, at Columbia University.

When I left Paris in November of '45, Gertrude did not seem ill. She was happy with her GIs and with the opera subject. She had met Donald Gallup, a young librarian from Yale who inspired confidence, and she had engaged to give him all her papers. A part of her occupation that winter was to reread all these and to destroy any that might embarrass others. No thought of death was with her, I am sure, for she planned, come spring, to buy a car again. And for the moment everything was happy, even though she must have been harboring for quite some time the cancer that was to destroy her.

France too was happy (all but the "*collabos*"), though working hard and living in discomfort to mend the sickness of its circulation system (its railways and roads and rolling stock and trucks, its lack of power and coal and gasoline). For food and clothing were not gravely lacking, but merely the methods of transporting them. And the transportation center that was Paris, though costly and inconvenient, was a haven.

Unfortunately it was also haven to a half-million or more GIs. One used to see them loafing on the streets, stuffed to the throat with all that GI food, bored with no place to go, and feeling sorry for themselves because the French population did not invite them home. There was food in France, but not enough for that. And there were not families enough to go around. As always, every family owned an American and loved him and spoiled him, in spite of low resources. But the unowned GIs, lonesome and unhappy, would wish that they were back in Germany, where everything, being run by the conquerors, was simpler, the black market easier to manipulate, and love available for merely cigarettes. In France the French were working for themselves and being as hospitable as they could, for the middle classes always like Americans. But the working-class French and the working-class Americans, probably from differences over communism, were suspicious and did not get along.

How thin the effective contact was I glimpsed in Lyon, where I made a trip as joint guest of the University and of our Embassy's Culture Office. I traveled there by train with perhaps three others, intellectuals from American universities now working for exchange of books and scholars with the French establishments. We had a half car, first class, to ourselves, though every other foot of space was occupied, everyone going somewhere needful, the corridors packed with luggage and babies and old folk. They did not show resentment of our privilege, but I was not happy with it. Had it not been for the sight of all those Frenchmen being helpful to one another and not complaining (a spectacle typically inside-France), I should have at the stops kept to my compartment, to hide my shame at using so much space.

My assignment was lecturing to university teachers of English; I spoke to them in French on "Words and Music." The eagerness of teachers, students, writers, artists, after a four-year cutoff from world access, their eagerness to know what had been done, to talk with other intellectuals, to trade experiences and books, was so alert one scarce could answer all the questions that came pouring out of them. And the attendance at American Libraries of Information was massive, with special interest shown in books on medicine (to bring them up to date) and in our building methods (very strange but fascinating to them because they would be rebuilding very soon). It is hard perhaps to realize nowadays, when French men of learning, business, industry have found their way back to the closed-in life that they prefer, how open and how willing to communicate they were in the first years after liberation. I say this with some reserves regarding business, for there was in those years a strike of capital, which refused to invest in French recuperation till it had become certain that there would be no workers' revolution.

The Communist party at this time was large, its voting power twice the membership. Their admirable organization of the Resistance had enabled them, moreover, to penetrate at the moment of liberation all administrations, including the police. The banking and investing *bourgeoisie* was naturally fearful lest the whole economy and government slip from its hands. And prying out of the civil service all persons possibly disloyal to investors turned out to be a graver operation than merely dismissing a few collaborators. It was like picking powdered glass out of a wound; and it would take years.

Our own industrial workers, detained at home in factories, were little represented in our troops abroad. So that union men capable of entering into communication with Frenchmen of their kind were too few for a people-to-people dialogue. The French workers despised our troops' political naïveté, and these saw a communist in every blouse. When "U.S. go home" began to appear as handwriting on factory walls, our soldiers knew they were not to be loved. And lest fighting break out in the industrial cities, they were shipped home, or back to Germany, or to country compounds where they saw only farmers and off the post would wear civilian clothes.

My coming home took place on a cargo ship packed tightly with GIs, sleeping on the floor and, as the ship tossed, rolling in one another's vomit. There had been no chance of an airplane passage; the best that could be done would be possibly one for Claude Alphand, whom Helen Reid enormously desired to sing at the Herald Tribune Forum. Hervé, then Permanent Secretary for Economic Affairs at the Foreign Office, was better placed than I to lay hands on a priority; but even he had trouble till I proposed that he cable his ambassador in Washington to please request it. So I stayed until this was accomplished, then took my troopship from a floating iron dock in the utterly destroyed port of Le Havre, along with two dozen other males traveling by permission to the United States.

We were twenty-four civilians in one cabin, sleeping on three-decker beds, and with no space outdoors worth trying to stand up in during the wild November storms. Almost all were businessmen of over forty and thoroughly companionable—especially an importer of Swiss watch-movements from New Jersey and a French salesman of Roquefort cheese. Nobody, in those cramped quarters, failed to be considerate; and I made one friend of genuine distinction. This was a physician, a blood specialist, Doctor Camille Dreyfus, who had spent the war in New York and was going back there after an inspection tour at home to close off his researches and move his family to France, a delicate, gentle man with whom one spoke of everything—art, science, politics, religion. One morning, having breakfast at the GI mess, forever loaded down with pork and ham, I realized he had been declining these. And so I said, "Could it be that you eat kosher?" And he replied, "When I can. Not strictly, even then, of course. But as a privilege. Because there are three things I am proud to be—an Alsatian and a Frenchman and a Jew. And I like to wear some badge of them, some sign."

And then eventually we arrived in Brooklyn, where Maurice Grosser met me in a borrowed car. It was a long, slow drive to my hotel. The paper had thought that I was never coming back. But they were pleased to have had all those Sunday articles *not* about politics and wars and armies. No other paper had published anything comparable; they did not mind that my stay had been expensive. Nor did they mind when I told them I was planning to make a wider tour the next year, to go lots of places, and to stay five months.

The year now ending had been full of things accomplished. My *Symphony on a Hymn Tune*, seventeen years unheard, had at last been played. And at the Philharmonic, of all places. For the new conductor there, Artur Rodzinski, had none of his predecessor's cause to shun me. He had already played, in fact, the suite from *Filling Station*. I had reviewed this performance (for a lark), remarking that he had got the tempos wrong. The symphony he asked me to conduct myself; and though I got the tempos right, the orchestra following like lambs, there had been tension at the first rehearsal from their resentment over my early reviews. The press was almost wholly disapproving. My colleague of the *Times* dismissed the symphony as "too trivial and inconsequential, too unoriginal in its material and flimsy in its structure to merit discussion."

On the other hand, a suite from *The Plow That Broke the Plains,* which I had conducted earlier with the Philadelphia Orchestra, was now published and was traveling rapidly through all the other orchestras (Boston excepted) to universal hallelujahs. My first book of Piano Etudes, introduced that spring by E. Robert Schmitz, had received what Broadway calls "mixed notices"; and it was not till a few months later, when Maxime Schapiro began to play this volume everywhere that certain numbers from it became popular. Also a recording, my first, had been brought out, myself conducting the Philadelphia Orchestra in Five Portraits. And a collection of my reviews and Sunday articles, entitled *The Musical Scene,* had received raves unstinted. And the film (by Ray and Houseman) *Tuesday in November* was pleasing to us all. (Today it seems even finer.) Also, I had conducted my Sonata da Chiesa, from 1926, in its first New York hearing. And that summer it had been proposed that I write an opera, also that I go to France for music's purposes. I suppose my cup could be called "running over."

In any case, the pattern was established that was to prevail for about another decade—namely, that I wrote music constantly and brought it through first performance and publication, that I also traveled widely, conducting and lecturing, also that I reported regularly from New York and elsewhere on the music life of Europe and America. I also kept up my wars with institutions; I enjoyed that. Busy, yes; but I had time for dinner guests and to give evening parties. My secretary, Julia Haines, would sum up my life, "Virgil is always fishing or mending his nets."

Europe in '46

Early in may of '46 I took the *Ile-de-France,* now returned to civilian service for a season but still with her wartime gray paint and all troopship inconveniences, such as giant cabins for many males or females. The violinist Zino Francescatti would practice in the men's washroom so as not to disturb his cabinmates. At other times one talked of France with the Francescattis, Yvonne de Casa Fuerte, and Marcel Duchamp. In Paris I found Gertrude Stein (quite thin) on the station platform; and as we kissed she said, "I'm not here for meeting you. Have you seen Richard Wright?" The Embassy had asked her to welcome a Negro novelist she was known to admire.

I arrived at my flat with ten trunks of consumer goods—transparent music paper for composer friends, plain music paper for students at the Conservatoire, old suits of clothes for everybody, nylon stockings, Turkish towels, quantities of soap, toilet paper, razor blades, cigarettes, and all kinds of packaged edibles. The previous year I had found out what was needed; and I had already sent by freight to the Chatelains a coffin-size box of such things, most of which had arrived. Chiefly the soaps were missing from it, and ladies' underwear. It seems the customs men would sometimes take things, thus enlarging distribution, after all. My own trunks and the electrical appliances for my landlord had been passed without inspection, thanks to the gangster.

My flat was a little dingy, but complete. And I brought home my pictures from the Chatelains, where Leonid had stored them when he rescued his and mine. (How glad I was to see the big Bérard!) From there came also plates lent and a couch-bed, both needed after three years' normal breakage. And the violinist Samuel Dushkin, emptying his apartment, lent a piano, My earlier housecleaner, Madame Jeanne, whose husband was retiring from the Banque de France, now moved back to La-Ferté-sous-Jouarre, leaving the conciergerie of the first house to her sister Elise. There was a new concierge for my house, the wartime one's husband (such a good cook!) having got into trouble by his less than perfect care for the possessions of those absent. And the new concierge, Madame Langlade, brought me a still younger woman named Catherine to clean and cook.

And cook she could, with evident delight. For she loved practicing her art, now that the things to cook well with were beginning to be available. For me almost everything was available through an American commissary recently established for the benefit of journalists and businessmen. So once a week or oftener Sherry Mangan's maid (for the Mangans were back in residence) would go by bus out to Colombes-sur-Seine and bring back for both our kitchens nets heavy with meat and groceries. There would be the usual crackers and spreads and cookies and cornstarch desserts, also tinned vegetables and fruits and dried things, butter and oil, sugar and coffee and tea and chocolate, and grandest of all (O luxury all legal and legitimate!) legs of lamb, fillets of beef, fresh fish, and real live lobsters.

So with Catherine to cook and with nothing to apologize for in possessing all this food, I began to have dinner parties for new friends and old. And Theodate's former lady's maid brought me table linens she had preserved. And Catherine would trot tirelessly the half-mile between my flat and hers to lend me silver when I did not have enough. And make peach tarts with custard filling, or strawberry ones, or greengage plum, because she found catered pastry not yet good enough to serve. Once or twice I gave cocktail parties; and for those she would make thin sandwiches and pound-cake. For the first of these receptions she had spread some crackers with peanut butter; and I noticed that the French guests would regard them with curiosity, take one bite, leave the remainder on the mantelpiece. She had warned me they would find its visual aspect unattractive, also that peanut butter was not for grownups.

I invited Gertrude Stein and Alice Toklas to have dinner with the gangster and his wife; they got on famously. Gertrude even invited the wife to come and see her pictures. Just at dinnertime a chauffeur had arrived with a hot dish of jugged hare (out of season), which delighted Alice, who loved strong dark flavors (and things illegal). I had brought out good wine to go with this (Chateau Lafite, I think), and I teased the gangster for calling it "nice" (*"gentil"*). I also teased Gertrude about something till Alice said, "Don't scold her. She may cry." I had not realized that her strength was low. She went off to the country not long after; I went to Luxembourg and Brussels to conduct. And then I went to Venice and Trieste.

Mr. and Mrs. Ogden Reid, in Paris that summer, invited the *Herald Tribune* staff to dinner at their hotel. And they gasped a bit when told that our postwar European readers were more exigent than New York as to both facts and reasonings; moreover, that New York editorial writers should ask themselves: "What will this read like in Paris?" Helen Reid would have liked to hire my flat for *Tribune* travelers, but luckily I had no right to sublet. Geoffrey Parsons had come to Germany and France, visiting his son, our editor, looking at the conquered, and hoping to drink a little wine in Burgundy. But he became ill in Germany, required surgery, and spent a month at the American Hospital in Neuilly, where I would go with Iris Barry of a summer afternoon to sit with him, swap jokes, and be affectionate.

In August, Lady Cunard came to stay at the British Embassy, where the Duff-Coopers, as she put it, were Ambassadors. So I took her to lunch with some others at the Ritz (much better by then). And I went to a party for her at the Embassy. It was there I saw for the last time Christian Bérard. He wore a dinner jacket and had washed. He was again making fashion drawings for *Vogue* and was designing sets and costumes for the theater—the world's finest of both. When he took me into a corner and said I must not think he had given up being a painter, for he was about to have a show, I assured him I had never doubted him. Actually, that spring in England, he had done large water colors, handsome and original. But back in France he did not persevere.

And a little later, after a police clampdown on the trade in opium, he ceased to smoke and drank a good deal more. He suffered a massive stroke in '49 at a stage rehearsal of Molière's *Les Fourberies de Scapin*. He was deciding whether to keep or to eliminate a certain slender spire in the background; and his last words were, "The minaret's all right." ("*Au fond ce minaret est bon.*")

I broadcast that year, as I had done the year before, programs of American music with original commentary. Both these and my musical coverage for the paper seemed, on the whole, less full of discovery than in 1945. I did review, however, at the opera, Méhul's *Joseph*. And seeing at the Cómedie Française another classic just as rarely given, the *Esther* of Racine, I realized that their actuality, their background of news interest, was the fact that the theme of both is Jewish resettlement.

With Nicolas Nabokov and Roger Désormière I heard a Sonata for Flute and Piano by a twelve-tone composer of twenty-one, Pierre Boulez. The piece delighted me because, in spite of its Germanic method, it sounded French, like an only slightly out-of-tune Ravel. Désormière acknowledged the Boulez talent as authentic, but had reserves about the work; he did not really hold with serial music. "You play around with dodecaphony," he said, "and all it does is falsify the ear." Nevertheless, as soon as Boulez wrote orchestral works, he became their chief exponent and interpreter. And Boulez, after Désormière was paralyzed in 1952, would go to see him constantly and sit with him and talk to him, though Déso, as friends called him, could not answer.

My comradeship with Boulez began in 1952, when we spent a whole night walking the streets and talking music. Nor was that the last time, for the eight-hour session was to become our norm. In a Sunday article of 1946 about atonality in France I had spent ten two-column lines on this young man, "the most brilliant, in my opinion, of all the Paris under-twenty-fives." I did not know till some years later that this was the first press notice he had received. After his world-wide success as a conductor in the 1960s, our meetings in Paris, New York, Los Angeles diminished in both frequency and length. I think he was embarrassed lest my prophecy might perhaps be coming true. For I had early warned him of the danger that lay in duplicating, even though not consciously, the career of Marcel Duchamp.

I said to him, "By using carefully thought out and complex ways, you produce by thirty a handful of unforgettable works. But by then you are the prisoner of your method, which is stiff. You cannot handle it with freedom; so you write less and less; at forty you are sterile. This is the trap of all style-bound artists. For without freedom no one is a master."

"*Bien sur,*" he sadly said, and changed the subject.

Now, at forty, he for the most part just conducts; he is careful of his time and energies; he takes forever to complete a work; and when he does, it seems to come out small. Bérard had skirted mastery, settled for success in illustration and in the theater. Duchamp refused to face, after his early remarkable achievements, the hazards of going on being a master. This was exactly what Picasso and Stravinsky, after an even grander youth, had not refused. Boulez, though far from self-indulgent like Bérard and not so self-destructive as Duchamp, may well have failed, all the same, as Europe's finest composing brain and ear, to bring his talent to fulfillment.

In the previous year I had sought permission to look at Germany, but without success. Our Paris editor had asked the military government to invite me, and the request had got as far as the commanding general, Mark Clark. His office, finding no slot for a music critic, suggested I come as a war correspondent. That status, however, would have required a two-or-three-week security check. This year, without any effort on my part, I was asked to several countries, including Germany.

The first of these trips was to Luxembourg and Belgium. In the former I conducted a concert of my orchestral works at the radio station, of which the musical director was Henri Pensis, who had passed the war in America. In that medieval-turreted and modern city I also encountered my first tape recorder, for the radio establishment still owned a prewar German machine, called in French a *magnétophone,* by which my concert was preserved for later broadcasts.

In Brussels I rehearsed for broadcast a concert of my chamber music, staying on the rue Royale in an eighteenth-century townhouse with fine pictures (even a Van Eyck), where my hosts Jacques and Jacqueline Errera were friends from their New York time as refugees. In bombed-out Antwerp I heard Flemish opera. In Malines I was entertained by the carillon, which I described as resembling in sound "a trayful of glasses, its climactic moments not unlike . . . that same tray dropped." And I got fun out of hearing an aria from *Samson et Dalila* on the chattering bells when what they should have been playing, I said, was John Cage. Belgium, far more than France, seemed to have recovered from the war; and being there was like being in a Flemish picture in which everyone is eating and laughing all the time.

Next, barely had I returned when Prince George Chavchavadze proposed that I visit him in Venice, where the princess had just reopened their apartment. Naturally I went; I had not seen Venice since Harvard Glee Club days. I went by a train that got me only to Milan. Then, after a day of waiting, there was another, which took all night to arrive at the watery metropolis. The apartment there was two whole floors in a grape-colored marble palazzo near the Accademia, which had belonged to an American, the late Princesse Edmond de Polignac. It had many rooms, and there were other guests. There would be twelve for lunch or dinner, and George would play the piano. The composer Gian Francesco Malipiero, still director of the musical conservatoire; the Liceo Benedetto Marcello, came to see me and to show me his establishment, with its secret rooms, where precious manuscripts had been hidden from the Germans and where he was now secreting tagless dogs, lest the municipal authorities cart them off for killing.

I was the first musician from outside Venice he had seen since before the war, and he could not have been more companionable. He brought to the house his newest group of string players, called Nuovo Quartetto Italiano, and they used to practice daily in our *sala,* where there was unlimited elbowroom and a cross draft. He showed me his composing pupils Bruno Maderna and Igor Gorini, along with their music. And once, while itemizing relics out of history, he put Richard Wagner's baton in my hand. It was thin, short, octagonal, and of mahogany, not the ebony broomhandle that his contemporaries used to grasp in the fist. And contactually it was impressive because it was his. I felt as if I had touched electricity.

For the holidays of the Holy Redeemer (the *Redentore*) there had been for houseguest a young British officer, the Honorable J. Hamish Saint Claire-Erskine, who asked me, "Could I possibly persuade you to come to Trieste and hear my opera company?" He was culturally in charge there; and Trieste was in the news, because the "Jugs," as we called our Jugoslavian allies, were threatening to take it, though it was technically in Italy. So I drove with him to the troop-filled seaport and reviewed the opera in the moated Castello San Giusto, its summer quarters. The company was indeed first class, with Margherita Grandi and Cloe Elmo for stars. We also visited in the hills above Udine a powerful radio field station captured from the Germans and still run by its German engineers, Nazis all of them, but too proud of their machine to sabotage it.

As I left for Paris, at the railway station I learned from that morning's *Herald Tribune* of the death of Gertrude Stein. In Paris I went straight to call on Alice, found her lonely in the large high rooms, but self-contained. Gertrude had been feeling tired all spring, she said, and they had hired a small house near Le Mans. There Gertrude had felt quite ill, had pain, and seen a local doctor. He had said, "You may need surgery. In any case you should go back to Paris."

At the American Hospital, an operation was recommended; but in view of her weakened state, it was thought best to postpone this till her strength could be rebuilt. Ten days later there was no change in her strength, and she was still in pain. The surgeon, though pressed, refused to operate. So she sent for the director of the hospital and said, "You will send me a younger surgeon, who will do as I ask." And when he came, she said, "I order you to operate. I was not made to suffer."

The words that have been quoted as her last were spoken while she waited for the wheel table that was to carry her to the operating room. As Alice Toklas told me, then and later, Gertrude had asked a little vaguely (for she was already under sedation), "What's the answer?" And Alice, to bring her back from vagueness, said, "What is the question?" It was in reply to this that Gertrude remarked, "I suppose if there is no question, there is no answer." She had earlier remarked, as her nephew's family, eventually to be her heirs, departed, "We don't have to see them again."

She is buried at the cemetery of Père-Lachaise in a double grave under a double stone designed by Sir Francis Rose, the youngest of the painters Gertrude had continued to admire. Half of it awaits to be inscribed for Alice Toklas. Alice herself, though then expecting little out of life beyond seeing through the press Gertrude's unpublished works and taking care of their dog's old age, has turned out to have a busy and thoroughly interesting existence—being visited by innumerable friends, traveling, and writing books herself (two cookbooks and a memoir). Though she believed, as Gertrude did, that "when a Jew dies he's dead," she could not be satisfied of that in Gertrude's case. Gertrude must somewhere exist, like Dante's Vergil. And since she exists, she can perhaps be visited.

It took Alice several years to plan her strategy, and much consulting with Catholic friends and priests. This time there really was a question; so there had to be an answer. The question was how to see Gertrude again; the answer was to become a Catholic. Since Gertrude, she could not doubt, was immortal, Alice had no choice but to take on immortality. But since in her case that could not be done through genius, her only chance was through the Christian faith. She puts it that she "went back to the Church," for she had been baptized, it seems, at twelve; a friend of her mother's, deploring the neglect of her religious life, had been permitted to arrange this. With despair and loneliness thus exchanged for hope, Alice has faced death serenely ever since, though life has clung to her for twenty years. At eighty-eight she had a cataract removed—for reading books and mail, no doubt, but surely too for seeing Gertrude clear.

And then I went to Germany and Austria, the trip arranged by Nicolas Nabokov, who was attached to our military government in a cultural capacity, being in charge of films, theater, and music for the American zone of Germany and for our sector of Berlin. My clearance in Paris took no time at all; and from the day in late August when we left by military plane for Munich till my return in mid-September from Berlin, everything was favorable to us—hotels, planes, trains, and chauffeured cars—because Nicolas, though civilian, held a colonel's rank, and also because he spoke four languages.

We only stayed a single night in Munich, then went by car to Salzburg, where the music festival was going on under American protection, for Salzburg was in the Austrian district administered by our army. The Oesterreichischer Hof, an officers' billet, was our hotel, with the grander Occupation officers, such as generals, installed in the grander country palaces. In every *Schloss* they held their social court, with many dinners, cocktails, picnic trips, the

VIPs lodged in the main palace, the younger set staying up late in an adjoining smaller one called the *Kavalierhaus*. And if life among these well-washed captains and their wives, short-haired lieutenants and their girls, was possibly less promiscuous after midnight than the prewar Salzburg festival house parties in those same quarters, it was luxurious in other ways, with the slightest expedition (to the opera, to some scenic spot, to Berchtesgaden and Hitler's ruined eyrie) a cavalcade of Packard limousines.

Charles Munch was conducting the Vienna Philharmonic, the pianist Nicole Henriot playing concertos with him. She also played ping-pong with me and beat me. And we visited Mozart's father's plain but not quite humble residence. Certainly we gaped like yokels at the grandeurs of Max Reinhardt's archiepiscopal Schloss Leopoldskron, with huge bronze animals all around the park. (Taken from Paris by Goering, these had not yet been returned.) I made friends with a young composer, Gottfried von Einem, who played me the first act (all there was then) of his opera *Dantons Tod* (all full of rhumbas). And I urged him on toward getting himself and some other young musicians made members of the festival's committee, which they did, then forced inclusion every year of a modern work. I also made the acquaintance of Herbert von Karajan, not yet conducting publicly again but already having prepared the new *Le Nozze di Figaro,* remarkable for dainty patterlike precision. We went to have tea with him and his wife on their sumptuous mountaintop. And the tea, as I remember it, was real. So also was its accompaniment, no doubt a luxury in that greaseless land, thin black bread laid with paper-thin raw bacon.

In Munich we visited in their bombed-out flat a Nazi's family known to us through Munch; their lack of access to food, heat, clothing was pitiable. And we called on Carl Orff (no Nazi), who played us recordings of his music, including the now popular *Carmina Burana.* Munich had been bombed chiefly with blockbusters; so that it looked worse than it really was, its redbrick piles only partially collapsed, all pink and whitish like a wedding cake that had been rained on. Frankfurt-am-Main, on the other hand, which had received incendiary bombs, looked actually better than it really was, with every house or public building gutted, its half-walls standing in lush gardens and already covered by luxuriant ivy, for incendiaries stimulate the growth of greenery.

There had been views of our local music officer, the conductor

Newell Jenkins, producing opera in Stuttgart whenever he could borrow the half-bombed house from our military, which used it desultorily for movies. Also of a similar setup in Wiesbaden. The duty of culture officers, I should explain, was to aid such Germans as could be denazified in restoring their intellectual institutions. I reported on all this in some detail regarding Salzburg, Berlin, and Dresden. Also on German composers and on the music life in general, for in the Grünewald district of Berlin, where we spent upwards of a fortnight in the house that Nicolas had rented complete with servants, we saw all the musicians there were, traveled freely to the Russian sector of the city, and fraternized with Germans, Russians, everybody—a way of life at that time not discouraged.

Nicolas's eighty-year-old father was staying with him, along with a somewhat younger wife, not his first. They had been living since Revolution times in Poland, a country from which postwar refuge seemed improbable. Then Nicolas learned about a Russian colonel who was in need of penicillin (in an army where venereal disease destroyed careers). So in exchange for the precious remedy, at that time our monopoly, the colonel had got exit permits for the Nabokovs.

My own chief Berlin friendly acquisitions were a German composer, the half-Russian Boris Blacher, and the Russians' music officer, Major Barsky, a great-nephew of Anton Rubinstein. Blacher explained to me why he and not Paul Hindemith should, and most likely would, take over the reconstruction of music teaching. Only a few years later, he had done exactly that; and Hindemith, returned from Yale to Europe with the same hope, was settled not in Germany but in Switzerland. Major Barsky, regretting my small acquaintance with Soviet music, took me to the Soviet music store in Unter den Linden and bought me a pile of scores two feet tall. When I asked him whether, if I went to Russia, I should hear music that was not available outside—in other words, was there an underground—he answered, "No, but you would find colorful folk stuff in the night clubs of Tiflis. And in Siberia, where the new industrial cities all have symphony orchestras, but where the players are just thinly educated Tartars, I think you would be amused by the Beethoven."

Our trip into the Russian zone of Germany came about through a high Russian administrator named Ivanov (just under Zhdanov, as I understood), whom we had met at a cocktail party. He got us the passes in three days (ordinarily it took three weeks) and regretted the delay. Since we ourselves had only three more days, it was proposed that we visit merely Dresden, where the palace of Prince Heinrich of Saxony had been turned into a house for foreign guests. And as our army regulations then required, we went in an army car with a GI driver. Along with us came (as guide, he said) an NKVD major most companionable. That is, he was companionable in Russian. At first he was reserved; then he broke into faint smiles, then guffaws at Nicolas's jokes; and before we were a half-hour out of town they were slapping each other's backs to Russian stories.

In Dresden we were VIPs, no question. The Russian music officer, a Captain Auslander, brought us everyone we asked for—school teachers, composers, publishers, art scholars, the head of the musicians' union. These were brought generally to table, where once we sat clean through the day, and where at every meal, including breakfast, there were red wine, white wine, and champagne. All these in addition to the vodka in your water glass. We went to neighborhood operetta theaters. Also to see the museum pictures, at that time hanging in the Pillnitz, an eighteenth-century palace outside of town. The old museum was completely down, along with the rest of the city's Baroque center—the cathedral, the opera house, the Zwinger palace. The people appeared gravely undernourished, especially all those moon-faced Saxon boys who, with scarcely any girth at all remaining, had shot up at twelve to six feet in height. The Russians sent us off, as we had come, with a basket lunch and bottles of white wine (plus vodka, naturally). Had there been time, they told us, we could have gone to nearby Meissen, where the china factories were. Since these establishments had been taken over by the Russian government, buying from them was not "trading with the enemy."

We chose, instead, one more look at Berlin, the most completely bombed-out great city there ever was. Steel girders from the canopy of a railway station had been wound up by the concussion into giant balls of wire. And the monumental center of the place— Unter den Linden, Schinkel's classic-revival library, the district of the Embassies—looked like the sterile craters of the moon. I had not known Berlin before the war and do not now believe that it could have been compared for grandeur to Rome, Paris, Vienna, London. But in destruction it was beautiful. Twenty years later it is still not much rebuilt, not at all on any monumental scale, though permanently there are shows of city planning held almost on the edge of its eastern sector, where all the city's major monuments await restoring.

On the troopship coming home there were Mary McCarthy and her about-to-be husband, Bowdoin Broadwater, she writing every day and discussing every sentence with him as if he were a valued editor. Indeed, he may have well been partly that, since her success as a writer seems to have grown to remarkable solidity during the fifteen or more years that they were married.

And there were commies, too, as on the *Paris* back in '33. Only this time, I think, not real ones, just fellow travelers from Harvard returning from a Youth Congress in Prague. They held meetings on board in which they tried to persuade us to take a "unified" (read pro-Russian) view of the cold war. Mary, always entertained by liberals, egged them on. I baited them, and to their leader remarked that his position, once clearly stated, was what was being called just then "appeasement." These yearning lads, I thought, seemed less straightforward, and certainly less confident in their country, than my friendly Russians from Berlin and Dresden, even than the NKVD major, who, when asked the state of his native city, Rostov-on-Don, had cheerfully thrown his arms aloft and cried, "*Kaput!*"

The Year I Was Fifty

I BEGAN *The Mother of Us All* on October 10 of 1946. On December 10 the voice-and-piano score was complete up to the last scene. I waited a month before composing that, feeling that I must back off and view the rest. In order to find out what the rest was like, I invited friends to hear me play and sing it. Through performing it for others, as I had done for seven years with *Four Saints*, I could find out how it moved and learn its ways. In January, I composed the final scene; by this time a partial cast was learning roles, with Jack Beeson as *répétiteur*. Otto Luening, who was to conduct, had as yet no orchestral score; but that was not urgent, since we were not opening till May.

The production was for Columbia University's Brander Matthews Theatre, where the house was small but the pit commodious. The cast was part professionals and part students; no one was paid for working in the show. The scenery and costumes were by Paul du Pont; staging was by the choreographer John Taras to a scenario, as before, by Maurice Grosser. I cast all the roles myself, holding auditions in my Hotel Chelsea drawing room. For minor parts we used Columbia students and trained them for understudying the leads. Among the finer singers who took part were Dorothy Dow (later of La Scala) and Teresa Stich-Randall (Mozart specialist and *Kammersängerin*, who now sings everywhere). The names of Belva Kibler, Hazel Gravell, Jean Handzlik, and Alice Howland are remembered by many in the music world, those too of William Horne and Everett Anderson. The stage was beautiful for sight and sound, though not to be compared to my Negroes-and-cellophane *Four Saints.*

The student orchestral players were pretty poor; and Luening, an experienced opera man, was patient, to prevent nervousness on stage. The instrumental textures, therefore, which I had laid out with transparency in mind, were likely to come out on any night with holes in them. Nevertheless, after the fourth or fifth performance, when I felt the players knew their parts as well as they ever would, I asked Luening to speed up the pacing. "Can you take twenty minutes off the running time?" I said. "Can do," he answered. And with no cuts made, the next performance came out shorter by that much.

Everybody up-to-date came to hear the new opera, and the press was receptive. The Music Critics' Circle, though reluctant to honor a member, even voted it a special award. Koussevitzky, still angry over criticisms, said to his neighbor (textually), "I do not like it to say it, but I like it." And wrote me to offer a commission for another opera. My colleague Samuel Barber, perhaps also smarting, remarked of my plain-as-Dick's-hatband harmony, "I hope you won't mind my stealing a few of your chords."

From its beginning, *The Mother of Us All* has often been produced by colleges, though it was never designed for amateurs and is difficult for young voices. I have not seen all these productions by any means; but in all that I have seen some charm has come through, for there is in both text and music a nostalgia for nineteenth-century rural America which makes any presentation warm and touching. Western Reserve gave it in Cleveland at elegant Severance Hall; and the orchestra, Cleveland's Philharmonia, was first class. Harvard performances in the Civil War memorial Sanders Theater, with only students singing (and not vocal students either), were so perfectly paced by their conductor, Victor Yellin, then a graduate student, that audiences laughed and applauded, wept at the end. Even at the University of Denver, with everything else precarious, an ingenious stage direction gave the spectacle security, enough at least for Stravinsky to comprehend. But it was not till eighteen years after its birth that it got interesting scenery. Then in 1965, at the University of California, Los Angeles, with Jan Popper conducting, an impressive young soprano, Barbara Gordon (my discovery), singing the role of Susan B., and with myself having coached everybody, including the choreographer, a visual investiture was created by David Hilberman which was as original, evocative, and appropriate as what Florine Stettheimer had created in 1934 for *Four Saints*.

The originality of this scenery lay in its representing neither buildings nor landscapes, but, of all things, people. It consisted of a set of giant cutouts painted to illustrate nineteenth-century ladies and gentlemen, for all the world like colored prints from some Victorian magazine. And all these flats could be moved horizontally to closed-in or to open stage-positions. They were dark blue in color, a tone rarely effective in painted scenery but one which, when lightly rubbed with red, can take light in glowing vibrant ways. And to the profiled figures slight additions of flowering branches, brief cases, flags, gave to outdoor scenes, to a departure, to a political meeting complete evocation. Moreover, the gigantic proportions of these pictured people reduced our singing actors to human size, a desideratum in not overlarge Schoenberg Hall, where any smaller scaling of the scenery tends to make giants of the actors and to trivialize them. The *Mother* sets were, in addition, airy. For all their largeness and somber color, they did not weigh on the spirit or box-in the play, but gave it space and lightness, as if great distances lay all about and the stage were just the segment of a continent.

That same spring there took place at Harvard a three-day Symposium on Music Criticism which I had been invited to address. I could not hope to compete for public favor with the English novelist E. M. Forster, planned star of the occasion; but the historians Paul Henry Lang, Otto Kinkeldey, and Edgar Wind, the pianist-pedagogue Olga Samaroff, the learned composer-pedagogue Roger Sessions, caused me no fears. I wanted to be first class, however, if I could. So after I had finished off in March my opera's six-hundred-page orchestral score, I wrote out carefully my assignment, "The Art of Judging Music," and showed it to Helen Reid, who was impressed. My speech was listed for the second of May; so with my opera already in dress rehearsal for opening on the seventh, I decided I could not spare the time for all three Harvard sessions, but would go only for the second, which was mine, also reviewing a concert that would take place that evening. For musical works had been commissioned too—string works by Schoenberg, Martinu, and Piston, choral ones by Malipiero, Copland, Hindemith, and dance works by Martha Graham to scores by William Schuman and Chávez.

Arriving on the night train, I gave my speech at Sanders Theatre in the morning. Next came a lunch in my honor to which Mrs. Kingsley Porter, widow of the Romanesque archeologist, still living at Elmwood, the James Russell Lowell house, had invited 120 people, a sit-down lunch with pasta and steaks and asparagus and an egg dessert, and with wine made on the place by her Italian servants. Back to Sanders Theatre for the questions and the arguments. Then at six-fifteen to the choral concert in chapel with organ and brass. Then to *The Harvard Crimson,* where I wrote my review of the concert and sent it by telegraph, returning to New York by the midnight train and finding in the morning at my door, when I arrived, the Late City Edition containing it. My Harvard speech was published in a volume, along with the other addresses. Also in the *Atlantic.* And I used it as title-essay for my next book of reviews and articles. It is a good piece, probably the best statement now in print of the whole experience involved in hearing music and describing it. But I have rarely used it as a lecture. Partly because any speech, once printed, goes a little dead. And also because the compactions of phrase I put this one through before publication have rendered it unmalleable for elocution. It now reads like a contract. The points are there, but all so close together that the language does not flow quite as it should for being listened to.

Then *The Mother* came on and played its nine performances. Also rehearsals for a broadcast on May 25 of *Four Saints.* I had most of my original cast for this, and I conducted. There was an excellent new tenor replacing Leonard Franklin, who had joined the war and stayed in service. Through all the galling labors and the errands involved in preparing two operas while doing my regular reviews and Sunday articles, it was Theodate Johnson, living in a small house hidden by the store fronts of Third Avenue, who gave me dinner regularly, went to rehearsals with me, provided rest between dates, was my almost constant evening companion. And for publishing *The Mother of Us All*, which she insisted must be done, she assembled subscribers to guarantee the costs.

Four Saints, also to be published, I had rescored a little bit, adding horns in place of saxophones, and two clarinets to relieve the precarious balancing required when woodwinds are only one of each. Ben Weber, a composer who lived off music copying, made me out a handsome new orchestral score. Was this completed also, with new orchestral parts, that busy spring? It must have been, because the broadcast, contracted for an early date in the Philharmonic's empty summer space, was played in the new version and so recorded. I conducted its recording in Town Hall. The RCA-Victor Company was not willing to record all of the opera; forty-five out of ninety minutes, a ten-side album, was their limit. With this in view, and with Maurice Grosser's help, I reduced the score by half through complex cuttings. Ten hours had been reserved for its recording; but three were wasted on a faulty seating plan, one that involved a dozen microphones and left balances to the recording engineer. On arriving at the hall, I had found this arrangement all set up, accepted it on trial against my judgment. After the morning session, we played the records back and found them, as I had known they would be, close-miked and dead. Robert Shaw, a consultant on the job, and Richard Gilbert, the company's classical-music man, agreed. "This afternoon," said I, "we'll do it my way."

I seated the orchestra therefore as for a concert, with chorus upstage, the orchestra and soloists down front. I used one mike, a large one, out by the balcony, and a small one near the choir to pick up diction. Then, with only seven hours to go, but with a layout in which I could control the balances, I began again at the beginning. Largely because of some vocal tones not ideal, the musical performance in this recording is short of perfect. But technically it is a good enough recording to have been reissued twice—as a long-playing disk in 1952 and with some acoustical embellishment again in '64. Its rarest excellence, beyond the charm of Negro voices, is its verbal clarity (up to 98 per cent).

In July I went to lecture in Vermont at Middlebury, stopping at Tanglewood in Massachusetts to address Copland's composition class on writing operas. There Koussevitsky, after tea on his fine terrace, took me by the arm, made over me. He had always had a gift for convincing every person that he was just the one the Maestro had been longing for. He could radiate, he could smile, he could touch you as if he were holding no reserves at all. In my case, of course, I knew that he held many. No farther back that year than February, I had attacked at some length in my column his attempt to suppress through legal action the publication of his biography by Moses Smith.

A Paris lawyer wired me in July that my flat, if left unoccupied, was in danger of being requisitioned against the housing shortage. I also had a cable from Suzanne Blum informing me I was named to the Legion of Honor. "Come over and let's have a ceremony." In Paris I got involved with "*collabos*," the first of these my good friend Bernard Faÿ, who had received just the year before, after a long-delayed trial, a whopping sentence (life imprisonment, seizure of property, and national degradation). Gertrude Stein, to whom I had introduced him, had been wretchedly unhappy at his imprisonment. I shall not try the case in this memoir; suffice it that Suzanne Blum and Paul Weill, who had no reason to love him, but quite the contrary, had found the trial a travesty and Bernard pitiable ("*digne de pitié*"). For Gertrude's sake, and out of friendship too, I essayed what little power I could wield. It was Suzanne who helped the most, for she was legal counsel to a ministry. And it was she, unless I am in error, who procured his removal from the Ile de Ré, an island fortress where his health was being injured, to a prison hospital on the mainland near Le Mans; and it was from this easier situation that a year later he escaped to Spain. In Madrid he taught history at the University, later moving to the University of Freiburg, in Switzerland, where he has remained. Subsequent revision of his case produced a pardon, the restoration of his property and voting rights. He goes now and then to Paris, publishes his books there. He has not been restored, so far as I know, his chair of *Civilization américaine* at the Collège de France.

At one point, discouraged about other help, I had asked the gangster for advice, and he had referred me to the President's secretary. But the secretary, who knew the case, assured me that nothing could be done just then. Several applications for a pardon had come to the President, he said; but all had been refused on account of pressures. Bernard, being intensely Catholic and royalist, and

389 · *The Year I Was Fifty*

through his eighteenth-century studies a specialist in Freemasonry, had denounced Freemasons by name to the Vichy government; and Masonry, under the Third and Fourth republics, was the cement of the entire electoral structure.

At another time I wished to help a singer, Kirsten Flagstad, who had come back that year from Norway. She had left New York in 1941 to join her husband, had not since sung publicly at any time. Now the husband, though she had had a perfect right to join him, had been a political associate of the traitor Quisling. When she was announced as intending to sing in America, there were public threats of picketing and of stink-bombs. Looking into the matter to decide my attitude, I learned from the Norwegian Embassy that although this artist had been no patriot, neither was there any juridical hindrance to her traveling in freedom and practicing her profession. I even received from the chief justice of the Norwegian Supreme Court a letter stating this. So I covered in Boston her first concert, incorporating this information in my review. There were minor demonstrations there and a few at her first New York recital. But by the next year she was singing again at the Metropolitan, all the more in voice from her six years' rest.

In Paris it had been requested that I "write something" to help a French opera singer, accused of collaboration and now living under house arrest. This time I replied to my beseecher, an American writer and literary hostess, that when this artist should be free to sing in public I should review her happily, because I had long admired her work, but that I could not try law cases in my column.

In September I went to stay with Suzanne Blum at Cap d'Antibes, along with the handsome Colonel Georges Spillmann. As commander of the First Moroccan Infantry, then in garrison at Villefranche, he suggested giving me my *Légion d'Honneur* with military honors. These consisted of a band, a headquarters platoon, and the regimental mascot, a bearded goat. And in their presence, in a public square in Nice, I was pinned and kissed while bagpipes and drums played *The Star-Spangled Banner* and *La Marseillaise,* both in the florid Moroccan style. Four years later my rank was raised from *chevalier* (or knight) to that of *officier.* That occurred in 1951, when Vincent Auriol, the same President of the French Republic who had signed my diploma, paid a state visit to America. Since it is customary on such visits to award decorations, it came about that Olin Downes, my colleague of the *Times,* was to receive a *chevalier's* ribbon; but since he had never been especially a friend of France (Germany and Finland his specialties, Russia his passion), the cultural attaché who recommended him must have thought it only right that I be moved up.

I never learned who had obtained me the first decoration. I thought it might have been Suzanne Blum, working through the Foreign Office. When I asked, she said that Hervé Alphand had been my official sponsor (*"a accepté de te patronner"*). Certainly it was Suzanne herself who solved the problem of my flat by suggesting that with my landlord's consent I sublet it to the colonel, about to be made a general and transferred to Paris. This consent involved a little bribe, a little blackmail. For the landlord did not want the place requisitioned (no profit in that); and the colonel, he knew, could requisition it. My proposal, suggested by Suzanne, was that the colonel be allowed to rent it furnished at twice my rent (a low figure) and that the difference be divided with the landlord. This arrangement lasted for twelve years, and the general was a model tenant. He discovered in the neighborhood a perfect *femme de ménage,* whom we shared; and whenever I arrived, he moved out, leaving every picture, ash tray, piece of soap, exactly where it had been when I left. My profit was just enough to keep the walls papered and the curtains fresh. And I had for Paris visits a flat that cost nothing.

I did not go to France, however, till five years later, when in 1952 I took abroad a *Four Saints* troupe. For the present I had one more European errand, showing to Beecham *The Mother of Us All.* Staying in London with him half a week, I sang and played him the opera, which delighted him. "I shall do this at the BBC," he said. But when it came to their considering it for his upcoming seventieth-birthday festivities, the BBC officials turned it down. Meanwhile I watched Thomas recording for His Master's Voice with his new orchestra, the Royal Philharmonic; and I also interviewed the other company, English Decca, deriving from both visits material for a Sunday piece. I also reviewed the Vienna Opera, then playing at Covent Garden. When the *Herald Tribune* bureau had asked for tickets, the reply had been that there were strictly none. However, since my presence would mean coverage, a special arrangement would be made.

I could witness Mozart's *Don Giovanni* from the royal box, under two conditions. The first was that I bring no one with me (presumably to prevent Beecham's coming along for a lark, taking a bow, creating a disturbance). The other was that I keep invisible. To occupy me during the intermissions, the house manager would take me for a walk, buy me champagne, show me the premises. The latter involved a royal ladies' rest room with no washstand or mirror and a royal men's room where a mahogany column, when opened, became a florid and flowing fountain. That was all, save for a flowered china pot embedded in upholstery in a covered box. There was also a downstairs sitting room, with furniture for holding champagne and cigars, where royal gentlemen could sit out whole acts.

The year of 1947 had begun with my making war on the ever-so-powerful Arthur Judson. The Philharmonic's conductor, Artur Rodzinski, had resigned, alleging interference from the manager. And since that manager was also president of Columbia Concerts, a corporation selling soloists to the Philharmonic, I took occasion, in defense of the conductor, to point out the conflict of interest that was involved. My article was a strong one, and the paper backed me up in an editorial. Judson informed me later that he had been angered by my denunciation, that he was now more than ever my enemy, and that he would remain so. This when Eugene Ormandy proposed to the two of us that Judson take on the management of my conducting dates.

My year ended in a small hassle with the Catholic clergy. In November the Pope's encyclical on art and music, *Mediator Dei,* had been printed in the Vatican's news organ, *L'Osservatore Romano;* and our Roman bureau chief, Barrett McGurn, had sent it to me. This encouraged the liturgical use of modern styles in both music and art, unless these are "unseemly in character" or "derived from a vain research for . . . outlandish effects." Naturally I printed it, translating from an Italian text such passages as dealt specifically with music. A flurry of querulous letters from priests editing Catholic papers hinted that the American clergy would have liked to bury the encyclical. And that is what their papers eventually did, publishing it only after many months and then in small sections, a little at a time, with no comment. I remembered that the American bishops had waited twenty years to implement the century's earlier

pronouncement about music, Pope Pius X's *Motu Proprio,* of 1903.
If now they showed a similar reluctance, that need not surprise. Nor
need it stop my cheering. The Pope was news; modern music was
my faith; their union was almost too good to believe. It almost
made up for the loss of modern music's chief organ of propaganda,
the League of Composers' quarterly, *Modern Music,* so brilliantly
edited by Minna Lederman, which at the year's beginning had after
nearly a quarter-century, in Léon Kochnitzky's phrase, "suspended
hostilities."

Five Years Go By

IN MY EARLY YEARS AT THE PAPER I did not write much music. I put my symphonies into shape and started them traveling. I orchestrated a dozen portraits for grouping into suites. I extracted other suites from films and from the ballet *Filling Station*. To already available chamber works, choral works, and songs, to organ works and other keyboard pieces, I added in 1943 a book of études for piano, the first of two. In 1945 John Houseman's documentary film *Tuesday in November* gave me a longer breath; after that I composed year after year symphonic works, concertos, chamber music, works in liturgical format, and many for the theater.

The Mother of Us All, completed and performed in '47, was followed in 1948 by a film, Robert Flaherty's *Louisiana Story,* for which I wrote an hour of symphonic accompaniment. I was able, moreover, to extract from this music two suites that have been played more, I think, than any other of my orchestral works.

Flaherty had neither Pare Lorentz's self-doubt nor Houseman's compulsion to self-torture. Patient, fearless, and trusting of himself, he could give a guy his head and let him work. And he worked too, went straight ahead, and with Helen Van Dongen, the most sensitive cutter of them all, slowly reduced his footage to the unchangeable timings that a music track must have. In the meantime I had looked up the folk music of the Acadian (or Cajun) people of the bayous. And I had thought too about the landscape music that would be needed for this watery region, which I remembered from my Air Force time in World War I.

But there was no point in going farther without a budget, and for some months there had been no money left. Flaherty had spent all he had on shooting and cutting; and the Standard Oil Company of New Jersey, subsidizers of the project, seemed disinclined to furnish further funds. But Bob went on showing his film (still music-less) to possible backers, until to one of these informal evenings Geoffrey Parsons brought Elmo Roper, public-opinion expert of the oil company, who was writing a column at that time in the *Herald Tribune*. And it was Roper, apparently, who procured the extra money to commission me and to pay for my music track's recording by Eugene Ormandy and the Philadelphia Orchestra.

Louisiana Story's music is of three kinds—folk music, scenery music, and noise-music. The Cajun people are represented by their waltzes and square dances and the tunes of the songs they sing. Natural scenery is depicted through musical devices adapted from Mendelssohn, Debussy, and other landscape composers. The noise-music used is the recorded sound of oil-well-digging machinery. I call it music because, as compounded and shaped by Helen Van Dongen into a rich and deafening accompaniment for a passage of well digging one whole reel (nine minutes) long, these noises make a composition. Also, I find this composition more interesting to follow than almost any of the industrial evocations, including my own, that musicians have composed with tonal materials.

The music track of this film has throughout its length a high presence, or decibel count. Flaherty saw no reason not to emphasize (up to the point of loudness at which visual attention would be disturbed) a symphonic accompaniment so little overlaid with dialogue. I know few films—indeed, none other recorded in America —in which orchestral color has been kept so vivid. Nominated for a Film Academy Award (an "Oscar"), the music was found unworthy of that honor, I was told, because the Philadelphia Orchestra's sound track was "unprofessional." That term meant, I was also told, that our engineers had failed to "sweeten the line"—a practice long observed in Hollywood by which the first violin part is recorded as a solo (*molto vibrato,* naturally) then superposed on the full "take," to add plangency. A Pulitzer Award I did receive, the only one yet given for a film score.

I worked on no more films till '57, when I scored *The Goddess*, by Paddy Chayevsky, and a United Nations atomic thriller by Thorold Dickinson, called *Power Among Men*. These I conducted myself, the latter with forty-five members of The New York Philharmonic. Chayevsky as a workman, though sincere, was hard to deal with, because he could give no one, save possibly his analyst, credit for brains. He confessed in full recording session, all the same, that I had been right and he wrong about a certain musical effect. Then later, with the sound track all complete, he took over the film from its director, John Cromwell, whom he disagreed with on the story's meaning. He thereupon cut out some twenty minutes, I helping him to find the spots where music could be broken. Whether he improved the film I do not know. It has quality and has won European prizes. For my taste, I find the music low in volume; but I liked Kim Stanley as an actress.

In 1964, for the New York World's Fair I worked with Houseman on a one-reel picture called *Journey to America,* to be shown four times an hour in the United States pavilion. Telling the history of immigration almost entirely through prints and still photographs, it is humane, grandiose, and touching. The scoring uses old hymns, folklore, the music of our peoples, much of it nostalgically dissonant. And as always happens when I work with Houseman, we experimented, this time with the timing of commentary. By knowing exactly where it would appear and vanish, I was able to score first softer and then louder and thus to avoid dial-twiddling by engineers. Unfortunately, as also can happen with Houseman, his co-workers did not realize that my scoring was exact, for by slightly misplacing the music track in certain spots they threw some of my results just that much off. My method here, I still think, was a good one; it should be of use in documentaries of which the text is poetry or compact prose. Applying it to jabber would not be worthwhile.

Going back now to the middle 1950s, my experience on a televised production of *King Lear* with Orson Welles and the English director Peter Brook was cartoon comedy. Welles played Lear, of course, but over Brook's head kept revising and cutting the script, directing everybody, and changing everything every day till in the final telecast nobody knew any more which lines were in and which were out. Orson himself, in a fury of improvisation, threw in five from *Richard the Third*. The show, a Ford-Omnibus

Spectacular, was for Sunday evening after an all-day dress rehearsal. On Saturday at midnight, as we broke, Brook had said gently, "Virgil, I'm short seven music cues. Do you suppose something could be done?"

"Certainly," I said. "Just show me where." Which he did.

So I went home and wrote them (in bed, as usual). My copyist came at seven in the morning, took them away, made orchestral parts for my eight (I think) musicians, delivered all to the theater at nine. We then rehearsed the new cues, timed them, and a little later put them in the show. At the telecast, I was in an upstairs studio, where I had a television set for watching the play, headphones for hearing it, a music stand, my score, and my musicians. I was alert in spite of my long night up; but I was also scared, having to bring music in on word-cues when almost nobody was saying the words he was supposed to say. I made no error at that, surprisingly. I was, however, late by half a second on a sight-cue; then right on the nose of my storm-piece came a crash of thunder, thrown in by a watchful engineer, just in case.

Possibly to make up for whatever needed making up for in this production, Orson later played *King Lear* at the New York City Center, this time with electronic weather by Vladimir Ussachevsky and other music by Marc Blitzstein. And this time he fell and broke an arm or leg beforehand, ended up by facing madness from a wheel-chair. I had salvaged from my own *King Lear* a funeral march, later used in Jean Giraudoux's *Ondine*.

The *Ondine* production, with Audrey Hepburn, was directed by Alfred Lunt; and I must say I enjoyed everything about it, even the star's husband, Mel Ferrer, whom Alfred did not care for. Lunt, like Flaherty, was a steady and straightforward worker, knowing infallibly what he did not want. With a director like that, one can use complex cueings and drench the play in music. For *Ondine,* as for *Louisiana Story,* I wrote lots of music cues, fitted them in without misunderstandings; and, helped by sets also of some complexity, we constructed a production at once light in texture and elaborate. Lunt called my incidental music the best he had ever heard; and I certainly found him, among the play directors I had worked with, the most efficient and the best organized.

The Grass Harp, by Truman Capote, was a fragile play sunk by scenery. An interior by Cecil Beaton full of bric-a-brac and china, a tree-house and a tree that filled the stage, were beautiful, all too beautiful. I tried to compensate for their luxuriance by using music sparsely, not too much of it. (My triumph was to fill a sky with falling stars by means of just one chord on a celesta.) Because we were opening in Boston, and the tree was tremendous, we held no dress rehearsal in New York. We gave, however, to an invited group of some two hundred Broadway professionals a last run-through in street clothes on a bare stage with only work lights. The play was touching; everybody wept. After we had got into our scenery in Boston, nobody out front ever wept again. That lovely tree, I thought, if fitted into some romantic opera, might survive for decades at the Metropolitan. Relieved of it, *The Grass Harp* has done well in colleges, little theaters, and clubs.

I worked also, in Stratford, Connecticut, on six more Shakespeare plays; and that was a pleasure because I like to work with Houseman. I like especially his constant worrying about everything. I do not share his penchant for tall women (a six-foot Juliet, for instance) or his fear of stars (assigning an assistant to handle Katharine Hepburn). For she too was a loyal workman who would worry until everything was right. About a music cue that he resisted, I said, "If it doesn't work we can always take it out. What are you afraid of?"

"You must remember," he answered tightly, "that *you* live in an ivory tower." I let that go. But the next day at breakfast, which we took in French, as always, I pointed out that he was the one who had spent twenty years in the limiting landscapes of Broadway and Hollywood, while I was a practical artist, traipsing from Vienna to Buenos Aires, from Mexico to Maine, Rome to Seattle, working in every species of show and concert, rehearsing and conducting orchestras, lecturing in the universities.

That was indeed my life, one third of it. The rest was reviewing music and composing. Among my works composed after 1945, those which touch me most are the Cello Concerto, which was my homage to a long-time friend, Luigi Silva; the Flute Concerto, which is a full-length and resembling portrait of another, the painter Roger Baker; a choral work with orchestra, *Missa Pro Defunctis* (or Requiem Mass), which exploits my skills in choral treatment and liturgical evocation; and *The Feast of Love,* for baritone and orchestra, my own translation from late Latin of the *Pervigilium*

Veneris, sex poem of all time. My other works I know will make their way; these also perhaps. But they worry me because I love them.

My reviewing, after 1945, or even earlier, worried no one save those who feared they might get scorched. As I reread these pieces now, I realize that they are written with a skill surprisingly dependable. I am sorry not to find them quite so interesting as the earlier ones. For those are passionate; they sing and curse. It is not strange to me that the collected books of my *Herald Tribune* pieces, appearing in '45, in '48, in '51, sold each a little less well than its predecessor.

At all times I had a vast correspondence, steady readers, and my continuing wars. The correspondence seems mostly out-of-date today. My wars, perennial, were of the David-and-Goliath sort—sling-shooting at the Metropolitan, at the trusts of concert management, at the Catholic hierarchy, at Arthur Judson, at Billy Rose. Between battles I wrote Sunday essays explaining modern music, also arguing that criticism is not just a whirling windmill, but truly an exercise of the mind. These pieces still express one man's experience in the making of music and in the observation of it. My point of view on both was strictly professional, strictly consecrated, and Franco-American. I never believed that geniuses were a special kind of man; I respected only sensitivity and workmanship. And I abhorred the vacuum that modern music had become in Germany, in Italy, and very largely in England, not to mention the emptiness of Soviet Russia.

On a trip made to America, recovering from one of his purgings, Dmitri Shostakovich had heard the New York Philharmonic. Now it happened that on that program, conducted by Stokowski, was a piece of mine called *Wheatfield at Noon.* In his diaries, transcribed for *Sovietskaya Muzyka,* Shostakovich remarked it "a very bad piece," "void of artistic content or meaning," and "most unpleasant to the ear." He had not cared for the Philharmonic either, or for Stokowski. I printed excerpts from his New York diaries in translation, including his opinion of my *Wheatfield.*

From the beginning I had carried on a guerrilla war against the great Toscanini, sniping constantly at his preoccupation with the "wow-technique," at his seeming preference for second-rate singers, at his couldn't-care-less attitude toward modern music, at the blasting sound of his brasses in Radio City's Studio 8-H, at the military-police ways of the ushers there ("the watch dogs of capital," Roy Harris called them), and at the overbearing nature of his publicity. When Stokowski, his associate, jeopardized his usefulness to the National Broadcasting Corporation, presumably by playing too much modern music, a severance was made in Toscanini's name on the pretext that having two conductors was bad for the orchestra. At this point I called attention to the constant presence there of guest conductors, to the fact that for half the week the NBC was a house orchestra anyway, and to the further fact that Leopold Stokowski had never been bad for any orchestra—in effect calling Toscanini a liar. Executives telephoned, of course; but the paper declined apology and stuck with me. There was rumor also that The Old Man would challenge me to a duel. He did not; he merely broke with Eugene Ormandy, whom he knew to be my friend. The latter, though regretful of his loss, made no appeal; nor did he mention to me the estrangement.

I always kept up coverage of the new books on music. Published music I did not review, esteeming its qualities too precarious, unheard. And recordings already had their Sunday column. But after this fell vacant, with new disks piling up, I sometimes would review a few of them. The trouble with record reviewing is the time it takes to listen, all the more tedious from solitary confinement. A concert takes time too; but you can have someone with you, see people there, or even doze. In addition, the recording of a famous work needs to be listened to with score in hand, if only for comparison with other versions. For instance, when in one month alone arrive four recordings of *Die Meistersinger von Nürnberg,* each four hours long, it is only fair to review them comparatively. But record reviews cannot be very long; they become too jubilant, bitter, or personal. And sixteen hours plus writing time for a half column, I could never persuade myself was justified.

My relation to the recording industry became strained after 1953 through my being a plaintiff, along with some thirty others, in a $150 million monopoly-lawsuit against the broadcasters and their affiliates (a lawsuit still unsettled, I may add). Until then my works had been recorded with reasonable frequency. After that time the frequency dwindled. In his pretrial examination another plaintiff, Gian-Carlo Menotti, alleging discrimination against the recording of his operas, replied, when asked whether the neglect could be ascribed to taste, "Impossible! I am the leading composer of operas." In my testimony that a certain work of mine, recorded two years earlier, had not been issued because the company "couldn't think of anything to put on the other side," though there was a work available, recorded by me with the same orchestra (and eventually issued as the verso), I described this quoted reply to my inquiry as "patently disingenuous." At this point the steno-typist and all the lawyers looked up: "What did you say?" "I said 'patently disingenuous.' Make what you can of that." I never knew what they made of it; but it became clear that at Columbia, where I had long been, at least musically, a friend of the house and where my works had caused no loss, I was not again to be recorded much, or soon.

There came also the usual honors—election to the National In-stitute of Arts and Letters in '48, to the American Academy of Arts and Letters in '59, to the American Academy of Arts and Sciences somewhat earlier. In '49 there were both a Pulitzer Award and my first doctorate (of Fine Arts, Syracuse, and to my surprise not honorary, but a working degree). Grosser had discouraged its ac-ceptance, "You shouldn't get mixed up with that world." But I insisted that as a reputable journalist working for a reputable pa-per, I could not refuse without discourtesy. And on the platform, also getting hoods, were figures indeed no end respectable—Ralph Bunche, of the United Nations, Lester Pearson, then Canadian Sec-retary of State for External Affairs, Nathaniel Goldstein, Attorney General of New York, plus other intellectual citizens. There was also a little pale-haired lady named Elizabeth Nightingale Graham, who turned out to be the cosmetics manufacturer Elizabeth Arden. When I told this to Grosser, it was his turn to say, "You see." I got even with him two years later by becoming a Kentucky Colonel, with a commission from the governor of the state. "Now sneer at that," I said. But being a Southerner, he did not try.

I did not accept membership on boards or committees unless I was prepared to do work. I really worked for the Arrow Music Press, of which I was a founder, for the Composer's Forum, and for New York University's Maison Française. I served also on committees at the Institute. And I met throughout its lifetime with the ANTA Music Panel—a group appointed by the American

National Theatre and Academy to advise our government in its program of helping musicians to go on tour in foreign countries.

This group was both good tempered and combative; rarely have I been so hugely entertained. The purposes of our existence were two—to select artists for quality, which only professionals can do, and to protect the State Department, through our independent status, against meddlesome congressmen. Very early we demanded veto power and got it; without our approval no musician could travel on the President's Fund or in ANTA's name. In addition, we were not paid, a fact which gave us even greater power. For he who buys advice need not use it. But he who receives it free from professionals has to follow that advice if he wants more.

All decisions were arrived at in our monthly meetings; only in emergencies did we vote by telephone. And the discussions were of a frankness and good will, an untempered hilarity I have never seen elsewhere, either before or since, employed as a committee's operating method. For with musicians like New York's William Schuman, Jay Harrison, Howard Hughes, and Carleton Sprague Smith, with Alfred Frankenstein and Raymond Kendall from California, John Rosenfield from Dallas, Harold Spivacke from the Library of Congress, Howard Hanson from Rochester, Arthur Loesser from Cleveland, and Nicolas Slonimsky from Boston, we were rarely at a loss for the truth about anything, and never for words.

Three panels—music, dance, and theater—had been formed in 1953. When ANTA was relieved by the State Department ten years later, the morale of them all was undermined. We understood that Senator Fulbright's disaffection from one of our musical decisions was causing the intellectual-exports program to be reorganized, and it is quite certain President Kennedy did nothing to stop that. Afterwards the meetings of the music panel were not lively any more and for decision making scarce worth going to. Those of us who have continued to attend do so, I think, in the hope that some day our authority may be restored. Those meetings are an exercise in group criticism, and the program they serve should implement the group decisions. To be effective, all such decisions must be professional, independent, and without any possibility of being bypassed— a point of view as applicable to art as to shipbuilding.

In the five years when I did not go to Europe at all, between 1947 and '52, I traveled the map of America from Maine to San

Antonio, Seattle to Savannah, Duluth to Houston, Denver to Louisville. I got to know my country's orchestras, its colleges, its newspapers, its hotels, its motels, and its restaurants. And I grew attached to Colorado, largely on account of Carol Truax, in those years an educational music executive in Colorado Springs, with whom I cooked, gave parties, organized a festival. One summer, teaching composition there, I discovered (later verifying elsewhere) that American students, even the best of them, though they can write in almost any kind of counterpoint and can sometimes orchestrate effectively, have not been trained at all in harmony.

When young composers went to California, they could call on Stravinsky or Schoenberg, but not both. Schoenberg, I think, was the more tolerant; Stravinsky did not permit divided loyalties. In my case there was no proscription or cause for any. I had no reason to offer Schoenberg overt homage. I did not really like his work that much, though I defended it; and a handful of letters bears witness to his gratitude. On one of my trips to Hollywood, when I addressed the Women's Auxiliary of the Los Angeles Philharmonic Orchestra, Schoenberg came to the lecture, pathetically smaller and thinner than I had known him. At the end I stepped down and went to him. He was happy to see me; we began to talk. But after about a minute his wife tugged at his sleeve, saying, "There is somebody important over here." The next evening he came also, this time to a critics' panel I was part of, sat close to the front, and tried to ask a question. But again she pulled his coat, and he sat down. He went on writing me when there was occasion; and I would send my greetings through the German colony of authors and musicians that had clustered, replacing their lost French Riviera, between the university and the sea.

Stravinsky made no protest at these minor infidelities. For twenty years we saw each other joyfully—in New York, Hollywood, Venice, wherever we were. There was a great deal of party giving too, at his house and mine, of dining and of drinking good French wines. He came often to hear my music, spoke well of it, advised Balanchine about making a dance-piece out of *Louisiana Story*, to be called *Bayou*. The less dramatic of the two orchestral suites, chosen against Stravinsky's preference, failed as a ballet.

At my New York hotel apartment Stravinsky first met Pierre Boulez; and the two of them sat talking on a sofa, in spite of milling guests, for two straight hours. This was after Schoenberg's death, when Stravinsky, guided by Robert Craft, who served as aide and musical adviser, was moving into the power vacuum, as politicians call it, left by the last to die of the twelve-tone triumvirate—Berg, Webern, and Schoenberg. In an earlier time he would not have wished to meet young dodecaphonists (there were plenty of those in southern California), least of all a polemical Parisian who used "neoclassic" as a dirty word.

Some have regretted that Stravinsky in his seventies should adopt Schoenberg's composition method. But even those who still deplore the surrender cannot but be happy that in his eighties he is still composing. As for myself, I find his twelve-tone serial music no less interesting than his neoclassic. Actually I believe it to be a continuation of his neoclassical procedures (using materials from turn-of-the-century Vienna) and neoclassicism itself, in Stravinsky's use, to be an outcome of his impressionist, or landscape, period. In impressionist music, places are evoked; in neoclassical, historic times. In twelve-tone writing it is almost impossible not to call on sentiments characteristic of Vienna between 1890 and 1910. There is, of course, no valid objection to that, nor to any method of composing, nor to any subject.

One can be sales resistant, however, to the publicity that surrounds the twelve-tone serial method, because of that publicity's messianic tone. And hallelujahs for the salvation of *le père Igor* are likely to be absurd from lack of humor. For Stravinsky by nature is himself a jokester, a jokester and a man of simple feelings. There is nothing about him tortured or self-reproachful; he has no overheated Jewishness, no German *Innigkeit* (or introversion). His Russian propensities are for piety, domesticity, and calculated violence. His use of double meaning comes from Paris. And if, like Satie, Picasso, Gertrude Stein, he can multiply his meanings without a smile, in the end (and I should say almost from the beginning) he is, save for the domestic sentiments, a dead-pan comic. For example, exclaiming very seriously in my house, "The oboe is one of the most beautiful instruments God ever created!" he might have been suggesting as a theme for William Blake or Milton *God Creating the Oboe*. It is also purest Stravinskyan *pince-sans-rire*.

For his eightieth birthday, when I cracked a joke myself, he did not like it or understand my malice; but he did not reproach me, and we continued to embrace. His wife, however, began avoiding me and looked the other way when I would pass. The purpose of my move was to test our friendship, to see if under blows it would survive. I did not care much whether it did or not, for I was finding his twelve-tone sanctimoniousness distasteful, and I deplored the celebrity apotheosis he had undergone. So I struck two ways at once. Reviewing *The Flood* for the London *Observer,* I praised the music, pointing out as well its artful irony. Then, in an American magazine, I slapped him hard. Jay Harrison's birthday-piece had been enhanced by four framed testimonials, requested. Shostako-vitch bore witness to the master's "great musical genius and en-dowments." Leonard Bernstein called him "a true immortal," Gian-Carlo Menotti "an indispensable item in a composer's workshop." I found him "a manneristic composer in a manneristic age" and re-called what the eighteenth-century Metastasio had said of himself, "a tolerable poet in an age of mediocrities." My attack's chief in-terest is its seeming lack of motivation. I had no reason for di-minishing a composer I profoundly admired, but we know what men will do to public monuments. And I do not regret it. Or do I? No. I can't. Living monuments are insupportable.

Coming back from trips, I usually stopped in Pittsburgh, Penn-sylvania, where my sister lived and where my mother spent the winter. Come spring, she always went back to Missouri, where she had sisters, cousins, nieces, countless friends. When she would visit me, say once or twice a year, Mother was a success, no question, in New York. For she had Missouri forthrightness along with Ken-tucky tact, and she could stay up late without fatigue. She thought any day a somewhat wasted day unless one went somewhere or had some company. Or in season, of course, did right domestic things such as dressmaking, canning, organizing a sickness, a wedding, a childbirth. So people came to our house, and we went to theirs. We went as well to concerts, the opera, the ballet, the United Nations, the horse show, the dressmakers' openings. And mornings she would mend, shine silver, or simply read, while after lunch, as a Southern lady, she retired. From eighty till her death at ninety-two she was constantly a guest, ever cheerful, easy to have around, never a weight.

The skill of her conversation became proverbial (and how not, for one who viewed life as a party?). When John Latouche asked her did she enjoy Gertrude Stein, she replied, "When I understand, I enjoy her very much. When I don't understand I just don't understand." And of John Cage's music for prepared piano, "It's pretty, but I never would have thought of doing it."

The most successfully explosive of her remarks was made to Betty Isaacs, who when asked, as people are asked in Missouri, what church she went to, replied that though she and the Judge were of the Jewish faith they did not go to temple very often. Mother hardly thought a second before observing, "I don't think it makes any difference whether people go to church or not, so long as they're good christians." She had used the last word as a common noun; the Isaacses loved her forever after.

When she became ill in 1957, I went to see her straightaway in Pittsburgh. "I hadn't planned it this way," was her apology. "I shan't get over this one. But that's all right. I've had a good life." Since I was to conduct shortly in Berlin, at the opening of the Kongresshalle, my sister wondered whether I should go. "Of course I must; Mother would think it foolish of me not to. And surely I can count on her for the tact not to die while I'm away." So I went to Berlin and came back. And then she did die, murmuring, "Open the door." And we took her to Missouri. And I went back to Europe for another engagement. She was a small woman, barely five feet, though plump; and she had been pretty. She never raised her voice. But in her gentle way she was a driver. She saw no reason for accepting in oneself, unless God forced it, any remediable imperfection such as ignorance, poor health, or a lack of manners. As my wartime buddy George Phillips used to say, "Your mother is the one with character, not you."

Nicolas Nabokov returned to Paris in '50 or '51 as world-wide director of The Congress for Cultural Freedom. His first major action there was to organize for 1952 a month-long festival of twentieth-century music. There were to be variants of this festival in Rome, 1954, still later in Venice, Berlin, and Tokyo, all of them comprehensive and costly. For the first one—L'Art du Vingtième Siècle, in Paris—he wanted passionately to show my *Four Saints in Three Acts*. The United States government offered him Gershwin's *Porgy and Bess*. He refused it as sociologically false (a white man's story) and culturally degrading to Negro actors (because sociologically false). Procuring the money for *Four Saints* was partly his achievement, partly that of my lawyer, Arnold Wiessberger. But it was procured; and I took charge of the production. We showed it first at the Broadway Theater in New York and then shipped it by plane to Paris—cast, costumes, and scenery—at the end of May.

Above left: Alfred H. Barr, Jr., first director of the first museum of modern art (New York, 1929) and the founder of modern-art scholarship. *Above right:* Philip Johnson, in the 1930s a showman of architecture. *Below:* Constance Askew, admired by artists and scholars, dealers and curators, poets and people of the theater.

Four Saints in Three Acts, 1934—St. Teresa photographed as if with Holy Ghost. *Below:* Florine Stettheimer's miniature theater for designing in real textures.

Left: Frederick Ashton (now Sir Frederick), for whom the saints moved gaily with decorum.

Right: Florine Stettheimer, drawing by Marcel Duchamp.

Below left: John Houseman, production director of *Four Saints*. *Below right:* Maurice Grosser, whose scenario was our basis for choreography and action.

Above: John Houseman, Pavel Tchelitcheff, Aline McMahon, and Orson Welles—V.T. too—had planned Webster's *The Duchess of Malfi* for Mercury Theatre. *Below:* Henry-Russell Hitchcock, architecture historian, with "Chick" Austin, museum director, in front of a picture by Balthus.

Above: Alexander Calder, who created for Satie's *Socrate* a mobile stage-set. *Below:* Jacques d'Amboise danced the lead in the 1957 revival of *Filling Station.*

Above: Pare Lorentz, author and director of the documentary films *The Plow That Broke the Plains*, 1936, and *The River*, 1937, for both of which I wrote the music. *Below:* Theodate Johnson (oil on canvas) by Maurice Grosser, 1938. She had a fine soprano voice, broke it doing war work in France, 1940.

Sets by David Hilberman for *The Mother of Us All* at UCLA, 1965. *Above:* A prologue showing Susan B. at home.

Above: Debate, Susan B. Anthony and Daniel Webster. *Below:* In the last scene Susan's statue is unveiled.

Above: V.T. at the New York *Herald Tribune* in 1940. *Above left:* John Cage, far-out composer, who wrote with Kathleen O'Donnell Hoover *Virgil Thomson: His Life and Music. Left:* The composer Lou Harrison about 1950.

Below: Geoffrey Parsons, Pulitzer-award-winning chief editorial writer and my mentor at the *Herald Tribune*.

Above left: Studio playback of *Louisiana Story* music—Helen Van Dongen, editor; Eugene Ormandy, conductor; Robert Flaherty, author and director; Bob Fine, recording engineer; and V.T. *Above right:* Henri Cliquet-Pleyel at seventy, correcting his *Concerto posthume* (sic). He died before its première in '63. *Below:* V.T. with Igor Stravinsky and birthday cake at Arnold Weissberger's, 1962.

Traipsing and Trouping

T HE JOINT PRODUCERS of *Four Saints,* the American National Theater and Academy and Ethel Linder Riener, had left all artistic decisions to me. Since most of my original singers had aged vocally in eighteen years, I held auditions and recast the work. Edward Matthews was still impressive as Saint Ignatius and his wife, Altonell Hines, unchanged as the *commère.* Inez Matthews, Edward's sister, though rather a high mezzo than a soprano, sang Saint Teresa I; Betty Allen, Saint Teresa II; Rawn Spearman, the tenor role of Saint Chávez. Among the dancers I find the name of Arthur Mitchell. In my chorus were Leontyne Price, Martha Flowers, Gloria Davey, Olga James, and Billie Daniel. It was a cast of pristine voices, most of them, like Leontyne, straight out of the Juilliard School and proud to be singing opera for pay. The next season, as once before, a new *Porgy and Bess* troupe used the best of them.

The Stettheimer stage-sets were impractical because cellophane, even if it were still available, would not be tolerated by the fire department. Tchelitcheff declined, with love, to do over Florine's opera. Esteban Francés also excused himself, unless there were considerable money to spend on spectacle. Eventually it was decided to reproduce as closely as possible the Stettheimer conception, using in place of cellophane a woven plastic material. I found this material droopy and greasy, its blue-green color dismal. But the costumes, at least, could be correctly copied; and anyway there was no artist available whom I would trust (or who seemed to have the courage) to redesign the opera throughout. It was also decided to reproduce the Frederick Ashton choreography, since this fitted the scenery and since there had remained from 1934 a prompt-book. The choreographer William Dollar, helped by Grosser and the prompt-book, did not do badly by the earlier conception. The musical performance, which I trained and conducted (and which Stravinsky complimented highly) was the presentation's really first-class element. But there was no all-over production brilliance, as in '34.

On my arrival in Paris I had encountered Orson Welles, who said, "Can I be of any help?" "You surely can," said I, "because you know the house; and we may have to adjust our lighting and stage movements." He came to a dress rehearsal at the Théâtre des Champs-Elysées, sat quietly throughout, then at the end showed our singers how to retract their large open patterns at the ends of scenes so as to be off the apron when the curtain fell. Whether he changed the way our lights were hung I am not sure. Grosser says no; my memory says he made certain that at least there were enough projectors in the house to light all those playing in front of the curtain line.

My orchestra was that of the Concerts Colonne, by courtesy of their regular conductor, Paul Paray, thanks to whose firm commitment, during five rehearsals and seven performances (O miracle!) not once did any player send a substitute. Neither the sight reading nor the discipline, however, was comparable to what we are used to in New York. Enthralled for certain by the Negro girls, my men half the time would turn their backs to me. For every entry of a soloist or section, I had to snap my fingers a good two measures in advance. That they could cooperate, however, was revealed at the last performance, when Inez Matthews had a cold. "Don't try to go on," I had said to her. "Leontyne knows the role." But she did go on. So I said to the orchestra, "Please take care with my soprano; don't make her sing loud all the time." Their anti-American resistance to me (three-fourth of them were commies) disappeared at once; and they followed lamb-like, hush-

ing volume at my slightest indication, their eyes on me instead of
on the stage.

It had been hoped to tour the new production; there had been
nibbles. Venice would have taken it in September, but we were
paying American salaries and could not wait. Barcelona could have
used us earlier, but our *première* was engaged to the Paris festival.
There was talk of our playing a week at Covent Garden; but we
were turned down, an executive of that house remarking that "the
Royal Opera [was] not quite the place for coons."

The Paris press, conditioned to Josephine Baker and to the
Katherine Dunham dancers, feigned some astonishment at our lack
of Negro sex display. They also found the scenery, though charming, tinsel-childish. They remarked the voices and performance as
first class. The work itself received mixed notices. Some critics
found the libretto nonexistent; others saw in it "the old Picasso
jokes" ("*Picasso mystificateur*"). Almost all viewed the music's simplicity as "arbitrary." One of them recognized my connection to
Satie but wondered regarding us both "whether [we] had renounced richness or merely resigned [ourselves] to poverty." The
most perspicacious of them (Marcel Schneider in *Combat*) found in
this "Sunday school entertainment," or "camped-up Mass . . . no
trace of impiety or sacrilege," merely "a modernistic golden legend." And

> to complete the illusion, Virgil Thomson's music, by perversity,
> imitates the village sacristan at a harmonium, with his con-
> stantly consonant chords, tonic and dominant. Purcell and
> Couperin are evoked, and other masters of the seventeenth and
> eighteenth centuries; but Thomson has managed to be different
> from them while appearing just to copy, with the result that
> this music, seemingly so facile, so conventional, achieves the
> utmost of sophistication; perfidious and perverse in its naïveté,
> it ends up as naïve through perversity.

There were attempts to laugh the whole thing off, as in New
York two decades earlier. There were also demonstrations in its
favor. Nadia Boulanger gave me a dinner for sixteen. My French
banker gave a lunch with rare wines at the Automobile Club for
two hundred. And on opening night I had found in my dressing
room a basket with fourteen kinds of flowers in it, bearing the

wishes of Christian Dior. The most impressive of these gestures was
a cocktail party, the hostess both a daughter and a widow of
academicians, the guests profoundly dowdy and distinguished, the
food and drink not showy, merely perfect, the whole an acknowl-
edgment of my long-held place, both personal and professional, on
the inside of intellectual France. (Said Marie-Blanche de Polignac
to Nadia Boulanger, "*Il était là comme un coq en pâte.*")

I was also asked to write for musical encyclopedias, to take part
in forum discussions and to serve on juries. What I actually did,
after ordering shirts and suits, was to go and visit Sauguet near
Bordeaux. Of all my French musical associates, he was the one who
had matured the most becomingly. In youth a thin man, he was
now portly; and his sharp-tongued spleen had given place to
warmth, revealing brains, benevolence, and heart. With the painter
Jacques Dupont we motored south and east, ending in Aix-en-
Provence at the festival. There we joined French music's in-group
—Poulenc, Roland-Manuel, the publisher Hervé Dugardin, and
more. My opera had not offended them by a too-small or too-large
success, and my prestige as a music-journalist gave them every
wish to please. There were English present also, but my fatal way
with them brought only tensions. The critic of *The Sunday Times*
took me to task for my overfrank review of Britten's opera *Billy
Budd,* shown also at the festival in Paris. And lunch guests invited
by the Dugardins to the garden of a hotel waited an hour for
Britten and Lord Harewood to come down. They were delaying,
we thought, to see if I would leave. When it turned out that I
was of the party, they sent word that one of them was not feeling
well.

In the summer of 1953 I conducted in California, Mexico, Newport, and Cambridge (at Harvard). And the following season I
conducted in Minneapolis, Cincinnati, Philadelphia, Baltimore,
Washington, and New York. There were recordings too, my last
for some time to come. And I worked on the *Ondine* with Alfred
Lunt. For several years I had been earning more from my music
and public appearances than from the paper. In the spring of '53 I
decided to resign as of October, thus giving the editors six months
to replace me. I was not bored with the job, but I could see boredom far off on the horizon. I had reviewed most of the artists that
there were and all the kinds of music. Going on for the sake of

a dozen novelties a year, if that, seemed less than urgent. On the contrary, as my mother had said of visiting, one should leave while both you and the others are enjoying it.

But just as I was about to give notice, Arthur Berger, at that time one of my assistants, told me of being offered at Brandeis University a professorship in musical composition with a good salary and four months' vacation. "Do you think I should take it?" was his question. "Of course you should take it," was my answer. But his resignation meant that I must postpone mine; I did not think it right that we leave in the same year. So he told our managing editor, George Cornish, that he would be leaving in the fall; and I told him that I would stay until the next fall.

The idea that I would relinquish a post so little demanding, so honorific, and so powerful was unbelievable to Cornish, to Parsons, to Helen Reid, and to young Whitelaw Reid. Unless perchance I was moving to another paper. But that, not. I had refused in 1941 *The New Yorker*'s offer to double my *Herald Tribune* salary. I was simply through with reviewing; I had had it. But not a one of them believed me. And for a year no plan was made for my replacement. Then Geoffrey Parsons asked me for suggestions. I said I did not think I should be allowed to name my successor. So we left it at that; and in late March of '54 I went to Europe to take part in another of Nabokov's music festivals, this time in Rome, and to indulge myself in a conducting tour.

This began in Barcelona at the gold-and-red-plush Liceo with a program of American music, all of it unknown to the orchestra and all of it to be learned in four rehearsals. It was a long concert with two intermissions, as is the custom there, and with a soloist, Bernard Greenhouse, to play my Cello Concerto. I had regretfully renounced Charles Ives's *The Housatonic at Stockbridge*, knowing that this five-minute work would take more time to learn than all the rest, time that would be needed for Copland's *Applachian Spring*, whose assymetric rhythms would give trouble. In fact, I spent so much time on those that as my last rehearsal was ending at the oh-so-Spanish hour of half past midnight, we had still barely read through *Louisiana Story*. I was announcing that I would take my chance on pulling that together at the concert when the violinist Casals, brother of the exiled cellist, made a speech, saying we had worked well within our given time but that we needed one half-hour more of practice, and proposing that the orchestra give that time free, in order to assure the concert's excellence. "We are after all in Barcelona," was what persuaded them.

In Rome I conducted, as part of the festival, my *Three Pictures for Orchestra*, difficult all of them, but by the radio orchestra well played. This festival, with some fifty composers asked, was devoted to the music of its guests and to commissioned works, of which there were twelve. The commissions awarded to Americans had been two, a Concerto for Violin and Orchestra by Ben Weber, with Joseph Fuchs as soloist, and some solo scenes from Lou Harrison's opera (after William Morris) *Rapunzel's Daughter*, sung by Leontyne Price. This last piece won a prize, in fact. Our American representatives made the best effect of any, I think—the composers Copland, Barber, Carter, Lou Harrison, and Ben Weber, the composer and conductor Carlos Surinach, the violinist Joseph Fuchs, the harpsichordist Sylvia Marlowe.

The festival, as if to prophesy the coming time, suffered from a plethora of overcomplex music. At the end of its ten-day term we were exhausted from digesting all those dense and chewy scores and from fighting for them against an indifferent public and a distracted administration. It had been thought appropriate to open the first concert with a fanfarelike work for brass by Giovanni Gabrieli. Three months went by; then just a week beforehand, Paris checking, it was revealed that the music could not be found in Rome. So Paris ordered it to be sent on from Venice. What should Rome know of a Venetian who wrote four centuries ago? Rome has its seven hills and three world powers. And music, as practiced by modern musicians, is not of interest to the Church, the Communist party, or the film industry.

As I left for my tour, Copland, also beginning to conduct, had written me, "Cut a wide swath so we can all go through it." And the next year he made a European tour himself. I conducted concerts of American music in Zurich, Paris, Luxembourg, and Vienna. I also made a trip through Scandinavia for reporting the June festivals. And in July I conducted in New York at the Lewisohn Stadium, giving *Four Saints in Three Acts* in the forty-minute concert version. By this time Edward Matthews was dead (of a motor accident) and Altonell Hines no longer singing well. So I persuaded Inez Matthews, a mezzo anyway, to sing the *commère,* using Leontyne Price and William Warfield for the leads. Leontyne, just two years out, was at her peak. I do not think she has ever sounded or looked more lovely.

I stopped at the office to see Parsons and George Cornish, because at last I had a successor to suggest—Paul Bowles, an excellent composer and a good writer, then living in Tangier. But by that time my successor had been named, the music historian Paul Henry Lang, of Columbia University. So I wished them all well and went back to Europe, where I had still a Paris radio concert to conduct. On a steaming July afternoon with no intermission, nor any time between works more than to put down and to take up scores, the program's ninety minutes, on my feet and sweating, were the most tiring I had ever spent.

It was through this, however, that I made a royal friend. Queen Elisabeth of the Belgians, herself a string player and the close friend of a cellist, heard the broadcast of my Cello Concerto with Maurice Gendron playing. She sent word thereupon by the singer Doda Conrad that she had found this the most interesting music she had heard in many years and that she looked forward to making my acquaintance. I wrote to acknowledge the message, but did not wait on her until the following year. Since that time, I have gone to her regularly, and we have talked of music and of politics. When she asked me hopefully, "You *are* a bit of a revolutionary, are you not?" I answered, "I am always against the government." "So am I," she said, and went off again to Russia. Still later, in the early nineteen-sixties, she spent a month in China. Coming back, she said, "Chou En-lai stays with peasants in their houses. He is a great man."

At this I comprehended her opinions. I had never doubted their sincerity, but I had not understood her need for them. As a Wittelsbach princess and a compassionate queen, impatient with parliamentary delays and bourgeois maneuvers, she found it right that a chief of state should visit his people and rejoiced at his care for the humble. Though German, she was no Junker; two wars proved that. On the contrary, she tended to believe that socialism justly administered can save time. I cannot agree with her or disagree; no matter what the government, I'm agin' it. But I did note that her leftist view was royal.

In Kitzbühel I tried to write a piano concerto that Minnie Guggenheimer, of the Lewisohn Stadium concerts, wished to commission. The effort came to nothing, so I studied scores. For I was to conduct at Town Hall in November a Mozart symphony, a suite by Bach, some songs of mine, and the Satie *Socrate*. Examining a manuscript of this, which I had never played with orchestra, I found written in, and signed by the composer Charles Cushing, an English version of the French text. Hooray, thought I, we'll use this. Then, as I went on examining it, I found, as always with translations, slight changes to make. I did not write to Cushing then; but after the *Socrate* had been sung by Phyllis Curtin and Alice Howland, I sent to him in Berkeley, California, a program in which the translation, as altered, was ascribed to both of us. It took him five years to forgive me. But he had still not seen my alterations. After five more years I sent him a vocal score containing my adjusted version. How deeply he resents my interference I may never know. But the work goes beautifully into English; that was his discovery.

Still in search of inspiration for a concerto, and in the rainy Salzkammergut longing for sun, I moved to the shores of Lake Garda at Sirmione, where I received a wire from Zermatt inviting me to hear Pablo Casals give lessons on the cello and to play, with the pianist Mieczyslav Horszowski, Beethoven's five Sonatas and the Variations. I said to Nicole Hirsch, "Let's go in your car." But she said, "I'm not invited." "I can fix that, I think," said I, "by wiring the management that I am bringing the music critic of the Paris *France-Soir*." So we went together by way of Milan and over the Simplon Pass to the cog railway's foot, then up to the high village by the Matterhorn, with its fine Victorian hotels and not one car.

In thirty years I had not heard Casals. Amazed by his musico-technical refinements, I acquired, as evidence, stenographic reports of his public lessons that I still show to players and to teachers. But what struck me most was his ability to play "white," as it is called, to move the bow very steadily, slowly, from point to heel, with no left-hand vibrato to conceal right-arm trembling, and with no such trembling anyway—this at seventy-seven, please remember. Eight years later, in Washington, at the White House, on an occasion when he played there after dinner, at the recital's end I went to look for him. In his greenroom I embraced him and turned to go, found myself nose to nose with President Kennedy. "Hello," he said. "What did you think of the music?" When I told him I had never heard the old man play more beautifully, nor Horszowski either, nor Alexander Schneider, and that their special excellence had been all for him (it could only be that way), he listened intently as if wondering, "Can I use this?" Then with a charming grin and a slight leer of complicity, as if asking for the low-down, he leaned toward me. "Is he really still as good as he ever was?" he wanted to know. For answer I described his bow-arm control. "Say, that will interest my wife. Let's tell her. Jackie, listen to this."

My last date that summer was Venice, where my Flute Concerto, composed for Elaine Shafer, Efrem Kurtz's wife, was to have its first performance. The program contained four new works; and the conductor, detained in Milan, would not arrive till the morning of the concert. It was proposed therefore that Bruno Maderna and I, since we were present (Miss Shafer, too), rehearse our works and get our pieces ready so that Nino Sonzogno, when he arrived, could spend his short time on the other works. This was done, and perfect performances resulted. Also showing in that autumn's festival was a Benjamin Britten opera based on Henry James's *The Turn of the Screw.* I heard this twice, admired it, was able to congratulate Britten sincerely. He even smiled. Since that time, though our paths do not cross much, he has not felt it needful to avoid me.

After my last piece appeared in the *Herald Tribune,* fourteen years from my first, I continued to lead the same life as before. I conducted, gave lectures, wrote music. I missed nothing about the paper but Julia Haines, for secretaries are habit-forming. Minna Lederman is said to have exclaimed, on hearing of my departure, "But how will he get his music played?" Curiously enough, it has gone on being played; my ASCAP reports show almost no decline. And since ASCAP chiefly reports radio performances, and since radio performances tend to follow the number of recordings available, the decline in my recordings would more than explain the slight diminution. And my whole income, cardinal test, has not diminished.

Right off, on my leaving the paper, Pierre Monteux had asked me to dinner. His intake that evening, in his eightieth year, consisted of a pint glass of Pernod with water, six oysters, a fillet steak with *sauce béarnaise* and soufflé potatoes, fresh asparagus with *sauce hollandaise,* ice cream, and for the four of us two bottles of champagne. "I can't drink red wine any more," he apologized. Afterwards, when the other guest had left, Doris, speaking for them both, with Monteux approving, said, "I hope you don't mind our asking about money. But without your *Tribune* salary, will there be difficulties?" I replied that their thought was most considerate, but that I had been independent of the paper for upwards of ten years. "Well, I'm glad," said she. "We were worried about you. And we want you to promise that if you should ever be short of funds you will let us know."

Actually, the only help I needed then was musical. As after my return to Missouri from World War I, after my return to Paris in 1925, my return to America in 1933 for producing *Four Saints,* my return to New York in the fall of 1940, whenever I have closed off an epoch in my life and opened another, it has taken a little time before the music flows. Relieved from deadline pressures and with nothing I had to do (evenings, at least), I seemed to write less music than before. I wrote songs to old English poetry and to Shakespeare, also songs in Spanish. I did six Shakespeare plays, three films, and a new ballet, *The Harvest According,* by Agnes de Mille (to excerpts she had chosen from existing works, with filling added). I traveled too, to South America, lecturing in Spanish and conducting, to Venice for two festivals, to Berlin for another, eventually to Japan. But I was not content with just moving about, nor with merely composing films, plays, and short recital pieces. It was not till I had completed a forty-five-minute work, the *Missa Pro Defunctis,* and in 1960 brought that through its birth pains in Potsdam, New York (with an orchestra of ninety, a chorus of three hundred), that I knew my reconstruction time was over.

A Distaste for Music

WHEN MEN OF LETTERS write about their century, literature inevitably gets star billing. That is the way they present the
times they live in, and we have all been brought up to believe them.
It has not been easy, therefore, for a mere musician to review six
decades. Nor has he attempted wiring these for sound. His only
effort toward consistency has been to leave out things not actually
seen by him. However, what he did see, and on some evidence remembers, is not quite the whole of this recounting, for verity required that he explain just why it was that he was where he was
and how he happened to be looking at what he saw. Which raised
the question: Who was he anyway?

And so it came about that a sketch aimed chiefly at describing
places, times, and persons got turned into a sort of self-portrait. It
had to be shown right off, for instance, that its Midwestern author
was not of the Sinclair Lewis–Sherwood Anderson–Ernest Hemingway line, all of them worried and preachy, but rather of the more
comic-spirited Booth Tarkington–George Ade–Mark Twain connection. He had also to be placed in the pre-World-War-I music
life of Kansas City, then in that of postwar Harvard, neither of
which was available in books.

Then came the discovery that France was more than just another
country, like England or Germany, or even very special, like Spain

or China, but a miracle spot like ancient Greece or the United States, where more comes out than seems to have gone in.

Next, joining the European 1920s, of which your observer instantly became a part, he seems to have learned quite early that these were not by any means the same 1920s that have become fixed in American romance as taking place against a frantic jazz accompaniment and peopled by a generation of good-looking young expatriates all happily, and some successfully, playing "lost."

The thirties also had to be explored—so different in Europe from in America but, like the twenties, consisting of two halves. Unlike the twenties, they are still virgin territory, for few historians have mapped the trails. Now that they begin to do so, I notice that the American trend is toward dramatizing the Great Depression, even monopolizing it, also toward monopolizing our progress toward workers' rights, as if the Léon Blum government of 1934-6 in France, with its advanced social laws and their enforced acceptance, had not offered a constant working example to our New Deal.

As World War II approached, it was the journalists who warned us. For four years or more they said it would take place. The statesmen of western Europe said it would not; the artists hoped it would not; the European rich from everywhere (manufacturers, bankers, men of business) mostly believed it would not, while both the British and French general staffs acted as if it could not. But when Hitler, bluffing, said it would take place, and nobody stopped him in 1936 from occupying the Rhine, the newsmen knew that nobody intended to stop him.

The intellectual and artistic life of America during that war, though largely still unplotted, is available for study. That of Germany under Hitler and of France during the Occupation still requires uncovering. And it does seem probable that the world's present state, particularly Europe's, will be easier to understand when those dark years shall have been lighted up.

My personal account of America during the 1940s remains that of a musician working on a newspaper. It is amazing what you do not learn there about contemporary history. You see nothing; the cables tell you nothing; the editorials explain nothing. I came to believe after many months fraternizing with them all—with Ogden Reid, Helen Reid, and Geoffrey Parsons, with the managing editor, the city editors, and the specialists—that they were not really on the inside of things. They could package the news, but they were too close to judge it. In prewar Paris times, the foreign correspondents from fifty countries, pooling their thoughts, had come closer to the truth (indeed, they still do) than those same reporters ever can once they are back home, holed up in the plant, and separated from their unofficial sources. The only better prophets, when I still had access to their analysis through Sherry Mangan, were the working Trotskyists. Communists of the Third International, whether Stalinist, Khrushchevian, or other, have never to my knowledge shown any special care for truth, past or present, or any prescience about things to come. Their conversation is Jesuitical; their acts are as often as not plain treacherous; their political faith is mythological and religious.

My column, which came to an end in 1954, reported little of the modern-music war that went on throughout the Eisenhower decade. That war, which was fought between Europe and America for world control over music's advanced positions, was won by Europe. Pierre Boulez, Karlheinz Stockhausen, and their aides now occupy lots of space in the world's press, ride high, make money, and instruct the young. John Cage and his associates enjoy honor at home and some in Asia; but they are virtually without influence in Europe save on those leaders just mentioned, the ones who early seized there all the paying posts. These posts are nearly all in Germany, where state-supported radio establishments are rich and where music publishers are the world's most prosperous and best organized.

The 1960s in America have seen the financiers of real estate take over much of music's distribution through building on slum-clearance property shopping centers for the performing arts. These developments are subsidized by philanthropic foundations and blessed by government. Recording and radio companies observe them carefully. Indeed, on almost any of their boards one finds a pair of television executives. These move in pairs for mutual protection, being not yet trained in art-trustee diplomacy. So far, these boards are openly conventional in taste and generally box-office minded. The broadcasting and publishing cartels of Germany, though no less greedy than our business combines, are at least engaged in furthering the composing art and do not shy away from modern music. They figure that sound investment in music's future can lie nowhere but in today's copyrights.

With music become on both northwestern continents a power-establishment; with, in Asia, Japan's high music literacy a stimulus to massive consumption in both the native and the European styles; and with India, once musically the mother of us all, rapidly becoming, through the All-India Radio, a pander to ignorance in every style (not to mention what has been done by radio toward destroying the Arab tradition through broadcasts in the Middle East and North Africa of musical artifacts from Cairo's Tin Pan Alley), the standardization of music everywhere, even when this takes place at a high taste level, is accompanied by a forced consumption repulsive to any but the untrained ear.

Myself, till I was twenty-five or six, I had a glutton's appetite for sound. After that, my need was more for giving out than taking in. So I went to concerts only for a reason—a work of mine, or of a colleague, or of a beloved world-wide living master. Though now and then, for purposes to me mysterious, as in my wartime practicing of Mozart, I would dig into the bedrock below some classic source.

As a result of this almost dietetic intake, my engagement to review for the New York *Herald Tribune* found me at forty-four with my mind unsaturated, my ear quite clean. And thanks to my bosses on the paper, who did not overload me, and to my continued functioning as a practical musician, which refreshed me, I did not go stale. In fact, I was a far more expert listener to music at the end than I had been when I started, fourteen years before.

All the same, I came to realize, once I had given up reviewing it, that I could not bear the stuff in any form. Moreover, observing my composer colleagues, I realized that they too were finding music unattractive. We know, of course, that virtuosos and conductors early dispense with going to one another's concerts. But privately they listen to recordings; they keep up. And in Europe composers can still be seen at musical events. In America, where the very air we breathe is oversaturated with processed auditory stimuli, the composer after forty, of a certainty by fifty, finds the whole musical hoopla unacceptable.

He does not give up composing, for that is his defense against exasperation. And performing can offer comparable absorption, as can shepherding others through rehearsals of his work. But in middle age the music producer is a poor consumer. And staying away from concerts, like fasting for the religious, can be a source of strength and serve good works.

The distaste for music of which I speak is not, however, merely a matter of age. It is a symptom sociologically observable almost everywhere but Buenos Aires and Tokyo, cities where radio still is not abused and where musical appetite runs strong. Elsewhere, more and more at musical occasions one sees only music addicts, unhappily a growing group. For as the music of our time has become progressively intellectualized (thanks to the progeny of Schoenberg), it has alienated more and more the intellectuals.

From Wagner through Stravinsky the musical advance, like that of painting, was applauded, publicized, and financially supported by philosophers, men of letters, intellectual hostesses, disinterested bankers, people of fashion, and far-out royalty. Go to a concert today and look at the faces. Few belong to the intellectual world. Nor do the overheard remarks express ideas, but rather conditionings. For they are a conditioned lot, responding to appreciation propaganda and to market studies; and they all look either vacant or preoccupied. Music can make them applaud or shout; but it never seems to lift them up, give joy.

I must admit too that if the audience for music seems unperceptive, especially as regards the music of our time, the performances of music that we hear (excepting for those that deal strictly with the new kinds) bear little resemblance to their publicity. The orchestras play off pitch, and the singers sing off pitch; no one bothers to blend, to balance, or to get a rhythm right. The effort seems to be toward a driving effect or toward a luscious sound, toward something easily salable in any case. Harmonious musical discourse, as a concept, seems to have disappeared pretty much everywhere.

Were not the performances of my youth still less efficient? Yes and no. The singers were better trained, the violinists and pianists just as communicative. The orchestras were nowhere near so good as they are now, man by man. But no group is any finer than its leader, and our leaders of today are no more sensitive to music than in their time were Mahler, Nikisch, Messager, and (in opera) Toscanini. Our players read faster, learn faster, save time and money; but every concert sounds like a rehearsal. How little the superior training of our symphony men counts for in the long run has been shown up many a time by Leopold Stokowski's lovely work with youth orchestras and Thomas Beecham's with the New York W.P.A. And all symphony men sound crude beside the devoted young who perform the difficult new music so delicately and so precisely for Gunther Schuller or for Pierre Boulez.

With performances overblown, overadvertised, and oversold, I often think that it would be a good idea for music writers to go underground. But I see no likelihood of their doing so. (And I imagine that if there were a musical underground, I should know it.) The twelve-tone serial composers, after spending nearly half a century outside the Establishment, are now a pressure group achieving power; they will certainly not resign from it now. Nor will the far-outs (percussive or electronic), whose training has ever been twelve-tonal and pressure-groupish. And just as certainly the pranksters, those charming rediscoverers of Dada who make us laugh, will not deny themselves the publicity for which their jolly jokes have been conceived.

Truth is, there is no avant-garde today. Dada has won; all is convention; choose your own. What mostly gets chosen in any time is that which can be packed and shipped. And for everything that can be shipped there is a conditioned public, from the universities, where Cage and Boulez are gods, to those cities, all too common West and South, where Mozart and Brahms are still a rarity and Beethoven's Ninth Symphony has not yet been heard.

Have we entered perhaps an epoch like to that of Louis XV in France, when there were no unsuccessful artists, no persecuted poets, no exiled philosophers (save the rich and vastly publicized Voltaire off in Switzerland), and when the intellectuals of Europe, no matter what their trade or discipline, made up a club that traveled, wrote letters, shared ideas, got one another jobs? This well may be our case. For with all governments except the Vatican and all the rich foundations going in for art, there is plenty of money around for everyone. In Europe, where the channels of art subsidy have been carved out by history, its formulas are not likely to change much. For professionals there—the poets, painters, and composers—are classically not only expenditure's recipients but also its advisers.

America's cultural enterprises—all but the public libraries and the state and Catholic universities—have for three centuries been controlled by amateurs, usually members of the business community. This privilege will not soon be abrogated. Federal government, however, may well be tapped for money. And this will entail some intellectual control such as the Smithsonian Institution exercises over a group of scientific, historical, and artistic enterprises. I have no fear for the ultimate result, given the general excellence of our intellectual establishments. But I do not think it realistic to dream romantically of poverty and persecution for the artist, of an underground, or of a permanent avant-garde.

The acceptance that we worked for from our youth began to take place in the middle thirties with the Works Progress Administration, and every President from Franklin Roosevelt through Lyndon Johnson has put weight behind it. Now we have it, the recognition of art and artists as national wealth. And if we still shall have to insist on our right, as artists, to guide public policies about art, we shall probably achieve influence sooner in the public sector than in that of corporate businesses like radio, television, and recording.

Of what, then, here and now, is music needful? A genius of the lyric stage, I say, a composer who will give stature to the operatic and poetic theater. We also need a music magazine, an organ to keep the intellectuals informed and to win back their lost interest in us. For without their faith and backing, the musical theater, like the concert world, is for its own money-raisers and for addicts.

Philosophical disputes about aesthetics died with Dada. The next steps toward understanding music and toward protecting ourselves from being taste-manipulated lie in two directions, both of them intellectual. The more urgent of these is the establishment of a musical sociology—an investigation of who consumes what and how they come to do it, in other words, a clarification of music's varied roles in our civilization. These studies are cardinal to a consumer industry, especially if federal government and the tax-exempt foundations are to assume a more than superficial involvement.

The other field is comparative musicology. And I don't mean just folkloring in the Orient. I mean the preservation, examination, and confrontation of the civilizing tonal arts of India, of the Indonesian regions, and of the Sino-Korean-Japanese complex. Analyzing their methods in detail and comparing them with our Western history of near two thousand years might answer the questions: What happens when? How does a monolinear music evolve? Does the discovery of the intervallic (or harmonic) phenomenon arrest that evolution? Are rhythm and meter incidental, or are they basic? And what are their possible roles in any music? In which of the great traditions is evolution now complete? In which still active? Hundreds of questions like these merit study, and their answers may indeed bring music back. For merely introspective, or philosophic, aesthetics has ceased to be a valid guide for growth.

There is no reason, I am sure, why music should not grow. Its present overproduction and overdistribution need not lead to eventual neglect and famine, though that may happen if we do not mend our ways, use our heads a little, and stop abusing the market. If the young, for instance, should decide one day to resist the market pressures, first losing interest, then, as they take things over a few years later, neglecting music's educational procedures, they might create a musical moratorium. But eventually music would start up again. And when it did, it might be worse than ever, with all the instrumental skills forgotten.

Seriously, I wish those called to serve the art would pool their brain power to study its operations. Awaiting that far-off moment, many of us, of course, will die. But the present writer, till he does, will fulminate. He will also (God willing) continue to compose. At the moment, a libretto in verse has been completed for him; and putting it to music seems vastly urgent. This book, besides, has gone as far as need be, as far as one man's memory can take it.

Index of Names

Index of Compositions:
Virgil Thomson

A NOTE ON THE TYPE

This book is set in Granjon, a type named in compliment to Robert Granjon, *type-cutter and printer—Antwerp, Lyons, Rome, Paris—active from 1523 to 1590. The boldest and most original designer of his time, he was one of the first to practice the trade of type-founder apart from that of printer. The face was designed by* George W. Jones, *who based his drawings upon a type used by* Claude Garamond (1510–61) *in his beautiful French books. "Granjon" more closely resembles Garamond's own than do any of the various modern types that bear his name.*

The book was composed, printed, and bound by The Book Press Incorporated, Brattleboro, Vermont. Illustrations printed by Halliday Lithograph Corporation, West Hanover, Mass.

Typography and binding design by

GUY FLEMING